S0-BAM-243

The Vocation of Business

The Vocation of Business

*Social Justice
in the
Marketplace*

John C. Médaille

CABRINI COLLEGE LIBRARY
610 KING OF PRUSSIA ROAD
RADNOR, PA 19087

continuum

NEW YORK • LONDON

 # 80917207

2008

The Continuum International Publishing Group Inc
80 Maiden Lane, New York, NY 10038

The Continuum International Publishing Group Ltd
The Tower Building, 11 York Road, London SE1 7NX

www.continuumbooks.com

Copyright © 2007 by John C. Médaille

All rights reserved. No part of this book may be reproduced, stored in a retrieval system, or transmitted, in any form or by any means, electronic, mechanical, photocopying, recording, or otherwise, without the written permission of publishers.

Printed in the United States of America

Library of Congress Cataloging-in-Publication Data

Médaille, John C.
    The Vocation of business : social justice in the marketplace / John C. Médaille.
        p.   cm.
    Includes bibliographical references and index.
    ISBN-13: 978-0-8264-2808-0 (hardcover : alk. paper)
    ISBN-10: 0-8264-2808-8 (hardcover : alk. paper)
    ISBN-13: 978-0-8264-2809-7 (pbk. : alk. paper)
    ISBN-10: 0-8264-2809-6 (pbk. : alk. paper)
    1. Social responsibility of business. 2. Christian sociology – Catholic Church.
  3. Economics – Religious aspects – Catholic Church.   I. Title.

  HD60.M414 2007
  261.8′5 – dc22

                                                                    2007002903

A morality that believes itself able to dispense with
the technical knowledge of economic laws
is not morality but moralism.
As such, it is the antithesis of morality.

—JOSEPH CARDINAL RATZINGER

Contents

Part I
THE HISTORICAL BACKGROUND

Part II
THE SOCIAL ENCYCLICALS

Part III
TOWARD AN EVOLVED CAPITALISM

Part IV
THE PRACTICE OF JUSTICE
IN THE MODERN BUSINESS WORLD

Preface

This is a book about the relationship of justice and economics, about equity and equilibrium, and about how this relationship is expressed in the actual practice of business. The overall aim of this book is a reform of business education. This reform is crucial, in my opinion, because in our culture it is largely the businessman and the bureaucrat who are, on a day-to-day basis, the makers of society. The world, such as it is, is largely what business has made it to be. And yet, when we look at business curricula, we find that it is not so much about education as about job training. Business, too often, is regarded as a set of purely technical skills, such as marketing, finance, operations, and so forth. The result is that the movers and shakers of our society have no grasp of the social, historical, and cultural realities in which they must operate. Thus, the very group who should be among our most broadly educated tend to be in fact our most narrowly trained. Each year, we send graduates forth to operate in an increasingly complex and dangerous world without any tools with which to comprehend either the dangers or the complexities.

This failure of business education is, I believe, a reflection of the failure of our economic theories. The reigning orthodoxies of the neoclassical and Austrian schools are themselves, in a very technical sense, an undisciplined conversation. That is, they make assumptions about the nature of human actions without reference to the discipline of psychology; they make assumptions about the nature of society without the discipline of sociology; about the development of economic man without the discipline of anthropology; they root their science in utilitarianism without the discipline of philosophy. They make statements about the "perfect system of natural liberty," but "nature" and "liberty" are terms from a philosophical and theological discourse, and this discourse must be consulted before one can say where the perfections of nature and liberty might lie. Economics assumes that all men and women are autonomous individuals always acting so as to maximize the benefits to themselves, and acting within a market environment that is considered the only possible means for the material provisioning of society. But psychology fails to confirm that men are motivated

xi

purely by self-interest, sociology fails to confirm a pure individualism, and anthropology finds in human history alternatives to pure market systems. Utilitarianism can certainly find support among the sages, but it turns out to be but one small stream in the great river of philosophy. Indeed, it would seem that the strength with which the economist holds to his assumptions is directly proportional to his ignorance of their sources.

As an undisciplined conversation, neoclassical economics, rather than being a true science, rises above ideology only with great difficulty. Every true science is disciplined by a higher science: biology is responsible to chemistry, and chemistry is responsible to physics. The biologist does not think himself demeaned by having to learn organic chemistry, nor the chemist by learning nuclear physics. But the neoclassical economist feels himself demeaned if he has to submit his assumptions to psychology, anthropology, sociology, philosophy, and theology. He feels, perhaps, that an appeal to such "soft" sciences will compromise the scientific nature of his study, and he stakes his claim to being a "scientist" on the empirical and mathematical nature of his work, or (as in the case of the neo-Austrians) on a system of *a priori* assumptions about human nature which are regarded as untouchable dogmas, not subject to empirical verification. However, a science that is disconnected from its neighbors in the scientific hierarchy is not a science at all, but a discourse that can never rise above the merely circular. Empiricism and mathematics are insufficient to make a study properly scientific. Indeed, astrology is both empirical and mathematical, but as it appeals to principles that find no root in the hierarchy of truth, it can never be a science. The economist who does not appeal to the higher sciences runs the risk of becoming an economic astrologer, forever drawing charts and making calculations that have but little root in reality.

But of all the failures of economics, the most important one is its failure to understand the relationship between justice and economics, between equity and equilibrium. This divorce of justice and economics is a rather modern development. From the time of Aristotle through the heyday of the Scholastics, economics existed totally, or nearly so, within a discourse of justice. It was only with the rise of a pure individualism that economics began to lose its footing in ethics. But in reality, this is not possible; every actual economic system will have, implicitly or explicitly, a corresponding notion of justice, a level of equity. If the system tolerates vast disparities of wealth and poverty, then it will tend towards social unrest and economic collapse, and some means will be required to redistribute purchasing power. This will usually take the form of a vast government bureaucracy or, more recently, the ponzi-scheme of consumer credit. Systems with higher levels of equity will require less government intervention and will be more stable.

However, at this point, we encounter a problem. Notions of justice in economics vary from the "Social Darwinism" of Herbert Spencer to the perfect equality of Karl Marx. Which standard shall we use? The standard adopted for this book is that of Catholic Social Teaching, a sustained meditation by the Church over the past 120 years on questions of social justice. Although I am a Catholic, the choice to use the Church's social doctrine is not so much a sectarian choice as it is a matter of convenience. Since one must start somewhere, the Church's meditation provides both a convenient standard and a rich literature on the subject. The choice is not meant to slight other and similar traditions; there is, for example, a rich evangelical tradition of social justice exemplified by such writers as Stanley Hauerwas, D. Stephen Long, and Jim Wallis. Nor is it meant to slight the Jewish, Islamic, or other non-Christian traditions, which have their own meditations on the meaning of social justice. Yet the surprising fact is that the differences in notions of justice between these traditions tend to be a lot smaller than the differences in Scripture, liturgy, theology, and governance might suggest. The Church's teaching, while hardly "binding" on any Christian, even a Catholic, is at the very least influential among the vast majority of Christians, and so may serve us as a starting point for discussion.

Throughout this book I have agreed with Adam Smith's claim that a nation that ignores justice is "going fastest to ruin." Yet here we encounter another problem. For while a nation that ignores justice may be on the road to ruin, the individual businessman who does so may be on the road to wealth. Indeed, his very avarice may confer an advantage over his more honest competitors. Therefore, business involves a real choice. I contend that business is a vocation, a *calling* to live life in a certain way, a way that contributes not only to one's own well-being, but to the well-being of all other members of society. Now, any individual entrepreneur may argue that in fact he does not have this choice; he may argue that the system limits his freedom and that he must comply or go bankrupt, and so it is useless to talk to him about freedom, choice, or vocation. I certainly have some sympathy with this argument, because it is certainly true that all social systems reward some behaviors at the expense of others; no individual businessman or -woman can be held responsible for the totality of the social system. Nevertheless, there is always *some* freedom of action, and with the proper use of the moral imagination, the entrepreneur can indeed contribute both to his personal good and the common good. While he cannot be responsible for the whole system, he is certainly responsible for his little corner of it;

there is always some space in which the entrepreneur or the manager can practice his or her vocation. Therefore, it is incumbent on a writer in this field not only to elucidate the principles, but to demonstrate them in practice, in practices which exist and which can be examined by those who have a mind to do so.

I would be remiss if I did not acknowledge those who guided my thinking on these matters. While there are too many to name, some in particular stand out. Among them are John Milbank, who taught me the practical relationship between theology and social systems; Garrick Small, who taught me about property and rent; John Mueller, for his brilliant critique of utilitarianism in economics; and Sr. Helen Alford and Michael Naughton, who elucidate management as a moral praxis. However, I must also say that the ideas in this book are mine; while these thinkers may claim ownership of any virtues this book has, I claim sole ownership of its errors, and will share the credit with no one.

I am also deeply grateful for the work of Christine Médaille, my wife, and Kate Bluett and Ann Médaille, my daughters, who were all my first editors and critics. Without their work, this work simply would not be, and to them I dedicate this book.

John C. Médaille
St. Nicholas Day, 2006
Irving, Texas

Part I

The Historical Background

Chapter 1

Justice and Economics

The Bible tells you how to go to heaven, not how the heavens go.

—ATTRIBUTED TO GALILEO GALILEI

SOCIAL TEACHING
AND THE BUSINESSPERSON

The modern world is separated from the medieval by the current belief that the world is entirely explicable in terms of natural science and that a study of the divine cannot really enhance our understanding of the "natural." This dichotomy between the "natural law" and the divine one has never sat easily with most people, even when they saw no practical way around it. Attempts to straddle the chasm between the divine and natural laws have often been perceived as outrageous. For example, when the Church intervened in matters of astronomy in the Galileo affair, she incurred the charge of exceeding her mandate, which indeed she did, and with disastrous results. The Vatican Librarian at the time, in a phrase often attributed to Galileo himself, noted that "The Bible tells you how to go to heaven, not how the heavens go." And so the world, particularly the modern world, seems to be caught between two versions of the "truth" with no real way to connect them.

But does the Bible really give its readers no insight on the movement of the heavens? More pertinent to this book, does it give no insight on the movement of markets? Even in the humane sciences (and economics must surely be reckoned as one of them), moderns seek a "scientific" explanation of things which could reduce the complexities of human life to some simple rules, after the manner of astronomy or physics, rules which would hold true no matter what the social, cultural, or religious milieu might be. Does Christianity — and the Catholic Church in particular — have nothing more to offer the modern businessperson than platitudes with no practical application? As Michael Novak has observed, no one conducts trade by camel train anymore; how can centuries-old teachings keep up with modern innovations and questions in business? Is life, both the life of the world and the

3

life of the individual, thus consigned to a kind of schizophrenia in which our moral life — the life of love and personal relationships and our deepest longings — is forever at odds with our "scientific" life, the life in which we earn our daily bread?

For more than one hundred years, the Catholic Church has addressed in great detail the situation of men and women in the modern world, particularly in their social, economic, and political situations. These teachings have commonly been referred to as "Catholic Social Teaching." Although these teachings actually have roots that go back at least to the Middle Ages, the "founding document" is generally considered to be Leo XIII's 1891 encyclical, *Rerum Novarum*. The title, which means "Of New Things," is appropriate because the modern world really did present the Church, as well as the working man and the entrepreneur, with situations that were unprecedented. On the one hand, economic philosophers believed that they were on the verge of penetrating all the perplexities of wealth and poverty, and finally resolving them. But on the other hand, the actual division between wealth and poverty seemed greater, and society itself always seemed on the verge of falling either into civil discord or into worldwide warfare. For all practical purposes, the result of economic science has been to present to the modern world a choice between two systems, or perhaps two collections of systems, socialism and capitalism — systems that are viewed as being radically opposed. Each system has, of course, its defenders and its particular scientific treatises, but neither side can claim the backing of the Church. For when the Church examined the question, she found that many of the differences between these systems are more apparent than real, and she offered a detailed critique of both sides. Naturally, this poses a problem for a laity raised in a milieu that tends to see the choice as a binary one; that is, either all one or all the other, or at best a compromise position more or less tending to one system or the other.

Partisans of each position have often tried to fit the Church's teaching into either a capitalist or a socialist framework. Some decide that what the Church teaches is really just socialism, and support or attack the teaching for that very reason, while others decide that it really is just capitalism, and support or attack it for that reason. In both cases, the Church's teaching tends to be viewed through partisan and ideological lenses. It is not that there are not other, non-ideological interpretations. Far from it. But such discussions tend to take place in the academic realm and rarely reach the level of the priest and pastor, much less the parishioner and the businessperson. Part of this failure to reach the laity relates to the general collapse of catechetics in the confusion following the Second Vatican Council. But the major problem has been a cultural milieu that preaches a "scientific" view, either socialist or capitalist, and tends to force all thought into one mold or the other, liberal or conservative, Republican or Democrat, Right or Left. Businesspeople are expected, by one interpretation, to feel guilty for their success and even for their professions and to spend their off-hours working for the overthrow of the system that provides their daily bread, or at the very least in lobbying the government for higher taxes on the wealthy and subsidies to one disadvantaged group or another. Or, by the other interpretation, the businessperson is told that capitalism is already God's own system, that in business matters God speaks with an Austrian accent, and that all one needs to do is conduct business with the proper "values" and resist to the death any attempt at government intervention.

But in neither case is the Church's teaching shown to be relevant to the businessperson's everyday professional concerns; a businessperson is not shown how the teaching will deepen his vision of the economic forces with which he must contend or how it will enlighten his grasp of managerial and industrial technique, things which are his day-to-day concerns. The premise of this book is that the Church's teaching is indeed relevant to the everyday concerns of businessmen and -women. Indeed, if the Church cannot impart any wisdom to businesspeople as such, there would be a great question about the value of a social teaching that could not be related to everyday social concerns. But there is ample reason to believe that the Church ought to be involved. Not just for the moral formation of businesspeople, which is of course critical, but also because the teaching is not just a series of abstract statements, but in fact leads to a *praxis* of business, one that can be examined in many successful implementations that provide examples for the daily decisions which businesspeople must actually make. A "teaching" which cannot be enacted in daily life and mundane concerns, which has no "practical" application, is not really a teaching at all, but a mere set of platitudes.

WHY A "SOCIAL TEACHING"?

But before we can begin our study, we must ask a prior question, namely, "Why a social teaching at all?" After all, isn't the Church's competence limited to matters of individual salvation? To return to our first question, can the Church really pronounce on economic or social matters without incurring a charge that she has exceeded her mandate, no less than she did in the Galileo affair, when she attempted to intervene in matters of astronomy? Shouldn't the famous statement of the Vatican Librarian apply equally well to statements about the movement of markets as it does to those about the movement of stars? In short, should not the Church be concerned just with heaven and leave the world to take care of itself?

This is a seductive view, since such an individualist notion of salvation and religion fits well with the American and the modernist character. Indeed, many people believe that the essence of religion is having a "personal relationship with Jesus Christ," unmediated by a church or any social institutions other than the Scriptures. If the relationship is "personal," then its applicability to "social" matters is at best ambiguous, confined at most to matters of the family or "public" morality. Further, the separation of church and state is (wisely) enshrined in our constitution, although the meaning of this separation is certainly open to interpretation. Ought not this separation be enshrined as well in our economy? Indeed, the question arises whether there can really be things such as "social" values at all. The prevailing political and economic orthodoxy views "society" as nothing more than the sum total of its individual parts and as having no real existence apart from the sum total of choices made by all the individuals that comprise a society. Therefore, all values may be considered "market" values, arbitrated strictly by the aggregate of market choices that individuals make. Each individual simply brings his or her "values" to the marketplace where they are fully arbitrated by the laws of supply and demand. The "values" themselves are rooted in nothing more substantial than personal preference; the market, and the market alone, is the arbiter of social values, and the role of the Church is merely to form the values that individuals bring to the marketplace. If this is true, can there really be a "social" teaching at all, given that society has no "real" or independent existence? Must not the role of the Church be confined to the formation of individuals and their values, which will then work their way into the marketplace, both the marketplaces of goods and of ideas?

Such an individualist view of society, however, is certainly open to question. In the first place, it simply does not match our own everyday experience of the world and the situation in which we each find ourselves. Are we really just a collection of disconnected individuals? Certainly we do not begin that way, but rather we are called by our parents into existence in the ready-made community of family, a structure that largely forms our values long before we are aware of its having done so. Most of what we are comes not by an individual "consumer" choice but by gift. Along with the gift of family, there are the gifts of language, nationality, religion, community, city, state, and nation. Our values are socially formed by these gifts of social context, and only after that formation do we find ourselves in a position to accept or reject our values. Our very being itself turns out to be already a "being-in-community" which mirrors in some fashion that ultimate community of persons that is at the root of all being, namely the Trinity. At their most basic level, humans are *social* beings, already formed by institutions "outside" themselves. These institutions precede the individual and will no doubt survive him or her, albeit in a changed form — a form changed by the individual's own actions. Thus individuals always finds themselves situated within a particular social context, a context that forms them and that they will in turn act to re-form; we always pass on to the next generation something different from that which we received.

That being the case, it would be very surprising if the Church — any church — did not address humans in their concrete *social* being. Indeed, we never really find a religion that fails to do so, whether well or poorly, nor do we ever find a society that is not totally indebted to its own moral views for the very structure of its social institutions, be they the family, the state, the market, and so forth. And what is true for all religions is even more true of Christianity, since for Christians all teaching is based on the "double charity," the law that is behind all laws, namely love of God and love of neighbor. In a real sense, *all* Catholic teaching is "social" teaching in that it concerns our relationships with either God or neighbor, and it all presumes social institutions. Each of the Ten Commandments, for example, presumes a social institution: the first through the third presume the church or synagogue; the fourth, sixth, and ninth, marriage and the family; the fifth through the tenth, the neighborhood; and the seventh and ninth, the market.[1] Our salvation depends (so we believe) on being incorporated into the Body of Christ, a communal structure that joins us to each other and to God in perfect community, and our liturgy is a public celebration of that communion with God and each other. In short, all the teachings of the Church are directed not to humanity as a collection of abstract individuals, but to humans as we actually find them in their social situations and as they actually relate to one another.

Of course, the "social teaching" per se refers to a specific portion of the totality of Church teaching which has to do with people's relationships in justice to the state, to society, and to the marketplace. And while we consider social teaching separately for the purpose of study, our study always presumes the totality of teaching without which this particular part could have no meaning. Since this is a business text, we will further refine our study to that portion of social teaching which has mainly to do with just relationships within the marketplace. Thus the central question to be examined in this book is, "What is the relationship between justice and economics?" And having pursued that question, to some conclusion we hope, we will want to know what impact it will have on our business practices and structures.

JUSTICE AND ECONOMICS

Concerning this relationship, it would seem that there are really only two possibilities: either that justice and a "proper" economics are things opposed, so that more of one necessarily means less of the other, or that they are things identical, so that a proper study of one exhausts the other. If the first possibility is true, if justice and economics really are things opposed, then it would seem that either the Church has no business in speaking of these matters (for manifestly the Church has no competence in economics per se) or that she must preach only a form of social poverty in which people voluntarily limit themselves in dealing with the things of this world and concentrate on the things of the next. Yet the Church refuses *either* to keep silent on economic issues *or* to be so otherworldly as to disdain completely the material things necessary for a dignified life in this world. Thus, from the Church's standpoint, the first possibility is excluded. On the part of the economists, the view that justice and economics are things opposed might force economists to acknowledge regretfully that theirs is the "dismal science" indeed, but insist that it is a science nonetheless, and follow it wherever it leads, which will be increasingly away from a moral order. Yet economists themselves are reluctant to concede such a point, and even those who claim a purely "scientific" view of markets nevertheless cannot resist speaking in terms of what "ought" to be, that is to say, to speak in the language of pure morality.

That would seem to leave only the second possibility, but here again we encounter a problem. If justice and economics are in some way identical, then either the theologians would dictate the content of economics, which hardly seems likely, or economists would determine the content of morality from their equations. While this option last may seem absurd, it was in fact (as we shall see) the position of the early capitalist thinkers, such as Malthus and Ricardo, who saw in the abstract formulations of economics the hidden hand of God. For example, they regarded such things as the so-called "Iron Law of Wages," which supposedly dictated that the poor will starve if they "overproduce," as simply the operation of divine providence — and something far more potent than preaching — working to curb the incontinent habits of the poor. Of course, it had no effect on those same habits among the rich. In other words, if the poor will persist in having too many children, then God Himself, manifesting Himself as the Iron Law, will punish them with more poverty, and there is nothing much that anybody can really do about it; rather, an abstract morality is displayed in the misery of the poor and the happiness of the rich, and any fool can read this catechism without the aid of a preacher. If providence really does work in such a mechanical fashion, then this book is superfluous, and one's economics text is all the guidance one will ever need in life. Obviously, we will not be taking this approach.

But if justice really does have some meaning beyond abstractions and platitudes, then it must be capable of really being embodied in real economic institutions, including the institutions of business, without conflicting with the inherent nature of those institutions. Granted that in a sinful world, and especially an originally sinful world, a perfect realization of justice is beyond our reach, and the hunt for utopias is more likely to discover dystopias. Nevertheless, this fact can never be a cause for despair, because as Christians we are the original and only true "progressives," believing that history does really move us closer to the Kingdom of God and that our immediate task is always to approximate it as best we can, to make concrete in the world and its structures the message of the Gospel.

Nevertheless, it seems intuitively obvious that a study of justice, by itself, will not lead to a particular economic system, because a vision of justice, no matter how perfect one's theological eyesight, does not by itself result in just systems. Justice, like any other virtue, must be embodied in concrete social structures and institutions, and that is a task for the society as a whole. Economists and businesspeople have a particular responsibility to develop such concrete systems, but the study of economics or business would be arid indeed if not related to some goal beyond the mere proliferation of production and consumption.

There is, I think, a third possibility we have not yet considered, and it is that economics and morality are indeed separate sciences, but *converging* ones (as all true sciences are). That is, they are mutually enlightening so that a real advance in one must somehow represent an advance in the other, and that no study of one is really complete without an understanding of the other. On the part of morality, we have noted that humans are social beings, and that morality can never be simply a collection of private choices but must be embodied in the social institutions in which everyone who has ever lived has found him- or herself situated. People are, to an extent, determined by the economic system — as well as all the other social structures in which they find themselves — even as they act to determine that system. A morality which confines itself to the personal and refuses to shape the institutions of society is divorced from the way people actually live. Such a morality consigns people's real lives, their concrete existence, to a moral desert. Therefore the proper economic life of mankind must be shaped by values which are moral in character, and this "shaping" works not only on individuals, but on social structures and institutions as well. Hence, a Social Teaching!

This answers the question of the Church's interest in matters economic. But can the same be said for economics and business? Is not economics a pure science answerable only to itself and one that moves by laws that are knowable by human reason quite apart from any theology or social theory? And is not the businessman or -woman answerable only to this science? Would not interference by the Church in this science be akin to interference in astronomy such as in the disastrous case of Galileo? Another way to state the case is, "Does the economist derive any purely economic insights by paying attention to justice? Does the businessperson gain any insight into managerial technique?" In order to answer these questions, we will have to understand the connection between economics and ethics at its deepest level.

THE EROTIC ECONOMY

Economics begins in desire, *eros*. We typically think of eros in regard to one type of desire only, the erotic, but in fact it refers to all desiring. We all have a range of desires, biological, personal, social. We must eat, we must love, we must seek the truth. But in general, we can only fulfill these desires in cooperation with each other; if we are to succeed in the world, we need each other, and hence we need some way of cooperating, some set of rules. The fulfillment of our desires therefore takes place in a *social* context. Economics is part of the social context, the part that deals with the rules of production and exchange. That is to say, we assume that everybody produces something, but is not able to produce all that he needs; therefore we must be able to exchange the surplus we produce for other things that we need.

Humans are made in the image and likeness of God. As such, we have a tendency to want not merely what is good, but what is perfect and complete. However, we live in a finite world, which means that the world can only produce goods that are imperfect, temporal, limited, recurring, and unable to satisfy us completely. Nothing we get from this world is capable of completing or perfecting us, yet we desire completion and perfection. This leads to the first of our economic truths, namely, that given a supply of good, useful, and beautiful products, demand, in the form of desire, will always exceed the supply. Desire, in the form of demand, is the final or ultimate cause of all production; it guarantees that, in general, there will be a market for the things we produce.[2] Because of imperfections in the economic system, demand in the form of purchasing power may not always be sufficient to clear the markets, but in general there will be the desire to do so. So long as we perceive that products are good, useful, and beautiful (whether or not they are actually so), we will *want* to have them.

The Structure of Desire

Desires, however, cannot be conceived of as simple and homogeneous. Modern economic theory reduces all desires to "self-interest," meaning egotistic and centered on gratifying immediate needs. Such a view excludes the possibility of any emotion or action not motivated by personal gain. However, this is a misapprehension of the human condition. Desire is not rooted in self-interest so much as it is in *self-respect*.[3] Jean-Jacques Rousseau defines self-respect as "a natural feeling which leads every animal to look to its own preservation and which, guided in man by reason and modified by compassion, creates humanity and virtue."[4] Self-interest and self-respect provide two contrasting views of the human person and, as we shall see, two very different notions of economics and justice.

Desire itself, far from being simple and homogeneous, is highly structured and hierarchical. While there can be a variety of ways to view this hierarchy, one of the more useful is given by the psychologist Abraham Maslow. He divides human needs in five levels. At the lowest levels stand man's physiological needs such as food, sleep, shelter, and sex. Next comes the need for safety and security. These two levels must be fulfilled at least partially if the higher level needs are to be realized; failure to fulfill these needs will limit the human potential to its most basic and animal-like level.[5] Next in importance are our needs for love and belongingness. These include the needs for a love and affection that is not conditioned on any reward or exchange, but simply given to the person as a person.[6]

The fourth level consists of the needs for "mastery and competence, for confidence in the face of the world, and for independence and freedom."[7] While in the previous level, affection is given to the person *unconditionally*, at this level respect is *earned* rather than based on celebrity or unwarranted adulation. Finally, the highest level consists in our need for aesthetic beauty and knowledge as ends in themselves. Therefore, at the highest level the need of a human being is a *moral* need. This need is categorical and unconditional; as Maslow puts it: "What a man *can* be he *must* be. This need we call self-actualization."[8]

While it is true that all people have these needs, it is also true that the needs become conscious desires through culture and a process of socialization. Therefore, as E. K. Hunt notes,

> The study of individual behavior must simultaneously be a study of society, and the evaluation of a social system must always be in terms of general human needs and the actualization of human potential.[9]

Given that the satisfaction of needs is a social process, economics is involved at every level. The fulfillment of the human person cannot be reduced to economics alone, but nevertheless such fulfillment is impossible without economics. Regardless of the economic theory one chooses, the actual *practice* of economics resides largely in businesses, and the choices that businessmen and -women make. Therefore business is critical in the process of forming a society in which our needs can be met and in which human persons can achieve their highest potential.

BUSINESS AS A SCHOOL OF VIRTUE

The production and distribution of products is the job of business. It involves determining, within the current resources and bounds of technology, what products are good and useful and beautiful, producing them, and finally allocating in some way the necessary purchasing power so that the products may be acquired.

Given that eros is at the base of economics, we immediately face a problem. From the standpoint of our desires, we all tend to be self-centered, to view the world solely in terms of our own needs and desires. Yet economics represents a *common good,* a good that encompasses the needs of all the members of society. The question is how we go from our self-centered needs to the common good. Our individual viewpoints will inevitably bring us into conflict with others. This conflict introduces *eris,* strife or discord, into both economic and business life. This is not by itself a bad thing. There will always be different points of view and indeed life is enriched by the clash of ideas and wills. However, conflicts which remain at the level of the eristic tend to be self-destructive. The problem is not strife per se, but how we resolve the discord and come to a common understanding; that is, how to come to some notion of the common good, a good that encompasses the good of each member of the society.

The most prevalent economic theories are based on *hedonism* or *utilitarianism,* the idea that the notions of "good" and "bad" are merely statements of individual preference based only on the pleasure or pain that a choice might cause, and that the common good, if it exists at all, is merely the summation of individual goods. These individual goods are arbitrated solely by market choice in a democratic fashion, on the basis of "one dollar, one vote" (in the economic order) or "one man, one vote" (in the political order).

Later we will examine the philosophic and economic claims of utilitarianism. For the present, suffice it to say that there is considerable room for doubt that self-interest, by itself, can ever provide an adequate basis for the common good. A society, including any particular business society, which is governed by pure self-interest, will always remain at the level of eris, of strife and discord. All questions will tend to be resolved on the basis of power relationships alone. Yet there is no particular reason why the best ideas, the ones that contribute the most to the common good, should be the same ones supported by the most powerful forces. Indeed, it is generally the case that those who have obtained the greatest privileges from the economic or political orders have done so precisely because they are powerful.

In order to reach the common good, we need some way to overcome eris in a way that transcends purely private considerations. Further, we must overcome narrow self-interest and be prepared to see things from the point of view of both others and the society at large. Transcending our private interests in favor of the good of others is an exercise of the *virtues*, and most particularly the virtue of *charity*. We have come to associate "charity" with the giving of money or time to a cause, but this is only a small part of charity. It is perhaps useful to use the Greek term, *agape*, or "brotherly" love, to describe it. It is, above all, a willingness to compromise or even sacrifice our own interests in favor of the greater good. The *agapaic* seeks to resolve disputes by finding the common good. It seeks not power relationships, but ethical relationships.

Charity is not "natural" to a fallen human nature, but is a learned response, requiring discipline and practice. For this reason, it may seem "unnatural" or naïve to connect the virtues with business and economics, especially an economics built on "natural" law. But in fact, business is only possible to the extent that the virtues are present. If some degree of honesty cannot be assumed, if people are not willing to work diligently, if people are not willing to exchange justly, then the economy is always in danger of destroying its own roots and tends toward chaos and collapse. Indeed, it is no accident that when virtue declines in a society, the role of lawyers and bureaucrats increases; we must increasingly depend on the courts and the government to play the role that virtue should play.

Business — and businessmen and -women — must cultivate the virtues if they are to succeed. Even a "cutthroat" business needs at least the virtues of prudence and courage. But in the long-term, more will be required, simply as a practical matter. For example, management of persons, which is a large part of the business of management, will require the virtues of justice and charity if the business is to gain the trust and loyalty of its employees. Given that: we all have desires; we must fulfill these desires socially, that is by mutual cooperation; cooperation is made possible by the exercise of virtues, then it follows that economics constitutes a school of virtue. This is not to say that piles of money cannot be made by immoral means. But it is to say that the use of such means strikes at the roots of social order and undermines the whole society. When such practices become commonplace, society, and its economic order, disintegrate.

THE VOCATION OF BUSINESS

We are presented with two possible ways of resolving the inevitable disagreements that arise in business and public life. One is the *eristic*, relying on power relationships to settle all disputes, and the other is the *agapaic*, which seeks to transcend mere power and find the common good. This is not to say that power is bad and should never be used; sometimes it is simply necessary for the proper authority to tell someone to shut-up and move on. But when the eristic becomes the only or the primary means of resolving disputes, then the business becomes a place where egotism and power struggles are the order of the day, then fear and loathing become its driving forces; the results are likely to be low morale, low productivity, and high turnover. Moreover, when such eristic techniques are the common order of business practice, then society itself becomes an exercise in egotism, and the likelihood of finding the common good becomes remote. Such a society is well on its way to decadence and collapse. Sometimes societies and systems collapse because of outside forces; invaders in the form of either men or microbes overthrow them by virtue of conquest or plague. But more often, societies collapse from internal pressures, from a loss of their moral bases, without which they cannot survive. A financial collapse will always be preceded by a moral collapse; moral bankruptcy precedes financial bankruptcy.

Business is indispensable to the common good; there is no way to reach it without the work that businessmen do, not only in providing the goods and services we all need, but in setting, to a large degree, the moral tone of society. Therefore business is a vocation, a calling from God, which involves not only building up of a business, but the building up of society as well.

Chapter 2

The Modern Moral Dialogue

All advanced civilizations pass through a period of "enlightenment"; some even survive it.   —THOMAS FLEMING

IS A MORAL DIALOGUE POSSIBLE?

We have advanced the idea that justice and all the other virtues are necessary
to business. Yet this immediately presents us with a problem, since these
are moral concepts and modern people have great difficulty in discussing
morality and coming to any well-assured conclusions. Indeed, we often find
that moral discussions quickly degenerate into acrimonious exchanges, as
anyone who has participated in a debate on, say, abortion or tax policy can
testify. One person will advance the principle of the right to life, while the
other will talk about the woman's right to control her own body. Or one
side will speak of a person's right to be secure in their property without
government interference while the other side will insist on the necessity of
publicly financed goods such as education or health care.

We instantly recognize these discussions, and very likely we have participated in them. We also recognize that a certain frustration often attends
these conversations; the other side fails to be persuaded by what we feel are
careful deductions from objectively valid premises. In other words, they are
the kind of arguments that *ought* to persuade, but rarely do. We may even
be left with the feeling that a moral dialogue is impossible or that the "other
side" will not listen to reason. Alasdair MacIntyre points out that all of these
arguments share three salient characteristics.[1] The first we may call "conceptual incommensurability." Each of the arguments is logically valid, or
may be made so, in that the conclusions follow logically from the premises.
But the premises themselves are based on quite different normative concepts;
the right to life is set against the right to moral autonomy and the control
of one's own body, or the right to property is set against the public good.
We have no way, in the current environment, of logically deciding between
these premises or rationally determining the proper relationship between

15

them; once we have worked our way back to the premises, no further debate is possible and we end up with assertion and counterassertion. At that point, the debates take on a shrillness that is always a hazard of conceptual incommensurability.

But this shrillness has another source as well. For if we possess no unassailable criteria that may be used to convince our opponents, then in making up our own minds it follows that we have made no appeal to such criteria, and something "non-rational" underlies all our positions.[2] But each of the arguments aspires to be impersonal; each speaker presupposes the use of criteria which are objective and independent of the attitudes of the speaker or the hearer. This imparts a paradoxical air to the discussions. If we attend only to the first characteristic, where argument lapses quickly into incommensurable premises, we might conclude that there is nothing here but a clash of wills. But this second characteristic, as MacIntyre points out, "the use of expressions whose distinctive function in our language is to embody what purports to be objective standards, suggests otherwise."[3] Even if one were to argue that such "objective" appeals were no more than a mask for an attempt to impose our will on others, we would still have to ask, "Why this masquerade?" "What is it about rational argument which is so important that it is the nearly universal appearance assumed by those who engage in moral conflict?"[4]

The third characteristic identified by MacIntyre is related to the first two: it is easy to trace the rival and incommensurate premises to their historical origins. The abortion debate pits a concept of rights which is derived from Locke against an appeal to moral law which comes from St. Thomas. In the second debate, ideas from Rousseau compete with those from Adam Smith. However, merely citing these names runs the risk of flattening a history which is long and complex. Why so many moral sources? When we examine the history of these concepts,

> we recognize that all those various concepts which inform our moral discourse were originally at home in larger totalities of theory and practice in which they enjoyed a role and function supported by contexts of which we have now been deprived. Moreover the concepts we employ have in at least some cases changed their character in the past three hundred years; the evaluative expressions we use have changed their meaning. In the transition from a variety of contexts in which they were originally at home to our own contemporary culture "virtue" and "justice" and "piety" and "duty" and even "ought" have become other than they once were.[5]

In other words, the concepts we employ and the words we use are relics from another era and have simply lost or changed their meanings. *All* of the concepts in these debates — freedom, rights, a universal moral imperative, etc. — have their place and they were once at home in some larger view. But now we have lost that larger view that gave them a meaningful relationship to each other, a relationship that made each of the concepts intelligible relative to each other. Instead of a coherent moral whole, we have fragments left over from a previous era, and we do not know how to put them back together; parts which used to fit together are now at war with each other. In order to recover an intelligible moral dialogue, it will be necessary to understand how we got here; we cannot find the way out unless we understand how we got in.

THE FRAGMENTATION OF
MORAL DISCOURSE

We begin our discussion with the so-called Enlightenment because it is at this point that we can most easily identify the fragmenting of moral discourse. The salient features of that era are the rejection of received authority and the attempt to root all things, morality included, in some non-religious base, such as idealism or empiricism. Perhaps by retreating into a realm of pure thought (as in Descartes) or by grounding it in pure observation (as in Hume), we could understand the moral realm, indeed all realms, apart from faith. This is not to suggest that the Enlightenment didn't have its own history; it did not spring full grown from the ground, but was itself a development of certain strains in Scholasticism, most notably the split between Scholasticism and Nominalism. The Scholastics had undertaken the task of "faith seeking understanding," of uncovering the rational hidden in the divine will. But Scholasticism never intended to divorce that understanding from the underlying faith upon which it rested so as to create an "independent" understanding which could stand apart from faith. Scholastic understanding was based on the *certainty* of faith.

The watchword of the Enlightenment was not certainty, but *doubt* and especially doubt about religious authority. To René Descartes, for example, doubt was not just a state of mind, but a *method* which served as the basis for all philosophy and hence all thinking. "Philosophy must begin not with a fact — as in Aristotle — but with a doubt."[6] This doubt is so radical that it is applied universally. "I will consider myself as without hands, eyes, flesh, blood, or any of the senses."[7] Descartes' next step was to find an idea that is so "clear and distinct" that it cannot be doubted. This idea was his own existence as a thinking principle, the famous *Cogito ergo sum,* "I think, therefore I am." For John Locke, on the other hand, this same doubt led in the opposite direction: we cannot trust the mind itself because everything the mind knows comes from sensations. If sensations were the root of all our ideas, then logically we must go back to the senses to understand anything, including morality. Where Descartes was without "hands and eyes," Locke was *all* eyes and ears and touch and taste. It is not necessary here to examine whether these ideas really function in the way their authors wish them to. Here we are concerned only with showing that doubt had replaced certainty and this already had led to a fragmenting of experience between the purely mental and the purely extra-mental. A *dualism* had replaced the unity of mind and body that was the hallmark of Scholastic thinking.

We must note here that none of the Enlightenment figures really doubted morality as such. Indeed, they followed as faithfully as anyone the ethics they had inherited from a former age; the problem was giving an account of why they should do so, an account that rested not on faith but on reason *alone* or on some indisputable fact of human psychology. The Enlightenment thinkers, and their heirs (which includes all of us) tried to follow one path or the other. Kant, for example, would opt for reason alone, while Hume and his successors would rely on the passions alone. We can examine the efforts of these two philosophers as representatives of each approach to see why each one is incomplete without the other, and why either approach leaves moral discourse in a fragmented and incomplete state.

Immanuel Kant

Immanuel Kant (1724–1804) attempted to give an account of morality based on reason alone. Central to Kant's thinking was the thesis that if the rules of morality are rational, they must be binding on all humans in just the way the rules of arithmetic are, and that they cannot depend on the contingent ability of actual persons to carry them out.[8] Kant's rationality excluded both an appeal to divine law and an appeal to human experience, such as considerations of happiness or pleasure; for Kant, practical reason is self-contained and has no criteria other than itself. Such reason must be both *categorical,* admitting no exceptions related to the circumstances and conditions of human beings, and it must be *imperative,* binding all humans, always and everywhere. Kant proposed the *categorical imperative* as an unassailable criterion of judgment for any moral principle which depends neither on God's will nor man's pleasure. Kant's test for this categorical imperative was, "Can we or can we not consistently will that everyone should always act on it?"[9] Statements such as "always tell the truth" or "do not commit suicide" are deemed to pass this test while ones such as "tell the truth only when convenient" do not. But in fact it is not clear that the latter statement does not pass such a test, and the arguments that it does are inconsistent. Further, it is easy to see that many immoral and non-moral statements can also be universalized, statements such as "never wear white after Labor Day" or "always persecute those who hold false religious beliefs."

Of course, Kant did not mean to include such statements, and indeed he felt they were excluded by a further criterion which had a specific *moral* content, namely, "Always act so as to treat humanity, whether in your own person or in that of others, as an end, and not as a means."[10] But is this a statement that can be proved by reason alone? It would certainly be immoral to hold that everyone ought to be treated as a means, but it can be held without inconsistency. It might be unpleasant to live in such a world of egotists, but to argue that such unpleasantness excluded egotism would be to introduce just those irrational considerations of happiness which Kant was attempting to eliminate from his "rational" considerations of morality. As MacIntyre notes, "The attempt to found what Kant takes to be the maxims of morality on what Kant takes to be reason therefore fails."[11]

David Hume

Where Kant eliminated the passions, David Hume (1711–76) eliminated reason and based all morality on the passions. In Hume's view, morality is the set of rules which help us to attain those ends which the passions set before us; morality is thus a kind of utility, something that aids us in attaining our desires. "Good" and "evil" are only synonyms for "pleasure" and "pain"; what is good is that which brings us pleasure, and the bad is that which brings pain. This is the philosophy known as *hedonism*, in which self-interest is the sole determinant of moral worth. Of course this immediately poses a problem, for if such rules as justice and promise-keeping are to be kept *only* because they serve our long-term interests, would we not be justified in breaking them when they do not serve our interests *and* have no further ill consequences?[12] At first, Hume denied any wellspring of altruism which could supply the defects of the argument from interest and utility, but later had to fall back on one, and labeled this wellspring "sympathy." Sympathy became for Hume, as later it did for Adam Smith, the invention which bridges the gap between following rules for reasons of self-interest and following them even when they do not appear to be in our self-interest. Like Kant, Hume was forced to introduce a purely "moral" notion that did not fit easily into the rest of his system.

No "Ought" from "Is"?

It would be wrong, however, to omit the negative reasons which Hume advanced to question the role of reason. Indeed, Hume questioned the very grounds on which any "reasoning" about morality can take place, because he did not see how, in a syllogism, a set of factual claims can lead to a moral conclusion. In other words, from statements about what *is,* can we conclude to what *ought* to be? The problem becomes clear if we look at the structure of the syllogism. "All men have two legs; Socrates is a man; therefore, Socrates has two legs." Note that the terms of the premises are connected by verbs of being or having; hence the terms of the conclusion must also contain these verbs. Hume's question was, how can you get an "ought" into the conclusion if it does not appear in the premises? If Hume is correct, and he certainly seems to be, can there be any reasoning about morality whatsoever? Can our choices ever be motivated by anything greater than mere personal utility?

Utilitarianism

Where Hume attempted to bridge the gap between a pure hedonism and altruism with a notion of "sympathy," other hedonist philosophers found no necessity to do so. Hume's teacher, Jeremy Bentham (1748–1832), advocated a pure hedonism.

> Nature has placed mankind under the governance of two sovereign masters, pleasure and pain. It is for them alone to point out what we ought to do as well as what we shall do.... In a word, a man may pretend to abjure their empire; but in reality he will remain subject to it all the while. The *principle of utility* recognizes this subjection, and assumes it for the foundation of that system the object of which is to rear the fabric of felicity by the hand of reason and law.[13]

Bentham believed that pleasure and pain could provide an infallible guide to law and morals through "hedonic calculus"; by simply adding up the pleasure or pain that a decision might cause, legislators could easily calculate the "greatest good for the greatest number." But to do this, they would have to rid themselves of any notions of altruism. "Dream not that men will move their little finger to serve you, unless their advantage in doing so is obvious to them." Bentham called his philosophy "utilitarianism." The public good is merely the sum of private and individual utilities. Only individual self-interest exists. However, it is not all that clear that individualism is capable of providing a notion of a public or common good. What might be in the best interests of a parent, an individual citizen, or a CEO may or may not be in the best interests of the family, the community, or the company, and this is especially true if "good" is defined in terms of mere "utility" or "pleasure." Moreover, it is not all that clear that "pleasure" is a particularly useful term in defining the good. Certainly some goods do bring us pleasure, but others do not. For example, it is difficult to explicate the sacrifices one makes to raise children or to serve in the army in time of war in terms of "pleasure." Further, there are any number of palpably evil actions which can bring "pleasure"; the thief or the rapist undoubtedly feels pleasure, but it is difficult to argue that theft and rape are "goods."

Nevertheless, utilitarianism came to dominate economics completely. Throughout the nineteenth century, prominent economists such as Jeremy Bentham, Jean-Baptiste Say, Nassau Senior and John Stuart Mill proclaimed utility as the only "scientific" basis for economics.[14] By the close of the nineteenth century the "marginalist revolution" gave utilitarianism a mathematical foundation. Eros, or desire, which founds all demand curves, is now just an expression of the "utility" that a product can give, and desires which cannot be measured by individual utility are deemed not to exist. The complex structure of human needs is reduced to a simple and egotistic calculation of benefits, and egotism replaces self-respect as the basis of human action. This becomes most clear with the economist Ludwig von Mises (1881–1973), the founder of the neo-Austrian school, who makes utilitarian calculation the heart of all human action while excluding any other considerations; selfishness needs to be so absolute as to exclude the notion of any pure charity.

> In this sense every action is to be qualified as selfish. The man who gives alms to hungry children does it, either because he values his own satisfaction expected from this gift higher than any other satisfaction he could buy by spending this amount of money, or because he hopes to be rewarded in the beyond.[15]

Utilitarianism's effect on the market is obvious. If all values are purely individual and irrational, then the market itself becomes the sole means of resolving values. The market is deemed to be the morally neutral meeting place where all individual values are correlated on a "democratic" basis (one dollar, one vote). What "value" do we place on charity? That is easily measured by the number of dollars contributed. What value do we place on SUVs? That is easily determined by adding up the amount we spend on them. Each person brings his or her values to the marketplace, a public space deemed to be the absolute and unchallengeable moral arbiter, and the market responds with a "public" answer measured purely by votes (that is, dollars) devoted to each segment or product. No public reflection on morals is necessary, or even possible, and indeed any such reflection which limits the market in any way would amount to the imposition of one private view and hence cripple the market's role. From a "public" point of view, morality is nothing more than legality and market viability. Abortion is allowed because no mother is forced to have an abortion (the child is as yet voiceless and hence can voice no opinion) and the market-necessary requirement of "freedom" is maintained. The proper level of public spending on education, medicine or welfare is merely the aggregate of the public's willingness to tax itself (or borrow) to support these things. In such an environment, pornography, Christianity, paganism, even war and peace, life and death, become merely competing products within the marketplace, products which the market, in its free and sovereign wisdom, values, or not, as the case may be. Morality thus becomes marketing.

Emotivism

One effect of utilitarianism is to render meaningless any judgments about "better" or "worse"; we are not permitted to say that philosophy is better than pornography or beauty better than ugliness. All we can say is that philosophy gives pleasure to this person, while pornography gives it to another. As Jeremy Bentham put it, "push-pin is as good as poetry." Without the ability to distinguish "better" from "worse" and "good" from "evil," the entire moral structure collapses, and all moral discourses become meaningless. What then *are* we doing when we discuss moral issues? G. E. Moore (1873–1958), in the *Principia Ethica* (1903), concludes that "the good" is a simple, indefinable, non-natural property which is incapable of either proof or disproof.[16] Of course, this removes the good from the realm of rational discourse and confines it to pure intuitions. From this *intuitionism,* it is but a small step to treat good and evil as simply emotional responses about which there can be no real discussion. Hence, the attempt to treat moral statements as an exercise of the rational powers can only be a mask for an attempt to impose our own views on others, for our own exercise of personal power. Thus the moral discourse can only be about *power* and not about morality per se. This philosophy is called *emotivism,* and it is the reigning orthodoxy of our contemporary political and economic world. In a pluralistic society, no group can advance any claims that have the authority to bind us in any way because all such claims are merely personal and not rational. The only way to resolve these claims is through the institutions of democracy, both political and economic. Morality becomes a set of legalisms we adopt not so much for "moral" reasons (which are, in any case, deemed not to exist) but for utilitarian purposes. For example, certain rules are required to insure the smooth operation of the market, such as the right of private property or the enforceability of contracts. The moral thus becomes the merely legal, and moral claims not related to the smooth operation of markets and public order are viewed with a suspicion that someone is trying to force a purely private set of moral standards on us. Should abortion be allowed? If standards of right and wrong (and hence of life and death) are mere legalisms reflecting a majority preference, how can it be denied? Should the poor be supported at public expense? That is a decision for the majority of the people as they vote their purely personal values.

We are therefore led, by a long historical process, into a strange situation. On the one hand, our moral discussions take place as if they were based on categorical imperatives; on the other hand, our political, economic, and social systems are based on a utilitarianism which denies such imperatives can exist. Therefore we live our moral lives in a kind of schizophrenia: we *want* our moral reasoning to be about something real, but our cultural environment denies that it can ever be so. Is there anyway to recover a meaningful moral dialogue?

RECOVERING THE MORAL DIALOGUE

The attractiveness of utilitarianism and emotivism in an environment where so many competing views exist side by side cannot be denied. Yet, at the same time, it leaves even its supporters with a certain uneasiness. Many a conversation about moral issues has been cut short with the statement "that's *your* opinion." While such a statement may end the conversation, it cannot end our disquiet; we feel somehow that a moral statement should be more than just an opinion. It is unsatisfying, even disturbing, to be told that the fate of a child or the fate of a nation rests on no foundation other than a collection of personal whims, even when those whims are dignified with the name of freedom. Nor can we entirely avoid the suspicion that something is fundamentally wrong with a system that treats both God and pornography as mere competing products. So we must ask, "Can a rational moral dialogue be recovered?"

Moral Logic

If Hume is correct about logic excluding any "ought" from its conclusions, then the answer to the above question must be "no." For Hume (and in general, for us as well) factual premises cannot lead to evaluative conclusions. But is this really so? It seems that we can construct syllogisms in which terms appear in the conclusion which do not appear in the premises. For example, take the factual premises, "This watch is grossly inaccurate" and "This watch is too heavy to carry about comfortably." From these we may conclude, "This is a bad watch." From the premises, "Mr. Jones gets a better yield for his crop, than any farmer in the district" and "His dairy herd wins all the first prizes at the fairs," we can validly reach the evaluative conclusion, "He is a good farmer."

> Both of these arguments are valid because of the special character of the concepts of a watch and of a farmer. Such concepts are *functional concepts*; that is to say, we define both "watch" and "farmer" in terms of the purpose or function which a watch or a farmer are characteristically expected to serve. It follows that the concept of a watch cannot be defined independently of the concept of a good watch nor the concept of a farmer independently of that of a good farmer. . . . Hence any argument that moves from premises which assert that the appropriate criteria are satisfied to a conclusion which asserts that "This is a good such-and-such", where "such-and-such" picks out an item specified by a functional concept, will be a valid argument which moves from factual premises to evaluative conclusion.[17] (emphasis added)

So long as there is a functional concept in the premises, there may be an evaluative statement in the conclusion, one that relates the facts to the function and comes to a judgment. So we *can* go from "is" to "ought," from factual premises to evaluative conclusions. *Function* always implies a "good" or "bad" in the particular performance of the function; we no longer are forced to divorce what "is" from what "ought to be." Further, we can note that all things, insofar as they have any meaning at all, have a function. We can barely use a term at all without some notion of how it functions in life or in language. This is true even of the most abstract concepts, such as pure number. For example, we do no violence to logic if, after a demonstration that "$1 + 1 = 2$," we state our conclusion in the form, "therefore, one plus one *ought* to equal two and does in fact do so." Indeed, the evaluative premise may actually be more secure than the purely "factual" one. Therefore we can root the moral discussion not merely in abstractions, but in an *ontology,* in what actually *is*. The "ought" is no longer banished to the realm of mere feeling and opinion, but rooted in the very concreteness of the world; the "is" and the "ought" are bound together as with iron hoops.

Rather than saying, therefore, "no ought from is," we should say, "an ought *only* from an is."

The Individual and Society

Having shown that logic does not exclude evaluative conclusions, we still have not solved the problem. For while we can determine with watch-like accuracy the function of a watch, we have to ask if we can do so for a human being. If the logic requires a functional term in the premises, what functional premise will we give to a person? Of course, every man or woman we actually meet, including the one we meet in the mirror, has a variety of functions. He or she is a sea-captain, a lawyer, a mother, a student, a businessman. And in each of these roles we may evaluate their performance. But when we strip away the roles, what is left? For the Enlightenment thinkers, what was left was the *autonomous individual*. This individual was complete in herself and had no natural good save the goods she chose for herself. This made the "good" purely the product of individual choice, having no relevance beyond the bounds of the individual. Hence, it became impossible to assign an overall good to man. Without such a purpose, as we have seen, it is impossible to engage in any moral logic whatsoever. It is for this reason that the Enlightenment project *had* to fail. If the "good" really only means "the good for me," if justice only means "what I take to be just," then all moral discussion is about subjective values that can't really be arbitrated in any logical way. Therefore the way was opened to a pure emotivism, in which "good" and "bad" become equivalent to "what I like and what I dislike." In such an environment, moral discourse becomes a war of opinion with domination as the goal.

But does this "autonomous individual" match any reality that we know or have experienced? It is true that we have been brought up, all of us, to believe in our own autonomy, to believe that we are our own persons and have only such connections and obligations as we choose to have. This individualism represents freedom: we as individuals are free from all restraint and especially the restraints of customs and traditions which impose a morality on us as something external, rather than something freely chosen on rational or emotional grounds. But is this really the case? Can a pure individualism really represent freedom? Indeed, does the autonomous individual really exist at all, or is this merely a cultural construct poorly related to what we actually see in the world? The question is, "What do we actually see, in ourselves and others?"

What we first notice is that none of us created ourselves but were called into being into the ready-made community of family. As we discussed in

chapter 1, we received from this community certain gifts, and not just material ones like food and shelter, but also the gift of language, a purely cultural
construct. We received all of our notions of right and wrong, proper and
improper as "ready-made" and complete. A person always finds him- or
herself *already* situated within a linguistic and cultural framework and always makes appeal to certain collective (though indeterminate) norms to
make sense of the world.[18] We did not freely choose our situation; it chose
us. Nor do our choices occur within a pure individual autonomy, but only
within a social discourse. The reality of human existence is simply that a
human being is a *social* being, and that every consideration of morality (or
politics, economics, etc.) that attempts to reduce humankind to a mere collection of individuals will profoundly distort the facts of human existence.
Society is not a mere epiphenomenon or accidental result of the grouping of
individuals, but the very thing which gives individuals both their being and
the context for all their actions.

But should we then begin our search for meaning at the social rather
than the individual level? This too is a problem, since we never see the
social except in individual actions. So we have a certain tension here: we see
the "social" only in individual actions, but we can interpret those actions
only in a social context which the actions themselves presume.[19] We cannot
begin our inquiry assuming a society which is merely the result of "freely
contracting" individuals, because all parties to this supposed contract are
already part of it before they are asked to sign on. Nor can we begin with
the purely social, since we cannot see the social except in individual actions.
Thus we must eliminate both a pure individualism and a pure "sociology"
as a complete description of man. If we cannot begin our inquiry with the
individual, and we cannot begin with society, what's left?

The Person as a Functional Term

We have already rejected both the autonomous individual and the collec-
tivity of society as the proper places to begin a moral inquiry. But we can
start from a term which unites them both. This term would stand for "the
individual-in-society," the only individual we ever actually meet. As it turns
out, this term already exists within the Western tradition, and the term is
person. Of course, we take the term "person" for granted today and use it
interchangeably with "individual." The term, however, does not exist in ancient languages; the word comes from the Latin *personare* which originally
referred to a stage mask. The idea of the "person" was a unique contribution of Christianity to the understanding of being human, and it arises from
reflections on the nature of the Trinity. The Christian narrative presented

a startling paradox: a God who was a unity within a community. Further, the names of the divine characters, all equally God, were the names of relationships: Father, Son, Spirit. One can only be a "father" in relation to an offspring, or a son in relation to a parent. While the term "spirit" may not seem like the name of a relationship, in fact its meaning in Christian theology is the spirit of love between the Father and the Son, and hence it too names a relationship. Thus God himself emerges, in the Christian narrative, as a divine community in which the "persons" are defined by their relationships. The Old Testament God, YHWH, the "I am," was the Lord of Being; in the New Testament, Being itself is subsumed under a community of love; the very "being" of the persons is a constant gift of love from each one to the others.

What is true for the divine persons is true, analogously, for the human person as well. The person receives his or her being as a series of gifts (grace) — being itself, family, language, culture, etc. — and accepts these gifts by refashioning them and passing them on. We can note here that the idea of "autonomy" is de-emphasized in favor of relationship. This is not to deny a certain autonomy; the term "person" already includes the term "individual." However, this autonomy is no longer abstract and absolute; rather it has a content, namely the receiving of gifts and the decisions relating to their use. It is an "autonomy-within-relationship." Further, the relational nature of the person implies that we only see persons in relationships, that is roles — parent, friend, business partner, student, etc. — and roles imply *function*. How do we function as a "good" student, parent, businessperson, etc.? Therefore the term "person" is a *functional* term, which is precisely what we need in order to have any possibility of a moral logic. We can root a real discussion of morality in the concrete reality of the human person.

We can also note that "person" is an "integral" term. It includes the totality of the person: thinking, feeling, acting, choosing, etc. Hence it is no longer necessary to fragment the bases of morality. For example, is stealing wrong because it is irrational or because we *feel* that it is wrong? The answer is "yes" to both. Certainly when we are the victims of a theft, we feel a wrong has been done. When we commit a theft, we feel either that we have cheapened ourselves or that we must find a way to rationalize our actions. In either case, we intuitively know that something is wrong, and this is prior to any reflection on the nature and consequences of theft. Nevertheless, we rarely leave it at the level of intuition, but reflect on the nature of honesty and what demands it can make on our actions. The reasons we act in a moral way, or at least desire to do so, arise from our character, from the habits we have formed. However, these habits are not, strictly speaking, rational.

Rather they arise from feelings, thoughts, and actions, that is to say, from the *whole* of human experience. It is no longer necessary to take one part of that experience, say rationality or emotion, and force it to stand for the whole of what it means to be human.

Values and Culture

We have demonstrated that a moral logic is possible and that the full experience of the human person can be integrated in our considerations of morality. Yet it seems there is further work to be done. If we look at the cases that started this chapter, we recall everyone began with "reasonable" but incommensurate premises; they were "logical" within their frames of reference but incomparable with other frames of reference. All sides in these debates acknowledge the validity of the premises of the other, but arrange them in different hierarchies. For example, in the abortion debate, no one would deny a certain "privacy" in making moral choices, and few would deny that living things have some right to continue living. But those who favor a legal right to abortion absolutize privacy and relativize life, while those who oppose it do the opposite. What is at stake, then, is not so much the validity of the premises, but the order in which they are arranged, our "moral hierarchies." So the question becomes, "Where do we get these hierarchies of value, and how may we compare and evaluate them?"

The answer to the first question is that we (mainly) inherit them; what will seem "natural" and "moral" to us (at least initially) will depend on the place, time, and circumstances of our birth. In the Greek city-state, a society that believed mainly in a worldly happiness whose fullness was available only to those with the "moral luck" to be born to the right class, a slave economy seemed "natural." In the medieval kingdom, where moral dignity was imparted to each human being, and where human destiny was ultimately in another world, a hierarchy of cooperating/competing powers represented by the guilds and other institutions was the norm. For the world of the Enlightenment — the world to which you and I are heirs — the moral ideal is the autonomous individual, and the cultural authority of any particular morality is dependent on its proper marketing. Now if we start from this last position, which indeed is where you and I have been taught to start, it is reasonable to take autonomy, and therefore privacy, as the highest value, and to make all other values relative to it. This goes a long way toward explaining why abortion is an issue of such great import for the heirs of the Enlightenment. But if you adopt the position of the Christian Republic, where all living things have an irreducible dignity, abortion becomes morally untenable.

Each of us, then, receives a certain hierarchy of values merely from the circumstances of our birth. These values are conveyed formally and informally by the institutions of our society: the schools, to be sure, but also the market, the political structure, the social customs, modes of dress, etc. All of these are educative. A culture, if it is to be alive at all, is always embodied in a given set of institutions and practices. Of course, this can't be viewed as a "mechanical" process such that a person born within a given culture also has, necessarily, a given set of beliefs. For one thing, a culture is never homogenous, but has various competing strains and nuances. For another, this is an historical process; culture changes over time. Older elements of the culture always exist side by side with newer ones, resulting in a certain tension. In our case, the Enlightenment ideals have never succeeded in completely annihilating the prestige and authority of the older Christian culture. But most importantly, while the human person is formed by culture, he also re-forms that culture in his every act; the person is capable of transcending the culture which forms her. And finally, no culture is complete, but contains within itself unresolved contradictions which always impel it forward. We can note, for example, that the Greeks (and the Americans until 1864) valued freedom yet lived in a slave society. In our own case, this dissonance resulted in the Civil War and later in the civil rights movement.

CULTURE, NARRATIVE, AND PRACTICE

In saying that our ideas are formed culturally, it is important to understand that a culture is not a set of statements such as might be found in a religious creed or a political platform. Rather, what a culture provides, primarily, are a *narrative* (or a range of narratives) which organizes the information we receive and a set of *practices* which embody that narrative. In our society, we tend to believe in the primacy of logic and that we organize, or at least *ought* to organize, our lives and beliefs logically. Therefore, the whole idea of all things being organized as a narrative may be counterintuitive to minds formed in the aftermath of the Enlightenment. The philosophers of the Enlightenment were, of course, fully aware that most men and women in most times and places had indeed organized their lives by some set of narratives, which they called "myths." Indeed, it was the prevalence of such narratives, whether Christian or pagan, which Enlightenment rationalism sought to overcome. But as we have seen, the Enlightenment could not find a firm foundation in logic and merely provided another and competing narrative.

Competing Narratives

We can get a better idea of how narrative functions in organizing the world for us by comparing two competing narratives with which all of us are familiar, those of materialism and Christian deism. In the materialist narrative, all things have their historical origin in the "Big Bang" and in the configuration of matter resulting from the motions originally imparted to them by this foundational event. Matter coalesces into the various lumps of fire and rock which we call stars and planets. By a continual ascent of material organization, matter becomes "living" and the living, by another long chain of events, becomes "conscious" and self-aware, and finally becomes man, society, history, war, love, etc., all of which *must* have their ultimate explanation in the arrangement and motions of matter.

The Christian narrative, on the other hand, posits a single God who constitutes himself in three persons by an eternal and continual act of love. This love overflows into the creation of beings who, although less than himself, are nevertheless capable of being raised up to a level of friendship and participation in divinity with him. Since they are less than divine, however, this participation can only be brought about by divine intervention in their affairs, in matter, and in time. Christians call this intervention grace, God's moment-to-moment care of the universe. The supreme grace is direct participation in the world and history, by which God actually becomes human in a sacrificial act which redeems humankind from its own folly.

These two accounts, though brief and therefore incomplete, are nevertheless complete enough to make some general statements about such organizing narratives (often called *meta-narratives*). In the first place, we can note that the foundational event in both cases cannot be explained. While the materialist event is arrived at by a chain of reasoning based on empirical evidence,[20] it has no prior explanation, not even in principle, because the singularity with which it begins destroys all information prior to itself and hence any possibility of reasoning about its causes. Both foundational events, the materialist and the Christian, stand by themselves as "singularities" in reason. Another quality we can note is that the narratives cover all of human and cosmic history; they begin with some foundational event and presume some terminal event. In the case of the narrative of materialism, it is either a death by fire in the re-collapse of the universe, or a "heat death" resulting from an ultimate expansion into the endless frozen void which is continually created. For the Christian narrative, there is a consummation in the Kingdom of God. And finally, we can note that the narratives slot all possible information into categories even before that information is received;

in a real sense, all information is "pre-judged" and assigned its appropriate position within the narrative.

Narrative and Rationality

Since the narratives do not rest on a "logical" foundation, are all encompassing, and pre-judge all possible information, does it not seem that we must exclude from them any notion of "rationality"? If we confine the "rational" to that which is logically demonstrable from secure and self-evident first principles, then narrative can never be "rational." There is very little that can, however. Neither the chemical composition of the moon, nor the act of love, nor the desire for honor and respect can be derived from first principles. Logic is a tool of human rationality, but not the whole of it. To get a better picture of what "rationality" means, we must return to the root word, *ratio*, and to the idea of "proportion" based on ratios.

The Enlightenment, following the tradition of medieval Scholasticism, tried to root all things in unshakeable first principles that did not depend on the Christian revelation. They succeeded only in establishing a new narrative; this narrative, however, required no less faith than did the Christian account on which it was at least partially based. Further, the effort to found morality on some single principle led to a fragmenting of human experience. But rationality — ratio — doesn't refer to just one element of human reasoning, but to its totality, to the relationship between "the world" and human experience. This allows us to include in our reason all aspects of what it means to be human: logic, emotion, sensation, experience, art, our innate moral sense, etc. Nothing need be excluded, but all put in proper proportion. And while no narrative can be logically demonstrated, they can all be rationally compared.

What form does this rational comparison take? Within any narrative there are areas which do not fit well into the overall schema. This leads to doubts or *aporias*, spaces where questions arise. For example, the materialist schema does not well accommodate the non-material realm, yet even thinking about "materialism" is non-material. It would seem that many areas of human life, indeed the most important ones, cannot be reduced to a material basis: love, honor, art, consciousness, etc., all seem to have something in excess of their material bases. It makes us uneasy to hear that "love" is just the movement of certain chemicals within the body. Whether it is true or not, we cannot get over a certain uneasiness because we simply do not experience love that way. The materialist narrative has difficulty accounting for the non-material elements of life, elements we experience as dominating our lives. The Christian narrative easily accommodates the material because it always acknowledges a "natural" base to all things human. Thus, for example, deism can easily account for the Big Bang, but materialism must exclude any notion of deism. The point here is not to settle the long-standing disputes between these narratives, but to suggest, however briefly, the way in which they should be compared. The primary point of comparison is to see their extent, to see what fits easily into the story and what does not. An "incomplete" narrative must flatten some aspect of the human to make room for an element taken to be more important, a circumstance which leads to "holes" in the story, holes which cast doubt on its rational coherence with the totality of human experience.

In returning to the examples that began this chapter, we can note that each set of premises, and the hierarchies which support them, are dependent on a meta-narrative. In understanding any of these positions, we must understand the underlying narrative that supports them, and the resulting hierarchy of values. Once the narrative is understood, the position it supports is essentially understood. Of course, the premises involved in any particular debate can be logically tested, but that will lead only to a partial understanding. In the end, the real question is whether a story which leads (in the abortion example) to a primacy of privacy (or to a primacy of life) offers a complete or a partial view of humankind; whether, that is, it is simply a better story. And since what is at issue is precisely this narrative view, issues really can't be "out-argued," but only out-narrated.[21]

The primacy of narration accords better with the way people actually think. As was mentioned before, we are not honest, in the first instance, because we have based it on some foundational principle, but because dishonesty does not accord with our narrative of human life; theft, whether we are the victim or the perpetrator, makes us uneasy. We may rationalize theft; we may even rationalize honesty; but in either case it is not the rationalization that moves us, but the discord theft causes with our own story of the world. Narration therefore is not so much a debate as it is a performance; the narration is alive to the degree that the story is performed, and performed not only in personal decisions, but in social institutions.

Narrative and Practice

It is important to reiterate that the narrative is primary. That is to say, we do not start with doctrines, premises, axioms, etc., but with a set of narrative "performances." For example, the Christian story does not start with an abstract doctrine of the Trinity; indeed the scripture doesn't mention the term at all. Rather it starts with a story in which God manifests himself in three distinct ways (such as at the Baptism of Jesus, Luke 3:21–22; Mt 3:13–17; Mark 1:9–11) and in which each manifestation is praised as God is praised, while, at the same time, God is praised as "one." This leads to a liturgical practice of prayer to the divine persons. It is only reflection on that practice and that story which leads to a *doctrine* of the Trinity, a process that takes three or four centuries to complete, if it really ever is "complete." In the same way we can note that capitalism, for example, did not flow from the meditations of Adam Smith; rather Smith reflected on what was already established practice within eighteenth-century England.[22] In each case, and likely in every case, the story is first performed before it is understood through reflection. Therefore, the question of "out-narrating" alternative views really becomes a question of establishing practices that embody the story and make it concrete in the world. The market embodies the world of individual autonomy and content-less freedom; it is the practice and not the theory that makes capitalism alive in the world today. Theory that doesn't result in practice is dead.

In sum, morality is both "deduced" and "discovered." There are certainly foundational principles involved, principles which can be resolved back to a "rational" standard, but also back to basic feelings and instincts. In addition, morality is discovered in our attempt to live in the social institutions we have inherited and to modify them according to the standards we have come to accept. But in the end, the only morality that counts is that which is "performed," made alive in the world by our actions.

THE CULTURE OF THE FIRM

In our world, this "performance" of the moral order takes place in large part within the confines of the business firm. Each firm is, of course, an expression of the wider culture that helps to create it, but at the same time each firm has its own culture in the same way that any other social institution does. A firm's culture will be determined in large part by how the controlling members of the firm view the purpose of the firm. Recall that in order to think morally, we must define a purpose or a function, and all moral decisions will follow more or less naturally. Firms generally view their purpose according to one of three possible models: the Shareholder Model, the Stakeholder Model, and the Common Good Model.[23] In the Shareholder Model, the firm's only purpose is to maximize shareholder wealth. While there are of course other goals, they are all subordinated to the idea of wealth creation. Now this is not all bad; wealth creation is certainly a necessary part of fulfilling human needs. However, wealth is not an end in itself, but a means to an end; it is a good, but not *the* good. The Shareholder Model reduces employees and the community to mere *instruments* of wealth creation.[24] This turns out to be problematic even in terms of business profits because it fails to recognize the value of the human contributions to the firm, which in fact are crucial. Firms advance and grow not so much on the basis of physical capital, but on the basis of "human capital," the creativity and innovation that each person is capable of bringing to the enterprise. Indeed, most people *want* to be enterprising at their work, but quite often the culture of the firm prevents their making a full contribution. "Organizations thrive by gifts of human excellence — skill, industry, and a spirit of cooperation that does not stop to count costs."[25] In a shareholder-only culture, these gifts tend to be thrown away, and agency problems (see chapter 17) tend to proliferate. We will visit these problems more thoroughly; suffice it to say for the present that the Shareholder Model runs the risk of creating values and practices that run counter to the integrity of the person while creating a culture of a relentless pursuit of profit over all other values.

The second model, the Stakeholder Model, attempts to correct the problems of the pure Shareholder Model by treating stakeholders — employees, customers, suppliers, and the larger community — as "quasi-shareholders."[26] This has the advantage of including a wider range of representation so as to achieve a balancing of interests of all the participants in a firm. However, it is deficient in several aspects. It assumes that the common good is reached by negotiation between stakeholders thought of in terms of "interest maximizers," thereby retaining the individualistic view of the human person.[27]

Both the Shareholder and Stakeholder Models of the firm retain the utilitarian view of the person and of the firm. But the utilitarian view can never reach the common good, or can do so only accidentally. But for any society to continue in being and to function reasonably well, some notion of the common good is required. The common good transcends a narrowly conceived view of the goods of each person and firm and allows wider goods to be realized, including the good of profit. Indeed, profit is a *foundational* good upon which other goods depend. But at the same time, all the other goods cannot be subordinated to profit without creating a culture that demeans both the individual person and the larger society. Common Good cultures are most often found in entities where the management or even ownership of the firm is dispersed throughout the enterprise. These are firms such as cooperatives, employee-owned firms, or firms that simply recognize open management and cooperative enterprise as core values. These firms are at least as profitable as any others, if not more so, yet are able to contemplate and achieve goods other than profit.[28]

This brief summary of models of the firm is not intended to be exhaustive. Rather, the intent is to show the connection between culture and practice, a culture that will be governed by a particular view of purpose and function. The business firm, no less than the human person and the economic order, requires some notion of *telos*, of purpose and function, in order to be rendered meaningful and intelligible. And since the firm is such an important part of modern life, the purpose that firms adopt for themselves will largely determine the purpose of society at large. The business firm forms a large part of our social experience; it forms a large part of our society. Therefore, the key to the reformation of society lies, in large part, with the reformation of the business culture.

CONCLUSION

We have discussed the impossibility of a moral discourse in the face of the Enlightenment fragmentation of mind and body, faith and reason. This fragmentation leads to a loss of the very idea of an *ought-ness* or *rightness*.

We have shown that the proper sense of rightness can only be recovered by discerning the function of things, their purpose or *telos*.

For humans, this purpose is always discovered not in the fiction of the autonomous individual, but in the reality of the person, a "being-in-relationship" with other persons, with family, with the community and society at large.

The term *person* is both a *functional* and an *integral* term. As functional, we can apply moral logic; as integral, we can reunite the fragments scattered by the Enlightenment: mind and body, faith and reason, logic and emotion.

The person always functions within a culture, a culture which forms the person and which is, in turn, reformed by his or her actions.

The culture itself is a set of narratives, which give meaning to all the actions within the culture, and a set of practices, which embody the narratives.

In our culture, these practices are performed, in large part, within the business firm, which itself is guided by a vision of its own purpose and function. The visions of a firm we can broadly classify as Shareholder, Stakeholder, or Common Good models.

Therefore, the reformation of society lies in large measure with the reformation of the business firm and with recovering a sense of the *common good.*

The common good itself is nothing less than a vision of justice. Every economic system, including our own, has embodied some notion of justice. But the precise idea of justice has shifted from culture to culture. Therefore we need to examine how justice has functioned as a term within economics.

Chapter 3

Justice in Economic History

Remove justice, and what are kingdoms but gangs of criminals
on a large scale?
                                                        —ST. AUGUSTINE

THE RECENT HISTORY
OF ECONOMIC HISTORY

Economic ideas, like all things human, are best understood in the context of
the history that produced them, because all human ideas are the products
of some history. Prior to 1972, that would not have been a controversial
statement, and it was generally required that graduate students of economics have at least one course in economic history. But in 1972, the University
of Chicago dropped this requirement, and most major institutions followed
suit. Underlying this decision was the belief that economics is a "hard" or
"natural" science rather than a humane one. As a hard science, economics would be totally independent of any "cultural" or "humane" influences.
Indeed, one of the most important economic history texts is Joseph Schumpeter's *History of Economic Analysis*, and the very title hints at the problem:
If economics is about analysis understood mainly in mathematical terms
rather than empirical ones, then the usefulness of a "history" is problematic; if economics is merely a matter of selecting the right equations, then
history is unnecessary since equations have no history.[1] Here we can see the
continuation of the Enlightenment project to free all things from the past and
root them firmly in the soil of pure rationality. But economics is a strange
science to desire its freedom from history, since all of its data is historical,
and its subject matter is human production, exchange, and consumption,
things that are beyond doubt culturally conditioned.

The result of this shift in economic education is a generation (or two) of
economists practicing in complete ignorance of the history of their art and
likely to have less than a full understanding of the ideas which they purport
to be using.[2] As Robert M. Solow noted:

My impression is that the best and brightest in the profession proceed as if economics is the physics of society. There is a single universally valid model of the world. It only needs to be applied.... We are socialized to the belief that there is one true model and that it can be discovered or imposed if only you will make the proper assumptions and impute validity to econometric results that are transparently lacking in power.[3]

It is doubtful that economic ideas (or anything dealing with human activity) can be properly understood apart from the history in which those ideas are embedded and of which they are part and parcel. If we are going to seriously look at the relationship between justice and economics, we need to see how this relationship has been handled by economists in history.

THE PREACHER AS ECONOMIST

Prior to the fifteenth century economics was normally discussed as a branch of ethics. The philosopher/theologian generally functioned as an economist because this was required to explicate the moral law. Hence we can call this period that of "the preacher as economist."[4] Of course, to explicate this "law," it was necessary to understand the "mechanics" of economics, which they did by inspecting the "natural law." However, this "natural law" is not a look at "raw" nature, as it came to mean in the seventeenth and eighteenth centuries, and certainly not a look at nature "red in tooth and claw." Rather, it was a view of nature bound up with a *teleology;* that is to say, a search for the true ends and purposes of natural things. These ends cannot be known scientifically but only morally.

The idea of the "preacher as economist" can be gleaned from the economic work of two of the greatest "preachers," Aristotle and St. Thomas Aquinas. The former was perhaps the first to produce an economic treatise; the latter expanded Aristotle's work in a Christian context. Together, the Aristotelian-Scholastic view formed a consensus that lasted until the sixteenth century.

Aristotle

For Aristotle, justice is not just a part of virtue, but "virtue entire, nor is the contrary injustice a part of vice, but vice entire."[5] Justice underlies all the virtues and deals with the relations of one human being to another:

And therefore justice is often thought to be the greatest of virtues, and "neither evening nor morning star" is so wonderful; and proverbially "in justice is every virtue comprehended." And it is complete virtue in its fullest sense, because it is the actual exercise of complete virtue. It is complete because he who possesses it can exercise his virtue not only in himself, but towards his neighbor also.[6]

It is within this relationship of one human to another, that is, within justice, that Aristotle locates economics. He presents a sophisticated analysis that includes a demand function, a distinction between use and exchange values, the function of money as the medium between value and demand (or "need"), and usury, among other things. Aristotle begins his reflection with the family, for "The family is the association established by nature for the supply of men's everyday wants."[7] It is the family, and not the individual, that is the starting point (contrary to modern economics) because only the family is self-sufficient; an individual in isolation can neither reproduce nor provide for himself.[8] Man, for Aristotle, is a social being always using language and reason and always embedded in a cultural milieu.

Crucial to our consideration of justice are two distinctions, Distributive and Corrective justice and Natural and Unnatural exchange.

Distributive and Corrective Justice. *Distributive* justice deals with how society distributes its "common goods." Aristotle defines these as "things that fall to be divided among those who have a share in the constitution."[9] This refers to the *common* goods of a state, a partnership, corporation, or some cooperative enterprise. For Aristotle, these things should be divided by "merit" based on contributions, but what constitutes this merit will be a matter that is determined culturally, "for democrats identify it with the status of freeman, supporters of oligarchy with wealth (or with noble birth), and supporters of aristocracy with excellence."[10]

Corrective justice,[11] on the other hand, deals with "justice in exchange"; that is, with transactions between individuals. In this case, justice consists in exchanging equal values, in "having an equal amount before and after the transaction."[12] This "equality in exchange" is the origin of "just price" theories. The problem is how to determine what values are equal when dealing with dissimilar products, which is nearly always the case. To use Aristotle's example, how many pairs of shoes are equal to one house? The only way to know this is by "need," which many economists understand as the demand function mediated by money. Thus the demand for houses and shoes can be compared by looking at their prices and the two can be equated in terms of money. Money, however, is a social convention: "this is why it has the name money (*nomisma*) — because it exists not by nature but by law (*nomos*)."[13] Thus the requirement for equality in exchange comes from the natural law, but the method of implementing it is legal or conventional. Although Aristotle uses money to make dissimilar items commensurate, he is not actually able to tell us how to do that, and admits to reaching an impasse on the problem.[14] The valuation problem, that is, *price*, remains central to economics.

Distributive justice, then, is a distribution of the products of a group to the members of the group, while corrective justice is between individuals. Distributive justice will be proportional to one's contribution to the group, and hence there can be unequal distributions based on unequal contributions. Corrective justice, on the other hand, will always involve equal amounts, like for like. The distinction between distributive and corrective justice remains central to economics, even if economists do not always recognize the distinction. Neoclassical economists generally cast economic questions in terms of free exchanges, that is, in terms of corrective justice. Many other schools have a tendency to see things in terms of distributive justice. This makes a profound difference in how they answer the questions, even when using the same data. To take a concrete example, we can ask if factor shares — the amounts of compensation given to capital and labor — are a question of distributive justice or of corrective justice. If the former, the shares will be determined by merit, which is culturally determined; if the latter, shares will fall under a calculation of the demand curves for labor and capital. Answering the question solely in terms of corrective justice suits the individualistic premises of neoclassicism because corrective justice is only concerned with exchanges between individuals; "social" questions do not intrude themselves. Therefore the notion of a social justice does not arise. Distributive justice, on the other hand, is always a matter of merit and contribution, questions which are answered in a social context. This distinction will therefore be a recurring theme in our examination of justice in economic history.

Natural and Unnatural Exchange. Also connected with justice is a "natural" limit on exchange. Aristotle recognizes that households need to have at least some wealth and property to survive.[15] But wealth can be pursued in two ways: one way is to get the things we need to live, and the other is to get money itself. The former is a necessary part of household management,[16] but the latter has no natural limit;[17] in the former case, men trade for what they need and cease when they have enough; there is no point in acquiring more bread than you can eat. But the latter case has no limit; money can be accumulated without end. This second type of exchange came about only after the use of money replaced barter.

Hence some persons are led to believe that getting wealth is the object of household management, and the whole idea of their lives is that they ought . . . to increase their money without limit. The origin of this disposition in men is that they are intent upon living only, and not upon living well: and, as their desires are unlimited, they also desire that the means of gratifying them should be without limit.[18]

The idea of some *limit* on exchanges strikes the modern person as strange, yet in an age of consumerism — consumption for its own sake and not to fulfill any real need — it is an idea worth recalling. Indeed, real wealth is impossible if we forget the reason for getting wealth in the first place.

St. Thomas Aquinas and the Scholastics

St. Thomas synthesized the work of Aristotle with a specifically Christian point of view to produce an economic view that reigned until the sixteenth century. Underlying his economic theories were two fundamental assumptions: "that economic interests were subordinate to the real business of life, which is salvation, and that economic conduct is one aspect of personal conduct, upon which, as on other parts of it, the rules of morality were binding."[19] Economic activity was regarded as a strong passion that needed restraint and boundaries; it needed to be put in its place, a place described by St. Thomas:

It is lawful to desire temporal blessings, not putting them in first place, as though setting up our rest in them, but regarding them as aids to blessedness, inasmuch as they support our corporal life and serve as instruments for acts of virtue.[20]

Here we have a view of economics as *bounded*, as existing within some limits. For example, self-interest, the mainspring of modern economics, was neither unknown nor condemned by the Scholastics. Indeed, it was required, since every man was required to provide for himself and his family.[21] However, self-interest was *limited* to providing the goods necessary for one's self and one's family only to the level called for by their "station in life"; beyond that, self-interest becomes the vice of greed.[22] The bounds of economics were given by Aristotle's idea of natural and unnatural exchange, the natural being that which supplies our needs, but the unnatural being for profit itself, unrelated to actual needs.[23]

Thus Thomas combines two ideas, the idea of a proper "station in life" and the idea of justice in exchange, to provide a synthesis between distributive and corrective justice. It is just this combination which, as we shall see, is often missing from neoclassical economics.[24] The idea of proper "stations" in life shows that equality was not a goal of Scholastic economics; while a race of sinless men could live from a common purse, communism was left behind in the garden.[25] The "stations in life" were embedded in a cultural milieu which required a hierarchy. The mechanism by which the Scholastics attempted to unite the distributive and allocative functions was the just price.

Just Price Theory. The Scholastics were aware of all the elements that go into modern pricing theory: utility, scarcity, supply and demand, costs, etc. However, they refused to reduce price to mere economic calculation. Most specifically, they refused the mainspring of modern pricing, utility, or "usefulness to the buyer." As one of the later Scholastics, Luis de Molina, put it,

> That one may not accept a higher price by reason of the advantage of gain of the buyer is proved from the fact that the advantage is not something of the seller's but the buyer's; therefore the seller may not accept payment for it; otherwise he would sell what is not his.[26]

Molina is repeating the words of Thomas from five centuries earlier, and the rejection of utility pricing is fairly consistent across the centuries dominated by Scholasticism. But if not utility, then what is the basis of the just price? For St. Thomas it is a matter of a price that "is neither more nor less than the worth of the thing."[27] But the worth of a thing is "not fixed with mathematical precision," but "depends on a kind of estimate, so that a slight addition or subtraction would not seem to destroy the equality of justice."[28] Thomas does not explicate the basis of a just price because the practice is already a part of the economic system of his time, and he assumes his audience already knows what he is talking about.[29] What seems hopelessly imprecise to us was more or less accepted as a "natural" part of the pricing system. Indeed, no pricing theory, right to our own day, has ever succeeded in being precise. What the Scholastics insisted on was that price reflect the wider social concerns expressed by the phrase, *common estimation.* Common estimation was not a result of market concerns, although it took those concerns into account. Rather, it was an ethical judgment about price that preceded the market; it was "an ethical judgment of at least the most influential members of the community."[30] In general, the Scholastic writers preferred prices that were fixed by law with due account given to market conditions; they were unwilling to give free reign to the market alone. The market was not sovereign, but constrained.

The primary factor in the common estimation was the wages of the workmen involved with the product, including the "worker" who is the merchant selling it. Just price theory was very much opposed to what is now called "economic profit"; the merchant was entitled to earn enough to support his station in life, but no more. His work deserved compensation, as did anyone's. At the same time, the worker was entitled to support adequate to his "station in life." Therefore wages were related to needs of the worker or the vendor, rather than a utilitarian valuation of the output.[31] The idea of the just price, from an economic standpoint, was that there should be no wealth without work, and that prices would be driven to costs, including and especially the cost of labor. Therefore the just price theory is often considered a precursor of the "labor theory of value" favored by Adam Smith, David Ricardo, and Karl Marx.

The theory of the just price conformed to the general practice of the Middle Ages which was to have a "free market" in natural produce (wheat or wool, for example) while attempting to control the rate of profit and wages. This control was exercised through the guild system and through positive law by setting fixed prices. The guilds themselves were associations of masters and journeymen that were granted monopolies over some trade in a given area in return for the pledge of a consistent level of quality and a fair price. Being monopolies, they were carefully watched.

Thus the just price was an attempt to drive price to the costs of production and eliminate what we would now call "economic rents." Modern theory finds the notion of a just price somewhat quaint and, to the extent that prices were fixed by law or monopolies, somewhat threatening. However, it should be noted that both modern and medieval pricing make the same claims, namely the elimination of unjust profits or economic rents by driving prices to costs; the just price may be equated with what is called the "long-term equilibrium price."[32] But the medieval theory makes another claim missing from modern pricing, namely that both the merchant and the laborer will receive adequate compensation to support them in their station in life, a station assigned by cultural forces. There would not be equality, but neither would there be massive wealth on one hand and destitution on the other; some notion of the common good would rule all classes.

THE ECONOMIST AS PREACHER

Between the fifteenth and the eighteenth centuries enormous changes took place in the economic life of Europe and most especially in England. Capitalism was by that time well established, but lacked a coherent theory to justify it. The ethical framework of medieval economics was under attack, but there was little to replace it. Or rather, what sought to replace it was a new concept which preached quite openly that "greed is good." This idea was most famously expressed in Bernard Mandeville's *Fable of the Bees: or Private Vices, Publick Benefits* (1714), "in which he put forth the seemingly strange paradox that the vices most despised in the older moral code ... would result in the greatest public good."[33] Further, we see a complete reversal of Aristotle's distinction between natural and unnatural exchange. Whereas natural exchange aimed at providing the goods necessary to live, for which money was merely a means and not an end, the *summum bonum* of the new ethic was the unlimited earning of money for its own sake.[34]

Into this ethical vacuum came the sages of the Enlightenment. If the older sages made economics a colony of ethics, the divines of the Enlightenment tended to reverse that order. Recall that the problem of the Enlightenment was to root all explanations in some naturalistic principle, be it logic or human psychology or induction based on observations of nature. God would be known not through written revelation, but through the revelation of nature. Thus the economist served a dual role: he interpreted the economic stars and read therein the will of God. God, or nature, was still invoked as a final cause but always operated through secondary causes which could be known "scientifically" and apart from any written revelation from the deity god-nature.[35] The major role for the "priests" of this god-nature was to answer the question raised by Mandeville: "How did 'private vices' become 'publick benefits'?" Without any conscious appeal to the common good, how could the common good result? For most of the classical and neoclassical economists, the market becomes a theodicy where god or nature is a Machiavellian sovereign who weaves long term benefits from purely private interests.[36] But as "nature and nature's God" are more thoroughly "understood," God himself becomes less necessary and nature becomes all we need to know. Thus the economist replaces the preacher. The "laws" of nature, interpreted by Enlightenment divines, become the hand of God in human affairs, and economics is raised to the level of ethics, if not actually surpassing it. The transitional figure in this process is Adam Smith (1723–90). There were, of course, Enlightenment treatises on economics before Smith, but by popular acclaim he is regarded as the founder of "classical" economics.

Adam Smith

Smith was a professor of moral philosophy at the University of Glasgow and was part of the Scottish Enlightenment. He was a Stoic philosopher and not a particular fan of Christianity. But he was a bitter enemy of the mercantilist class and a friend to the working classes. His writings on economics were a response to the "Mercantile Pamphleteers," a group of writers who aimed to influence government policy in favor of the English merchant class. But Smith's real aim was to do for political economy what Newton had done for astronomy: reduce the seemingly endless complexity to a simple natural rule. As Newton had "tamed" gravity with the inverse square law, Smith hoped to find a similar law for political economy.[37] The problem was, however, that Smith found not one, but two "Newtonian" principles, the Labor Theory of Value and the "Invisible Hand" theory, and they were opposed to each other; one theory emphasizes conflict and the other emphasizes harmony.[38] Hence Smith ends up being an iconic figure for two opposed economic philosophies, capitalism and communism. In the Invisible Hand theory we have the foreshadowing of what will become "neoclassicism." But from the Labor Theory of Value [LTV] is born Marx's theory of capitalism.[39] We will take each theory in turn, and then try to discover why there are two of them.

The Labor Theory of Value. According to the LTV, the exchange value of a commodity is determined solely by the amount of labor required to produce that commodity.[40] This value forms a "natural" price and is the equilibrium price around which the actual market prices tend to fluctuate; the forces of supply and demand push prices to this "natural price."[41] Thus labor forms a universal standard of value:

> Labour, therefore, it appears evidently, is the only universal, as well as the only accurate measure of value, or the only standard by which we can compare the values of different commodities at all times and at all places.[42]

Although labor is the real standard of value, Smith points out that it is never purchased at full price, but treated as any other commodity.[43] Smith notes that "in that original state of things, which precedes both the appropriation of land and the accumulation of stock, the whole produce of labour belongs to the labourer."[44] But, "As soon as the land of any country has all become private property, the landlords, like all other men, love to reap where they never sowed, and demand a rent even for its natural produce."[45] Further, men stand in need of a "master" and an advance on materials and wages.[46] Wages depend upon a contract, but the two parties are not equal in negotiating the wage contract. While masters can easily combine and the law does not prohibit such combinations, the law (at that time) prohibited them for workers. Masters can hold out longer than the workers.[47] Thus Smith identifies *actual* wages as the result of a power relationship between masters and workers and not a result of purely "economic" forces.

Smith is often viewed as an unequivocal supporter of capitalism, a friend to business, the prophet of selfishness, and the mystic of the "invisible hand." John Mueller has labeled this picture of Smith "Smythology";[48] the real Smith is far more complex. For example, far from being a supporter of mercantile interests, Smith was extremely suspicious of them: "People of the same trade seldom meet together, even for merriment and diversion, but the conversation ends in a conspiracy against the public, or in some contrivance to raise prices."[49]

Smith believed that the interests of the merchants were generally contrary to the interests of the laboring and land-owning classes; while the fortunes of these two rise and fall with the fortunes of the country as a whole, it is the opposite for the merchants:

> But the rate of profit does not, like rent and wages, rise with prosperity, and fall with the declension, of the society. On the contrary, it is naturally low in rich, and high in poor countries, and it is always highest in countries which are going fastest to ruin. The interest of this third order, therefore, has not the same connexion with the general interest of society as that of the other two.[50]

For Smith, the "liberal reward of labour" is crucial to the success of society:

> But what improves the circumstances of the greater part can never be regarded as an inconveniency to the whole. No society can surely be flourishing and happy, of which the far greater part of the members are poor and miserable. It is but equity, besides, that they who feed, cloath and lodge the whole body of the people, should have such a share of the produce of their own labour as to be themselves tolerably well fed, cloathed and lodged.[51]

> The liberal reward of labour, as it encourages the propagation, so it increases the industry of the common people. The wages of labour are the encouragement of industry, which, like every other human quality, improves in proportion to the encouragement it receives. A plentiful subsistence increases the bodily strength of the labourer, and the comfortable hope of bettering his condition, and of ending his days perhaps in ease and plenty, animates him to exert that strength to the utmost. Where wages are high, accordingly, we shall always find the workmen more active, diligent, and expeditious, than where they are low; in England, for example, than in Scotland.... If masters would always

listen to the dictates of reason and humanity, they have frequently occasion rather to moderate, than to animate the application of many of their workmen.[52]

This passage gives us a clue to what Smith was doing with the LTV; it is a theory about *equity,* that is, about distributive justice. Smith was doing two things: First, he was attempting to find a principle for economics equivalent to Newton's inverse square law for gravity.[53] Second, he was trying to establish the right of the worker to a sufficient wage based on pure natural law grounds in such a way that it could not be denied by reason or, one hopes, by employers. In explicating the LTV, Smith abandoned completely the idea of utility in pricing, something that had been connected to price theory since Aristotle. Further, his explication of the theory was totally inconsistent, and it would remain for later thinkers, such as David Ricardo and, more recently, Piero Sraffa to work out the details. Nevertheless, the Labor Theory of Value was influential in classical economics, so much so that John Stuart Mill (1806–73) could say of it, "Happily, there is nothing in the laws of value which remain for this or any other future writer to clear up; the theory of the subject is complete."[54] But Mill did note the difficulty of distribution; the values returned to the laborer were nothing like the full values that the Labor Theory of Value indicated. This led Mill to conclude that while the laws of production "Partake of the character of physical truth," the laws of distribution are "of human institution solely" and could be made "different, if mankind so chose."[55]

The "Invisible Hand." When Smith speaks of the LTV, the rhetoric is very much about social discord and class conflict. But Smith has a second theory, a theory of social harmony and economic welfare. This is the so-called "Invisible Hand" theory. The term originally appears in an earlier work, *The Theory of Moral Sentiments:*

[The rich] consume little more than the poor, and in spite of their natural selfishness and rapacity, though they mean only their own conveniency, though the sole end which they propose from the labours of all the thousands whom they employ, be the gratification of their own vain and insatiable desires, they divide with the poor the produce of all their improvements. They are led by an invisible hand to make nearly the same distribution of the necessaries of life, which would have been made, had the earth been divided into equal portions among all its inhabitants, and thus without intending it, without knowing it, advance the interest of the society, and afford means to the multiplication of the species.... In ease of body and peace of mind, all the different ranks of life are nearly upon a level, and the beggar, who suns himself by the side of the highway, possesses that security which kings are fighting for.[56]

In this view, the "security of kings and beggars" is equal, and all have an equitable share, a share that would be no different even if there were a more equitable distribution of property. Yet by the time Smith wrote the *Wealth of Nations,* he seems to have come to a different view. In the *Wealth of Nations,* the "invisible hand," which actually appears but once in the text, has a somewhat different meaning:

> By preferring the support of domestic to that of foreign industry, he intends only his own security; and by directing that industry in such a manner as its produce may be of the greatest value, he intends only his own gain, and he is in this, as in many other cases, led by an invisible hand to promote an end which was no part of his intention. Nor is it always the worse for the society that it was no part of it. By pursuing his own interest he frequently promotes that of the society more effectually than when he really intends to promote it.[57]

Here the term is used in connection with foreign trade and only means invisibility from the government bureaucracy. Smith held that if each man would look after his own business, the interests of trade, foreign or domestic, would take care of themselves. Smith had concluded that a government of, by, and for the mercantile classes did not benefit society. Everywhere Smith looked, he saw a system of subsidies, bounties, tariffs and restrictions all designed to grant privilege to the wealthy, and this fact filled him with righteous anger. The rich could no longer be depended on to make an equitable distribution of rewards, and government, he concluded, "is in reality instituted for the defense of the rich against the poor, or of those who have some property against those who have none at all";[58] the rich had captured the government to such an extent that it nearly always favored them over the poor.[59]

What does tie the two views of the "invisible hand" together is the idea of self-interest. As Smith expressed the idea:

> Whoever offers to another a bargain of any kind, proposes to do this. Give me that which I want, and you shall have this which you want, is the meaning of every such offer; and it is in this manner that we obtain from one another the far greater part of those good offices which we stand in need of. It is not from the benevolence of the butcher, the brewer, or the baker, that we expect our dinner, but from their regard

to their own interest. We address ourselves, not to their humanity but to their self-love, and never talk to them of our own necessities but of their advantages.[60]

The context of the passage is that of exchanges between individuals, or corrective justice. "Self-interest" here is simply descriptive of the reason people trade with each other. Nor was Smith the Prophet of Selfishness; rather, he makes a clear distinction between self-interest and "private interests" and always uses these terms in opposite ways. Self-interest is merely a man taking care of his own business and is generally beneficial to the public good; private interests are the combinations of merchants that attempt to seize monopoly power, subsidies, and other privileges from the government to the detriment of the public good. "Self-interest" for Adam Smith did not have the meaning that selfishness had for Mandeville or that it would later have for the utilitarian economists; these regarded selfishness as the only proper (or even possible) motive of human action. Self-interest had for Smith the same meaning it had for the Scholastics: the obligation each man had to take care of himself and his family through his own work and efforts. Since it was an exchange theory, it was also a theory of social harmony, since corrective justice (unlike distributive justice) is always an attempt to achieve equality in exchanges.

The Fragmentation of Economics. Many readers of Smith have noted a kind of schizophrenia in his work. For example, E. K. Hunt notes:

When Smith examined capitalism from the vantage point of production, he was led to a class conflict view of the economy; when he examined it from the vantage point of exchange, he was led to a social harmony view.[61]

But this was not schizophrenia; it was merely the recognition of the two kinds of justice which *must* be a part of any economic system. However, Smith could not join the two necessary halves of economic theory into a coherent whole. The unity that ancient and medieval economists had attempted was now shattered, and this fragmentation was reflected in the divisions in the economists who followed Smith. They tended to view the economy either from a distributivist or social justice viewpoint, or from a corrective or social harmony viewpoint. On the one hand there were the *labor theorists*, who concentrated on the social aspects of production and exchange, and on the other there were the *utilitarians*, who concentrated on the individual aspects of exchange only.[62] The two traditions continued in parallel for the next hundred years, with each side talking about *either* distributive or corrective justice, but rarely about both. That is to say, they each talked about half the economy, and hence talked past each other. This continued for a hundred years until the *neoclassicists,* working with exchange theory alone, discarded distributive justice entirely.

David Ricardo

Whereas Smith was a philosopher, David Ricardo (1772–1823) was an investor, who made a fortune in the stock market and retired at the age of forty-two to write about economics. His viewpoint is very different from Smith's; whereas Smith always wrote from the vantage point of a philosopher in sympathy with the worker, Ricardo wrote from the vantage point of the investor, and his chief concern was maximizing returns to investment. One important event that happened between the times of Smith and Ricardo was the publication off Thomas Malthus's (1766–1834) *Essay on Population,* discussed in the next section. Ricardo combined Smith's analysis with Malthusian pessimism. Nevertheless his contributions to economic theory were substantial. Here we shall be concerned with just two of them, the Law of Rents and his refinement of the Labor Theory of Value.

It is important to understand the historical context of Ricardo's work. Industrialization had reduced the working class to subsistence levels by 1750; the standard of living deteriorated during the second half of the eighteenth century, and any increase in the opening decades of the nineteenth century was slight at best.[63] The living conditions can be glimpsed from the report of a government official about slums in Glasgow:

> Although the outward appearance of these places was revolting, I was nevertheless unprepared for the filth and misery that were to be found inside. In some bedrooms we visited at night, we found a whole mass of humanity stretched on the floor. There were often 15 to 20 men and women huddled together, some being clothed and others being naked. There was hardly any furniture and the only thing which gave these holes the appearance of a dwelling was fire burning on the hearth.[64]

These conditions, however, were not really the concern of either Malthus or Ricardo, who both accepted them as the natural condition of the poor and part of the providence of God, who punished the poor for their improvidence and fecundity. Rather, they were concerned with a debate between the two wings of the English ruling class, the old landed gentry and the new industrialists. Malthus endeavored to show that high rents were justified and useful, while Ricardo, a representative of the capitalists, wanted to demonstrate that the landlords added nothing but cost. The specific occasion for their dispute was the debate over the Corn Laws, which imposed high tariffs on the importation of wheat, thereby raising the price of bread (the staple of the poor) and the rent on land.

The Law of Rents. David Ricardo developed the Law of Rents partially to validate Malthus's Theory of Population (the so-called Iron Law of Wages) and give it a stronger theoretical foundation. By the Law of Rents, the rent on any particular parcel of land will be equal to the difference in the product of that parcel and the product of the least productive parcel in use, that is its "marginal productivity."[65] For example, if one parcel A of land, the least productive in use, produces one bushel of wheat per acre, and another parcel, B, produces three bushels per acre, the rent on parcel B will be two bushels per acre, while A will command no rent at all. If a less productive parcel of land, C, is put into production, perhaps because of population pressures, and that parcel produces only one-half bushel per acre, the rent on parcel A will rise to one-half bushel and on parcel B to two and a half bushels per acre. An increase in population would force marginal land into production, thereby raising the rents on all other tenants. The least productive land that can be used is that which provides subsistence, so that eventually, as more land is placed in production, wages will sink to subsistence levels. Indeed, it is not just wages, but all non-rent returns, both returns to labor and to capital, which are limited by the Law of Rents.

The Law of Rents rests on three assumptions: one, that land is necessary for production, that is, there is no substitute for land; two, that land has varying productivities; and, three, that demand is rational, informed, mobile, and driven by financial calculations of value.[66] Assumptions one and two seem to be self-evident. The third assumption is "no more than the assumption of a perfect market. If actual markets are near perfect, then this proposition will be true. Hence, the operation of Ricardo's rental relationship will be an indication of how closely an economy is to the perfect market ideal."[67] It would seem then that the Law of Rents should hold, at least in an idealized state. When all the land in a country is owned, then land forms a kind of monopoly and rents rise to absorb all the increased values that arise from productivity improvements or population increases. The landlord is rewarded not for any services he provides nor for anything he has done to the land, but merely for the fact of ownership. Ricardo concludes that since the Law of Rents demonstrates that the landlord absorbs any increases in productivity at the expense of both capital and labor, "the interest of the landlord is always opposed to the interest of every other class of society."[68]

Although Ricardo mentions the interests of the laborers, he is not really interested in them. In fact, by the Iron Law of Wages, the real wages of workers cannot be increased above subsistence (labor's "natural price") for any length of time. This is because as the real wages are increased, the population rises. This causes more marginal land to be put into production to provide food for the increased population, which, by the law of rents, raises the rent and hence decreases the *real* wages of the worker, leading to a cycle of misery, death, and decreasing population. The Iron Law of Wages has in practice turned out to be made of straw, and this was true even in Ricardo's own day; for example, population growth from 1820 to 1870 was 0.79 percent per year, but per capita income growth was 1.26 percent per year, an effect contrary to the predictions of the theory.[69] Indeed, wages and population have always been more likely to rise and fall together, rather than move in opposite directions. Yet, despite the lack of empirical evidence, the theory remains with us both in an unbroken line of dire predictions from Ricardo's day to our own, and in the theory of an equity-efficiency trade-off, by which we are to believe that increases in wages at the lower end of the pay scale necessarily lead to increases in unemployment. However, what Ricardo had stumbled across in the Law of Rents was the theory of marginal utility as the limit on wages, of which the Law of Rents was merely a special case. It would be another fifty years until the "marginalist revolution" before anybody realized the implications of the law, but when they did, it changed economics forever.

On the basis of these arguments, Ricardo opposed the Corn Laws because they increased the price of bread and hence the cost of subsistence, and no one could reduce costs below subsistence wages for any great period of time. Ricardo's heart went out to the investor as Smith's had to the worker; profits must find their limit merely because the worker insisted upon eating. The solution was to find a way to lower the cost of bread by importing wheat. This led to the doctrine of comparative advantage, by which nations could profitably trade, "profit" here meaning "lowering the cost of subsistence and hence increasing the rate of profit."

The Labor Theory of Value. It was Adam Smith who originated the LTV, but he could never give it a consistent formulation because he could never quite account for the capital component of production. Ricardo solved this problem because he realized that capital — the tools and machinery of production — were merely the intermediate products of labor, created only because they contributed to the eventual production of a commodity for consumption.[70] Therefore capital is the embodiment of past labor in current production and always regresses to labor (and to other capital, which in turn regresses to labor).[71] Therefore capital is a series of "time-dated" labor inputs to production. Now all the outputs could be expressed in terms of labor that is expended either in the current period or past periods. This assumed that prices represented the cost of production;[72] this could be assumed if supply and demand worked to force prices to production costs.

If prices are always equal to the labor embodied in a product (including the past labor known as "capital"), then profit must be equal to the total amount of labor needed to produce the whole product minus the portion required to produce the subsistence necessary for the laborer. For example, if a product had ten hours of labor (and hence a price equivalent to ten labor-hours), and four hours were required to pay for the subsistence of the laborer, then profit would be equal to six labor hours, minus land rents. Therefore there are but two ways to increase profits: lower the cost of subsistence, or lengthen the number of hours the laborer works. Ricardo's distributive theory assumes the worker is entitled to no more than subsistence.

Although Ricardo used the LTV to defend high profits on the grounds that it added to capital accumulation, later labor theorists used it to justify higher wages, since profits were the surplus over subsistence, and there is no logical reason why all of these values should go to the employer. Therefore the capitalists abandoned the LTV and began to rely totally on utilitarian arguments, arguments that generally excluded a theory of distributive justice. But those interested in distribution continued to use the LTV.

Karl Marx

It may seem odd, so long after the collapse of the major communist states and the conversion of others into quasi-capitalist states, that it is necessary to discuss Karl Marx (1818–83). Yet Marxists have not accepted that the Stalinist states were a real implementation of Marx's theories, and that only events unfolding in *capitalist* economies can validate or refute Marx's thought.[73] But however one treats the "test" of Marxist economics, the great joke about Marx is that he *accepted* the capitalist system as a necessary development in human progress; he looked beyond capitalism to a later stage in development that would inevitably correct the defects of capitalism, but his critique of capitalism presupposed his acceptance of it. He was an enthusiastic supporter of large-scale production and economic concentration of the means of production. These laid the groundwork for a socialist state, and the capitalist phase could not be avoided. Marx had a mystical view of history. In his view, history had a hidden purpose and moved inevitably toward its consummation in the victory of communism. Thus for Marx, the atheist, history became a substitute for god. If, as Marx believed, religion was the opiate of the people, history was the opiate of the Marxists. The great value of capitalism, for Marx, was that it destroyed the previous religious culture and hence prepared humanity for the next stage in its development.[74] As capitalism had destroyed religion, communism would destroy capitalism in the final consummation of a mystical notion of history.

Marx was profoundly influenced by Adam Smith and David Ricardo. He reasoned that if Smith was correct that all values were traceable to labor, and Ricardo correct about subsistence wages, then the capitalists' share, that is, the difference between the price and subsistence wages, was a "surplus value" that belonged to the capitalist merely by virtue of his being a capitalist. Hence capitalism was inherently the exploitation of workers by the taking of the "surplus value." Marx, writing from within capitalism, was in fact able to make real contributions to economic theory. He refined Ricardo's LTV, giving it a more precise formulation, and contributed to the understanding of business cycles and depressions, a topic which had mystified, and continues to mystify, utilitarian economists. Marx was a great admirer of capitalist industrial technique. He believed that sheer volume of output would render the question of just distribution redundant and that for the new human being, with all of his material needs easily satisfied, the last barriers to autonomous freedom would be removed.[75] Therefore justice, as such, was not really the aim of Marxism; volume production would solve the problem.

One curious effect of Marx's historical mysticism is that the present moment is always sacrificed in the name of the future. Capitalism, being just a stage in the building of the worker's paradise, is justified as a necessary historical development that will one day be replaced by something better. The practical effect is that communist governments have always been able to rationalize present horrors in terms of future benefits. Having abandoned the present for the future, Stalinism and other tyrannies could, like capitalism, be justified as mere historical "stages." Marx's mysticism provides a convenient excuse for dictators.

More profound than his effect on capitalism was Marx's effect on socialism. Before Marx, "socialism" was a diverse set of movements which, in general, sought to restore to the worker the rights he had enjoyed in the pre-capitalist era. In general, these movements did not look to the state, but to voluntary associations; they were quite different form the "modern" notions of socialism, being, if anything, mostly opposed to state power on the whole rather than supportive of it. Guild socialists and syndicalists, for example, looked to forms of association which would annihilate the sharp distinction between "owner" and "worker" that was the centerpiece of capitalism. Marxism displaced these "socialisms" with "scientific" socialism that relied solely on gaining control of the state and the government bureaucracy. As G. D. H. Cole put it,

> Marx had "infected" socialists with an "economic fatalism" which made them acquiesce in centralization and top-down control of industry as an unavoidable precondition of economic efficiency. Instead of taking concrete steps to counter hierarchical authority in the workplace, they staked everything on the hope that socialist parties could gain control of the state.[76]

Marxism may have scared capitalism, but it destroyed socialism, or at least any rival form of socialism. Socialism became a kind of "state capitalism," with bureaucrats replacing industrialists as the real owners of capital and lords of production, and "socialism" acquired the meaning is has today. The real test of Marxism is not with the communist tyrannies, but with the "Fabian" socialists who gained control of much of Western Europe. As a consequence, socialism in the West morphed into a form of Keynesian welfare economics, which was itself a variety of neoclassicism.

After Marxism swamped all the other labor theorists, the movement lost much of its vigor. The LTV itself would not become a consistent theory until the work of Piero Sraffa (1898–1983). But by then, leadership in economics had passed to another group.

THE UTILITARIANS

Despite the prestige of Smith and Ricardo, LTV was not the only theory of value, or even the predominant one. LTV was an attempt to hold on to the values of the old order, most especially the idea that there should be no wealth without work. Merely owning capital could not be a moral basis for wealth; only putting it to use in work could justify rewards. But the labor theorists were swimming against the tide. As we showed in the last chapter, "values" were losing their objective character and becoming a matter of mere personal preference. The hedonism of Bentham was becoming the utilitarianism of economics, where "value" becomes nothing more than the market correlation of individual preferences, and egotism was the only valid motivation for action. Hence the utilitarians concentrated on economics as the science of exchanges. Specifically, they purged economics of any notions of a labor theory of value and any notion of distributive justice.

They reduced all value, indeed all human action, to a rational calculation of utility.[77] All "normative" considerations are ruled out in advance. "Justice," insofar as it figures in utilitarian economics at all, merely means voluntary exchanges, and liberty is no more than freedom to exchange goods.

Thomas Malthus

Thomas Malthus (1766–1834) is most famous for his theory of population. In fact, he has two such theories, one predicated on there being too many workers and the other predicated on there being too few.

Malthus's thesis was very simple: "Population, when unchecked, increases in geometrical ratio. Subsistence increases only in arithmetic ratio."[78] The "check" on population was starvation, the limit of what the land could produce. For Malthus, the "liberal reward of labor" would lead only to the poor reproducing faster than the food supply with the inevitable result of starvation for some and low wages for all:

> A man who is born into a world already possessed, if he cannot get subsistence from his parents on whom he has a just demand, and if the society do not want his labour, has no claim of *right* to the smallest portion of the food, and, in fact, has no business to be where he is. At nature's mighty feast there is no vacant cover for him. She tells him to be gone, and will quickly execute her own orders....[79]

Malthus was equally clear on the solution. Instead of working to ameliorate poverty, the authorities should increase it and work to raise the mortality rates among the poor:

> Instead of recommending cleanliness to the poor, we should encourage contrary habits. In our towns we should make the streets narrower, crowd more people into the houses, and court the return of the plague. In the country, we should build our villages near stagnant pools, and particularly encourage settlements in all marshy and unwholesome situations. But above all, we should reprobate specific remedies for ravaging diseases; and those benevolent, but much mistaken men, who have thought they were doing a service to mankind by projecting schemes for the total extirpation of particular diseases.[80]

Malthus's *Essay on Population* (1798) swept England and the continent with its apparent simplicity and logic. It inspired Charles Darwin to formulate his theory of evolution, and variations of this theory remain popular today — despite the contrary evidence — and especially in dealing with less developed countries.[81] But it also turned economics, so optimistic under

Adam Smith, into the "dismal science," a calculation of limitations where resources were scarce and only misery abundant.[82] Malthus justified this "melancholy hue" of his work with a theodicy: misery and vice were the necessary conditions to rouse man from the "torpor and corruption" that were the "original sin of man."[83] Poverty in this account is not the result of oppression or injustice, but of the unalterable Will of God operating on the incontinence of the poor. Of course, it has not the same effect on the rich. For the rich, all those extra mouths to feed become the limit on the returns to capital; there will be starvation for the poor and inconvenience for the rich.

Malthus had a second theory of population as well, one connected to his analysis of "gluts" (we would say "depressions"). It seemed obvious that such gluts could only be the result of an insufficient demand. Malthus believed that the cause of this insufficiency of demand was that as capitalism progressed, there was a tendency for capitalists to receive too much income. But these excessive profits needed to find investments if there was not to be a shortage of demand. However, new investments required new workers, and it was obvious that the supply of workers could not be expanded as fast as the growth in capital, since it takes sixteen to eighteen years to bring new workers into the market; in other words, there were too few workers to absorb the new capital. When Malthus examined the shortage in spending, he found that the workers already spent all they earned. The capitalists, however, were too busy accumulating to be able to properly spend their fortunes. But landlords, Malthus observed, were gentleman of leisure. Since their income was from rent, which required no effort, they could spend their time consuming. Therefore, high rents would make up for the insufficiency in demand caused by the too rapid accumulation of capital combined with the too slow growth of the workforce.[84]

The constant in the two theories is high rents. In the first instance, high rents help to keep down the "excess population," and in the second high rents work to make up aggregate demand caused by a lack of population. And while we may be tempted to smile at the self-serving nature of these theories, the fact is that the justification of economic rent remains an embarrassment to economic theory right up to the present time.

Jean-Baptiste Say

The industrialization of England led to widespread discontent and labor unrest. The wealthy in England had before them the example of the French Revolution and became increasingly alarmed. They attempted to suppress worker's movements by outlawing unions. This left the workers with no legal means of resistance; hence they resorted to illegal means. Riots and "sabo-tage" (jamming a sabot, or wooden shoe, into the machinery to wreck it) increased. Upheavals occurred in 1811–13, 1815–17, 1819, 1826, 1829–35, 1838–42, 1843–44, and 1846–48. Most of these were spontaneous manifestations of an utterly wretched working class.[85] England was in a state of low-level but near continuous civil war. The authorities responded as authorities do in a state of war: with utter ruthlessness. Sabotage was made a capital offense, and laws against unions were enforced with feroc-ity. Furthermore, economic depressions occurred with appalling regularity, making the situation of the poor, desperate even in good times, even worse.

In such conditions, the task for the utilitarian economists, who were all defenders of the system, was to show that the wealth of the industrialists was just, the low wages fair, and that the gluts were at best temporary phenom-ena which would pass quickly. Typical of these economists was Jean-Baptiste Say (1767–1832). Say's Law of Markets, usually stated as "supply creates its own demand," is considered by many as "essential to any defense of free markets."[86] What the law says is that a free market will always adjust *automatically* to an equilibrium in which all resources, including labor, are fully employed.[87] As a consequence, there can be no "gluts" or depressions. Any appearance of gluts would be illusory. While there may appear to be too much of one product, what is actually happening is that its price is too high, while the price of some other commodity must therefore be too low. Since this is simply a pricing question, the market in its wisdom will auto-matically correct the problem; the price of one commodity will be raised and the price of the other lowered. As Say put it, "If there is an overstock, of many kinds of goods, it is because other goods are not produced in sufficient quantities." "That [commodity] which sells above its cost of production will induce a part of the producers of the other commodity to the production of ... [the higher-priced commodity] until the productive services are equally paid by both."[88] Say had proved, by unaided reason alone, that the depres-sions which caused so much misery were in fact impossible. Whether or not one considers Say's method to have been effective, the idea of finding an "au-tomatic" way of achieving equilibrium would remain part of the utilitarian agenda.

Nassau Senior

Nassau Senior (1790–1864) was perhaps the most influential economist of his day. While most of his specific analysis has been rejected, the agenda he established for utilitarian economics became the basis of what would later be known as the "marginalist revolution." Key points of Senior's agenda were to show that markets were "self-adjusting" and "gluts" were impossible; to free economics from any considerations of "value" (the "methodological" question); and to find a way to reduce the three sources of income — rent, profit, and wages — to one common principle.

Gluts. Like Say, Senior believed that gluts were impossible. Since the desire for wealth was insatiable, the idea that there could be "too much" on the market was nonsensical. Both Say and Ricardo had made much the same argument, but they at least recognized that such gluts, impossible as they were, had in fact occurred. Senior, however, did not seem to take notice of the actual economic crises that did happen in his lifetime; he simply ignored them.[89] Senior seemed unable to believe that while desire might be infinite, cash might be in short supply.

Methodology. Senior believed that economics should not be concerned with social welfare, since this would involve the economist in normative and ethical considerations; economics should be concerned only with wealth, not happiness. Therefore, economics could not be based on the ends or purposes of an economy, since that would involve ethical questions. Rather, the "science" should be rooted in "a very few general propositions, the result of observation, or consciousness, and scarcely requiring proof, or even formal statement."[90] Senior selected four propositions which in his mind "scarcely required proof": all men desire more wealth with as little sacrifice as possible; Malthus's law of population; industrial production can be indefinitely increased; farm production, on the other hand, is subject to diminishing returns for each additional unit of labor.[91]

There are two problems with Senior's "scientific" principles. The first is that they are not scientific. The principle of a science gives a rule or measure to which all objects in that science are subject. For example, gravity provides a foundational principle for physics in that the relationship of all massive objects can be measured by the rule of gravity. Senior's principles would not seem to do this. In the second place, they are arbitrary; there seem to be other principles which are far more "foundational" that could just as easily have been selected. For example, it seems obvious that he could have selected this principle: "A society must produce enough food, clothing, shelter, and other goods, so as to support its members and provide for the continuation of the race." This would seem both to be more fundamental and to provide a measure for the success of the economy.[92] What really happens in a methodology like Senior's is that the "principles" are in fact selected to support conclusions already reached; the pretense of "science" is merely a cover for one's own bias.

Distribution of Incomes. Senior's big challenge was to provide a justification for rent and profits. His strategy was to show that all the factors of production — land, labor, and capital — derived their incomes from the same principle. If this were so, then there could be no reason for one group to attack the basis of the income of another group, or grounds for complaint about one's own income. Profits, Senior claimed, were a reward for abstinence; the rich were rich because they abstained from pleasures, hoarded their cash, and invested wisely. The hardest of these to justify was rent. Rent for both Smith and Ricardo was a suspicious category, since it seemed to be a payment based not on any work the landlord did, other than collect the rent, but for a merely legal form, ownership. But recall that Smith and Ricardo were still wedded to the medieval idea that wealth should arise only from work. For Senior, rent was unproblematic; it was simply "the revenue spontaneously offered by nature."[93] Senior accepted the division of property uncritically. Senior then went on to show that profit was really rent "as soon as the capital, from which a given revenue arises, has become, whether by gift or by inheritance, the property of a person to whose abstinence and exertions it did not owe its creation." Finally, Senior claimed that wages were just another form of rent given to the laborer as the "proprietor of a natural agent"[94] (that is, his or her ability to work).

Senior's method meant that he was forced to reverse himself, conceding that profit was *not* a reward for abstinence, at least not for the current recipients. Further, wages are not a form of rent; no one is paid for their *ability* to work, but only for the work they actually do. But although Senior's attempt was a failure, the quest for a single principle of income would occupy a major place in utilitarian economics. Before that quest could be fulfilled, the utilitarians had to go through one more step, the "marginalist revolution."

The New Poor Law of 1834. The Poor Laws were England's welfare system. They were established in the sixteenth century and necessitated by the fact that so many of the peasantry were thrown off the land and into the cities — cities that could not provide all of them with adequate work — that revolution was a constant threat. Then as now, "welfare" systems engender resentment both on the part of those forced to pay for them and those forced to depend on them. Senior more than resented the laws, he wished to see them abolished, along with all publicly supported relief. He felt that the poor were merely lazy, and the Poor Laws supported that laziness. Only by degrading the poor could they be forced to work, never mind that there was not enough work to employ them. Senior felt that the poor must be excluded from political life and repressed by military power, if necessary:

There seem to be only three means of governing a densely peopled country in which [the poor] form the large majority. One is to exclude them from political life. This is our English policy.... Another is the existence among them of a blind devotion to the laws and customs of the country.... A third plan is to rely on military power — to arm and discipline the higher and middle classes, and to support them by a regular army trained to implicit obedience.[95]

In 1834, these laws, which already gave only meager support to the poor, were re-written under Senior's direction to further stigmatize poverty. The new law forced all the poor to go to the workhouse where they would live in appalling conditions, work from sunup to sundown, wear prison clothing, and be fed a diet substantially less than that afforded by the lowest wage offered in the free market. "Outdoor" relief (support apart from the workhouse) was outlawed, and families were broken apart and forced into the workhouse as a punishment for destitution. Senior felt that such harsh measures were necessary because of "the threat of an arrogant laboring class, resorting to strikes, violence, and combinations [unions], a threat to the foundations not merely of wealth, but of existence itself."[96] Such was the tone and temper of utilitarian economics in the nineteenth century. The tone would shift with the coming of the marginal revolution; one wonders if the temper ever will.

SUMMARY

From the beginnings of conscious reflection on economics, there was a unity of ethics and economics, in thought if not always in practice. Aristotle discussed both in his *Ethics* and *Politics,* and considered them part and parcel of each other. He also recognized two "sides" to justice, the distributive and the corrective. The latter includes the exchange economy and is more or less constant in every culture. But the former, distributive justice, is irreducibly cultural, and this kind of justice, which includes the processes of production and distribution, will vary with the ethical orientation of the particular society.

The synthesis of ethics and economics, of distributive and corrective justice, held sway until the sixteenth century, but under the pressure of the new mercantilist class, this synthesis began to give way. Virtue was no longer seen as necessary to the economic order. Indeed, new individualist notions of being human, and especially of the human being as primarily an egotist, engendered the view that vice, and not virtue, was the proper foundation of economic activity, an idea that leads to Mandeville's paradox of private vices as the basis of public benefits. This is the state of affairs toward the end of the eighteenth century, when Adam Smith begins his reflections on the economic order. Smith was a moral philosopher and well aware of the unities in Aristotle and the Scholastics. He was unwilling to abandon either corrective or distributive justice. Unfortunately, he was not able to unite them under a single theory, but ended up with two incompatible theories, the Labor Theory of Value and the "Invisible Hand" theory; the former corresponds to a distributive principle and the latter to a corrective principle.

The economists of the nineteenth century tended to emphasize one of these theories, to the exclusion of the other. Thus there was a fragmentation of economic thought, with neither side being able to produce a consistent, comprehensive, and coherent theory. Nevertheless, utilitarian theories began to dominate, theories which called for the complete divorce of ethics and economics in order to place economics on a "scientific" basis. In general, the utilitarians excluded all notions of distributive justice. But they, no more than the labor theorists, were not able to define this "science." This sets the scene for the next stage in the development of economic theories, the marginalist revolution.

Chapter 4

The Disappearance of Justice

There is no such thing as "society."

—MARGARET THATCHER

THE MARGINALIST REVOLUTION

Marginal Utility

Utilitarian economics required four things that classical economics could not provide. The first was a theory of equilibrium which was "automatic"; it was necessary to show that the market would quickly move to correct any imbalances between supply and demand. Say had attempted this task in his Law of Markets, but the task looked incomplete. The second was Senior's project of finding a single principle for all sources of income — land, labor and capital. The third project, also from Senior, was to provide a "scientific" or "natural law" basis for economics which would forever remove it from the realm of philosophy and ethics. Finally, economics needed a coherent price theory, one that did not depend on distributive justice. Neither the Labor Theory of Value nor total utility was able to provide this. Utility, for all the fervor of its supporters, was no more successful than the Labor Theory of Value in explaining economic realities.

It was this last category, price theory, which proved to be the key to the whole problem. Many economists hit upon the solution more or less at the same time, including W. S. Jevons (1835–82), Léon Walras (1834–1910), Carl Menger (1840–1921), and Alfred Marshall (1842–1924). The solution was to use not *total* utility, but *marginal* utility — that is, the value of the last increment. This marginal increment is not as valuable (or "useful") as the next-to-last increment. Marginal utility has a charming simplicity about it. Think of being thirsty. At such times a glass of water or soda will have a certain value to you which can be expressed as the price you are willing to pay. But after the first glass, the second is much less valuable, and the third has no value at all. Each successive increment has a *marginal*

63

utility, that is, the change in utility from each successive increment can be expressed mathematically as the first derivative of total utility. Marginal utility proved to be a universal solvent, washing away all the problems of classical economics and fulfilling the agenda laid out by Say and Senior.

Marginal Utility in Exchanges. W. S. Jevons applied this principle to a general theory of exchange. Underlying his general theory was a theory of the human person based on Bentham's hedonism. As Jevons put it, "Bentham's ideas...are...the starting point of this work." "I have attempted to treat economy as a calculus of pleasure and pain and have sketched out...the form which the science must ultimately take."[1] This assumption is important because marginal utility only makes sense if people normally act to maximize their "marginal" pleasures. In any other theory of the human person, marginal utility would be extremely limited. But assuming such a model of human behavior, one could easily show that such "humans" would be forever comparing prices and utilities at the margin and adjusting their purchases to maximize their pleasures. For example, if one had two commodities, x and y, and could only get another x by giving up some y, then one could compare the ratios of one's own subjectively determined marginal utilities for the products, MU_x/MU_y, with the prices of the two commodities, P_x/P_y. If the ratio $MU_x/MU_y > P_x/P_y$ then one could gain some utility by trading some x for some y. The process of comparing utilities and prices would continue until one had exhausted the gains possible by exchange.[2] This application of the equations of differential calculus to questions of human behavior was considered a great advance; the "Invisible Hand" of Adam Smith acquired a visible mathematics.[3]

Carl Menger used this same explanation to explicate the laws of supply and demand. All consumer prices were ultimately determined by marginal utility through Menger's Law of Demand: the quantity of a commodity that people were willing to purchase depended on the price, and the quantity demanded and the price were inversely related to each other. The higher the price the lower the volume, and the reverse. Economics now had what it had lacked, a coherent theory of prices. This was something that neither the labor theorists nor the "total" utilitarians could supply, and it did not depend, like medieval theory, on a cultural variable such as one's "station in life."

General Equilibrium. By applying marginal utility through a complex set of mathematics, Léon Walras was able to show the existence of a general equilibrium model under conditions of perfect competition involving a large number of small firms. Equilibrium means that supply would equal demand in every market and that there would be full employment of all resources, including labor. Of course proving the existence of such a model and proving it actually works in practice are different things. It is obvious that people are willing to exchange at non-market-clearing prices from the simple fact that people do not know what such prices are. Therefore Walras posited the existence of a "crier" who would announce all the prices. Buyers and sellers would then announce their intentions to trade at the announced prices, but if this was not the equilibrium price, then the crier would announce a new set of prices. This process would continue until the equilibrium prices were discovered, and only then would trade take place.[4] Despite the obvious drawbacks of the model, it has been a central part of economic theory ever since it was developed. Walras himself recognized the weakness of the solution, but believed that the economy would find equilibrium by a process of "groping."

Distribution of Incomes. However, there was a problem. In order to make marginal utility work, it was necessary to treat the three factors of classical economics — land, labor, and capital — under the same mathematics; that is, they had to be treated as *homogeneous* quantities. But quite obviously, they are not, not in the real world. They are *heterogeneous*. Land is not labor, and labor is not capital. Empirically these are three different things that operate according to different laws. Capital, for example, refers to human-made things that can be extended and substituted. That is, the supply of capital goods can, in principle, always be extended; you can always make more of it. Further, one kind of capital can, in principle, be substituted for another; if there is a shortage of commodity "A," you can usually substitute some other commodity in greater supply. Land, on the other hand, is a fixed commodity whose supply cannot be increased and for which there is no substitute. And the worker — a human being — differs from the other two factors in ways too obvious to mention. Land is no substitute for human beings. Machines may be substituted for workers only when an employer requires mere physical exertion. But if the requirement is qualitative, if what is required is creativity, innovation, expertise, management, etc., then only humans can provide these. How then could these heterogeneous commodities be described under the same mathematics?

The problem was "solved" by John Bates Clark (1847–1938). Clark set himself the task of solving the problem raised by Nassau Senior; that is, showing that all incomes — wages, profits, and rents — originate from the same principle. On the opening page of his textbook, *The Distribution of Wealth*, he declared:

> It is the purpose of this work to show that the distribution of the income of society is controlled by a natural law, and that this law, if it

worked without friction, would give to every agent of production the amount of wealth which that agent creates.[5]

Clark's solution was to treat capital as an abstraction with no actual *physical* content. Capital-goods are, of course, physical entities — machines, tools, buildings — and these things are always consumed in the process of production. But capital itself is indestructible, perpetual, fluid, and mobile.[6] Capital is no more than continuity of ownership, with the precise content of the things "owned" constantly changing. What applies to capital comes to be applied to all factors. There are no landlords, laborers or capitalists, only owners of inputs labeled *a, b, c*, and so on. Hence you would get a production function $x = f(a, b, c \ldots)$.[7] The system of mathematics is perfected by making a clean break with any actual reality. There are no longer such things as shovels and men and plots of land; these are mere appearance only. In reality, they are all just little bits of the capital fund, with each little bit expressed in the formulas as $a, b, \ldots z$.

Clark went on to show that in a profit-maximizing firm each of these bits gets employed until it reaches it marginal product, that is, the value of the last unit which can be profitably employed. Under conditions of perfect competition, all resources will be employed and each resource will receive the value of its marginal product, which is deemed to be the "amount of wealth that the agent creates." Further, these factor payments exhaust the value of the total output, meaning that no surplus values are created. In other words, there is no such thing as "profit." As Clark explained it:

> Normal prices are no-profit prices. They afford wages for all the labor that is involved in producing the goods, including the labor of super-intending the mills, managing the finances … and doing all the work of directing the policy of the business. Beyond this, there is no return, if prices stand at their normal rate; and the reason for this is that *entrepreneurs* compete with each other in selling their goods, and so reduce prices to the no-net-profit level.[8]

This is the equivalent of saying that the normal level of profit for entrepreneurs is the same as their marginal product as employees, that is, that the employer makes no more than the employee.[9]

Clark's theory had an astounding result: justice was no longer a virtue, a matter of human intentionality, but the unavoidable result of an "automatic" and mechanical system. Distributive justice disappears into the logic of exchange; corrective justice supplies the place of distributive justice, but only when people are working to maximize their own self-interest. Presumably, a person *not* working in her own self-interest, say Mother Theresa, would destroy the logic of exchange and actually be working against justice. The order established by Aristotle and St. Thomas, in which distributive justice precedes the corrective (rewards must be distributed before they are exchanged) is reversed, and Mandeville's paradox of "Private Vices; Publick Benefits" is given a mathematical form. Justice itself is no longer about right relationships between a person and his neighbors, but relationships between humans mediated only by money; justice is no longer about the right relationship, but about the right price.

Neoclassicism

Marginality became the major analytic tool of economics: marginal costs, marginal products, marginal revenues, etc., everything could be described in terms of numbers and analyzed in terms of margins. In fact, enthusiasm for the concept was such that some believed that all things could be explained by marginal utility. For example, Ludwig von Mises wrote a great tome on what he calls *Praxeology,* in which he argues that not only the economy, but also love, sex, society, and everything else can be explained in terms of human selfishness working through marginal utility. In Mises, marginal utility becomes not just a physical principle, but a psychological and anthropological one, indeed the mainspring of all human action.[10] This new system of economics, though it bore some continuity with classical economics, was so different that it got a new name, *neoclassicism.*

Marginal utility allowed the complete realization of Nassau Senior's project. Economics is no longer a branch of moral philosophy, but a *science.* The economist could now become a "scientist" and be free from any purely moral considerations. Economics had at last found its "Newtonian" principle; as inertia explained all physical movements, marginal utility could explain all market movements. As Jevons put it, the lack of a "perfect system of statistics . . . is the only . . . obstacle in the way of making economics an exact science"; once the statistics have been gathered, the generalization of laws from them "will render economics a science as exact as many of the physical sciences."[11] However, as we saw with Clark, it could become a "physical" science only by divorcing it from anything physical. Only by severing the connection with the empirical world could economics become pure mathematics.

As a "science" economics is, as its supporters claim, a science of exchange only. Even production is viewed as "an exchange with nature."[12] Price, equilibrium, and incomes could all be explained, and explained by corrective justice alone, without resorting to the troublesome cultural implications that are always involved with distributive justice. Indeed, the individual never need concern him or herself with justice, since it operates automatically; it arises solely from the individualistic pursuit of hedonistically conceived self-interest. Moreover, this change in economics tracked the change in society at large and in the philosophical fashions we have already traced. The philosophic subjectivism that formed the basis of emotivism was mirrored by the methodological individualism of neoclassicism. It is in fact a radical individualism that roots the entire theory.

Individualism. For the entire system to function people must be conceived of as utility-maximizing individuals; this is the *methodological individualism* upon which the whole structure rests. However, this cannot be a conclusion of economics; rather it is a metaphysical assumption that is prior to economics and, as such, is beyond question from the standpoint of neoclassicism.[13] Economists simply are not trained in the fields which give insight into human actions. Statements about what human beings are like come from other sources, generally theology, philosophy, psychology, and introspection. These give other answers to the human questions, answers that are problematic for the use of hedonism as a foundation. Theology will have very little to do with hedonism, while for philosophy it is but one small stream in the great river of human thought, and a muddy one at that. Psychology simply refuses to confirm the existence of the person as a utility maximizer with well-ordered scales of preferences. Rather, as we saw with Maslow, persons have a dense and complex scale of needs which relate them to themselves, to others, and to the eternal order, and these needs cannot easily be reduced to mere "utility."

But our most immediate knowledge of the human person comes from introspection, from taking an honest look at ourselves. For we are both the subject and the object of our study. When we look in the mirror, we see two things: an egotist, and someone who is embarrassed by his egotism. With respect to the first quality, we would be able to confirm all the findings of neoclassicism, were it not for the presence of the second quality. For we do not like to think of ourselves as pure egotists, but will attempt to rationalize our actions, even (or especially) our worst actions, in terms of doing them for somebody else's benefit. Even neoclassicism attempts to justify itself on the grounds that its *Private Vices* lead inevitably to *Publick Benefits*.

The neoclassicist is likely to respond at this point that the individual is the only source of action because only individuals act. He is likely to reiterate, along with Margaret Thatcher, that "there is no such thing as society" and that we cannot refer any decision to that non-existent entity. But as strange as that statement is from the head of English society, it is no less strange from anyone who owes his origins to a family and his social position to the existence of a society. It is quite true that we only see actions in individuals, but it would be a mistake to conclude that these are the actions of *autonomous* individuals, rather than individuals fully situated in a cultural and social matrix which influences, and often wholly determines, their choices. When a businessman puts on a coat and tie in the morning, he is not making a purely "free" choice, but is fulfilling certain social expectations imposed on a man in his social position. He may "autonomously" choose the color of the tie, but not the fact of the tie; that is a social constraint.

Natural Law. John Bates Clark was convinced that he had found a "natural law" solution to all the problems of economics, one that was a direct insight into the Divine Law.[14] Such a view would be free of any purely cultural constraints or systems of values. It would be, like the inverse square law, universally valid and binding on all peoples. But can "natural law" be applied to human systems in this way; can there be a "value-free" law for humans?

The answer to this question depends on one's view of natural law. The older view of natural law situated it within a discernment of the meanings of things, that is, within their *natures* and *ends*. Thus, natural law would always involve a *teleology*, a perception of final meaning, but such perceptions involve philosophical, theological, and cultural questions. The Enlightenment version of natural law sought to divorce natural law from any moral or theological authority. Is this actually possible?

Let us take a simple deduction from "nature": "Lions eat lambs; therefore the strong prey on the weak!" The conclusion would seem to be an unavoidable deduction from the indubitably factual premise, a pure instance of a "natural law," blissfully free of any moral or theological foundation. But in fact it contains a hidden assumption: the premise concerns animals, but the conclusion is applied to humans. Is this valid? Yes, if the human being is no more than an animal; no, if the human being transcends the animals. If the latter is true, then natural law can never be just a "reading" of nature, but must be guided by a consideration of the end and nature of being human. Can the issue be resolved one way or another by an appeal to pure reason? No, because both views rest on a purely theological foundation. Humans may or may not be just advanced animals and nothing more. Certainly, humans are advanced animals, but the status of the "something more" cannot be proved — or disproved. Certainly, both humans and lions enjoy a leg of lamb for lunch; quite possibly, speech is no more than an advanced form of roaring or baying. There is simply no "proof" that humans transcend, or do not transcend, the animals; it is a matter of faith and faith alone. Therefore, the question of whether the proposition is a valid deduction from natural law depends not on the raw "facts" (which cannot be disputed) but on the theology by which one reads those facts. And this will be true for every statement which purports to be a conclusion from natural law. The only question is whether the values are explicit or hidden; if the latter, people will delude themselves into thinking that their thinking is "value-free," when in fact it is a mere attempt to impose their values on others. The solution is never to proclaim a "value-free" conclusion, but to make the values that underlie the conclusion explicit.

At a more practical level, we find all of our economic terms firmly embedded in cultural terms; any attempt to idealize the economy in terms of pure number, let's say an "ideal production function," turns out to be a purely cultural exercise. For example, in this ideal function, how many hours per week does the worker work? Forty? That is the result of a particular historical circumstance and something dictated by no "natural" law. Will the formula assume private property? But many types of land tenure systems are possible (see the next chapter). Will sanctity of contract be assumed? Or will contract depend on violence, as it does in places where the government is weak and the mafias strong? And so forth. Nearly every "pure" number in the formula will be shown to have a cultural basis. The project of the Enlightenment, in economics no less than in morality, fails once again; the real cannot be divorced from the moral, and our perception of the world cannot be divorced from faith.

Equity and Equilibrium. It is not the claims of a bogus scientism or natural law which make neoclassicism interesting. Rather it is its specifically moral claims which command our attention. For indeed neoclassicism, despite its claims to be value-free, makes some quite specifically moral claims, and it is these claims which require us to dig deeper to see its true basis. What neoclassicism claims is that it is the "perfect system of natural liberty," which is able to deliver an abundance of goods at a price which is *exactly* equal to the cost of production, including fair remuneration for all the economic actors, workers and investors alike. Indeed, since there are no profits, no economic rents, returns to both worker and investor are normalized so as to eliminate any great differences between the two and to guarantee a good life to all who come under its care. Further, it promises equilibrium and stability, the ability to adjust and heal itself and return quickly from any departures from the balance of supply and demand, while providing full employment for all who wish to work.

What is remarkable about these claims is that they embody precisely the hopes of the ancient and medieval economists: a society free of rents, providing equity and equilibrium to all its citizens. Whatever one may think of the methods and arguments for or against neoclassicism, it is clear that it has chosen the correct goals and standards. And it is according to these standards — its own — that neoclassicism must be judged. It requires no outside source, no extrinsic critique; its own goals are sufficiently lofty, serious, and humane. In the coming chapters, we will evaluate neoclassicism, but we will do so by referring mostly to the standards that neoclassicism sets for itself.

THE KEYNESIAN REVOLUTION

A World in Turmoil

One of the major promises of capitalist theory is that of equilibrium, the ability to adjust imbalances between supply and demand quickly, and thus avoid the economic shocks known as depressions or recessions, or simply "gluts." But in fact, as capitalism became more predominant, it became less stable, not more so. In the United States, for example, there were only two severe economic crises in the first half of the nineteenth century (beginning in 1819 and 1837). But in the second half of that century, the crises increased in both number and severity, with five major shocks (1854, 1857, 1873, 1884, and 1893). The experience in England was similar, only more severe. In the first half of the nineteenth century England experienced four crises (beginning in 1815, 1825, 1836, and 1847), but that number increased to six in the last half (1857, 1866, 1873, 1882, 1890, and 1900). By the twentieth century, the situation had grown even worse, with frequent depressions culminating in the Great Depression of the 1930s.[15]

Thus it was clear that despite the advances in economics, the models did not seem well-related to actual business conditions, which continued to have seemingly intractable problems of business cycles, chronic unemployment, and poverty. The economic engine seemed to be rather selective in its workings and favored the rich over the poor, which was contrary to the predictions of equity. Neoclassical theory was having difficulty explaining it all, much less coming up with a remedy. Capitalism was losing its grip on the people. The communists had come to power in Russia, while Fascism and Nazism ruled in Spain, Italy and Germany. Socialism was on the rise across Europe, and the world seemed headed for war.

It is in the midst of the crisis of the Great Depression that John Maynard Keynes (1883–1946) does his theorizing and comes up not just with an explanation, but with policy prescriptions that have become embedded, for better or worse, in the policies of every single developed country. Although Keynes is often considered a radical, the truth is that he accepted the neoclassical model nearly without change:

> Our criticism of the accepted classical theory of economics has consisted not so much in finding logical flaws in its analysis as in pointing out that its tacit assumptions are seldom or never satisfied, with the result that it cannot solve the economic problems of the actual world.[16]

The Failure of Equilibrium

When Keynes mentions solving the economic problems of the actual world, he means giving policy prescriptions to governments. Neoclassicism could not or would not do this, since the theory allowed for only a minimal economic role for governments. Indeed, neoclassicism had difficulty even recognizing the problem, since the theory of an automatic, self-adjusting equilibrium did not account for the frequent depressions, nor did it recognize any involuntary unemployment. According to the theory, labor, like any other commodity, had a market-clearing price, and full employment could always be achieved by lowering the wage of the worker and increasing the profit of the entrepreneur. Therefore whenever unemployment existed, it was only because the workers refused to take the wage cuts necessary to bring the wage rate into equality with the marginal product of labor, and hence it was always *voluntary* unemployment. Keynes did not dissent from this analysis,[17] but he pointed out that there was another way to lower the wage rate: the price of goods could be increased while the wage rate was held constant, that is, by inflation. Workers who would not often agree to a pay cut might accept inflation more peaceably.[18]

Inflation can be easily influenced by government policy when the government controls the money supply. And it was Keynes's intention to "select those variables which can be deliberately controlled or managed by central authority in the kind of system in which we actually live."[19] In other words, Keynes was attempting to identify the tools by which the government could effectively manage the economy in the hopes of eliminating the disastrous business cycles which had plagued the system. In contrast to other neoclassical economists, Keynes recognized that the economic system did not automatically provide equilibrium and stability, but rather,

> it seems capable of remaining in a chronic condition of sub-normal activity for a considerable period without any marked tendency towards either recovery or collapse. Moreover, the evidence indicates that full,

or even approximately full, employment is of rare and short-lived occurrence.[20]

Implicit in Keynes's writing is the notion that equilibrium is not *automatic* but *intentional*, that is, equilibrium can only result from policies deliberately designed to bring it about; it cannot be left to *laissez-faire*.[21] Equilibrium at full employment only occurs in a very rare and special case of the relationship of the propensity to spend and the inducement to invest.[22] Note that "propensity" and "inducement" are terms drawn more from psychology than from economics. Keynes's insight is that equilibrium depends on the psychology of markets and on distributive justice. It is in these areas that Keynes makes his unique contributions to economic theory.

The Psychology of Markets

The human person had been shrunk by neoclassical theory to a mere shirker and egotist. A shirker, because he desired only wealth without work (Nassau Senior),[23] and because work itself was considered such a great disutility that only the greatest inducements could overcome the "aversion" to work. As Jeremy Bentham put it, "Aversion is the emotion — the only emotion — which *labour*, taken by itself, is qualified to produce...*love of labour* is a contradiction in terms."[24] These inducements consisted of the prospect of high profits for owners of capital and the threat of starvation for those who owned only their own labor.

Keynes recognized that markets were made of human decisions and could not be understood apart from the human person. He had a more complex notion of the person and his or her effect on the market. Therefore Keynes introduced four terms that were purely psychological in character: the *marginal propensity to consume*, the *marginal propensity to save*, *liquidity-preference*, and *market expectations*. The first two terms govern how much people are willing to spend or save out of their incomes, and vary with the level of income. The lower the income, the greater the propensity to spend, but this propensity is diminished as one's income increases. These factors help determine *effective demand* (the amount that can actually be purchased, sometimes called *aggregate demand*) in the economy. The liquidity-preference determines the demand for money and is made up of three motives: the transactions-motive, which is the need for cash for current business and personal expenses; the precautionary motive, the desire for excess cash to meet contingencies; and the speculative-motive, which has the object "of securing profit from knowing better than the market what the future will bring forth."[25] The liquidity-preference (demand for money) interacts with the supply of money to determine interest rates. Market expectations are simply the expected future yields from capital assets and are equivalent to the Marginal Efficiency of Capital.[26] Together, these factors influence nearly every other economic term, and interact in complex ways to produce the shape of the market, and especially to produce the business cycle.

The Business Cycle. In contrast to the theory of a stationary equilibrium of neoclassicism, Keynes proposed a theory of shifting equilibrium "meaning by the latter the theory of a system in which changing views about the future are capable of influencing the present situation."[27] It was (and is) indisputable that economies go through cycles of euphoria and depression, of boom and bust. The major culprit, according to Keynes, is a sudden change in the *Marginal Efficiency of Capital* [MEC] (that is, the discounted present value of a capital asset, the amount of money one expects to receive in the future for the purchase of a capital asset today). Of course, the MEC is highly dependent on market expectations, but the basis of such expectations is highly speculative and uncertain.[28] When the MEC is above the interest rate, money flows easily into a market. After all, if one expects an asset to pay, say, 10 percent per annum and can borrow the money to acquire it for 5 percent, it makes sense to invest. Eventually the market becomes "overbought" and when the inevitable disillusionment sets in, it falls with "sudden and catastrophic force."[29] The MEC falls so rapidly (being no more than a measure of optimism) that it falls below the interest rate, hence no one wishes to invest. Keynes described the process thus:

> It is an essential characteristic of the boom that investments which will in fact yield, say, 2 per cent. in conditions of full employment are made in expectation of a yield of, say, 6 per cent., and are valued accordingly. When the disillusion comes, this expectation is replaced by a contrary "error of pessimism," with the result that the investments, which would in fact yield 2 per cent. in conditions of full employment, are expected to yield less than nothing; and the resulting collapse of new investment then leads to a state of unemployment in which the investments...in fact yield less than nothing. We reach a condition where there is a shortage of houses, but where nevertheless no one can afford to live in the houses that there are.[30]

In other words, as euphoria turns to pessimism, the market psychology creates the conditions which make the pessimistic predictions actual conditions. Investors rush for the exits to avoid getting caught in a collapse, and thereby create the very collapse they would avoid. There are runs on banks that would otherwise be sound, as fear encourages people to withdraw their funds. Yet there is no shortage of capital, labor, demand, or any other purely "economic" factor, but only a shortage of the faith which keeps the whole system together. Keynes argued that in conditions of *laissez-faire,* it is impossible to avoid panics without a far-reaching change in market psychology, and such a change is unlikely to come about spontaneously.[31]

The interest rate, meanwhile, increases because a collapse in the MEC precipitates a sharp increase in the liquidity-preference; that is to say, people would rather have cash than investments. This gap between the interest rates and the MEC is the major cause of the cycle. The neoclassical theories, however, tended to confound the two numbers[32] and hence could provide no coherent explanation for the repeated failures of equilibrium.

The sudden fall of the MEC also impacts the marginal propensity to consume,[33] which causes a further drop in demand, which leads to a further round of lay-offs, and so forth. Further, the decline in output is accompanied by a reduction in working capital, which is a further element of disinvestment, one that may be very large.[34]

The neoclassical solution to crises is to maintain a "flexible wage policy," i.e., simply make pay cuts. The lowered wages will lower production costs, increase the volume of employment, and thereby stimulate effective demand,[35] and employment is uniquely correlated to effective demand. But as Keynes pointed out:

> Moreover, the contention that the unemployment which characterises a depression is due to a refusal by labour to accept a reduction of money-wages is not clearly supported by the facts. It is not very plausible to assert that unemployment in the United States in 1932 was due either to labour obstinately refusing to accept a reduction of money-wages. . . . Labour is not more truculent in the depression than in the boom — far from it. Nor is its physical productivity less. These facts from experience are a *prima facie* ground for questioning the adequacy of the classical analysis.[36]

The question is far more complex than neoclassicism allows. Lowering wages would have a variety of effects, some of which would increase and some of which would decrease effective demand.[37] A moderate decrease in wages would likely have no effect, while an immoderate one would likely shatter confidence and destabilize the situation even further. In any case, the expectation of lowered wages, or outright job loss, would be likely to lower the propensity to consume and thereby lower effective demand. Further, only under socialism could a flexible wage policy be administered, and it would not be practical in a system of free bargaining.[38] What governments can do is work through a flexible monetary policy, which analytically comes to the same thing; wages could remain the same while the money supply was increased, and with it, prices.[39] But whatever strategy is adopted, Keynes was clear that government action was necessary to ensure full employment. He was convinced of the need for central controls to bring about an adjustment between the propensity to consume and the inducement to invest.[40]

The remedy for an economy in the midst of a crisis was very simple: the government could simply borrow money and spend it to raise effective demand. It would be best to spend the money on socially useful projects, such as housing for the poor. But in any case it should spend money at times when money wasn't being spent in sufficient quantities. If necessary, the Treasury could fill old bottles with banknotes, bury them in disused mines, cover them up with rubbish from the town dump, and then sell the "mining" leases to private companies to dig them up again.[41] Anything to get the "money pump" going again.

Equity and Equilibrium

Keynes's ultimate goals were greater than just making minor adjustments during depressions; his real interest was in distributive justice, but not just from the moral perspective, but from the view of practical economics. The remedy for the business cycle "would lie in various measures to increase the propensity to consume by the redistribution of incomes or otherwise."[42] His point was that vast differences in wealth and poverty were themselves the cause of unemployment and depressions. This was based on the practical and undeniable proposition that the wealthy had a lower marginal propensity to consume than did the poor.[43] Thus purchasing power would be lost to the economy, and with this loss comes the loss of employment. Therefore, in the face of vast inequalities, equilibrium was impossible. It is here that Keynes locates the primary failure of neoclassicism: "The outstanding faults of the economic society in which we live are its failure to provide for full employment and its arbitrary and inequitable distribution of wealth and incomes."[44]

Keynes also wished to increase the stock of capital to the point where it ceased to be scarce.[45] This would eliminate the scarcity premium on capital and be the "euthanasia of the *rentier*," one who earned an income not by work but merely by the ownership of an asset, which involves "no genuine sacrifice."[46]

In this concern with distributive justice, Keynes was not aiming at a perfect equality:

For my own part, I believe that there is social and psychological justification for significant inequalities of incomes and wealth, but not for such large disparities as exist to-day. There are valuable human activities which require the motive of money-making and the environment of private wealth-ownership for their full fruition.[47]

Nor was he attacking the individualist base of neoclassicism:

Let us stop for a moment to remind ourselves what these advantages [of individualism] are. They are partly advantages of efficiency ... the advantages of decentralisation and of the play of self-interest. The advantage to efficiency of the decentralisation of decisions and of individual responsibility is even greater, perhaps, than the nineteenth century supposed; and the reaction against the appeal to self-interest may have gone too far. But, above all, individualism, if it can be purged of its defects and its abuses, is the best safeguard of personal liberty in the sense that, compared with any other system, it greatly widens the field for the exercise of personal choice.[48]

What Keynes was doing was showing the technical connection between *equity* and *equilibrium,* between distributive justice and corrective justice. Just as Aristotle concluded, distributive justice was a *social* question, which would require involvement of the social institutions, such as government, to achieve. Deliberate policies to redistribute income, thereby raising the propensity to spend, and controlling the supply of money, thereby decreasing the cost of capital, were necessary to ensure full employment, stability, and social peace. Nor would these measures be prejudicial to the capitalist (except for the pure *rentier*) since the growth of wealth, and of the economy, depended on the propensity to consume, a propensity that was hampered by vast inequalities.[49] What Keynes did was to join the individualist and the social concerns, because the human being is both an individual and a social being, and no theory that appeals to the social alone (socialism) or the individual alone (neoclassicism) can ever be sufficient, either intellectually or economically.

It is precisely this aspect of Keynes's work that causes his critics so much consternation. Yet one wonders why. The predictions of J. B. Clark's *The Distribution of Wealth*, the standard neoclassical text on the matter, are exactly the same as Keynes's: namely, incomes for both capitalist and worker normalized to each other, the elimination of economic profits (rents), a stable economy, and full employment.[50] In other words, both systems of thought have equity and equilibrium as their goals. The dispute therefore is not about

ends, but about means. The neoclassical economists exclude distributive justice and believe that all the good effects can come about accidentally, without
anybody intending justice. They look to "automatic" laws that operate apart
from human intentionality.

Yet the results of this "automatic" system have not been as promised.
The more "libertarian" the economy has been, the more unstable, the more
inequitable, and the more miserable it has been. Libertarian and instability
have gone hand in hand, with more of one leading to more of the other,
and no amount of theorizing can change the sad facts of history. The experience of the eighteenth, nineteenth, and the first part of the twentieth
centuries, when utilitarian ideals held sway, speak more clearly than can
any tome or textbook. A theory is justified by its results, and measured by
what it promises. Just as communism failed to dissolve governments and
bring prosperity and equality to the people, as promised, and so must be
condemned on its own ground, so too has utilitarianism failed to dissolve
the vast differences between wealth and poverty or bring economic stability,
and so must be judged on its own terms. The words of the poet Oliver Gold-
smith still hold as true today as they did in the eighteenth century, when he
witnessed the growing accumulation of wealth and the destruction of the
English working class:

> Ill fares the land, to hast'ning ill a prey,
> Where wealth accumulates, and men decay;
> Princes and Lords may flourish, or may fade:
> A breath can make them, as a breath has made;
> But a bold peasantry, their country's pride,
> When once destroyed can never be supplied.

The Impact of Keynes

Shortly after Keynes published *The General Theory* (1935), World War II
broke out. The world's misfortune was, in a sense, Keynes's fortune because it immediately necessitated the expansion of government expenditures,
putting his ideas to an immediate test. The results were judged to be spec-
tacularly successful. Since the War, Keynes's prescriptions have become an
integral part of the economy of nearly every advanced nation. In 1946,
Congress passed the "Employment Act" which required the government to
use its taxing, borrowing, and spending powers to maintain full employment, and Keynesianism was thereby legally mandated.[51] And there can
be little doubt that since his policies have been so widely implemented,

depressions have become more mild (reflected by the name "recessions") and less frequent than in the days of pure neoclassicism.

Some of Keynes's critics accuse him of being a socialist, but the truth is otherwise. The fact is that the hopes of socialism have died in the Keynesian synthesis of neoclassicism and distributive justice. Since the War, Western economies have been not precisely "free market," but "managed" economies, to a greater or lesser degree, a policy "that brought the sensational novelty of mass affluence to the peoples of the United States, Western Europe, Japan, and all the other countries that followed their path."[52] The conservative economist Milton Friedman somewhat impishly suggested that "We're all Keynesians now!" Judging by the number of regimes that have adopted the theory, in whole or in part, Keynesianism is the most successful economic theory since Adam Smith. The most conservative governments (e.g., Reagan and both Bushes) pursue Keynesian strategies as aggressively as do liberal ones, if not more so.

Still, the results have not been an unmixed blessing. In the first place, the easiest way to accomplish the recycling of funds has been through military expenditures, through the growth of what President Eisenhower called the "military-industrial complex." Some have therefore charged that Keynes has encouraged a militarism that was no part of his intent. In fact, it has not been a real militarism, which would at least involve the virtues of discipline and courage, but a corporate shadow of it which calls for much in the way of subsidy and nothing in the way of sacrifice, except sacrifices on the part of the young men and women sent to a succession of foreign wars.

Further, Keynes's redistributive policies concerned only the redistribution of income. He was certainly aware of the need for spreading the ownership of capital, but he could provide no policies in that direction. Income redistribution will always require a vast and intrusive government bureaucracy to collect and disperse the funds. In the process, it tends to make each person a mere client of the state rather than a true citizen; where subsidies are to be given or funds paid, the idea of a common good, so crucial to Keynesian analysis, dissolves into a war of economic interests and often spurious "rights." And once these bureaucracies and mechanisms are in place, there is every likelihood that they will be captured by the most powerful corporate forces, who then use them as their private preserves, setting up a sort of reverse Keynesianism, transferring funds from the middle class to the rich. And further still, the vast government intrusion into business seems to work *in favor* of large business and *against* small businessmen, because the cost of regulation is small relative to big business and large relative to small businesses.

Finally, there is the serious question of whether Keynesian policies can be maintained in the face of mounting debts. These debts are not a necessary part of Keynes's prescriptions, because the debts built up in bad times were to be repaid in good times. But such debts may be a practical consequence, since it is politically easier for governments to incur debts than to repay them. The age of Keynes may be coming to a close simply because we can no longer afford it. But what can possibly replace it without returning us to the days of economic turmoil and misery? There can be little doubt that in an age of war, communism, fascism, and turmoil, Keynes saved capitalism for the capitalists. The question now is whether capitalism can be saved from Keynes.

UTILITY TRIUMPHANT

Chicago and Austria

Despite the success of Keynesian policies in stabilizing the capitalist system, there was an inevitable counterattack on the part of utilitarian economics. Or perhaps it is more accurate to say that *because* of the success of Keynesianism, there was a counterattack; after all, it is difficult to preach the automatic stability of the free market in a time when so many people are out of work. But after the crisis has passed, it is again possible to renew the attack. Beginning in the 1970s, neoclassical economists, especially those of the Austrian and Chicago schools, began to displace the Keynesian consensus that had arisen after the war. By the 1980s and 1990s they were ascendant in the centers of economic orthodoxy, the major universities, the government, and in a series of well-funded "think tanks." They were aided in this effort not merely by the force of their arguments, but by the rise of "neoconservatism," a marriage of liberal ideology and evangelical morality (see chapter 12).

The leading economist of this period is Milton Friedman, a "Chicago" economist and Nobel Prize winner. Friedman is a radical libertarian who advocates the abolition of: corporate taxes, the graduated income tax, free public schools, regulations on the purity of food and drugs, the licensing of doctors, the post office, government relief for natural disasters, minimum wage laws, laws against usury, and laws prohibiting heroin, cocaine, and the like.[53] Both the Chicago and Austrian schools of thought would probably agree on most of Friedman's prescriptions, since both reduce the human being to a "utility-maximizer," and both view economics purely as the "science of exchange" (that is, corrective justice). Even production, which is surely a part of economics, is viewed as an "exchange with nature." One wonders how nature negotiates the terms of the exchange, or just what she receives in return for giving up her food, fiber, and mineral wealth. Beyond that, the differences between the two schools are subtle, although the fights are bitter. Austrians tend to be rationalists, deducing their beliefs (in the manner of Senior) from "first principles" regarded as "fundamental." Chicagoans tend to be more empirical, though they also accept "utility" as a metaphysically given principle. In this debate, we can see the Enlightenment fragmentation of the rationalist and empiricist approaches being played out before our eyes. Indeed, both are "modernist" philosophies, which D. McCloskey (herself a Chicago-school economist, though a dissenting one) describes in these terms:

> Modernism promises knowledge free from doubt, metaphysics, morals, and personal conviction; what it delivers merely renames as Scientific Method the scientist's and especially the economic scientist's metaphysics, morals, and personal convictions. It cannot, and should not, deliver what it promises. Scientific knowledge is no different from other personal knowledge. Trying to make it different, instead of simply better, is the death of science.[54]

Most of the Austrians would object to being described in these terms because they see themselves as highly ethical. However, they exclude ethics from economics itself; ethics are to be confined to the "moral-cultural" system which should support capitalism without actually modifying or affecting any of the economic system's principles or assumptions;[55] hence there are no practical differences. Perhaps the most basic way to see the differences in the schools, such as they are, is to look at their attitudes to something really basic. Something like sex, for example.

Sex, Marriage, and Utility

In order for utilitarianism to be a self-consistent view of the human being, it must define *all* human activities, including sex and marriage, in terms of utility. Most economists have mostly avoided the implications of this, but recently the Chicagoans have faced the issue squarely. For if there really are no such things as objective values and a human being really is naught but a utility maximizer, then the difference between the criminal and the law-abiding citizen is not in their moral character, or so the Nobel Prize winning Chicagoan Gary Becker argues, but in the fact that their "benefits and costs differ." "Frauds, thefts, etc., do not involve a true social cost but are simply transfers, with the loss to the victims being compensated by equal gains to criminals."[56] Criminal activities therefore provide a social value in gains to the offenders and should be treated as any other industry that creates a "diseconomy" to others, such as factories that produce smoke and other public nuisances.[57]

The same analysis can be extended to sex. Richard Mackenzie and Gordon Tullock point out, in good Chicago fashion, that "sex is a service produced and procured" like any other product. Hence, for utility-maximizing individuals:

> It follows that the quantity of sex demanded is an inverse function of the price ... the rational individual will consume sex up to the point that the marginal benefits equal the marginal costs.... If the price of sex rises relative to other goods, the consumer will "rationally" choose to consume more of other goods and less sex. (Ice cream ... can substitute for sex if the relative price requires it.)[58]

Gary Becker extends this utility-maximizing analysis of sex to love and marriage:

> It can be said that M_i loves F_j if her welfare enters his utility function. ... Clearly, M_i can benefit from such a match with F_j, because he could then have a more favorable effect on her welfare — and thereby on his own utility — and because the commodities measuring "contact" with F_j can be produced more cheaply when they are matched than when M_i has to seek an "illicit" relationship with F_j.[59]

Richard Posner, a follower of Becker's, carries this line of argument to its logical conclusion. Commenting on prostitution and marriage, he says "The difference is not fundamental."[60] Responding to this Chicago analysis, the Austrian Robert Nelson points out that women were traditionally held as property, which has an economic advantage:

> The incentive of the owner (husband) to invest in the human capital of the wife may be much greater when the wife is not free to leave to take a better offer — just as owned cars are often treated much better than rented cars. The wife in turn is likely to be much more devoted to the welfare of her owner (husband) when she knows she has no place else to go.[61]

Such is the quality of the "debate" between Austria and Chicago. In either case, decent married women and mothers end up regarded as prostitutes, property, or both; decent husbands and fathers become merely their clients or their pimps. The problem becomes clearer when we look at Jennifer Roback Morse's *Love and Economics*. Ms. Morse is a former Chicago economist who emigrated to the Austrian view after she had a child. Her book is a beautifully written account of love, marriage, and parenting, and a polemic against what she calls the *"Laissez-faire* family." Had the book been entitled simply *Love* there would be no problem, but she added *and Economics*. Yet her outlook has no impact on her economic views whatsoever, and she even denies that it can.[62] Marriage remains for her, as for the Chicagoans, a purely private matter with no impact on the "value-free" nature of economics. What Morse and all the utilitarians fail to realize is that there are no "neutral" social institutions, economic or otherwise. They reward some behaviors and punish others. If "utility is all," then marriage must be about utility; if egotism is the only force, then we must force egotism into the bedroom. If "love" gives you "utility," that's well and good, but it remains a "private" choice with no more privileged position in economics than any other private choice.

One might easily find the Chicago analysis repugnant, yet one is forced to concede that it is internally self-consistent and intellectually honest; if the human person really is naught but a pleasure maximizer, then surely love and marriage must come under that analysis. The Austrians, on the other hand, merely wish to have their cake and eat it too; they want to treat the human being as an egotist in the marketplace and an altruist at home; they preach both value-free institutions *and* the importance of values, but only on the "private" level. This schizophrenic view of being human is simply not tenable and constitutes a mere intellectual evasion. Or to carry the baking analogy further, the Chicagoans would lace the economic cake with the arsenic of egotism; the Austrians have no objection to the poison, but want the cake to have a moralistic icing. In either case, it would be wise to skip dessert.

THE DISAPPEARANCE OF JUSTICE

The trajectory we have traced in economic history moves from economics as a moral endeavor to economics as a "pure" and "value-free" science; "justice" disappears as a specific concern of economics. Instead of economics being evaluated in terms of ethics, ethics, even sexual ethics, are evaluated in terms of mathematics, the mere relation of utilities between "M_i" and "F_j." This movement entails a breaking of the unity of distributive and corrective justice and stakes all on corrective justice alone. One wonders why it is so necessary for the utilitarians to confine economics to the study of exchanges. After all, exchange, corrective justice, has been well understood since the time of Aristotle, and there seems to be little to be gained from translating Aristotle from Greek into calculus. As a mere logical necessity and empirical fact, production and distribution are prior to exchange; nothing can be exchanged until something is produced and the output dispersed. So what is going on?

The narrowing of justice does make sense if we view it against the background of the narrowing of the human person into an "autonomous individual" that took place during the Enlightenment. Both utilitarian economics and hedonistic philosophies were part and parcel of the same movement. Distributive justice deals with social relations, and "society" was a suspicious category for the Enlightenment sages. Margaret Thatcher is completely in line with the Enlightenment spirit when she proclaims that "There is no such thing as society," only autonomous individuals freely contracting with each other to maximize their individual utilities.

Exchange has another advantage that fits well with the Enlightenment prejudices. It can be easily quantified and reduced to mathematics. This makes it a perfect candidate for "Hume's Fork,"[63] by which anything that is not reducible to numbers should be "committed to the flames." Since distributive justice always involves an ethical and social judgment, not reducible to "number," then by utilitarian reckoning, it can only be "sophistry and illusion."

However, it was not so easy to get rid of distributive justice; its absence leaves a yawning gap in economic theory that cannot be covered up by mere appeals to freedom of exchange. Hence the importance of the project of Nassau Senior and J. B. Clark to show that a just distribution will result from mere corrective justice alone. No human intervention or concern with justice is necessary because it is an "automatic" process; just as sure as the stars keep their courses without ever "intending" to do so, so too must justice find us so long as no one intends that it should. Of course, this day of just distribution must wait upon the day of perfect equilibrium, which is the day of secular salvation promised by neoclassical economics. Like the Second Coming, it is a long time in coming; but like that Second Coming, it will be a day of justice. But whether it comes or no, it is important that distributive justice be "swallowed up" by corrective justice; otherwise you will have to introduce considerations of the human person and his/her social context that are impermissible in utilitarian thought.

We must be grateful for Becker, Posner, Morse, and McKenzie for showing us the logical outcomes of a pure utilitarian economy. No arguments against the system would be as damaging as their arguments in favor of it.

And at this point, we must make a choice: Either we must accept Becker's analysis of the human person, and all the economics that flow from it, or we must seek another model, and with it another economics. We will not be permitted, if we are honest, to take the Austrian evasion, to force the person to divide his/her time between being an egotist and an altruist. Rather, we must recognize that being "economic man" is a part of being human, and that the "parts" must comprise a whole. The burden of the remainder of this book will be to examine the human person through the teachings of historical Christianity, and to attempt to discern the implications of these teachings for the economic and business order. This will *not* be a task of "inventing" an economic system, but of examining practices which have worked or are working and of seeing how they can be or are being applied to the modern situation. Or, to put the task another way, of seeing how the call of Christ relates to the Vocation of Business.

Chapter 5

Property, Culture, and Economics

[Property is] that sole and despotic dominion which one man claims and exercises over the things of the world, in total exclusion of the right of any individual in the universe.

—*BLACKSTONE'S DICTIONARY OF LAW*

PROPERTY AS THE FOUNDATION OF WEALTH

All wealth begins as a gift from the Earth. The earth itself is the indispensable beginning of all life and all the sustenance that life requires. Thus the primary "capital" has always been the earth. The concept of "capital" becomes complex and embraces all sorts of things, including money, equities, intellectual property, machinery, etc., but all capital and wealth are still founded on the land. Therefore the distribution and possession of the land is the key element in the distribution of wealth.

All wealth is distributed based on some rule of property, either property in land, in goods, or in one's own labor. But basic to everything else will be property in land. Even in the infinite expanse of "cyber-space" one needs a place to place the server, some ground to bury the cable or set the tower. Therefore we must deal with the question of property before we deal with anything else touching on our material well-being. Societies distribute property according to their understanding of what "property" means and what "justice" means. The concept of justice controls the meaning of "property." The idea that there could be different meanings comes as a surprise to us, since we regard the concept as self-evident. And indeed, there is something self-evident about private property: that which we make should belong to us, and this idea is more or less constant throughout all societies and cultures. But there is a kind of property that we do not make: land, air, water, mineral wealth, the electro-magnetic spectrum, etc. Who "owns" such property, and how did they come into possession of it? The property in things *given* is fundamentally different from the property in things *made* by human beings; this kind of ownership is a social relationship, and always different in different cultures. Further, it will determine, more than any other factor, all other economic relations within a society. Indeed, we normally name economic systems after the form of property ownership that dominates in that society. So, for example, capitalism, socialism, feudalism, tribalism, all refer to different ways of owning land.

Therefore, any rational exploration of justice, and the economic and business systems that implement justice, must begin with a study of how the society governs land ownership. Such ownership is prior to any production or exchange, and the first thing a society must distribute is the land. Every society will make this distribution according to its own notions of justice, notions that vary from culture to culture. However, underneath these varying notions are some themes and issues that play themselves out in every culture as it develops through its history. The most basic theme is the distinction between ownership and use.

Ownership and Use

The classic position on ownership of the land in Catholic Social Teaching comes from St. Thomas Aquinas. For Thomas, there is no particular reason why a "particular piece of land should belong to one man more than another" (*ST* II-II, q. 57, a. 3). Nevertheless, St. Thomas gives an excellent defense of private property:

> [Private property] is necessary to human life for three reasons. First because every man is more careful to procure what is for himself alone than that which is common to many or to all: since each one would shirk the labor and leave to another that which concerns the community, as happens where there is a great number of servants. Secondly, because human affairs are conducted in more orderly fashion if each man is charged with taking care of some particular thing himself, whereas there would be confusion if everyone had to look after any one thing indeterminately. Thirdly, because a more peaceful state is ensured to man if each one is contented with his own. Hence it is to be observed that quarrels arise more frequently where there is no division of things possessed. (*ST* II-II, q. 66, a. 3)

The thing to note about this defense is that it is *pragmatic:* things just work better when there is private ownership. But then Thomas identifies a second aspect of property, its use. He writes, "The second thing that is competent to man with regard to external things is their use. In this respect man ought to possess external things, not as his own, but as common, so that, to wit, he is ready to communicate them to others in their need" (Ibid.).

Thus Thomas identifies two aspects of property: *ownership* and *use*. One dictates a *private* aspect of property and the other a *public* or *common* aspect. What is the relationship between these two aspects? According to Thomas,

> Community of goods is ascribed to the natural law, not that the natural law dictates that all things should be possessed in common and that nothing should be possessed as one's own: but because the division of possessions is not according to the natural law, but rather arose out of human agreement which belongs to the positive law.... Hence the ownership of possessions is not contrary to the natural law, but an addition thereto devised by human reason. (Ibid., ad 3)

Indeed, the common claims on property are so strong that theft is allowed in cases of need: "In cases of need all things are common property, so that there would seem to be no sin in taking another's property, for need has made it common" (*ST* II-II, q. 66, a. 7, sc).

For St. Thomas, then, there is a common aspect of property that is governed by the natural law and a private aspect which is governed by positive law, or prudence. Now we can better understand Thomas's pragmatic defense of private property: it is a method, governed only by prudence, of ensuring that the "natural" common values of property will be available to all; it is a way to ensure that property will be properly developed so as to be useful to the whole community, since property always needs to be developed in some sense in order that its values be made available to humans. Now, if St. Thomas is correct, we would expect to see in the history of property ownership a variety of prudential methods based on the interplay of the common and private values in land. Further, we would expect that these various methods of ownership and use will vary according to how cultures perceive the natural law as it applies to justice. We will test this thesis by looking at four different systems of ownership: the "Sabbath Land" of the Old Testament, the "private" system of the Greek city-states, the feudal land of the Middle Ages, and our own system of modern capitalism.

PROPERTY AND CULTURE

Sabbath Land

If religion and economics are separate and distinct things, you would never know it from reading the Bible. The Old Testament especially is an "economic" document which specifies a system of land ownership (indeed, several systems) and calls for "justice" from nearly every page. The land is a primary theological and economic category in the Old Testament, particularly the "Promised Land."[1] The Bible does not present us with a series of moral abstractions, but embodies its strictures in concrete situations, specifically in the way the people are to relate to the land. As the faith of the ancient Hebrews waxes and wanes, so too does their relationship with the land. For this reason, we find not *one* system of land ownership in the Bible, but six.[2] The oldest of these is the Sabbath Land codes found in Leviticus 25–26, Deuteronomy 15, and Exodus 23.[3]

Taken together, these chapters present a picture of the land as bound by the Sabbath. That is to say, not only do the inhabitants of the land observe the Sabbath, but the land does as well; the land itself rests one year in a week of years. The overriding premise of this system is *covenant*, an agreement between God and humans with obligations on both sides. An overview of the covenant is given in Leviticus 25, while chapter 26 provides a series of blessings for keeping the covenant (3–13) and a series of curses for violating it (14–39). Both the blessings and the curses relate primarily to the land, its fruitfulness and security, and only derivatively to the inhabitants. Among the blessings we find that the Lord promises that the land will receive rain in due season (26:4), the threshing will overtake the vintage (5), dangerous animals will be removed (6), and the land shall be secure from attack (6–8). But chief among the blessings is the physical presence of the Lord: "And I will walk among you, and will be your God, and you shall be my people" (12). The curses, however, outweigh the blessings "seven-fold" (21) and include disease, famine, loss of political independence, wild beasts, and exile.

The central premise of the covenant is that the land cannot be sold because it cannot be owned: "The land shall not be sold in perpetuity, for the land is mine; with me you are but aliens and tenants" (Lv 25:23). Even this tenancy of the land does not reside so much in individuals as in the clan or tribe, and the kinsmen always retain the right to "redeem" the land (that is, buy it back after a "sale").[4] Here we see most clearly the distinction between modern and Levitical notions of land ownership; while in the modern world, the individual is sovereign over his own land, in Leviticus the land cannot be alienated from the clan or tribe, and the individual himself is a mere "tenant" even though he holds a life-time tenancy.

The specific terms of the "lease" required that the Hebrews:

1. Not sell the land in perpetuity. Rather, it could only be leased to another for up to seven years. Even then, the kinfolk of the one leasing the land had the right to "redeem" it. But whether or not it was redeemed, the land had to be returned to its owners every Sabbath (seventh) year.

2. Permanent slavery for Hebrews was forbidden; those placed in debt servitude had to be freed every seventh year.

3. Every seventh year the land had to lie fallow, the "land Sabbath." This probably referred to a normal crop rotation system rather than *all* the land being uncultivated in one year.

4. The poor had the right to harvest whatever grew on the fallow fields, as well as the right to glean the other fields. Thus the land provided work and sustenance for both for the "owners" and those who owned no land at all.

5. Since "ownership" of the land was vested not in individuals, but rather in the clan or tribe, the current tenants merely used the land and "possessed" only as much as they could use themselves. There was no concept of land as a capital asset which one could hoard or exchange for a profit. In fact, the only way to draw income from the land was by personal labor,[5] and as such, the land was available to both "rich" and "poor" members of the extended family or tribe.

This system of land tenure rested upon the Hebrew view of the purpose of life. The ancient Hebrews had only the vaguest notion of an "after-life," a concept that came much later to the Hebrew religion; rather, the land *itself* was the promise. A peaceful life on their own land, free from foreign rule, with each man tending his own vines, was the ideal; "salvation" meant having a home and living by one's own efforts. The land itself was not a "commodity" to be bought and sold, but a gift from God for all generations, not just the current one. The Sabbath land system is typical of tribal land ownership systems found throughout history, including the tribal cultures of our own day. To put the matter into modern terms, "one could consider the land the joint property of all members of the tribe, past, present and future, with present members having only a leasehold interest."[6]

We can see from the story of Naboth's vineyard (1 Kings 21) that the ideals of the Sabbath land system were not just pious admonitions, but rather were a functioning system. King Ahab desires a field belonging to Naboth and offers to buy it from him. But Naboth will not sell because, as he tells the king, "The Lord forbid that I should give you my ancestral heritage" (v. 4). Naboth cannot sell the land because he does not "own" it; he is merely the current user of the land. On this basis, the commoner can stand his ground (literally) against a king. The king can do nothing but return to his palace and sulk. However, the king has a wife named Jezebel who is not Jewish but a Canaanite princess, a foreigner from a land where the king's word is law and all land belongs to the king; hence she is amazed at her husband's weakness. "A fine ruler of Israel you are!" she taunts him (v. 7). Taking matters into her own hands, she has Naboth framed on a charge of blasphemy and killed. Ahab then takes possession of Naboth's field. But as he does, he is confronted by the prophet Elijah, who accuses him, "After murdering, do you also take possession?" It seems the violation of the land laws is as abhorrent as the murder. The story testifies to the persistence of the old laws.

Nevertheless, the laws were sufficiently disregarded so that land and power were being concentrated in fewer and fewer hands, which caused an angry response from the prophets, such as when Isaiah says, "Woe to you who join house to house and field to field until you are left to dwell alone in the midst of the land" (Is 5:8). The final chapter comes when the kingdom of Jerusalem is besieged by the Babylonians under Nebuchadnezzar. The Prophet Jeremiah tells King Zedekiah that the key to lifting the siege is to free the slaves. The Hebrews promise to do so, and immediately Jerusalem's ally, the Pharaoh Hophra, takes the field against Nebuchadnezzar, who lifts the siege to face the new threat. Seeing the Babylonians depart, the nobles renege on their promise and fail to actually free the slaves. In the meantime, Hophra takes one look at Nebuchadnezzar's army and changes his mind; his army retreats to Egypt and Nebuchadnezzar resumes the siege. Jeremiah tells them what the result will be:

> Therefore, thus says the Lord: You have not obeyed me by proclaiming liberty, every one to his brother and to his neighbor; behold, I proclaim to you liberty to the sword, to pestilence, and to famine, says the Lord. I will make you a horror to all the kingdoms of the earth. (Jer. 34:16–17)

And that is exactly what happens.

Hebrew society, like any other, did not remain static, nor did its spiritual life. The spirituality that supported the Sabbath codes was weakened by internal stresses and by long contact with the more urbane culture of Babylon.

After the return from exile, the Sabbath laws were re-written into the Jubilee codes, codes more "sympathetic" to private wealth. These re-written codes are similar in form to the Sabbath codes, but the year of freedom occurs not every seventh year, but every seven times seventh year. Thus land can be leased and slavery imposed for forty-nine years, or pretty much for one's whole adult life. Further, the right to harvest the fallow fields was taken from the poor and retained by the owners. This all constitutes a "privatization" of property rights and follows closely the trajectory that will repeat itself time and again throughout history: the gradual accumulation of property in the hands of a few, and the "privatizing" of what had previously been common rights to the land.[7] We can see this pattern at a later stage in looking at Aristotle's Athens.

Aristotle's Athens

The ancient Greeks, like the ancient Hebrews, were a tribal people and had a system of land ownership not too very different from the Hebrews with ownership vested in the family or tribe.[8] But by the time of Plato and Aristotle, new and private forms of property were rising. "Young Greeks recognized that their standard of living could be enhanced by buying land privately and working it. The product from this enterprise did not have to be shared with relatives."[9] Plato regarded this kind of ownership as vulgar and forbade it to the "guardians" of his ideal republic. Aristotle, however, took the opposite tack, arguing that property was a practical necessity. Why did this "privatization" of property become practical and necessary when it had not existed before? The answer lies in the transition from a rural and tribal society to a city-state. The great problem with tribal societies is tribal rivalries and warfare. Such warfare can be disastrous, the ruination of whole societies, as we can see today in Africa or in parts of the Middle East. The challenge of the city-state was to channel the strife into economic competition, which sustains agriculture and trade,[10] and to provide for the support of a military class, which becomes the aristocracy. For Aristotle, the warriors should be the land owners. He accepted private property, but only when connected with an obligation for common use in the form of defense and production.[11]

This privatization of property, and the consequent concentration of wealth, was connected with what might be called a privatization and concentration of virtue and happiness. Full happiness could only come from the practice of virtue, and full virtue was limited to the aristocrats; slaves, women, children, artisans, the poor, the ugly were all barred from full happiness and the exercise of complete virtue.[12] Since being an aristocrat was an accident of birth, happiness was a matter of "moral luck" and available in its fullness to only a lucky few. This might be called a kind of Pagan Predestinationism, in which a few are preordained to happiness (or at least its possibility) while the rest are condemned to various degrees of unhappiness, with the slave at the bottom of the heap. Slavery was in fact a cornerstone of Greek economics and fit in well with the conception of morality. Indeed, the moral, cultural, and economic systems are always intertwined and interdependent. The Greek system maintained both the common and private aspects of property but emphasized the private, as opposed to tribal systems, which emphasized the communal.

We can see a trajectory of movement from more communal values to more individual values in both the Greek and Hebrew societies, with a complete privatization of land and a disregard of communal values as the society deteriorates. This happened to the Hebrews before their exile and to the Greeks before their fall to the Romans. In the same way, Roman property follows this same pattern. Toward the end of the empire, land tended to be concentrated as soldiers on extended active duty lost title to their land, and the power and influence of the landowners grew while the free farmers declined in number and significance right up to the collapse of the empire.[13] However, the Middle Ages were able to reverse the trajectory in new and interesting ways.

The Middle Ages

The barbarian invasions gave impetus to the concentration of land as the need for defense increased. The former free soldiers and farmers became serfs (slaves) on their own land. Europe entered a dark age from about the fifth to the ninth centuries; there was a near total loss of trade and commerce, of government, even of the domestic arts, such as farming; security became the primary concern. Life expectancy declined to perhaps as little as twenty-four years, while crop yields plummeted, some say to as little as five grains per head;[14] while that number is unlikely, it was certainly true that farming declined. Part of the decline had to do with the fact that the northern lands required different techniques than the Mediterranean farms; the soils were rich but heavier and harder to work; the available "scratch" plows, for example, made little impression on the soil, and the existing harnesses constricted the horses' chests which limited the amount of weight they could pull. What were needed were new methods and even a new economics.

And that is precisely what happened. As Europe emerged from the Dark Ages around the ninth and tenth centuries, there was a technological explosion. It was not one invention, but dozens of little ones such as the moldboard plow, the horse collar, three-crop rotation, the use of legumes, the spiked harrow, and horseshoes.[15] Farms became very productive once again. The increased production meant a revival in population and trade, not to mention improvements in the health of the people. By the eleventh century, for example, the average height for European men reached 5′ 8″; it began to decline after that and men did not again reach that stature until the twentieth century,[16] contradicting the popular view that life in the Middle Ages was "nasty, brutish, and short." This increased productivity raises a question of why problems in farming that had existed for centuries suddenly were solved in so short a period of time. What was at the root of the trend toward innovation and constant improvement? To understand this development we must understand the system of medieval land tenure, the feudal system.

As we noted previously, at the start of the Dark Ages the mass of people had been reduced to slavery. But slavery, especially when it is so widespread, has both military and economic drawbacks. In the first place, slaves do not make good soldiers; it matters little to them what language the master speaks, and they are not likely to risk their lives over the issue. In an era of warfare this is a serious shortcoming. Nor do slaves make good workers; they may work for free, but as long as the master gets all of the values above bare subsistence, they will not work harder than subsistence requires and are not likely to invest the effort in innovation or experimentation on which improved output depends. If the estates were to progress, they could only do so by granting a measure of freedom, both political and economic, to the slaves. Thus it gradually happened that by the ninth or tenth century the term *servus* no longer meant a slave but a serf and very nearly a peasant.[17]

To understand how this happened, we need to look at land ownership. The predominant form of land ownership was in "fief." All title was held by the king (as the representative of the people) who in turn granted estates for a fee (fief). This "fee" was not a "rent" in our sense of the term, but a complex system of rights and responsibilities. We have extensive records from these estates because the bailiff, a combination of CEO/accountant for the estate, was required to give detailed accounts of the estate, thousands of which still exist. The estates were divided into three portions. The first of these was the demesne or the domain which was the lord's private farm, usually occupied by the bailiff. This might consist of about a third of the land. Another portion was that worked by the serfs and cottagers and owned by them in all but name. The third portion was the commons, on which both the lord and the serfs had certain rights.[18]

Each serf held about twelve acres of land in tenancy.[19] His rent was largely in goods and in labor. He was required to pay ½ *d.* on November 12 along with a peck of wheat, four bushels of oats, and three hens. At Christmas, he must pay a cock and two hens, and 2*d.* worth of bread. At Michaelmas (September 29) he would pay a peck of seed wheat. In addition, he must plow, sow, and till half an acre of the lord's land, work three days at harvest, and do such work as required by the bailiff, which could be several days per week. Compare this with the expected yields from his land of thirteen bushels per acre of wheat or twenty of barley, sixteen of oats, or fourteen of peas. The cottagers paid between 1*s* 2*d* and 2*s* for their cottages and were required to work at haymaking one or two days for ½ *d* per day. They were also to work four days at harvest during which they were fed at the lord's table. During the rest of the year they were free laborers, usually employed on the estate for money.

In return, the lord was expected to maintain the infrastructure of the estate (roads, canals, bridges, etc.), provide for the defense and the policing of the estate and hold courts for minor offenses and disputes. In addition, the lord owned the mill which everybody was required to use for grinding their grain, for a fee, and the brewery at which everybody made their beer, also for a fee. Finally, the lord had the best pastureland and the right to all the oak and ash trees, which could be cut only with his permission.

The fact that the fees were fixed had profound economic and social consequences; it meant that any improvements in productivity would go to the serf rather than the lord. The servile condition implied by the term "serf" had all but disappeared, and the tenant regarded the land as his own. True, he could not sell it, but neither could he be evicted, and he could pass his title, such as it was, to his sons. What improvements he made to the property accrued to his own benefit. Under such conditions, men willingly worked and eagerly improved the land. These rents were not economic, but customary; what would later become the so-called Law of Rents, by which the landlord got the benefits of all values above that produced on the worst piece of land, held no sway. The rents were not based on the value of the land, but on the value of the services provided to the land.[20] Adam Smith correctly identified the fees not as "rents" at all, but as taxes, that is, what someone pays the ruling authority for police protection, infrastructure, etc.[21] In an economic sense, there were no rents at all. This explains the great improvement in agricultural technique and productiveness. For when people can keep the output of their industry, they get very industrious indeed, and very creative. It is no small irony that great economic results were obtained by ignoring what would later be called the "laws" of economics. It is clear from the records that there was a security and fixity of tenure and well-distributed property. The picture we have of a few who owned the land and the many who worked it in misery is simply not correct. The peasantry was prosperous, secure in their land, well-fed and, if Professor Steckel is correct, tall.

The expansion of farming also meant the revival of town life and with it the revival of trade and industry, for there can be no town life unless there is a surplus of food to support it. The industry in the towns was organized into *guilds:*

> A Guild was a society partly co-operative, but in the main composed of private owners of capital whose corporation was self-governing, and was designed to check competition between its members: to prevent the growth of one at the expense of the other. Above all, most jealously did the Guild safeguard the division of property, so that there should be formed within its ranks no proletariat upon the one side and no monopolizing capitalist upon the other.[22]

The guild controlled all production within the towns and was made up of both the workers and the owners. Being a "worker" in a trade was itself a temporary condition; after a period of apprenticeship all the workers could become masters.[23] Note that the guild did not actually do away with competition, but merely competition on price; the masters still competed on matters such as quality, artistry, and service. Trade and industry flourished under this system and great wealth was created, as can be ascertained by the amount of surplus available for projects such as cathedrals, castles, public buildings, roads, and canals.

What emerges is not a simple political/economic hierarchy, but a complex system of multiple authorities reflecting a moral equality within a political hierarchy. The guilds, the towns, the estate, and the religious authorities, all had their own laws, rights, and customary rules which were regarded as more or less "sacred" and could not easily be tampered with by other authorities. Everyone, from the peasant to the aristocrat, was conscious of his rights and willing to assert them against all threats. Property was well distributed so that even the meanest peasant had rights to the common lands. Although legal "ownership" was vested in the sovereign, actual ownership was vested in the lords, the tenants, and the townsmen. The system not only created a vast amount of wealth, but distributed it well to high and low alike. The system of customary rents, rather than economic ones, worked well. However, the system began to evolve from one of labor rent to one of cash rents. Landlords preferred to receive, and peasants preferred to pay, cash in lieu of service.

By the middle of the fourteenth century, there was very little of the old serfdom remaining. At first, the payments in lieu of service worked well for both sides, but things changed rapidly after the plague (1348), which reduced the population of England by one-third.[24] Wages rose rapidly, and the cash commutations for service were no longer sufficient to hire replacements. Attempts to force the serfs to labor on the old terms failed, since workers could just flee the estate with the assurance that they would find work at high wages elsewhere.[25] The high wages meant that the remaining serfs could buy their freedom and could pay a money rent for farms, which led to the rise of the yeoman-farmer. As the wages rose, and the profits of the old system declined, the landlords attempted to re-impose serfdom, but with little success. Indeed, wages were so high that in 1351 the Statute of Laborers attempted to cap the wages at pre-plague rates and imposed treble damages on lords who paid more than the statutory rate.[26] However, the law had little effect; demand for labor was high and the peasant had too many alternatives.

> The labourers gained all that the landlords lost, and could extort what terms they liked from the necessities of their employers. This attitude was met by the Statute of Labourers.... The attempt failed. Year after year, almost century after century, the Parliament complained that the Statute of Labourers was not kept, re-enacted it, strove to make it effective, were baffled, adopted new and harsher expedients, and were disappointed.[27]

By the end of the fifteenth century, wages had reached their highest level; a peasant could provide food for his family for a whole year by fifteen weeks of work, and a craftsman by ten weeks.[28] England enjoyed, for a century or more, the novel experience of general prosperity with high wages and full employment. It was no accident that such a system developed in Christian Europe, for it well reflected the values of the medieval Church. For Christianity the end of life was not in this world, as it was for the Hebrews and the Greeks, but in the next. Therefore mere accumulation could not be part of the final end. Moreover, this end, union with God, was available to rich and poor alike; there was a moral equality even in the face of social inequality. In such circumstances, slavery withers and dies and the classes tend to converge. Since the kings had lost their divine status, they could no longer be absolute monarchs (as they were before and would later become) but were hedged in by a system of rights at all levels of society.

However, there were problems developing. The move from service to cash also meant a move from a society based on custom to one based purely on money.[29] The new system also affected the revenues of the crown, which were based on the old "suit and service" system. When Richard II imposed a poll-tax in 1381, in keeping with the new cash economy, there was a wide-spread rebellion under Wat Tyler that nearly succeeded in establishing popular government in England.[30]

The Modern Era

The sixteenth century opened with England in prosperity, a prosperity that was well distributed to workers and farmers through high wages for the one and low fees for the other. By the end of that century, wages had collapsed and vast numbers of peasants had been dispossessed from the land to become a landless proletariat in the cities. A system of "welfare" became necessary, in the form of the Poor Laws, to support a rapidly growing underclass. Obviously, some catastrophe had intervened to change the character of England and the balance of economic and social forces. That catastrophe was the seizure of the monasteries (1536) and a new view of property. This seizure itself was in line with a growing discontent among landowners with the feudal system. They wanted to obtain not merely customary fees but the full economic values of the land for themselves. To do this, they would have to break the power of the working and peasant classes. Further, large tracts of land had been taken out of the feudal system, both by the monasteries and by grants to individuals, and became "freeholds" paying no fees to the crown. This meant that the revenue which formerly flowed from these lands had to be made up by increased taxation.[31]

By the sixteenth century, the Church controlled fully a third of the land in England, making the Church the single largest landowner aside from the king himself. The Church's lands supported not only the monasteries themselves, but were part of the charitable and educational infrastructure. The universities, for example, were largely supported by scholarships funded by the Church, so that the collapse of the monasteries very nearly meant the collapse of the universities. The monasteries were also a part of the pension system, by which "corrodies" were purchased from abbeys. These were a kind of annuity, in which a sum of money would be given to the monastery in return for the right to be supported by the monks for the rest of a beneficiary's life.

The Dissolution of the Monasteries was not the result of the Protestant Reformation; it was the cause. King Henry VIII regarded himself as a Catholic, and indeed persecuted dissenters with the same zeal as had his father. Rather, it was the work of a combination of factors. The first was the growing resentment of the power of the clergy and of abbots who seemed more interested in wealth than in religion. Anti-clerical Catholics hoped that seizure would allow the funds to be used for education and public improvements. Their hopes would be thoroughly disappointed. The second factor was the profligacy of the king, who had emptied his treasury and sought to refill it by confiscation. The third group were those who hoped to get the land on easy terms, which in fact they did.[32]

It should be noted that the seizure of the monasteries, by itself, did not actually change things in England. Had the king merely taken over the Church lands, he would have become the richest and most powerful force in England, and perhaps in Europe. But the life of the peasants would not have changed all that much; instead of paying fees to the officers of the Church, they would have paid them to the officers of the king, and things would have proceeded as before. But in point of fact, the king did not actually get the land.[33] The king was in no sense an absolute monarch; his bill had to pass the parliament, and parliamentarians then were like parliamentarians now: each member had his own price.[34] Each member of Parliament (and they were all drawn from the land-owning class) had his eye on some tract of land that he had coveted, and, as the price of his vote, he got it, often for a price of pennies on the pound. Instead of refilling his treasury, the king spent his capital and ended up as poor as before.[35] The wealth that should have flowed to the king passed through his hands and into the hands of a new class. This land-owning class already owned outright in the demesnes a fourth to a third of all the village land. Now a further fifth to third was added to that, making them the masters of half the land in England.[36]

Nor was that all. The land-owners wanted to *enclose* the village commons, that is, take them out of common ownership and make them "private" property. "Enclosure" was a movement that had been undertaken in a small way prior to the seizures and that had been roundly condemned by the king's chancellor, Sir Thomas More. But with the removal of More and the change in the balance of power, there was little to check the disappearance of the commons into private hands.[37]

Adding to the woes of the working class, Henry VIII sought further remedy for his finances by debasing the currency. Workers found that the prices for everything but their labor increased, doubling and then doubling again. Henry and his successors reduced the value of the coinage by as much as 60 percent before the old measure was restored by Queen Elizabeth a century later.[38]

The looting of English land continued through the reign of Henry VIII's weak successor, a sickly child, so that by the beginning of the reign of Queen Mary, there was a powerful class of capitalists, a weak and impoverished crown, and a degraded and landless peasantry; power in England had passed to a new group of men. The dispossession of a large number of former peasants resulted in the creation of a landless proletariat, who clogged the cities in a search for work or turned to brigandage on the highways; further, there was a century of civil wars culminating in the Revolution of 1660 as the new landowning class asserted its power; finally, and perhaps most importantly, the common people had lost their bargaining power on wages. Henry had unwittingly accomplished what the Statute of Laborers could not; wages were finally limited not by the law but by the economic system.[39] A century before the seizures, the peasant could provision his family by fifteen weeks of work and the artisan by ten; by 1543, it took the peasant forty weeks of work and the artisan thirty-two.[40]

Society passed from a system of well-distributed land at easy rents to a system of consolidated estates rented on the unfavorable terms[41] of what would later be known as the Law of Rents. It amounted to a "new conquest of England."[42] The intense land speculation forced a rise in land prices, and the new owners had to squeeze every penny from the tenants to make the land pay. Thus with the new owners of England came a new attitude. When some peasants objected to the seizure of their common lands, the new landlord told them:

> Do ye not know that the King's Grace hath put down all the houses
> of monks, friars and nuns? Therefore now is the time come that we
> gentlemen will pull down the houses of such poor knaves as ye be.[43]

The new attitude was based on a new view of property. The fine balance between common and individual values gave way to a purely "private" notion of property; the feudal system, which enmeshed property in a complex relationship of rights and responsibilities, became an *allodial* system, where property is held free of any obligations. While we accept this today without any critique, in fact it took some doing to "sell" it to a public that still remembered the commons and the system of customary duties. Moreover there is always the problem of how one gets original title to land. You and I hold a piece of property most likely by right of purchase. But how did the first person come into exclusive control of that property? Obviously the land originally belonged to no one but was common to all. The philosopher of the new view of property was John Locke (1632–1704). He begins, as St. Thomas does, with a common view of property but moves to the question of how to take property out of its common use and put it in a purely private domain, free of any common responsibilities. His answer was to appeal to the "property" we all have in our own labor:

> Though the Earth and all inferior Creatures be common to all Men, yet every Man has a Property in his own Person. This no Body has any Right to but himself. The Labour of his Body, and the Work of his Hands, we may say, are properly his. Whatsoever then he removes out of the State that nature hath provided, and left it in, he have mixed his Labour with, and joyned to it something that is his own, and thereby makes it his Property.[44]

By working the land, then, one takes it out of "common" use and makes it private property. Moreover it becomes *radically* private, with no public obligations whatsoever; the obligations implied by St. Thomas's view of common use do not apply.[45] Finally, for Locke not only does one's personal labor entitle him to take land from the common domain, but the labor of any under one's control does as well. This means that ownership is now in principle infinite with no natural limitations whatsoever. For Thomas, private property was a conventional arrangement intended to further the common good; for Locke, the reverse is true: ownership is natural and any "communal" values are purely conventional, a matter of positive law; the connection to the common good disappears entirely and all values are purely individualistic. Note how well this accords with the new individualism that becomes the hallmark of the Enlightenment. Recall also how the Enlightenment fragmented human experience while reducing all values to the purely logical or psychological. Thus the communal and personal nature of property, connected to some degree in every civilization, is now fragmented, and the only values are the satisfaction of personal desires freely determined by the individual.

PROPERTY AND ECONOMICS

Economic Rent

We have previously seen that while classical economics recognized that the income from land (rent) was different from the income from either labor or humanly created capital, neoclassical theory attempted to treat all sources of income as springing from marginal utility. At equilibrium, this would drive all prices to costs and eliminate any economic profit. But this is simply not possible when it comes to property in land; land will always collect an economic rent. *Economic rent* is a payment to a factor of production in excess of that which is needed to keep it employed in its current use. Another way to think of economic rent is that it is collected on a fixed resource which is not consumed in the transaction. Neoclassicism claims, like all economic systems, to be able to eliminate economic rent, for the most part. When we are dealing with humanly created capital items, this is likely true. If a maker of widgets is in a position to charge economic rent for his product, that is, when there are excess profits, other entrepreneurs will be attracted to the widget business, thereby raising the supply and lowering the price until the economic rent is eliminated. But land cannot be manufactured. It has neither production nor depreciation costs, hence *all* payments for land will be in excess of its production and depreciation costs. If economic efficiency means paying no more for an asset than that which is required to keep it in production, then economic rent is the precise measure of economic inefficiency. Therefore, the question of economic efficiency cannot be addressed apart from the question of economic rent. We have just seen how the use of non-economic (customary) rents in medieval England caused an explosion of creativity and economic expansion. Later (chapter 14) we will see how the elimination of rents had similar effects in modern day Taiwan, Korea, and Japan.

Property ownership confers another advantage related to economic rent, that of the *unearned increment*. The price of raw land (not including the improvements to the land) is not determined by the land itself, but by what happens to the surrounding properties. Think about buying a plot of raw land in a sparsely populated area near a large city. As time goes on, there is a tendency for the population to expand and for development to find its way to the outlying areas. As the population increases and surrounding tracts get developed, the price of the land rises, and it does so without the owner having to do anything to the land whatsoever. This increase in value constitutes the unearned increment, an amount accruing to the land with no effort on the part of the owner.

Insofar as equilibrium depends on efficiency, land rents will constitute an irreducible element of inefficiency in the economy. The effects of this inefficiency will be vastly exaggerated by the concentration of land ownership. Societies that have a small landowning class will have high rates of poverty, unemployment, and underemployment, a fact that may be easily verified since there are, alas, many such economies both present and past. Further, what is true for land is also true for capital; the more it is concentrated in ownership, the more difficult will be the tasks of development, equity, and equilibrium. Thus to a large extent the distribution of incomes in a given society will be largely determined by the distribution of property. This fact has profound implications

The Mystification of Property

To most people, and to most ages, "property" refers to something physical in the real world. However, property no longer has this meaning within economics; it loses any purely physical properties to become a pure abstraction and, we might say, a purely mystical concept. Recall that J. B. Clark had drained capital of its actual content so that it became no more than "continuity of ownership," a kind of "transmigration";[46] ownership rather than use becomes the determining factor. As Hernando de Soto points out in *The Mystery of Capital: Why Capitalism Triumphs in the West and Fails Everywhere Else*, "capital" now becomes not a "thing," but a "representational system" where "we can disengage the resource from its burdensome material constraints."[47] A house, then, is not capital, but only the deed to the house, "an economic concept *about* the house, embodied in a legal representation."[48] In other words, property becomes a purely *cultural* construct with a merely tenuous connection with reality; the "reality" becomes the deed, the actual house being no more than a footnote to the deed.

The cultural nature of "capital" becomes more evident when we see what happens when a capitalist system is suddenly imposed on pre-existing systems in both the so-called Third World and the former communist countries. We tend to view these people as desperately poor because they have no capital. The poverty is indeed widespread, but so is their capital. As de Soto points out, not only do the poor save, but the value of their savings is immense — forty times all the foreign aid received throughout the world since 1945.[49] The poor have houses, land, machinery, farm implements, and other things commonly thought of as capital, but they do not have capital in the capitalistic sense. For example, in Peru, the value of extra-legally held real estate amounts to $74 billion, or five times the total valuation of the Lima Stock Exchange, fourteen times the value of foreign investment, and eleven times the value of all government enterprises.[50] Yet, in order for a claim to land to be registered in Peru, 728 steps are required, a process beyond the means or patience of most of the peasant entrepreneurs.[51] Thus the "new" capitalistic system becomes a means of social control and exclusion.

Throughout most of the world, the "extra-legal" segment of the economy is as large as or larger than the legal segment. The poor trade houses and land, have informal banking systems, produce goods on their farms or in their workshops, but are still not capitalists. Not for want of trying, but because of deliberate exclusion. More than anything, what separates the capitalist from the non-capitalist is not the actual existence of capital, but the social and cultural constructs that surround Western notions of capital and property.

A QUESTION OF VALUES

We have come to view all arguments about property as arguments between an absolute ownership as embodied in capitalism or "public" ownership as embodied in socialism. But the historical question is far more complex, always being some combination of the two. The particular combinations are not given by an abstract vision of economics, but by the vision the society has of the end and purpose of the human person and society; it is in view of its final values that a society allocates the relative public and private values of land. R. H. Tawney put the case like this:

> [The Scholastics] while justifying [private property] on grounds of experience and expediency, insisted that its use was limited at every turn by the rights of the community and the obligations of charity.... Society is a hierarchy of rights and duties. Law exists to enforce the second, as much as to protect the first. Property is not a mere aggregation of economic privileges, but a responsible office. Its *raison d'être* is not only income, but service. It is to secure its owner such means, and no more than such means, as may enable him to perform those duties.[52]

Thus we see in a highly communal society like the ancient Hebrews a communal view of land with ownership in the tribe and use in the family; moreover, it is a view of moral equality that lets the commoner stand his ground even against the king. For the Greeks, the ideal was an aristocratic one, where the private values are more emphasized, yet the communal values are present in the form of the support of the soldier and the advancement of commerce. For the people of the Middle Ages, there was "public" ownership with private use circumscribed by custom with a diffusion of rights and responsibilities throughout all levels of society. For our own age, the question of the relative merits has been fragmented into two opposing views that make absolute either the individual values (capitalism) or the communal values (socialism). In actual practice, in both "socialist" and "capitalist" countries, this means a strong view of the "private" nature of property with the communal values recovered by taxation. All of these views were "economic," in the sense that they established viable and relatively stable economies that produced great wealth for their citizens.

Economics, then, emerges as a tool by which people and societies provide for their material needs within a certain moral framework. People, and societies, are *relatively* free to choose their own ends and to build the kinds of systems that support those goals. The answer is not given in advance by an abstract economics, but freely chosen and discovered through actual practice.

Part II

The Social Encyclicals

Chapter 6

Rerum Novarum:
A Scandalous Encyclical?

It gradually came about that the present age handed over the
workers, each alone and defenseless, to the inhumanity of employers and the unbridled greed of competitors . . . so that a very
few rich and exceedingly rich men have laid a yoke almost of
slavery on the unnumbered masses of non-owning workers.

—POPE LEO XIII

READING THE SOCIAL ENCYCLICALS

The social encyclicals are a group of papal writings beginning in 1891
with Pope Leo XIII's *Rerum Novarum*, "Of New Things," and continuing
to the most recent, *Centesimus Annus*, "On the Hundredth Anniversary"
(of *Rerum Novarum*) in 1991. They deal with topics that are prudential,
contentious, and current. They deal with government, politics, economics,
wages, and the like. In other words, they deal with subjects that are the common traffic of everyday news, daily work, and economic and political life.
These topics are the very stuff of politics and ideology; hence, many readings of the encyclicals have an ideological character. Commentators often
"pick and choose" those elements which match their ideologies and ignore
or downplay the rest. But the whole point of the encyclicals is to transcend
the narrow ideologies of contemporary politics. The best antidote to an
ideological reading is for the student to read the documents in their original while attempting to incorporate *all* elements. It is important to give the
closest reading to the parts which raise the biggest challenges to one's own
point of view. This is not to imply that one accepts them unreflectively, or
even that they must be accepted at all. But before one comes to a judgment
one way or another, one should be absolutely sure that one has understood
the idea on its own terms.

109

THE HISTORICAL BACKGROUND

The eighteenth and nineteenth centuries saw a sea-change in the economic life of Europe, one that did not bode well for the working classes. The mercantilists, whose activities were well documented in Adam Smith's *Wealth of Nations,* had consolidated their hold on the economic and political life of much of Europe. Mercantilism was that peculiar combination of private privilege and government power which resulted in an enormous increase of wealth for the mercantile class. Further, as we noted before, the closure of the monasteries and the enclosure of the commons had dispossessed the people of their land, and land itself came to be regarded as "private" with little in the way of communal values other than taxes. Even the term "working class" heralded a new set of conditions, since in the prior age most men did not think of themselves in that way; they were farmers or craftsmen working their own professions rather than "laborers." A new class of landless peasants, the "proletariat" who were dependent on wages, had been created.

But the new economics made wages independent of need. Labor was a commodity like any other, the price determined by supply and demand and limited by marginal utility in theory, but by power relationships in fact. By the time of Benjamin Disraeli (1804–81), England had become:

> two nations between whom there is no intercourse and no sympathy; who are as ignorant of each other's habits, thoughts, and feelings, as if they were dwellers in different zones or inhabitants of different planets; who are formed by different breeding, are fed by different food, are ordered by different manners, and are not governed by the same laws.[1]

Just how different these two nations were may be gleaned from some of the statistics concerning the poor:

- In the 1880s, more than a third of all Londoners were living in families huddled six to a room, and more than one in eight dying in the workhouse.

- In the 1870s the height of eleven- and twelve-year-old school boys from upper class schools was five inches greater than boys from industrial schools; this reflects an enormous difference in diet and health.

- In 1917, under the more relaxed recruitment standards of the British army, 10 percent of potential recruits were found unfit for service, 41.5 percent had marked disabilities, and 22 percent had partial disabilities.[2]

The situation was paradoxical, because the new economics had undoubtedly raised production to unprecedented levels. But the results seemed to be unevenly distributed: Dickensian poverty for the masses and wealth for a relative few. "Why, in the presence of so much wealth, are the poor so many?" became the question of the age. Neither the classical economics of Smith, Mill, and Ricardo nor the neoclassical, marginalist economics held the answer. Indeed, instead of the full employment and equilibrium promised by the system, there were high unemployment and cycles of boom and bust.

If the marginalists could not supply an answer, the socialists had one ready made: property was theft! It was the privatization of property that was causing all of the problems. Socialism in the nineteenth century was not one thing, but had many strains: guild socialism, trade union socialism, utopian communes, etc. But toward the end of the nineteenth century the distinguishing feature of "true" socialism was a belief that all property should be controlled by the political officers of the state.[3] The most frightening form of socialism was that preached by Karl Marx, so-called "scientific socialism" or communism, which promised to rectify the situation. And after a string of actual revolutions swept Europe in 1848, with support not only from the lower classes but from the middle class as well, the prospect of socialism or worse seemed real enough.

The Catholic Response

At first, the Church responded to the deterioration of the working class as if it were a problem of charity, but rarely asked why the sudden increase in the number of poor people. It missed the rise of a new class and new conditions; in other words, it missed the rise of new *structures*. By misreading the new conditions, it was losing the allegiance of the working class.[4] During the revolutions of 1848, the French bishops called attention to the insensitivity of employers and called for reforms leading to a sense of partnership between owners and workers.[5] But the most serious work was done by the man often called "the founder of social Catholicism," Bishop Wilhelm Emmanuel Ketteler (1811–72), Archbishop of Mainz, whom Leo XIII called "my great predecessor."[6] Ketteler was instrumental in drawing attention to the *structural* problems of the economic system and the faulty intellectual underpinnings that supported it. Further, he insisted on the right of the Church to concern itself with temporal affairs and to judge them from a moral standpoint.[7] Along with Ketteler's analysis, there was a growing awareness of the problems among prominent churchmen: Cardinal Manning in England, Cardinal Gibbons in the United States, Baron von Vogelsang of

Austria, and others.[8] But without a doubt, the growing influence of socialism was a spur to action.

READING THE ENCYCLICAL

Whenever we read a text, we bring a certain amount of "baggage" with us: attitudes, beliefs, prejudices, convictions, and our own social context and education. This baggage often forms a barrier between ourselves and the text; we judge it by our subjective expectations and beliefs. But the really perceptive reader will make every attempt to understand a text on its own terms before engaging in any critique. This requires a certain "distance" and objectivity. We have to put our own conceptions and preconceptions in the background while we attempt to absorb what the text has to offer. Later, of course, we will summon up our own beliefs and compare them, but the first task is just to understand what the text actually says. With this in mind, let us first try to glean as much as we can from a reading of the encyclical, and later try to analyze it.

From its very title onward ("Of New Things"), the encyclical acknowledges the existence of new conditions, which of course were, by that time — 1891 — no longer new, but sanctioned by long tradition. The opening sections clearly lay out the results of these new things, namely that it

> gradually came about that the present age handed over the workers, each alone and defenseless, to the inhumanity of employers and the unbridled greed of competitors... so that a very few rich and exceedingly rich men have laid a yoke almost of slavery on the unnumbered masses of non-owning workers. (*Rerum Novarum* 6)

The statement about the destruction of the guilds (6) is not a throwaway line, but a key to the pope's analysis: the removal of the old systems resulted in the loss of protection, solidarity, and property by the workers.

Socialism and Property (7–17)

Leo rejects the socialist scheme of doing away with private property as injurious to the workers (7–8). He advances a view of property that is based in natural right, but which is fundamentally different from the capitalist view. On the one hand, he upholds property as the "[worker's] wage under a different form"; the very reason to work "is to procure property for themselves and to retain it by individual right as theirs and as their very own" (9). But on the other hand, property does not cease to serve the common good. Those who lack land provide labor, and thus the land provides for all (14).

Property itself is "human" because, while the earth brings forth her gifts in abundance, she does so only by the work of men; the worker "leaves impressed, as it were, a kind of image of his person, so that it must be altogether just that he should possess that part as his very own and that no one in any way should be permitted to violate his right" (15). Man can provide for the future by using his reason, but only the land can give him this kind of stable and continuous support (12). Property is not a right deriving from the state, but from the nature of man (13). The laws of the state can only be just when in accord with this natural law (17).

Family (18–23)

The teaching on property is intimately connected with the teaching on the family and the necessity of providing for it; property rights have a greater validity because of their connection with family life (18). The family has rights and duties prior to and independent of the state (20), including the right to provide for its children. Hence there is the natural right of inheritance (19).

The state may interfere with the family no more than necessary. If a family is in such poor shape that it cannot provide for itself, then its distress should be remedied by the community. If there is a grave violation of mutual rights within the family, the state may intervene to restore these rights. But further than this the state cannot go (21).

The Role of the Church (24–25)

The Church must instruct the minds and regulate the morals of all classes, and only the Church can do this. Therefore it is the right of the Church to intervene in economic matters. It is the duty of the Church to protect the workers, and the state can be employed for this purpose only within limits. In reality, only a return to Christian morals can heal society (41). It is the Church's duty to form men's consciences (40).

The Duties of Rich and Poor (26–32)

Leo affirms that class differences are natural and that labor is unavoidable (26–27). However, the rich and poor cannot be set against one another, because each needs the other (28). The classes must be united by recalling them to their duties (29). The duties of the workers are to perform the work agreed upon and not to harm the property of their employers, to refrain from violence or rioting (30). The duties of the employers are to establish a wage in accordance with justice, not to gain by oppression or usury, and to protect the workers from violence (31–32).

The Proper Use of Wealth (33–39)

The just use of wealth is distinguished from just ownership (35). While things may be owned privately as a natural right, they must be used as if they were common and readily shared with those in need. This is a duty not of justice but of charity and hence cannot be enforced by law (36).

Duties of the State (45–60)

The state cannot act as a substitute for charity (45), but it, too, has a role in the proper use of wealth (45–46). The state must serve the common interest. The first duty is to insure the moral environment:

> Now, States are made prosperous especially by wholesome moral-
> ity, properly ordered family life, protection of religion and justice,
> moderate imposition and equitable distribution of public burdens, pro-
> gressive development of industry and trade, thriving agriculture, and
> by all other things of this nature, which the more actively they are
> promoted, the better and happier the life of the citizens is destined to
> be. (48)

The state must exercise due care in safeguarding the rights of non-owners (49). The wealth of nations has no other source than in the labor of workers:

> Equity therefore commands that public authority show proper concern
> for the worker so that from what he contributes to the common good
> he may receive what will enable him, housed, clothed, and secure, to
> live his life without hardship. (51)

The state has a right to intervene in families only when no other remedy is available (52). But the state should mandate sufficient time off for religious duties and should prevent immoderate work or work not suited to age and sex (53), labor that is too long (56), and pay that is inadequate (56). The rights of all must be protected, but special care given to those of the weak and poor (55). Nevertheless, Leo opposes an "absurd equality" and violence.

The Just Wage (61–66)

"Free consent" of the parties alone does not guarantee the justice of a wage, since labor is the only means for most to earn their daily bread. Work is both *personal* and *necessary* (61–62). Insofar as work is personal, the worker can give consent to any wage. But as work is also necessary, since only a wage can give most men the means of survival, the "wage shall not be less than enough to support a worker who is thrifty and upright" (63). Furthermore, the wage must be sufficient to allow a thrifty worker to save and acquire a little wealth of his own (65). By this means, there will be a more equitable division of goods, and the differences between the classes will be lessened (66).

Associations (68–80)

Leo gives great importance to associations, and especially workers' associations which have "first place" (68–69). The state cannot forbid such associations except when they have aims in conflict with public morals (72). However, Leo believes that the worker associations of his day are under the control of "secret leaders" with anti-Christian motives, and he urges Christian workers to form their own associations (74). These associations should provide for workers in need (77–78).

THE STRATEGY OF *RERUM NOVARUM*

At the center of *Rerum Novarum* are three crucial points: the just wage, the distribution of land, and worker associations. The just wage is the means by which workers can both obtain what they need today and save to get the capital for land of their own. *Land distribution* is at the heart of the strategy,[9] and the just wage at the heart of land distribution. The goal of this strategy is for the workers to achieve independence for themselves. That is why it was so necessary to defend private property, especially the private property of the poor.

The third part of the strategy is worker associations. Leo had something in mind more akin to guilds than to the unions of his day. Leo suspected, correctly in many cases, that the unions were largely socialist and sought the overthrow of society in general and of Christianity in particular, which socialists viewed as a mere prop of the established order. But he would not deny the right and the necessity of the workers to unite to protect their own interests and bargain in their own behalf. He wanted them to do much more, and to take on the burdens that both the socialists and the capitalists wanted to shunt off to government. Here Leo is affirming the importance of intermediary institutions in the life of society. Leo also carved out an important but *limited* role for government. The political authority formed a court of last resort to protect the rights of all, but most especially the rights of the poorest members of society. But its interventions (especially in family life) were to be limited and were to endure no longer than absolutely necessary. In the same way, its economic interventions were to be no more than necessary to preserve good order. The primary centers of authority in society would be the family and various kinds of associations.

THE SCANDAL OF *RERUM NOVARUM*

On one hand, *Rerum Novarum* would seem a staid and conservative encyclical: it upholds private property as a sacred right; it is suspicious of unions; it condemns socialism outright and in very round terms; it condemns the call to revolutionary and violent action. On the other hand, it has a revolutionary call of its own. In making the just wage the lynchpin of Catholic Social Teaching, the encyclical began a controversy which continues to this day.

The economists of Leo's day, and most of those of the present day, held that wages, like any other commodity, are to be bought at the lowest possible rate. This price is dictated by a supposed "natural law," and its moral rightness is assured by the mutual consent of the labor contract. Thus wages, they would argue, no matter how low, are justified by economic science and Christian morality.

In affirming the just wage, Leo cuts wages loose from either free consent or economic "law." Leo denies that the worker has a right to work for less than the just wage,[10] which seems to violate freedom. And in affirming that the just wage is dependent on the needs of the worker, he appears to violate economic science. Economic dogma has held that wages are set by supply and demand and limited by marginal utility. Recall that at this time, economics was discovering utilitarianism and transforming itself into a "science"; along comes a Roman priest imposing a "non-scientific" requirement.

One of two things is happening here: either Leo has located a fault in economic theory, or he has made an absurd statement, one comparable to the Galileo case, in which well-meaning churchmen tried to dictate the content of a pure science. Further, Leo makes the *distribution* of property a central issue; indeed, one of the purposes of the just wage is to insure that workers have a chance to get property of their own. Such distributions were simply not considered an issue among the economists of liberalism.

The just wage formed the fault line along which opinion about Catholic Social Teaching would divide. On the one hand, supporters of the just wage would propose a new way of looking at economics which challenged its very basis; on the other, neoconservatives would introduce an interpretation of Catholic Social Teaching which would at various times ignore or downplay the just wage, or identify it simply with the free market wage, or simply deny the whole theory.[11] However much the sides may disagree, they have at least identified the correct issue: Catholic Social Teaching stands or falls on the validity of the just wage. The central question remains, "Is labor just another commodity in the process of production? Is the worker just another 'thing'?"[12]

Rerum Novarum is revolutionary in another sense. By placing importance on the subsidiary institutions, it defies the reigning individualist orthodoxy of both the Right and the Left (or at least of certain strains of thought on both sides) which affirm the individual as the only real unit and the state as the final authority. This issue has a particular importance today, when even "conservative" administrations seem to accrete more and more power at the federal level, and when the role of the so-called "faith-based organizations" in delivering social services is being debated.

Finally, *Rerum Novarum* is revolutionary in that it moved the Church from the position of treating economic questions as purely charitable ones to treating them as structural ones. The Church's response is not limited to calling for more donations to charitable organizations, although it certainly continues to do that, but requires calling into question the very structures and organization of society and economic life.[13] For the next hundred years, the discussion would be primarily concerned with structures.

Chapter 7

Laborem Exercens:
Work as the Key to the Social Question

Hence in every case a just wage is the concrete means of verifying the justice of the whole socioeconomic system and, in any case, of checking that it is functioning justly. —POPE JOHN PAUL II

THE POLISH POPE

Karol Wojtyla was born in 1920 of working class parents in the village of Wadowice, near Krakow, Poland. Born in a free country, he saw it conquered first by the Nazis and later by the communists. As a young man, he attended an underground seminary, since the Nazis had closed the universities and seminaries. He worked at a quarry and a chemical factory to support himself. Throughout his life, the great events of the twentieth century were not mere stories in a newspaper, but living realities experienced on a daily basis. The struggles against the Nazis and the communists were all too real and too close.

It is little wonder, then, that as Pope John Paul II he took social systems very seriously indeed, and that he was willing to live a life of struggle against what he saw as the materialism at the heart of the current economic system. And least surprising of all should be the fact that he brought a new perspective to the issue, specifically, looking at it from the standpoint of the worker and seeing in the worker the whole key to the social question.

READING *LABOREM EXERCENS*
Work as the Key to the Social Question

Man's life is built up from work (3), and hence the meaning of work must be examined (6). The solution to the social question must be sought in the direction of "making life more human," and human work is decisive in understanding this problem (11).

118

Work today is affected by changes as important as those which occurred in the Industrial Revolution, changes that are impacting the dignity of workers. These new conditions require a re-ordering of the structures of the modern economy and of the distribution of work (3). The commitment to justice must be closely linked with commitment to peace (7). The disproportionate distribution of wealth and poverty calls for ways to ensure the just development of all nations (8).

Work and Man

Work is a fundamental dimension of man's existence on the earth (12): "Man is the image of God partly through the mandate received from the Creator to subdue, to dominate, the earth" (13), and that activity reflects the very action of the Creator, who worked for six days.

Work is a *transitive* activity which begins in man and is directed toward an external object (14). Through this process, man orders the external world and so confirms his "dominion" over the earth (15). This is the *objective* sense of work, and in this sense it embraces the whole set of instruments known as technology which facilitates and perfects his work (19). However, "technology can cease to be man's ally and become his enemy...through exalting the machine, it reduces man to the status of a slave" (19). The use of machinery provides grounds for looking at human work in new ways (17), and for showing that man is the proper subject of work (18).

Man is in the image of God; that is, he is a rational being capable of acting in a planned and rational way and having a tendency toward self-realization. His actions serve to realize his full humanity and to fulfill his calling. He is therefore the subject of work (23). It is in this *subjective* dimension that we must seek the dignity of work (26), just as Christ did when he worked as a carpenter. "The primary basis of the value of work is man himself, who is its subject" (27).

The Priority of Labor over Capital

Work is for man, not man for work. Therefore work can never be treated as a commodity or a kind of merchandise or an impersonal force ("workforce"); this treatment is the premise of "materialistic Economism" (29). This is a "reversal of order" in that it treats man "on the same level as the whole complex of material means of production and not in accordance with the true dignity of his work." It is this reversal of right order that "should rightly be called 'capitalism'" (30).[1]

The economistic premises of liberalism safeguarded initiative for the possessors of capital alone and treated the workers as mere instruments of production. Capital was considered the basis and purpose of production (34). In response to this consideration, there must be "ever new movements of solidarity of the workers and with the workers" (37) whenever their dignity or rights to a just wage are threatened.

Work is a good thing for man because only through work does he achieve fulfillment as a human being (40). In being the object of human work, matter gains in nobility, but this cannot come at the expense of the lowering of the dignity of the worker (41). The good of work also goes beyond the individual's good, for work is the foundation of family life (42). Work provides subsistence for the family, and the worker first learns to work in the home (43). Work is also the foundation of all social life (44).

The Conflict between Capital and Labor

The conflict originated in the effort by entrepreneurs to establish the lowest possible rate for labor (48) and was transformed into a systematic class struggle carried on by ideological and political means (49). In essence the conflict stems from the violation of "the principle of the priority of labor over capital" (52): labor is the efficient cause of production, while capital is merely an instrument. Capital is always the result of prior labor (55). The first phase of work "always remains the relationship of man with the resources and riches of nature." That is, it begins with the gift of the Creator (54). Therefore, "We must emphasize and give prominence to the primacy of man in the production process, *the primacy of man over things*" (57). Man is the subject of work, and capital a mere "thing" (57).

Capital therefore cannot be separated from labor, or labor opposed to capital; a labor system can be right only if it overcomes this opposition (58). At his workbench, whether in a workshop or an office, man "enters into two inheritances": what is given to all of humanity in nature and what others have already developed on the basis of that gift of nature. These developments of technology and capital condition man's work, but man and his work do not depend on them (59).

The error of economism, which considers humans solely according to their economic purpose, is an error of materialism (60). That is, economism includes a conviction of the superiority of the material and subordinates the spiritual and personal to "material reality." Such practical materialism judges the material alone to be capable of satisfying all of man's needs (60). This error did not originate with a theory, but with the practices during the time of rapid industrialization. From these practices, "in which what was mainly seen was the possibility of vastly increasing material wealth," developed theories and philosophies that gave primacy to things over persons.

New practices and theories must be developed which restore the primacy of persons (62).

The Church's view of property is radically different from either the collectivism of Marx or the individualism of capitalism.

> Christian tradition has never upheld this right [to ownership of property] as absolute and untouchable. On the contrary, it has always understood this right within the broader context of the right common to all to use the goods of the whole of creation: *the right to private property is subordinated to the right to common use,* to the fact that goods are meant for everyone. (64)

Property cannot be possessed "against labor" or even for "possession's sake." The only legitimate title to property is that it should serve labor and thereby achieve the "universal destination of goods" (65). "From this point of view, one cannot exclude the *socialization,* in suitable conditions, of certain means of production" (65). Socialization can be accomplished by associating labor, insofar as possible, with the ownership of capital.

The Church rejects the right of private property as "an untouchable 'dogma' of economic life" (66). This right must be adapted, perhaps by joint ownership of the means of production, or sharing in management and/or profits, etc. (67). But this socialization of property cannot be achieved by merely eliminating private property, which would simply take the means of production out of the hands of one group of people and put them in the hands of another group (68). We can say that property is properly socialized only "when on the basis of his work each person is fully entitled to consider himself part owner of the great workbench at which he is working with everyone else" (69). Labor should be associated with the ownership of capital as far as is possible, and there should be a wide range of bodies mediating between private ownership and public good with real authority and autonomy (69).

The Rights of Workers

The worker has a relationship with two employers. The *direct employer* is the one "with whom the worker enters directly into a work contract," while the *indirect* is all those other factors which determine the work contract and the justice or injustice of the relationship therein expressed (76). This includes the persons and institutions which determine the whole socio-economic system (77). Also included are the links between states, since no state is self-sufficient anymore (78). This can result, for example, in highly industrialized states fixing the prices for raw materials at the lowest possible levels and the prices of finished products at the highest possible. Direct employers in this situation may not be able to pay a just wage (79). But the worker's rights cannot be doomed by a system "guided chiefly by the criterion of maximum profit" (80).

The lack of work is a great evil, and the indirect employer must "act against unemployment." The common use of goods dictates that unemployment benefits — i.e., subsistence — be provided when work cannot be found for all (82).

The just wage is the key issue of social ethics (88), and the common use of goods the first principle (89). The just wage is the concrete means of verifying the justice of the whole socioeconomic system (89).

Elements for a Spirituality of Work

Work is a sharing in the activity of the Creator in which man in a sense continues that activity (113). Awareness of this ought to permeate "the most ordinary everyday activities" (115). The power of work is not opposed to the power of God (116): Christ himself was a worker (118). By work not only do we alter things and society, but we develop ourselves as well (122). This realization allows us better to understand progress, which must be understood in terms of "greater justice, wider brotherhood, and a more humane ordering of social relationships," all of which are greater than technical advances (123).

A PRACTICAL SPIRITUALITY OF WORK

Laborem Exercens begins and ends with a spirituality of labor. This spirituality stands in contrast to the pope's condemnation of "economism" as an error of materialism. The encyclical is therefore best read as a dialogue between the materialistic and spiritual views of labor. This spirituality is not something "disembodied" or other-worldly, but rather something with concrete dimensions and practical consequences. The first and foremost of these consequences is that human labor cannot be considered as just another tool of production, but rather as the whole point of production. Following on this first consequence are other consequences which actually affect the workplace in profound ways.

Work as Transitive and Intransitive

Work is both transitive and intransitive, and in both aspects it is spiritual as well as physical. Transitively, the worker transforms some object in the world — makes steel into cars, wood into houses, money into loans, etc. — and thereby participates in the work of creation. This ability to transform the world is part of man's dominion over the Earth and hence is not a tyranny: man cannot do whatever he likes, but must work to infuse the material world with spiritual values by making good, useful, and beautiful things. But in addition to this transitive aspect, this transformation of the world, work is also *intransitive:* the work that a man does stays with him and transforms him. Work is the primary way of fulfillment as a human being. Therefore work is something *good;* it is not, as often depicted, a punishment resulting from the Fall. That punishment is *toil,* whereby nature resists man's efforts with thorns and thistles. Even in the original state, man tended the garden and guarded it (Gen 2:15).

A practical consequence of this dual nature of work is a philosophy of job design that allows for the growth of the worker on one hand (the "intransitive" values) and, on the other, the ability of the worker to make use of these intransitive values in contributing to the "transitive" values of the product itself. Indeed, companies often do themselves harm by ignoring these principles; they act is if they are hiring the work and not the worker. But the worker makes the products and services, and the worker alone can discover added value over and above what is currently produced. Given that business, properly understood, is about adding value to material things, businesses often throw away one of their greatest assets in the evolution of their products and services. This philosophy of capturing all the values, subjective and objective, transitive and intransitive, is often called "Human-Centered Design."[2]

The Priority of Labor over Capital

John Paul II calls for the "socialization of property," a term that cannot fail to sound suspiciously like "socialism" to ears raised in a capitalist culture. But the pope uses a line of reasoning that is not socialist at all. Rather, it depends on recognizing the true nature of property in both its private and social roles. Our own view of property discards the social values in favor of the private ones. Property, no matter how it is owned, must serve the common good, or even the basic economic values fail to find equilibrium, fail to function at a practical level. When that happens, massive government inputs are required to sustain demand. Add to this the fact that *all* capital is the result of prior labor, and labor applied to resources that are, in the first instance, a pure gift. We are given already the world and its riches, a gift of the Creator-God, but we can only make use of them by labor.

Taken together, these add up to an absolute priority of labor over capital. This is a reversal of the order of capitalism, whose very name gives priority to the possessors of capital. In capitalism, capital is considered the cause of wealth while labor is a mere instrument. This reversal of right order is the essential and practical materialism at the heart of capitalism. This fundamental materialistic error leads to the error about property (the primary and most original form of capital). Both capitalists and socialists tend to absolutize property (the former making it an absolute good, and the latter an absolute evil), but the Church sees property as a relative and subordinate good, one subordinated to the common destination of goods. Property which no longer serves this purpose loses its legitimacy.

The Direct and Indirect Employers

By recognizing that there are social factors and laws that determine the conditions of employment and the whole socioeconomic system, we all become the "indirect employers" of labor. We are all a part of this system; we cannot absent ourselves and say that it is somebody else's responsibility. True, the indirect employers have only an indirect responsibility, but it is a real one nevertheless. Once we understand this — namely that we are all, more or less, part of the "indirect employer" — the need for solidarity becomes obvious.

The Spirituality of Work

Work, then, even in its purely economic aspects cannot be understood as purely economic. There are no "separate realms" in which to segregate the objective and subjective aspects, but each interpenetrates the other. Christ himself dignified work by becoming a worker, and the Father worked "for six days" on creation. When we understand both aspects, we can more clearly evaluate what really constitutes progress and what does not; we can more easily discern which management practices are productive and which are not.

Chapter 8

Centesimus Annus:
The Uncertain Victory

We have seen that it is unacceptable to say that the defeat of so-called "Real Socialism" leaves capitalism as the only model of economic organization. —POPE JOHN PAUL II

THE DEFEAT OF COMMUNISM

Centesimus Annus ("On the Hundredth Anniversary of *Rerum Novarum*") was written as communism was falling across Russia and Eastern Europe, accomplishing the end of the Church's century-long struggle. It is difficult to convey the sense of euphoria and triumph that swept through the West. I recall being in Berlin as the communist regime was falling in East Germany. There was a continual party at the Berlin Wall, which was covered, every square inch, with graffiti and a riot of color. In East Berlin, the *Unter den Linden* was covered with handmade political posters expressing opinions that only months earlier would have earned their makers, at the least, an interview with the state police. Throughout the West, the feeling was that a century and a half of struggle was coming to an end, a struggle that had included wars both hot and cold.

For the Catholic Church in particular it was a heady moment in history. The empire which had made war against the Church and placed so many of her sons and daughters in its gulags was crumbling like a house of cards. The ideology which had promised the destruction of religion was itself discredited and nearly destroyed. Pope John Paul II was particularly mindful both of the peaceful nature of the victory and of its beginnings with the Solidarity movement in his own homeland. As huge armies had maneuvered for half a century on either side of the Iron Curtain in preparation for a war that never came, and faced each other down with nuclear weapons, the decisive movement came from an electrician leading the workers in the shipyards of Gdansk, Poland, and marching under the banner of the very "solidarity"

125

that the Church had urged. And all this was accomplished with hardly a shot being fired.

Yet for all that joy, the struggle against communism is only one-half of the Church's struggles for economic and social justice. The other half is concerned with the economism, materialism, and consumerism that characterize economic liberalism. With the discrediting of "real socialism" (as the pope terms it), the Church could turn her attention more fully to the problems of the "business economy" of the West. The themes that John Paul II had stated in *Laborem Exercens* and *Sollicitudo Rei Socialis* could be developed in the light of a post-communist world.

READING *CENTESIMUS ANNUS*

Characteristics of Rerum Novarum

In his first chapter, the pope invites us to re-read *Rerum Novarum* and apply it to our own day (3). The "new things" about which Pope Leo XIII wrote are a new form of property (capital) and a new form of labor (wages). Labor had become a commodity to be bought by capital with no regard to "the bare minimum required for the support of the individual and his family" (4). The key to reading *Rerum Novarum* is understanding the dignity of the worker, a dignity that arises from the personal nature of work, which is the exclusive property of the worker, but is at the same time social, connected to the family and the common good. Property also is a right, but "not an absolute value." It is subject to the universal destination of goods (6).

Since work is both personal and necessary, wages cannot be determined by the free consent of the parties. Work's necessity means it is governed by the obligation to preserve life. Thus, *Rerum Novarum* affirms the right to a just wage (8).

Rerum Novarum criticizes both socialism and liberal capitalism. It also repeats an "elementary principle of sound political organization": the fewer resources one has to fall back on, the more defenseless one is, and the more one requires intervention from the State (10). There are "necessary limits to the State's intervention," however, since the individual and the family are prior to the state. The guiding principle both of *Rerum Novarum* and of the Church's social teachings is "a *correct view of the human person*" as having an essential dignity which includes, but is not limited to, the work that a person performs (11).

Toward the New Things of Today

This chapter begins with a consideration of the errors of socialism, which are primarily errors of atheism. The largest error is anthropological: the person becomes nothing more than a molecule in a "socio-economic mechanism," a cog in a machine, and disappears as an agent of free moral decisions. By depriving the person of something to call "his own," socialism makes him dependent on the state and those who control it. This hinders the building of a truly human community. The atheism of the system denies man his "transcendent dignity" and reorganizes society along the lines of this denial. Man can only discover his own transcendence in responding to "the call of God contained in the being of things." Each individual must respond to this call, "and no social mechanism or collective subject can substitute for it" (13).

The pope now recalls the teaching of *Laborem Exercens* concerning class warfare. *Rerum Novarum* condemned it, but did not mean to condemn every form of social conflict. Indeed, such conflicts are inevitable, and Christians must often take a stand "honestly and decisively." Class warfare as such must be replaced by the struggle for universal social justice; privilege for any one class must be sought within the context of the common good. Conflict must be restrained by ethical and juridical considerations, and "by respect for the dignity of others (and consequently of oneself)" (14).

State control of the means of production has the effect of reducing citizens to mere cogs "in the state machine." This does not mean, however, that economic matters are excluded from "the State's range of interest and action." The state has the task of ensuring the proper juridical framework exists so that no party is powerful enough to reduce the others to subservience. The state must also protect workers from unemployment, by insurance if necessary, and ensure wage levels sufficient to provide for "the worker and his family, including a certain amount for savings." The state's actions are guided by two principles: according to the *principle of solidarity*, the state acts directly to defend the weakest; according to the *principle of subsidiarity*, the state acts indirectly on the economic system by creating conditions for the free exercise of economic activity (15).

The pope praises the attempts which followed the Second World War to preserve "free market mechanisms"; however, the market cannot be the only point of reference for social life. This leads to a consumerist society which attempts to defeat Marxism on the level of materialism: this society satisfies more of man's material needs than does communism, but it agrees with Marxism in reducing man to an economic cog. Like Marxism, the consumerist society denies "value to morality, law, culture and religion" (19).

The Year 1989

The year 1989 was crucial in overturning the effects of the Yalta Agreement, which had delivered Eastern Europe into the hands of tyranny. The pope points with evident pride to the fact that the upset began with the Solidarity movement in his homeland of Poland and proceeded peacefully using the means of negotiation, witness to the truth, and appeal to conscience without recourse to the means of class warfare (23).

The inefficiency of the Marxist system was not just a technical matter; it was a matter of the violation of human rights, including those to ownership and freedom. The Marxist system also failed because it misunderstands man as being merely economic, when in reality the person is always situated within a culture, which includes language, history, and certain attitudes toward "the fundamental events of life, such as birth, love, work, and death." Cultures are ways of facing the ultimate question of the meaning of life, and without ultimate meaning, cultures become corrupted (24). In totalitarian regimes, force trumps reason, and coercion overrides conscience, which is the foundation of any authentically free order. The struggle for social justice is not yet concluded, however; there remain in developed countries the excessive promotion of utilitarian values and the appeal to appetites which obscure the "the hierarchy of the true values of human existence." In some countries, new forms of fundamentalism are arising which restrict the right to preach the Gospel (29).

Individual freedom is conditioned in many ways which make its exercise more difficult. Primary among these is, of course, original sin. But not even original sin can destroy freedom, any more than any society can. Individual interest and freedom cannot be sacrificed to social good; rather, ways must be sought to bring individual and common interests into "fruitful harmony." This cannot be done by turning politics into a "secular religion" and attempting to create a temporal paradise on earth (25).

The end of Marxism did not rid the world of oppression and injustice; much work remains to be done. Some, in pursuing this work, have sought "an impossible compromise between Marxism and Christianity." Only in the Church's social teaching and its teaching about the human person can "an authentic theory and praxis of liberation" be found (26).

Private Property and the Universal Destination of Goods

Private property should be regarded as an extension of human freedom which affords each person and family scope for autonomy. But property has a social function based on the common purpose of goods. Therefore, property cannot be an absolute right, but only a subordinate one (30).

God gave the earth for the sustenance of all men; this fact is the basis for the "universal destination of the earth's goods." Work is needed to reap the earth's goods, though, and the work one puts into the earth makes part of the earth one's own. Land and work are the foundation of all wealth, but their relationship has changed over time. Whereas land was once the primary factor in wealth, now the human person himself is (31). Know-how, technology and skill are another form of ownership, and initiative and entrepreneurial ability are necessary aspects of the creation of "wealth in today's society." Like manual labor, these immaterial factors depend on a just price obtained through mutual agreement. Mankind's principle resource is the person himself, who discovers the earth's resources and who, by disciplined work in cooperation with others, creates more extensive "working communities." The modern business economy is based on human freedom. The person is the greatest resource, and that resource must be given the freedom to develop and realize its potential (32). The modern system has its risks and problems, however: despite the advances, "the human inadequacies of capitalism and the resulting domination of things over persons are far from disappearing" (33).

For responding to needs and utilizing resources, the free market is the most efficient instrument. But this refers only to needs which are "solvent," or which actually have purchasing power, and to resources which are "marketable," or which can actually obtain a satisfactory price. Many human needs can find "no place on the market." Nonetheless, "there exists something which is due to the person because he is a person" prior to the logic of exchange (34). Market mechanisms ignore any good which cannot be bought or sold; they carry the risk of market idolatry, an idolatry of commodity (40).

Since this is the case, one can, indeed, struggle against an economic system if it is "a method of upholding the absolute predominance of capital, the possession of the means of production and land, in contrast to the free and personal nature of human work." However, the struggle cannot result in socialism, which is merely state capitalism, but rather must result in "a society of free work, of enterprise, and of participation." In other words, the free market must be "appropriately controlled" so as to meet the basic needs of all members of society. The defeat of socialism does not mean that capitalism is the only viable model of economic organization. Profit, while indicating a business's level of efficiency and success, cannot be the only measure "of a firm's condition" (35). The books can still be balanced while the employees are cooked.

One of the ways in which society can appropriately control the free market is through education and the creation of certain lifestyles. These lifestyles, like all cultural choices regarding production and consumption, stem from "an overall understanding of life" and of the human person. Consumerism is a lifestyle which fulfills material and instinctual human desires without regard to the comprehensive nature of the person; it is "objectively improper and often damaging to the person's physical and spiritual health." But an economic system has no criteria in and of itself for evaluating comprehensive views of humanity and human need. Consumers must be educated "in the responsible use of their power of choice," and this education can include intervention by the state. Consumption cannot be directed at "having" rather than "being"; one should not live merely to *have* more but to *be* more. Enjoyment is not an end in itself. Societies must "create lifestyles in which the quest for truth, beauty, goodness and the communion with others for the sake of common growth are the factors which determine consumer choices" (36).

One consequence of consumerism is the ecological problem, the consumption of the earth's resources in a disordered way. This problem arises from a poverty of outlook in which we desire to possess the world rather than relate to it in truth. We forget that the world is a creation with a "prior God-given purpose," and in doing so we betray that purpose (37). We are equally at fault in forgetting the purpose of the human environment. Our outlook is conditioned by the social structure, which can either help or hinder a person's ability to live in accordance with the truth. "The decisions which create a human environment can give rise to specific structures of sin which impede the full realization of those who are in any way oppressed by them." Human ecology demands the creation of "more authentic forms of living in community" (38).

The life of "having" instead of "being," a life of "false and superficial gratifications," leads to alienation. Alienation is "the loss of the authentic meaning of life." This is not Marx's definition of alienation, which the pope rejects, but it is a reality of Western life. Work organized solely for maximum profit and without concern for the workers alienates by replacing supportive communities with relationships marked only by competition and estrangement, in which the person is a means and not an end. Alienation is a reversal of means and ends, and it can only be righted by recognizing in ourselves and others "the value and grandeur of the human person." It is only through the free gift of ourselves that we find ourselves; we must be oriented to true ends — people — and to God. It is only in the light of this, the "correct scale of values," that "ownership of things may become an occasion of personal growth." But human growth is hindered by mass communications which impose fashions and opinions through repetition without scrutiny of the premises (41).

The real question is, Should the Third World pursue capitalism as the path to economic progress? That depends on the definition of "capitalism." If one means by capitalism "the positive role of business, the market, private property" and free creativity, then the answer is a resounding "yes." But the pope adds that this should not be called capitalism, and suggests calling it the "business economy," the "market economy" or simply the "free economy." If, on the other hand, capitalism denotes a system in which economic freedom "is not circumscribed within a strong juridical framework which places it at the service of human freedom in its totality and sees it as a particular aspect of that freedom," then the answer is no. Millions live in material or spiritual poverty; there is a danger that a radical capitalist ideology could spread which would blindly entrust these poverties to market forces, believing *a priori* "that any attempt to solve them is doomed to failure" (42).

The Church does not offer solutions because they must arise from concrete historical circumstances; rather, she suggests her social teaching as "an indispensable and ideal orientation" for finding those solutions. Any real solution will give persons precedence over things: businesses are not just societies of capital goods but societies of persons with different responsibilities. Workers' movements "directed towards the liberation and promotion of the whole person" and associated in a progressively expanding chain of solidarity are a necessary part of the solution (43).

Ownership of the means of production is "legitimate if it serves useful work." Illegitimate ownership is that which "is not utilized" or which "serves to impede the work of others in an effort to gain a profit which is not the result of the overall expansion of work...but rather is a result of illicit exploitation, speculation or the breaking of solidarity among working people." The pope concludes this chapter by noting that "The obligation to earn one's bread by the sweat of one's brow also presumes the right to do so. A society in which this right is systematically denied, in which economic policies do not allow workers to reach satisfactory levels of employment, cannot be justified from an ethical point of view, nor can that society attain social peace" (43).

State and Culture

The question about socialism and capitalism leads naturally to one about totalitarianism and democracy. The Church values democracy and rejects the idea that agnosticism and relativism are the philosophic attitudes which correspond to it. Without truth there is only power to guide politics, and "as history demonstrates, a democracy without values easily turns into open or thinly disguised totalitarianism" (46). Totalitarianism rejects objective standards of truth because they provide the criteria upon which the state and its statesmen can be judged (45). While asserting the need for a truth to guide politics, the Church is equally aware of the dangers of fundamentalism and fanaticism by which some would "claim the right to impose on others their own concept of what is true and good. Christian truth is not of this kind" since it does not imprison politics in a rigid schema. The Church respects freedom, but knows that "freedom attains its full development only by accepting the truth" (46).

Even in democracies the truth is not always respected. Issues arise which are decided not on the basis of the common good and the demands of justice, but on the "basis of the electoral or financial power of the groups promoting them," as is the case with "the scandal of abortion." Such a situation both reflects and feeds an "inability to situate particular interests within the framework of a coherent vision of the common good" (47).

In the interest of the common good, the state must guarantee conditions of individual freedom, private property, a stable currency, and efficient public services. The state must also oversee and direct "the exercise of human rights in the economic sector"; the primary responsibility for this, however, lies with individuals and the groups that make up society. If these groups are unable to fulfill their responsibilities, the state can exercise a "substitute function," but such interventions ought to be for urgent reasons and must be brief. An example of this is the state's right to intervene against monopolies. The welfare state has increased such interventions, leading to a loss of human energy and an inordinate increase in public agencies. Any intervention by the state must respect the principle of subsidiarity: higher-level agencies must support lower-level ones, not swallow them (48).

By supporting agencies and communities at different levels — families, businesses, worker associations, etc. — governments support levels of relationships by which society becomes "personalized." But the individual today is often suffocated between the state and the marketplace; he seems to exist only as a producer/consumer or as the object of state administration. In order to overcome today's individualistic mentality a widespread commitment to solidarity and charity is required (49).

The Person Is the Way of the Church

Our true identity is revealed only in faith (54). Theology is necessary for interpreting and solving present day problems: Atheistic solutions ignore the spiritual dimension of man, while consumerist solutions convince him that he is free from every law and imprison him in selfishness (55). Although "Real Socialism" has collapsed, the West must not see this as a "one-sided victory" without reforming her own systems (56).

The social teaching of the Church is not a theory but a basis for action; the witness of actions gives credibility to the teachings, and this concerns not only material poverty, but cultural and spiritual poverty as well (57). Reform requires a change of lifestyles, of models of production and consumption, and of the structures of power which govern today's societies (58). This is an interdisciplinary effort to "incarnate the one truth about man in different" economic and political contexts. There is also an "experiential dimension of this teaching, which is to be found at the crossroads where Christian life and conscience come into contact with the real world" (59).

AN ENDORSEMENT OF CAPITALISM?

No encyclical has been as much a subject of partisan and ideological debate as this one. When it was first issued, the *Wall Street Journal* proudly proclaimed, "The Pope Endorses Capitalism." The *Journal*'s headline was well supported by commentators especially from the neoconservative schools (Weigel, Novak, Neuhaus)[1] and from the radical traditionalists (Budde, Brimelow).[2] Indeed, the pope has positive things to say about profits, the business enterprise, free markets, a limited role of the state, free enterprise, and many other aspects considered "capitalistic." However, he never offers unalloyed support for these things, but always points out the problems with them. In fact, throughout *Centesimus Annus*, and consistent with all the other encyclicals, the pope refuses to use the term "capitalism" as a positive term, but instead identifies it with a reversal in the proper order of values. Indeed, the pope states that "We have seen that it is unacceptable to say that the defeat of so-called 'Real Socialism' leaves capitalism as the only model of economic organization" (35).

So what is going on? Is the pope endorsing capitalism or is he urging us, after the model of *Laborem Exercens*, to seek other models? It is important to keep in mind that capitalism is not a term which has a precise definition; the definition that the pope gives it, namely a system in which the right order of values is reversed, precludes him from "endorsing" it in any way. But at the same time, we have a tendency toward "binary" thinking, in which all that is not socialism is capitalism. The popular definition of capitalism includes things which either have nothing to do with it (business subsidies, for example) or are parts of many other economic systems. It would seem, when one reads the various commentators on this encyclical, that they are not always reading the same document. Commentators like the radical Michael Budde, the liberationist Donal Dorr, the neoconservative George Weigel, and the traditionalist Rupert Ederer all take on different aspects of the encyclical; it is important for the student to note not only what they leave in, but what they leave out, and to determine which readings are really the most inclusive of all the elements of *Centesimus Annus.*

From a purely economic standpoint, the technical superiority of capitalism over socialism is evident. Capitalism still exhibits the same errors of practical atheism, however, because capitalism always elevates things over people (33). Given that statement, can *Centesimus Annus* be considered an endorsement of capitalism? Some statements that are problematic for this thesis include: the market cannot be the only point of reference in a society (19); the market ignores the existence of goods which cannot be commodities and leads to an idolatry of the market (40); it is right to struggle against a system of the absolute predominance of capital (35); an all-encompassing consumerism leads to objectively improper lifestyles (36); work organized solely for profit leads to alienation (41); the pope refuses to call what is good about the business system "capitalism" (42); most of all he refuses, consistently with Catholic teaching from the earliest days, to absolutize private property. Against this, one must also note the pope's acknowledgement of the superior efficiency of the free market and the importance of the role of profit.

THE UNCERTAIN VICTORY

In reflecting on the victory over "real socialism," the pope points out that the fundamental mistake of socialism is not something technical, but a mistake about the human person. Socialism reduced man to a cog in a socio-political machine; it deprived him not merely of property, but of the power of personal decision and made him dependent on the state. At the heart of socialism lie the errors of atheism. In claiming to be able to lead mankind toward perfect goodness, the communist state sets itself above all values. Hence it cannot tolerate any objective criteria of truth that can be used to judge its actions, and this is true of all totalitarianisms. However, it is not just communist and totalitarian states that suffer from this disregard for truth, because in the developed countries as well there is "an excessive promotion of utilitarian values" and an appeal to "immediate gratification" (29). Indeed, truth has, if anything, a lower value in capitalist states than in communist ones. In a communist society, the truth is so important that those who hold a different account of it can be imprisoned or persecuted. But in a capitalist society, truth is relativized and marginalized. The market alone stands as the arbiter of truth, and philosophy, the search for truth, is reduced to good marketing technique. You are "free" to believe what you like, but truth itself can have no public space because that would limit the freedom of the market. In both systems, truth is banished from the public square.

This is why the debates about the "endorsement" of capitalism profoundly miss the point. And the point is this: just as communism fell not through its "technical" errors, but from its atheism and mistakes about the human person, so capitalism is in danger of falling victim to its own innate materialism and consumerism. Capitalism commits the same sin of economism and the same materialist errors about the human person. And unless there is a profound reform of the capitalist system, it is likely to suffer the same fate. In the fifteen years since the encyclical was issued, there has been no basic attempt at reform. Has this made any difference? That is to say, "Is there a danger of a crisis of capitalism?"

The paleo-liberals and the neoconservatives share an intense optimism about capitalism, namely that it will lead, by a sort of automatic operation, to a more just society, even if it begins in circumstances of outright oppression. Yet events have overtaken theory. It is of course debatable whether the United States is itself growing more like an oligarchy, with sham elections involving very little real difference between the political parties and a very narrow range of political debate. But what is not debatable is that capitalism has proven itself highly adaptable by totalitarian systems; indeed, its success in totalitarian and nominally communist China must give us pause, and the situation in Russia raises the same doubts. This really isn't news, since capitalism worked to produce viable economies in Nazi Germany and Fascist Italy, but these could be passed off as aberrations.

Is the liberal/neoconservative optimism justified, or is the system in need of fundamental reform? Currently, we are borrowing two billion dollars a day to finance our imports, while our manufacturing capabilities are slipping overseas. There are grave doubts that we can cover our debts, public or private, and major social systems, such as health care and retirement pensions (both public and private), are insolvent. But most of all, our lifestyle is largely financed by credit, often at ruinous rates, and there is some serious doubt that we can continue indefinitely to spend tomorrow's dollar on today's consumption. The pope has issued a clear call for reform, not a partisan political tract. This reform must be systemic, must be a reform of the financial, political, and economic systems. But beyond the technicalities, it must begin with a conversion, a change of heart, a rejection of materialistic lifestyles. Without this, we may find ourselves in a prolonged period of instability with no real way out. We must recognize that these deeper needs will be satisfied by the social systems that distinguish business as a mere job from business as a vocation, a calling.

Part III

Toward an Evolved Capitalism

Chapter 9

The Social Teachings and Economics: Ideas in Tension

The prestige accorded to mathematics in economics has given it rigor, but alas, also *mortis*.   —ROBERT HEILBRONER

SOME "ECONOMIC" PRINCIPLES OF CATHOLIC SOCIAL TEACHING

A "Catholic" Economics?

The Church is the arbiter of justice, not economics. Therefore there can be no such thing as a "Catholic" economics. The Church does not claim competence beyond the realm of theology, but justice falls within this realm and the Church is competent to declare standards of justice that economics must observe. A society ignores such standards at its own risk, risks that involve the stability of society and even the profitability of investments. The Church regards economics as *normative* or "architectonic"; that is, a set of tools and principles by which societies realize, at a concrete level and however imperfectly, their own ideas of justice. In this view, economics is an arena of human freedom that allows a wide variety of systems. The architectonic view contrasts with the "positive" view of many economists who prefer to see economics as a positive science, akin to physics and therefore devoid of freedom. In the positive view, one is forbidden to think of "freedom" in the laws of supply and demand just as one would not think of "freedom" in the movement of the stars. After all, if economics is a positive science, like physics, then disagreement over its laws and facts is moot: one may not like gravity, but one *will* abide by it. If, however, economics operates not by law alone but by choice as well, then multiple economic systems are possible. Thus, we can see that the question of a Catholic economics is really a question of the freedom of economics. The Church comes down on the side of freedom, and that has implications for the way it seeks justice in social institutions.

139

With that in mind, let us first isolate some of the more important criteria given by the Church's social teaching and then note the tensions that occur with a purely "scientific" view of economics.

The Ultimate Purpose of the Economy

The Church has a *teleological* understanding of the universe. That is to say, it believes that everything has a proper purpose and end. Humanity's proper end is eternal happiness with God. Institutions are part of the quest humans have for ultimate meaning and eternal happiness with God. Thus the Church includes all human institutions within the moral order. Cultural institutions help direct humans to their final end. Recall that we can only discuss a moral issue when considering something with a *purpose,* and apart from some notion of a purpose, we cannot apply reason to moral statements. The ultimate purpose of human beings, the attainment of final happiness, presupposes a journey through space and time which imposes certain requirements on each person. One of these requirements is that he must work, and this work will always occur within some social setting which requires cooperation. There are both *physical* and *spiritual* aspects of work and cooperation. Science will have much to say about the former, but nothing at all to say about the later. This is because human "work" is not merely the expenditure of energy that it is for a machine or a mere physical process, but an aspect of the human person, something that always escapes a purely scientific analysis. The "positive" or "scientific" view isolates the "individual" from the person and treats this individual as a part of a machine.

This is the key to the difference between the two views: the Church treats of "persons" rather than individuals; that is, a person's individuality is not something isolated and abstract, but is always embedded within some social context, first and primarily the family, then larger associations of communities of various kinds, and eventually the whole human family. The human person is the measure of all things. Since the human person is the measure of all things, and since the person exists within social structures, the measure of any social structure is how well it serves the human person. And further, since the person must work, and that work will be organized by economic structures, it then follows that the measure of those structures ought to be how well they serve the purposes of human work. Here we have a standard which allows us to engage moral reasoning in thinking about the economy.

Human Work

Work is both natural and spiritual. Work is treated at both a natural and a spiritual level. Work is part of the process by which humans achieve "dominion" over the earth. By work humans participate in God's own creative act and have the opportunity to refashion the things given in the creation of the world into things that are useful, good, and beautiful.

Work is both transitive and intransitive. As transitive, human labor goes out of the person and into some object, re-creating it, as it were; this is the *objective* dimension of work. But work is also intransitive; the work remains within the man or woman who performs it. While we are busy forming the world, our work is forming us as well. Work is how we express ourselves and part of how we grow and develop.

Work is both necessary and free. Work is free since we freely choose our work, freely contract for it. But work is also necessary, since it is only by work that we earn sustenance for ourselves and those in our care. Hence the "freedom" of the work contract is bounded by the necessity implicit in the duty to survive and provide for those in our care.

Property

Property is a sacred right, but not an absolute one. Property allows us scope for freedom, self-expression, and security. However, property is not a part of the natural law, but a human addition designed to serve the common good, and it loses its legitimacy when it ceases to serve this good. Property is originally given by God to humans for their common use and sustenance; property is therefore subject to the universal destination of goods. Therefore, property is a *means, not an end.* Property must serve work and the common needs of humankind.

Property originates in work. We acquire valid title only by placing the stamp of ourselves upon the land, that is, by work. It is labor that makes property "proper" to a person. But property in land or minerals is a finite resource; huge accumulations for one can only occur by depriving others of even the possibility of acquiring property. This is true even for more abstract forms of property, such as financial capital; while they are in theory unlimited, they are at any given moment finite, and an imbalance of ownership by a few limits the ability of the many to acquire property of their own.

The Primacy of Labor

Capital is the result of labor. Only by labor do states grow rich. *Labor is therefore the primary and efficient cause of wealth,* and capital a mere instrument. Therefore labor cannot be separated from capital, or capital set against labor. Indeed, capital can only be considered legitimate when it serves the legitimate ends of the labor in which it originates, that is to say, when it serves the authentic needs of the human person. Capitalism, as long is it represents a division of capital and labor and gives a false priority of capital *over* labor, *always* represents a reversal in the right order of values.

The Just Wage

The just wage is the primary criterion of a just economy. We have seen that all title to capital originates in labor; that the entire purpose of private property is to serve work and the common destination of goods; that work is necessary to humans, both in a physical and spiritual sense; that in both senses, people must work and must both earn their daily bread through work and express themselves through their work. From all this it follows that an individual's work must feed him or her and his or her family; hence a "just wage" is not only a moral requirement of an economy, but indeed the only real way to measure an economy's success.

Subsidiarity

Subsidiarity implies a "bottom-up" view of society. It starts with the family as the basic unit of society. Only the family, and not the individual, can perpetuate itself, and therefore only the family can be the ongoing basis of society. All economic, social and political activity is built around the family and serves its needs. But because no family is self-sufficient, families in turn require their economic and social contexts, including government. Higher social formations have a right to interfere in the affairs of a lower organization, including the family, but this is only a limited right; such interventions can only be used to correct egregious failures, and may last only for as long as necessary to correct the failure. Some problems, of course, don't go away, such as unemployment: as long as the economic system is unable to offer all persons meaningful employment, then society must provide other means for their dignified subsistence. But this must be clearly seen as a defect of the system, in the same way that the need for a police force or an army is really a defect arising from original sin. From the viewpoint of subsidiarity, society is highly "textured"; instead of a simple system of an "individual/government" relationship, there should be a rich collection of levels within society, each with its own realm of competence and authority. At present, government has absorbed functions which used to belong to the Church or other authorities such as the guilds. Marriage, education, charity, and commercial regulations had been guided by other bodies, even if their decisions were enforced by the state.

Solidarity

Solidarity is complementary with subsidiarity. Subsidiarity provides the vertical dimension of life, while solidarity provides the horizontal dimension; subsidiarity is a connection among elements of society viewed as a hierarchy, while solidarity provides the connections among the elements viewed as if they were on the same level. Solidarity connects us with the common good and impels us, in the name of Christian charity, to act for the good of all. There can be no vision of the common good unless there is solidarity among all the elements of society.

CONFLICTS WITH ECONOMIC THEORY

We can now contrast these conclusions of Catholic Social Teaching with the assumptions common in standard economic texts.[1]

A "Neutral" Economy?

In direct opposition to the Church's teleological view of the economy, there is a tendency among neoclassical economists to regard economics as the application of "value-free" laws and therefore as being beyond any moral judgment. The sole criterion is often stated as a value-free "efficiency." But efficiency is an empty term; it needs an object to have any meaning. In other words, we must ask, "Efficiency at what?" At producing the largest pile of goods possible? Or at providing an equitable distribution of the goods necessary to life? These are two very different kinds of "efficiencies" and result in two very different views of economics. The first view, efficiency in production, is usually stated as something like producing the largest amount of goods for the least amount of inputs. While this may sound "value-free," in fact it contains a host of "values." For one thing, it focuses economic thought entirely on the production of goods, but surely that is a "value." For no particular economic reason, "more" is equated with "better." An exclusive focus on production inevitably leads to a culture of consumerism; after all, one must do something with the efficiently produced pile of goods. If the duty of the economy is to make as many things as possible, the duty of the citizen must surely be to buy them, or the system collapses. Consumerism may or may not be an economic truth, but it is certainly not "value-free." Further, this view hides other value judgments, namely that profit is the sole criterion for success. This lurks as a hidden but powerful assumption of the "efficiency" measure, and is a value-laden assumption. In the final analysis, the refusal to address the question of values does not produce a "value-free" science, but merely an ideology in which values are hidden and therefore unexamined.

Mere efficiency in production cannot express the totality of economic values; we expect more than just "things" from an economic system. For example, an economic system must provide meaningful work for all its members. Or we can ask for a certain level of distribution, even to the lowest members of society. These are possible values. But if efficiency is limited to the production function, then distribution values cannot even be considered. Can this really be a complete description of an economy?

Furthermore, the "value-free" premise is a thoroughly individualistic view. Social values, if they are acknowledged to exist at all, are considered to reside solely in the rules of exchange between individuals, without any relation to the social content of the exchange. "Values" in this view have meaning only to individuals and cannot be allowed to determine the economic system. This view breaks the solidarity that is the foundation of any rational view of society, and hence any rational view of economics.

Work as a Commodity

It is interesting that "work" is not even listed in the index of *The Economic Way of Thinking*,[2] one of the more popular undergraduate economics texts, nor is "labor" discussed in itself, but only the division of labor and its subjugation to laws of supply and demand. There is hardly a sentence in the book where some other term, let us say "pig iron," could not be substituted for the term "labor." For example, we read, "a smaller quantity of labor services will be demanded as the price that must be paid to obtain them goes up."[3] If you substituted "pig iron" for "labor services" in that sentence, it would retain its meaning. Therefore in such a view labor is meaningless in itself; it is just another commodity. Nowhere in the text could you discover that labor, unlike pig iron, is the source of all economic values as well as the source of all capital. Nowhere would you discover that labor, unlike pig iron, has a variable rate of efficiency, one tied to its rate of compensation and the culture of the firm.[4] This is really not so surprising, since in the economistic view labor is just another "commodity," a factor of production, a means and not an end, and one hardly deserving of any separate treatment than would be received by any other factor of production. Labor as such is invisible in such a system, and noteworthy only when it causes problems, such as strikes or demands for better conditions. Such a view of economics is clearly abstract and unrealistic, and unable to describe, much less predict, actual market and business conditions.

In fact, labor in neoclassicism is something to be eliminated, insofar as possible. We often hear that investment "provides jobs," but this is not really an accurate description of what happens. The normal use of investment is to "economize" on labor; that is, to eliminate, downgrade, or outsource it. One grows rich by reducing the labor content of goods, not by increasing it. For example, if society devotes the work of 1 million laborers to producing all the widgets it needs, then one will grow rich if one has a method to produce the same number with half a million men. This is not all bad of course, but we must at least be able to describe accurately what is going on. It may be that the reduced cost of widgets will increase the market for widgets and absorb the laid-off workers, or that the capital freed up will find them new positions. But that is not a given and will lead at the very least to some temporary dislocations, and perhaps even permanent ones.

Labor is often treated as a very problematic machine, a resource that happens to be "human," as the ubiquitous title of "human resources department" indicates. It is problematic because unlike other machines, it can rebel, join a union, call in sick, be insubordinate, etc. Much better to have a real machine than a human one. Recall that Malthus regarded labor as a drag on the economy, a kind of thinking that is still prevalent. Labor is not regarded as a source of wealth, but as a competitor for it. What is missing from this view is an idea of labor as that which is at the heart of the values and purposes of an economy. Even if eliminating certain kinds of "toil" from labor is to be desired, labor by its true nature is a good.

The Absolutism of Property

It is in the treatment of property that the Church's position radically diverges from both socialism and capitalism. Both systems absolutize property, treating it either as an absolute evil (Marxism) or an absolute good (capitalism). The Church's view avoids the twin evils of collectivism, which denies the private character of property, and of individualism, which denies the common good and common use of property. Since property has a *dual constitution*, neither socialism nor capitalism can provide a complete description of property. Again, many standard texts such as *The Economic Way of Thinking* do not delve into the nature of either property or of title to it; private property is merely an assumption, and an unexamined assumption, of the text. Under the individualistic assumptions of capitalism, property is an *unrestricted right* that can grow infinitely. Yet, if we consider the fact that certain forms of property, such as land, exist in finite quantities, it is appropriate to ask if it can accrue to a small group of owners infinitely without impacting the common use.

The Primacy of Capital

The presumption of the primacy of capital is not always stated, but it is always implicit; everything is ordered toward the concentration of capital, and people are constantly told that it is capital that creates jobs. The presumption is often made explicit in debates over tax policy, where we are constantly urged to lower marginal rates on capital income and place more of the burdens on labor income and consumption. But the presumption of the primacy of capital does not match economic reality. Summarizing the research of J. W. Kendrick and Theodore Schultz, John Mueller has noted that capital accounts for only one-third of economic growth, while human capital accounts for two-thirds.[5] Thus capital is not primary in the economy, but all depends instead on labor, that is, "human capital."

The presumption of capital's primacy confers political prestige and economic power. In the naïve belief that capital is primary to growth, government policy applauds the concentration of capital in ever larger corporations, and often ignores its own laws by granting enormous privileges and favorable tax treatment. As Daniel Webster noted, "power naturally and necessarily follows property." Webster's law is inflexible; the concentration of property, whether in land or other capital, inevitably leads to concentrations of political power and oligarchy.

Commodity Pricing for Wages

No idea from Catholic Social Teaching seems as strange to "positive" economics as the just wage. Indeed, as we previously noted, any discussion of wages in neoclassical economics is problematic, since a "wage" is just a special name for the price of one particular commodity, labor; if labor is a commodity, its price must follow the rules for other commodities. Hence it is no surprise that *The Economic Way of Thinking*, in a chapter on the "Distribution of Income," finds that there really is no way to affect income distributions. "Because income isn't really distributed by anyone, it can't actually be redistributed. No one is in a position to apportion shares of the social product."[6] This is, of course, a restatement of the "Iron Law of Wages," and it is contrary to actual experience. Distributions of income vary widely from culture to culture and country to country.[7] But mostly, this statement removes economics from the sphere of human freedom and intentionality. The positive economists identify the production half of economics as an arena of human creativity and effort, which is certainly true, but then imprison distribution in "un-freedom" and constrain it by laws as ironclad as those laid down by Malthus and Ricardo, laws which have failed the test of empirical verification for two hundred years. Whether or not these laws are true, they leave one with a profound sense of disappointment. Why, if half of economics is creative, must the other half be iron-bound and servile? Distribution is half of economics; there is something unsettling about saying that we can do nothing about half of the "science." Wages form the bulk of demand; it is somewhat mysterious how one can understand the demand distribution without understanding the distribution of incomes, which for the most part for most people means wages.

"Limited Government"

No other principle is so firmly enshrined in rhetoric and so routinely ignored in practice as is the principle of limited government. We witness "conservative" administrations vastly expanding the power, reach, and cost of government. But this is not new. Since the growth of mercantilism/capitalism in the sixteenth and seventeenth centuries, government has always grown with the corporate world. This is less surprising than it seems. As wealth accumulates into fewer and fewer hands, so does power, and power always seeks advantages for itself, advantages which can be best obtained from a large and powerful state apparatus. Capitalism thus catches democracy in a conundrum: the more wealth it produces, the more it concentrates power, and the more power is concentrated, the more true democracy is weakened. Thus the Church's warnings on the concentration of property have a political dimension as well.

Individualism

Both solidarity and subsidiarity look to some shared notion of the common good in both the vertical and horizontal relationships within society. But capitalism takes no note of the common good, at least not directly; all "social" values are merely the summation of individual choices, choices made not for the common good but for private utility. In such circumstances, the very notion of a "common good" becomes problematic at best, and a matter of marketing at worst. Capitalism is built on the values of the Enlightenment, values that presupposed the individual as the measure of all things and ignored the person, the "individual-in-relationship."[8] This flattens all social relations and "privatizes" all values. There is nothing between the individual and the government, and the richly textured social fabric of intermediate organizations is reduced to a series of lobbying interests.

CRITERIA FOR AN ETHICAL ECONOMICS

Before we can find a way to reconcile the tensions we have just noted, we must examine the questions that are posed by economics — any economics — and establish some criteria for judging the answers that a particular economic theory might give. Without such criteria, it is simply impossible to think about economics in an orderly or disciplined way.

The Economic Problem

What is Economics? "Economics is about social provisioning, or how societies provide for their material reproduction."[9] This definition deals with a more basic problem than do the more common definitions of economics, which generally involve "the allocation of scarce resources among alternate uses." Resources must be allocated, but such definitions leave out the purpose of these allocations. Further, the neoclassical definition biases the conversation in favor of "scarcity" rather than abundance, but the whole purpose of resource allocations — the whole reason for economizing — is to allow for a relative abundance. It is the means (resources) which may be scarce, but not necessarily the ends. We will take up the question of scarcity and abundance in relation to means and ends in a later chapter. For the moment we can note that the more basic question involves social provisioning. In answering this question, we must deal with three further questions: What to produce? How to produce it? To whom should the benefits be distributed?[10]

What to produce? What a society produces is a direct reflection of its dominant values, or at least of the values of those who dominate society. It would seem that some things *need* to be produced and are therefore *natural* and beyond cultural considerations. But while things like food, clothing, and shelter are necessary, the forms they actually take are always cultural. For example, we must eat to live regardless of what language we speak, but what we actually eat — spaghetti, or egg foo yung, or hamburgers — is always a cultural product.

How to produce it? This is a question both of human technology and abilities. There must be a means of assigning tasks, something which normally has a large social content. For example, tasks will be assigned at least partially on the basis of education, but who gets educated and who doesn't is largely a social decision.

To whom should we distribute the product? This question has both discretionary and necessary aspects. Certainly the product must be divided so that enough members of society can subsist and reproduce the next group of workers. Beyond that, distribution has strong discretionary elements. Normally, the actual distributions will depend on the values of the society at large, or perhaps will reflect the values only of the ruling class. The solution is largely a matter of power relationships rather than of some "pure" economics.[11]

Solutions: Tradition, Command, and Market

The answers to the questions of social provisioning can come from three sources: Tradition, Command, or the Market.[12]

Tradition: The past guides the present: What to produce this year is guided by what was produced last year; sons follow their fathers' professions. There is little change and less freedom. All three questions are answered, but answered, as it were, "in advance" and with little option for growth and change.[13]

Command: Command economies rely on some central authority to provide all the answers.[14] While this ensures that all the questions are answered, the quality of such answers may be open to some doubt, especially if the values of the planners are at odds with the values of society at large. The planners can be seeking either the interests of the common good or their own interests. Nevertheless, economies heavily dependent on command have functioned successfully and left behind great monuments such as the pyramids.

Market: The forces of supply and demand dictate the answers, with each individual responding to price signals in order to maximize utility. In this way, it is believed, the market is self-organizing and capable of creating order out of chaos. But as Charles Clark has noted:

> This is the myth of the market. Markets are not natural phenomena, but are socially created. In the real world the market mechanism is best at dealing with small changes to an already existing economic order, providing the signaling function of adjusting relative prices so that a small number of market participants can adjust their behaviour. Markets, however, cannot generate this order. All markets are social institutions, embedded in particular societies and in history. They have rules of behaviour, laws and customs. These come from tradition. Also they have property rights and methods for enforcing these rules and customs. These come from command. Without the proper context, markets are inefficient and chaotic, as Russia is currently demonstrating to the world.[15]

Clearly, markets do not generate order, but are based on a pre-existing social order which they then help direct. But they can also help to destroy that order. Indeed, the assumption that all things can be based on self-interest destroys the very basis of virtue which is presumed by the market. A pure market system has never been attempted, because it cannot be attempted; markets require fully socialized and ethical participants in order to function. It is no accident that as the force of custom and virtue diminishes, the role of law — and lawyers — increases. So too does the role of politics and bureaucracies; force, legal or political, must replace the virtues that a "pure" market system helps to undermine.

Values: Normative and Positive Economics

Some wag somewhere has said that "scientific" economists suffer from physics envy. And indeed, many economists lay claim to a "positive" or "value-free" view of economic relations based purely on precise measurement and complex mathematics, just like physics. But astrology is also based on precise measurement and bewildering mathematics; its status as a science — and its relation to reality — is not thereby established. Economists may bristle at the comparison, but it is clear that math and measurement are insufficient to establish a science. In the first place, mathematics is not an empirical science; it is a set of formal and idealized relationships and is indifferent to any particular reality other than its own axioms. There is nothing in economics that is driven by a mathematical logic: time, money, culture, and uncertainty prevent this.[16] The *homo economicus*, the "pure" economic creature, simply does not exist, and were we to meet such a creature, we would regard him as grotesque.

In the second place, measurement itself depends on theory and all theories require value judgments. For example, in measuring unemployment, the economist must

> first start by making the decision that it needs theoretical explanation and second [he] must define what unemployment is, both of which are blatantly value-laden (and political) activities. Furthermore, the choice of what methods to use to investigate this phenomenon also involves value judgments, as does selection of the critical criteria about what will be accepted as the "final term" in the analysis, the bases of what arguments will or will not be accepted. However, values and value judgments enter into theory construction on the ground floor by giving the theorist the "vision" of the reality s(he) is attempting to

explain. This "vision" is pre-analytical in the sense that it exists before theoretical activity takes place.[17]

Neoclassical economics are therefore, like everything else human, value-laden; it cannot be a question of a false dichotomy between "values" and "facts." Rather, it is a question of examining the values by which the facts are explained or even perceived. That will be the burden of the next chapter.

Chapter 10

Toward an Evolved Capitalism

By acting according to the dictates of our moral faculties, we
necessarily pursue the most effectual means for promoting the
happiness of mankind, and may therefore be said, in some sense,
to co-operate with the Deity, and to advance as far as is in our
power the plan of Providence.   —ADAM SMITH

ECONOMISM

What's Love Got to Do with it?

The primary value of neoclassical economics is expressed by the term
"economism," the reduction of all possible social values to economic ones.
For example, *The Economic Way of Thinking*, an introductory economic
text, is fairly typical of much economic literature in claiming that all economic thought is derived from one fundamental presupposition, "All social
phenomena emerge from the actions and interactions of individuals who
are choosing in response to expected additional benefits to themselves."[1] In
other words, at the heart of all human interaction is selfishness, the benefit to
oneself. The text goes on to *deny* that this constitutes selfishness, but offers
no further explanation of why it shouldn't be so called.[2] The text further
explains that everything from rush hour traffic, to charities, to government
bureaucracies, to the operations of IBM can be explained by economics.[3]
The authors claim that all persons "choose their actions on the basis of
the net advantages they expect."[4] The authors also claim that they "[do]
not deny the reality or importance of generosity, public spirit or any other
virtue,"[5] but they do not explain how these fit into their theory.

The authors do not attempt to justify the presupposition of self-interest;
it is to be accepted as an article of faith. But at least one economist has
attempted to give a better explanation of this thesis. This economist was
Ludwig von Mises, who attempted to raise utilitarian reductionism to the

level of a serious school of philosophy which he called *Praxeology,* a philosophy he explicates at great length in his tome *Human Action.* Mises is attempting to reduce all human activity to marginal utility. Recall that with the discovery of marginal utility, economists had a powerful analytic tool which they felt moved their discipline from the realms of philosophy to those of pure science. The founders of the marginalist revolution were motivated by the need to find a useful term in the mathematics, one that would allow them to construct powerful economic formulae. However, it is an open question as to how far these models could claim to represent all possible economic relations. Mises attempted to solve this problem by rooting marginal utility neither in mathematics nor even in the physical world per se, but in the very structure of human action; that is to say, it becomes a psychological principle. If marginal utility can be shown to be the sole determinant of human action, then everything human can be explained by marginal utility, and the whole social world falls under the dominion of economics.

Mises starts with the thesis that all human action results from uneasiness or discontent.[6] He assumes a "methodological individualism,"[7] which isolates all human actions from their social context. As Mises puts it, "The hangman, not the state, executes a criminal."[8] Mises then assumes that all of our actions are marginalized in that we attend to our most urgent need first and, having satisfied that, move on to the next most urgent need, etc.[9] Actions must be marginalized because means are always limited;[10] that is to say, we always want more than we have. From this "principle," which is taken as self-evident, Mises goes on to derive all possible supply and demand curves and thus establish classical liberalism on a "self-evident" psychological foundation; after all, if human action is governed by marginal utility, then everything human must also submit to the marginal utility. Utilitarianism is all.

Human Action is indifferent to questions of human will and motivation. Delving into the will "would not add anything to our knowledge,"[11] while questions of motive simply do not affect the theory.[12] And yet, one wonders how one can adequately deal with human actions apart from human will and motivation. However, the theory does *in fact* take account of motivations, but assumes that *all* motivations are the same, namely to maximize benefits to oneself. All actions, according to the theory, begin in discontent, proceed through evaluating scarce means, and terminate in actions intended to increase personal benefits. However, this turns out to be circular logic, unrelated to actual experience, and unnecessary in any case. It is circular because it *assumes* what it intends to prove, namely that all human action is dependent on marginal utility; this may or may not be true, but it must be demonstrated rather than presumed *a priori*. Nor does the theory square with the facts of our daily experience. Everyone who has an important paper to write or client meeting to prepare for, yet sits on the couch zoning out in front of a tired TV re-run, recognizes instinctively that human motivations are complex, multi-layered, dense, and often impenetrable even to the person him or herself. The diligent Praxeologist will no doubt respond that at that particular moment, leisure was more "useful" than work. But if this is true, it is trivially true; if "utility" merely means we do whatever we do, it cannot enlighten us as to the source or structure of human action; if we cannot say *why* one action was more "useful" than another, we cannot give an account of human action solely in terms of usefulness.

In any case the theory is unnecessary for establishing the validity of marginal analysis; marginal utility is a physical principle, not a psychological one. It arises from the finite nature of the physical world. All physical processes, because they are finite, tend to be non-linear at some point. We add a spoonful of sugar to our coffee and stir. The electro-chemical bonds in the coffee take up similar bonds in the sugar and the sugar is dissolved. We add a second spoonful, but now there are not as many unoccupied bonds, so less of the second spoonful gets absorbed. We add a third spoonful, but now there are few bonds left, and the majority sinks to become a sludge at the bottom of the cup. Marginal utility can explain why the third spoonful adds less sweetness than the first, but cannot tell us why anybody chooses to add that third spoonful. And failing to explain this very human action, it fails as a theory of human action. Human actions are far more complex than physical processes and demand more from the philosopher and the psychologist than a simple reductionism.

Working from a dubious principle to an unnecessary conclusion, Mises thinks that he has made economics "scientific" and immutable, the product of unchangeable laws as solid as those which dictate the movement of the stars. Indeed, Mises claims that Praxeology has the same epistemological status as do logic and mathematics, stating that it is "unconditionally valid for all beings endowed with the logical structure of the human mind."[13] But what has actually happened is not that human action is explained by a comprehensive theory, but that human action is flattened to conform to a narrow ideology. It is not a question of excluding utility from human action, for that will always be a factor, a part of the density of relations and motivations; rather it is a question of mistaking the part for the whole; the whole range of possibilities for human action is reduced to utility, scarcity, and personal benefit, and all other considerations excluded.[14] People do indeed marginalize their actions according to utility, such as when they rank the items on a "to-do" list in order of importance, but this prioritizing is always the result of training, discipline, and character, and not something necessary, inevitable, and automatic.

Mises excludes the one question that would make the subject both interesting and useful, namely, the question of why some things are more useful to us than others. The real question here is why we love some things rather than others, since it is only love of one sort or another that makes anything "useful." Answering this question will lead us in quite a different direction and should have a different impact on the way we model economic behavior. Ultimately, what this economism represents is a confusion of means and ends, or even a priority of means (things) over ends (persons). Mises takes a principle that properly applies to things and applies it to persons. This confusion can distort even obvious economic truths into palpable falsehoods. Take, for example, the case of scarcity.

Scarcity, or "Can There Ever Be Enough to Go Around?"

Scarcity is the most obvious and self-evident economic principle: we live in a finite world. Indeed, scarcity is what makes economizing necessary.[15] However, when ends and means are confused, scarcity itself becomes not something self-evident, but something evidently false.

Let me illustrate with an anecdote. When I was a boy in New York City, we lived in an old brownstone apartment on Manhattan's West Side. We did not have a car; indeed there was only one person who owned a car on the whole street. And anyway, the street wasn't all that amenable to cars, being cobblestone. However, for fifteen cents one could buy a subway token, and for that fee the cultural and recreational wealth of New York City was ours, even as small children. My brother and I loved to go to the American Museum of Natural History to see the great skeleton of Tyrannosaurus Rex that dominated the lobby, or the great blue whale that hung in the basement. Or we would go to the Metropolitan Museum of Art and see the armor exhibit, with knights in shining armor mounted on steeds covered in steel plate, lances lowered so that, when you entered the room, they looked like they were charging directly at you. Or for the same fee, we could go to the beaches at Coney Island or Far Rockaway. We were indeed men of the world at the age of seven. But mostly, we were independent; we were free. It was a poor neighborhood, but we were rich in cultural and recreational resources. By contrast, my children grew up in an affluent suburb in Texas. Everybody on the street had at least two cars, but my children had very little transportation. The means of transport were not available to them independently, and hence parents and children were bound together in a relationship similar to that of a lord and his chauffeur; both children and parents lost some of their freedom. It was perhaps good that there so few places to go, and that the major cultural resources were the mall and the movie theater.

In one case, there was a scarcity of means and an abundance of ends and in the other an abundance of means and a scarcity of ends. In one case, cars were scarce and transportation abundant, and in the other cars were abundant and transportation scarce. Properly considered, scarcity should apply to means, not ends. If we reverse the terms, we end up manufacturing our way into scarcity, and an expensive scarcity at that. In place of robust systems designed according to some notion of the common good, we have narrow systems designed from the premises of individualism which always make the ends, transportation in this case, more problematic, and more problematic the more you invest in them; we spend huge sums of public money on systems that limit access rather than expand it. This same pattern of spending ourselves into scarcity can be seen education, health care, the military, etc. Expenditures for higher education increase while access to college declines, for example. What is lacking is a purpose, a *telos*, that is to say, a vision of the common good, and a proper distribution function informed by that vision.

The Economic Stork

The methodological individualism of neoclassicism shifts the focus of economic thought from the family, where it rested in Aristotelian and Scholastic economics, to the individual. However, the individual, by him or herself, is sterile and not a self-sustaining entity. Neoclassicism thus has no way to explain how new workers come into the economy, and hence it has no way to explain growth. John Mueller has characterized these shortcomings in economics as "The Economic Stork Theory" (EST). In the Economic Stork Theory, workers arrive in the economy fully grown, fully trained, and fully socialized. These stork-borne workers are a "given"; that is, there is no way to explain the growth in workers or their level of training and socialization, and hence little reason to support them with political or fiscal policies. Mueller describes the theory as follows:

> I call this the Stork Assumption, since it literally means that adult workers spring from nowhere, as if brought by a large Economic Stork. Under the Stork Assumption, the accumulation of workers' tools — buildings and machines — is the only possible source of economic growth that can be affected by policymakers. Moreover, under these

assumptions the total tax burden not only should, but inevitably must, fall entirely upon the incomes of workers (who by assumption cannot avoid such taxes by having fewer or less-educated children, though property owners are assumed able to avoid taxes on property income by investing less in property). The Stork Assumption, not economic theory, underlies the perennial proposals to abolish taxes on property income, which are advocated by a cottage industry of (mostly my fellow Republican) economists centered in Washington, DC.[16]

As a corollary to the Economic Stork Theory, the only "useful" work done in the economy is work done for wages or other economic rewards, and hence there are only two kinds of human activity, work and leisure. Hence, there are only two kinds of individuals in this theory: *Partially Useful Individuals* (PUIs) and *Totally Useless Individuals* (TUIs).[17] The PUIs are partially useful because they spend some of their time at "work" producing things in the money economy. The TUIs, however, don't "work" at all. Rather, some of the TUIs, otherwise known as "mothers," spend their time in such leisure activities as taking care of the household pets; some of these pets are called "cats" or "dogs," and others are called "children," another form of TUIs.

Since the standard of living in the EST is the result of a positive capital-to-labor ratio, increasing the number of PUIs does not increase the standard of living unless the amount of capital is increased by at least an equal amount. In other words, you can increase the standard of living by decreasing the number of people, or at least slowing the growth of the population. Therefore the crucial element in growth is capital, and people are problematic. The policy implications are that capital should not be taxed, only people, in the form of labor or consumption taxes. This will help to discourage the formation of new PUI/TUIs, while raising the capital-to-labor ratio.

Mueller points out that the EST's most glaring error is the failure to recognize that the family is the basic economic unit. And within the family, the choice is not so much between work and leisure as it is between production for exchange and production for immediate use. Of course, economic theory simply has no way to account for production for use, even though it is actually the whole point of production for exchange; we work to provide money to buy meat and potatoes which we then use to produce dinner. Production for use does not show up in the GDP, but in fact the GDP presupposes such production. What the TUIs known as "mothers" are doing is crucial not just to the continuation of the economic system, but to the continuation of civilization itself. There is no economic growth without mothers and the job they do. Moreover, the social shifts of the last fifty years have moved us away from production for use to more production for exchange. Now, one may debate as long as one likes the soundness of this move into the workplace in terms of, say, women's liberation. But as the feminists point out (quite rightly), if mothers were paid a salary for everything they do, they would earn a hefty salary indeed. But the attempt to monetize the work of mothers, to convert it from production for use to production for exchange, is futile and leads to endless debates that have no possible resolution. There simply isn't enough money to replace what mothers do everyday. The transfer of work from use to exchange does indeed show up as an "increase" in the GDP, but not as an increase in any actual output of goods and services, and likely involves an actual *decrease* in such services and in their quality. Do day-care centers really provide the same level of "care" as does a family? Do fast-food stands really substitute for family meals?

Moreover, the policy implications are '. Differential rates of taxation between capital and consumption (or labor) misallocate resources and send the wrong signals. If you have the good fortune to be a robot, your "income" would be calculated by deducting the costs of your production, maintenance, and depreciation from your net receipts. But since you are merely a human, these expenses are treated with contempt by the taxing authorities and by the economic theories on which they rest. A robot reading this book can deduct the cost from his net; alas for the mere student it is a consumption item, and will get no favorable tax treatment.

The Distribution Function of Wages

The commodification of labor is the most glaring and economically untenable example of the confusion of means and ends. The liberal economists are certainly correct when they point out that labor, like any commodity, has a market clearing price fixed by supply and demand; hence, all unemployment is voluntary. However, price is not an absolute, nor is it determined absolutely by supply and demand, even in our own "free-market" economy. Rather, it is an allocation method influenced by a number of factors. Recall the "just price" theories of the Scholastics and how they actually functioned in the Middle Ages through the guilds and a combination of market forces and social regulations. This was not an invention of the Middle Ages, but something that occurs naturally and always occurs to some extent. Since there are no "pure" market systems, there are no "pure" market-wage systems.

One implication of the fact that prices are part of the allocation system is the conclusion, intuitively obvious, that wages are the part of production allocated to the workers; indeed, wages form the bulk of demand in a capitalist society; through its wages, labor is expected to clear the market of the bulk of goods. But how can one commodity — priced as a commodity — be expected to clear the market of all other commodities? How could the monies received for *any* single commodity, let's say wheat, clear the market of all other commodities? Herein lies the central conundrum of liberalism that Chesterton noted:

> When most men are wage-earners, it is more and more difficult for most men to be customers. For the capitalist is always trying to cut down what his servant demands, and in doing so is cutting down what his customer can spend.[18]

Of course, output is distributed not only by wages, but by rents, interest, and profits, that is, by "factor shares." However, the factor shares for interest and profit get distributed for the most part to a small group; most men and women get their incomes from wages. In 1998, 17 percent of income went to 1 percent of the families, with a further 40 percent to the next 19 percent. That gives 57 percent of the income to the top 20 percent, with the remaining 80 percent of the people to split 43 percent of the total income.[19] This 43 percent of the total income is not enough to purchase all the goods and services we produce, or even 80 percent of it. To keep the economy going, workers must spend as much as they can. Here we see the thrift paradox: If people stop spending and start saving, will there be a shortage of consumption?

The economy requires a transfer of purchasing power from the top to the bottom (or at least to the middle). This has been understood for some time. Two methods are Keynesian transfers (welfare) and consumer credit. The former implies a "nanny state" with burgeoning bureaucracies and redistributive taxes; it tends to make each person a "client" of the state rather than a citizen. But consumer credit carries an obvious contradiction when used as a transfer mechanism to sustain consumption. Consumption can be increased by a borrowed dollar today only by decreasing consumption by that same dollar — plus interest — tomorrow. This increased debt burden requires even larger transfers via credit, and a vicious cycle is set up. This is the classic ponzi-scheme.[20]

The Utopia of Usurers

There can be little doubt that the American economy is addicted to debt, both in its public and private accounts. Without this debt, the economy would simply contract, perhaps disastrously. Our international debts require that we borrow $2 billion a day to finance our consumption. America is now a debtor nation, and foreign nationals and governments now have a great claim on our goods and productive resources. This gives them tremendous leverage in dealing with the United States.

Debt is therefore at the heart of our distribution system, a fact which should lead to serious reflection on the nature of debt and the advisability of using it as a transfer mechanism. Yet there has been very little reflection on the nature of debt, and especially on the subject of *usury.* This is somewhat odd, given our addiction to debt, and especially since discussions of usury were a staple of economic analysis up until about a hundred years ago. Usury has typically been prohibited or restricted in most societies. Today, however, these restrictions are considered primitive and outmoded. Nevertheless, in light of our present predicament, it may be well to re-examine the theory.

The definition of usury tends to shift with the culture. In some places and times, it was *any* interest whatsoever, in others it was interest on non-productive loans, and most recently it was simply excessive interest.[21] At the heart of all of these definitions, however, was the notion that nobody should make something from nothing. That is, you should not be able to make a profit without producing something of value, without increasing society's stock of goods and services. To do so is to "use up" the social stock rather than increase it, hence the name "usury."

The most sophisticated discussions of usury come from St. Thomas Aquinas and the Scholastics. This analysis has been relegated to the realm of religious superstition by most economists, but the questions it raises cannot so easily be disposed of. One economist who realized its value was Lord Keynes, who said,

> Provisions against usury are amongst the most ancient economic practices of which we have record. The destruction of the inducement to invest by an excessive liquidity preference was the outstanding evil, the prime impediment to the growth of wealth, in the ancient and medieval worlds. . . . I was brought up to believe that the attitude of the Medieval Church to the rate of interest was inherently absurd, and that the subtle discussions aimed at distinguishing the return on money-loans from the return to active investment were merely jesuitical attempts to find a practical escape from a foolish theory. But I now read these discussions as an honest intellectual effort to keep separate what the classical theory has inextricably confused together, namely, the rate of interest and the marginal efficiency of capital.[22]

Usury for the Scholastics was not merely interest, but interest on a non-productive loan. What they were attacking was wealth without work. Consider the case of someone who lends his neighbor a cow. The cow produces milk and perhaps a calf, and the lender has a right to some portion of this produce. The cow "fructifies," produces something. Compare this with money. Money does not "fructify," and charging interest on it is getting something for nothing.

However, money combined with human work can fructify, and the lender then has a right to collect a share of the profits. In other words, lending as an investment in some productive enterprise is entitled to share in the profits of that enterprise, since it also shares in the risk. Loans will then be liquidated by the success of the enterprise, or will be written off with its failure. But in either case there will be no additional burdens on the stock of society, hence no "usury," that is, no "using up" the stock of society. But if the loan produces nothing, then nothing can be charged for the loan, or else it is a simply a wealth transfer rather than real growth. The Scholastics also recognized the right to receive compensation for certain "externalities" of money, namely for risk and the loss of the use of the money. But beyond these legitimate claims, usury is simply a transfer of wealth from one class to another that produces nothing of itself: it is wealth without work. This is especially true of consumer loans. They are merely a claim against future earnings without contributing to those earnings. An economy that depends on consumer lending to fuel consumption is in fact merely borrowing from consumption in future periods.

Usury, aside from its character as avarice, as the desire for wealth without work, has troublesome practical consequences as well. On the one hand, it "covers up" problems in the distribution system, that is, with the allocation of factor shares. If we did not inject massive amounts of consumer credit, there would be a massive failure of demand and the problems of factor shares would become apparent to all. As it is, these problems are hidden and will remain so until the ponzi-scheme collapses (as it must), as it does in depressions. On the other hand, usury detracts from the amount of capital available for productive investments; the absurdly high rates of interest make investment in production less attractive than investments in financing consumption.

The problems associated with usury and with the mounting debt are likely to be the major concerns of the next decade. The solution is to find real growth, not just a growth predicated on short-changing the future. So what is the source of real growth?

PERSONALISM

Self-Interest vs. Self-Respect

We have seen how the assumption of the human person as a pure "utility-maximizer" leads to an anthropology which treats humanity's deepest aspirations and most basic relations as mere calculations of individual benefit. Even love and sex must be reduced to computations of costs and benefits, while family life itself, the very origin of humans, is treated as no more than an exchange of utilities. Indeed, the primary anthropological assumption of utilitarian economics has not changed since Mandeville's *Fable of the Bees* in 1724; but as Robert Faulhaber notes:

> the transformation of the water of "self-interest" into a wine of public interest [is] a fake miracle. No matter how free markets and society might be, they cannot make individual perversities sum up to a total good...the apparent success of market civilization depended...upon an endowment of ethical and institutional capital which it steadily consumed and, in the nature of the case, cannot replenish....In addition...the countervailing motive of self-sacrifice has gradually lost its status and force. Simple selfishness as "self-interest" has become generally respectable and expected behavior, and its opposite an object of suspicion.[23]

Faulhaber points to the importance of "ethical" and "institutional" capital without which the market cannot function. Neoclassical economics rarely recognizes the importance of these and in any case has no way to account for them in a "positive" science; after all, what dollar value would one put on honesty or on fair dealing? Yet without an expectation of honesty in the market, the market cannot function. The same author also points to the importance of self-sacrifice without which no family, city, or society could prosper.

The main reason that a pure self-interest cannot add up to a public good is that it cannot add up to a private good. Self-interest is not something known in advance. It is, rather, *discovered* through the process of living and interacting with others. Rarely do we know with any degree of clarity where our self-interest lies. For example, does our self-interest lie with immediate or delayed gratification? Well, sometimes with the one and sometimes with the other; it is usually impossible to say until *after* the choice has been made. Self-interest is particularly inappropriate when conceived of in terms of "utility maximization," the starting point of neoclassicism. This is because our needs are ordered and complex and the term "maximization," which implies a numeric ordering, simply does not apply. It is true that we have purely physical needs which lend themselves to a numeric calculation. But our higher order needs, needs such as love, professional recognition, and self-actualization, are never a matter of quantity but of intensity; for example, every man needs love, but a man's "love-utility" (so to speak) is not maximized quantitatively by having a harem, but intensively by learning to love one woman ever more intensely. But this love is never subject (*pace* Becker and Posner) to a calculation of self-interest; as soon as it is, it ceases to be love and therefore ceases to have utility.

Nevertheless, it would seem to be very difficult, or even naïve, to drop the premise of a pure self-interest. It is undeniable that when we go into business we hope to gain some advantage for ourselves, some advantage that might not be obtainable when working for another. And as businessmen, we certainly hire others hoping thereby to benefit ourselves. Are we thereby stuck with the premise of utility maximization and with its grim anthropology?

Some economists would handle the problem by limiting the scope of self-interest to the business world while reserving altruism for the home and other places.[24] Yet this requires a bifurcated human being, one who operates under contradictory sets of motives depending upon his location. Further, it requires a bifurcated economics, since the family, no less than the firm, is also an economic entity, or at least an entity with economic aspects. We seem, then, to be caught in a dilemma: either we surrender to a purely utilitarian anthropology, or we divide the human being into pieces and parcel him out by time and place. Neither solution seems palatable. To escape the dilemma, we need a term that includes, yet transcends, self-interest. That term, suggests Robert Faulhaber, is *self-respect*.

Self-respect includes self-interest because every self-respecting person takes care of him or herself and his or her family; she does not allow them, if it is in her power, to become a charge on the charity of others nor fall below a certain level. By the same token, a self-respecting person does not allow herself to be dominated by egotism or by mere things (consumerism). Self-respect allows us to give due consideration to the higher-order needs, that is, our need for love and belongingness, for competence and professional mastery, for independence and freedom, and finally our need for the pursuit of beauty and knowledge as ends in themselves.

The indignant Praxeologist might respond at this point that these higher level needs can be described in terms of self-interest, but that is not really correct; indeed, the methodological individualism of the utilitarians presumes an egotism that "leads every individual to make more of himself than of any other [and] causes all the mutual damage that men inflict upon one another."[25] The self-respecting person, on the other hand,

> takes nothing from others since he is the incarnation of the universal in himself. That he loves and desires in himself as well as in others, whereas the egoist loves only his particular self, or better, the self which others can be made to see.[26]

Self-respect, unlike self-interest, allows us to perceive and act on a common good, without which civil society is impossible. Self-interest proposes an alchemy that transforms private interest into public interest by a mere arithmetic summation, but this alchemy simply does not work. The issue here may seem unnecessarily "philosophic," but in fact it is closely related to both economics and business practice. Self-interest, conceived of in terms of "utility maximization," lies at the heart of all utilitarian economics, and such economics are impossible without this assumption. Any economic system serves what is perceived to be the good of the person. If that "good" is conceived of in merely numeric and subjective terms, the higher order goods, as well as the common good, are likely to get short shrift or be ignored entirely. This is an economic tragedy, because it is the human person who is the source not only of all "spiritual" values, but all material and economic values as well. For at the heart of economic growth and prosperity stands not capital, but the human person.

The Source of Economic Growth: Persons

The economic policies fostered by neoclassical models tend to regard the creation of capital as the main source of growth. Indeed, at the current moment we are witnessing efforts to increase capital by shifting the entire tax burden to wages and consumption, on the neoclassical theory that capital investment drives growth. However, this assumption was challenged some forty years ago by Theodore Schultz, who noted that the neoclassical model could, at best, account for only one-third of the growth we actually witness.[27] As Schultz put it:

> The income of the United States has been increasing at a much higher rate than the combined amount of land, man-hours worked, and the stock of reproducible capital used to produce the income.... To call this discrepancy a measure of "resource productivity" gives a name to our ignorance but does not dispel it.... Unless this discrepancy can be resolved, received theory of production applied to inputs and outputs

as currently measured is a toy and not a tool for studying economic growth.[28]

Where does the other two-thirds of growth come from? Schultz offered the hypothesis that missing growth came from "human capital," the growth in the population and in their skills. Thomas Kendrick was able to verify Schultz's hypothesis and showed that "human capital," the rearing of children and education, accounted for 63 percent of growth, intangible capital (research and development) accounted for 5 percent, and tangible capital for 32 percent.[29] Note how well this fits in with the Church's teachings that it is the worker that is the source of all wealth and capital the mere instrument, precisely the opposite of what neoclassical theories teach. Indeed, people are problematic in neoclassical economics. In neoclassicism, productivity increase is a function of the increased ratio of capital to labor. The more workers you add, the lower the ratio becomes unless you can add capital faster than workers. Hence, "people," the only legitimate object of any economy, become problematic at best. Based on these false notions of growth, we see a concentration on population control policies especially for developing countries; our sages will venture into the most thinly populated places, such as Africa, declare them overpopulated, and start passing out condoms and birth control pills. These, combined with the bizarre investment strategies of the World Bank, do indeed lead to increased capital-to-worker ratios, but they also lead to increased poverty and a reversion to tribalism.

We can think about this problem by reflecting once again on the situation of our tenth-century farmer on the cusp of the medieval agricultural revolution.[30] It was not an increase of capital that brought about this revolution, for the amounts of capital involved were trivial, even by the standards of the time. Rather, it was the action of the serfs in experimenting with dozens of small changes that produced the wealth that fueled the next four centuries of growth. And these changes were themselves enabled by a change in the land system which allowed the serf to keep the greater part of his output. It was not the return to capital that was crucial, but the return to labor. In fact, capital was forced to accept a smaller share, albeit of a much larger output.

Clearly, economic growth requires an investment in child-rearing and education. These are regarded by the neoclassical theory as "consumption" rather than as investments. Thus, what should be the whole point of the economy, sound and stable families, becomes a mere "consumer choice" without any real theoretical or practical importance. Here we see the problem with neoclassicism's choice of the "individual" and not the family as the basic economic unit. Whether a person has or does not have a family is, in the standard theory, a meaningless choice in itself. But, of course, it *is* meaningful. It is the family, and not the individual, that is the basic economic unit because only the family is capable of reproducing and sustaining itself. Further, as we have seen, it is only the family that can provide the main instruments of growth. People are fond of saying that "children are our future," but we find that our future has no place in our economic theories.

The Entrepreneurial Firm

It may seem tautological to talk of an "entrepreneurial" firm, since all firms are entrepreneurial in the sense of being founded and run by entrepreneurs. But as long as the entrepreneurial spirit is confined to the owner or the general manager, the firm will not really be fully "entrepreneurial," and the potential that is inherent in all the "human capital," the persons who make up the firm, will simply go to waste. Employers, raised on an intellectual diet of utilitarian economics, which considers work to be a "disutility," end up ignoring their most important assets. Indeed, every self-respecting person wants to make a contribution to the workplace and to his fellow workers. There are, to be sure, slackers in the world, but more likely the work environment discourages real contributions by its very assumptions that entrepreneurship is a scarce commodity, rather than a general quality of human beings.

What the idea of "entrepreneurship" often comes down to is a question of authority. "The meaning of 'authority' embraces authorship, as the word implies."[31] The "author" may be the person who founds a company; what his authority means is that he is the author of some idea of making a product, no less than the poet is the author of a given poem. As author, he is the instigator, champion, and promoter of the idea, and this confers authority. This is the "original" authority of the firm, which often comes to be a delegated authority that works through the board of directors and the managers. The corollary of authority is discipline, for there is no authority in the company without the ability to command. Discipline will be most easily accepted when there is a perception of shared risks and rewards. To the extent that employees see their most important interests and their advancement tied to the interests and advancement of the firm, they will accept the discipline necessary to build an enterprise.[32] But to the extent that they see the rewards going elsewhere, and their contributions dismissed or taken without compensation, monetary or otherwise, they will turn to law, lawyers, and unions for their protection. Managers and owners may fear or despise unions, but they cannot deny that they themselves are the enablers of unions by their own attitudes toward work and workers.

But in addition to the authority that comes from the "author" of the firm, there is an authority that comes from the shop floor. This too is an "original" authority that arises from the process of production itself:

> The shop-floor worker knows what has to be done and has often discovered, or will discover by trial and error, how best to do it. This knowledge represents the accumulated wisdom of shop-floor experience.... Thus authority in business is another name for the willingness and capacity of individuals to submit to the necessities of co-operative systems.... The most efficient form of management will be that which engages the consent and co-operation of the workforce by aligning formal authority with the inner authority that comes from the job and the people who work the shop floor ... there is a large reserve of productivity latent in human attitudes on the shop floor. It is the single biggest resource we have. If we could tap that resource, the growth of productivity would be explosive. Nothing holds us back from increased production but ourselves.[33]

Work is necessary to the growth and fulfillment of the person. Once a manager realizes this fact, his or her attitude toward job design and management changes. Once each person in the firm is regarded as a potential entrepreneur, they tend to become entrepreneurs, creating values for themselves, the firm, and the community (customers). The legitimate authority of both management and workers must be acknowledged; the authority of the former is delegated from the "authorship" of the firm, and the authority of the latter from their connection with the production process. To be truly successful, there must be a shared sense of authority and discipline based on a common purpose. A shared or common purpose can only be reached through a sense of justice that recognizes the legitimate concerns of all who are involved in the firm. As George Goyder puts it:

> In its relations with the workforce the ultimate source of management's authority must be its concern for justice. This means holding to a purpose that seeks to balance the interests of those it serves. Holding a just balance in human affairs is no light task. It means working to principle rather than expediency, taking long views which may require times of waiting and recuperation from adverse market forces.[34]

Lest anyone view this as a mere platitude without practical application, let it be noted that there are highly profitable business organizations built on just this model,[35] a model where, as Fr. José Arizmendiarrieta puts it, "Everyone is an owner and everyone is an entrepreneur, without discrimination, in good and bad times, contributing with the available capital and the needed work."[36]

The Mother's Problem, or "Ludwig, Listen to Your Mother!"

There is an economic problem which makes the questions we have been dealing with less abstract; by putting the question into concrete terms, it provides a challenge for anyone who purports to be able to explain economic choices. That problem is called "The Mother's Problem" and was originally proposed by Philip Wicksteed in 1910 in *The Common Sense of Political Economy*. His idea is that an economic theory should be able to explain, in its own terms, what actually occurs in an ordinary household when, for example, a mother allocates the scarce family resources among members of her family. In doing so, she evaluates the needs of each member of her family against both the current resources and the need to save for longer-range goals, such as education, etc. When she buys something, say milk, she must weigh the price against her family's needs and against alternatives. In the utilitarian description of the world, she must be acting out of the utility she derives from each member of her family; she gets such and such an amount of "utility" from the baby, another amount from her husband, from her children, and from her cat, and dispenses the milk in accord with the utility she derives from each one of them; whichever one is more "useful" to her on that day will get the first allocation of milk.

But this is nonsense; the mother does not have children, change diapers, cook and clean, and attend to the education of her children for reasons of the utility she derives, but for reasons of love. She evaluates the allocation of milk not in terms of benefit to herself but in terms of the needs of each member of her family. So in this case, it is likely that the needs of the baby will come first and be satisfied before anyone else's needs. Then the children will receive their milk at breakfast, her husband will lighten his coffee, she will use some for a cake, and if there is anything left over, the cat will get a saucer of milk. As John Mueller points out, the mother is actually doing two things: she is ranking people as ends and things as means. People in the family are regarded as an end in themselves and their needs evaluated against the means at the family's disposal. And this is true of *all* human action: "it is done not by individuals for 'utility,' but by persons for persons" out of motives of love.[37] Sometimes, it is motives of self-love, and here the utilitarian argument holds sway as everything is viewed from the standpoint of self-interest. But when self-interest is the dominant motive, whether in the family or in society at large, we label that family or that society "dysfunctional." Without love, and especially love of others, neither society nor the family can function.

This point is precisely denied by Mises:

> Social cooperation has nothing to do with personal love or with a general commandment to love one another.... [People] cooperate because this best serves their own interests. Neither love nor charity nor any other sympathetic sentiment but rightly understood selfishness is what originally impelled man to adjust himself to the requirements of society...and to substitute peaceful collaboration to enmity and conflict.[38]

Thus in reality, the final source of action in Mises is not utility at all, but violence or the fear of violence, and this is true for every materialist philosophy; we cooperate not out of love but out of fear. Utilitarianism, as expounded by Mises, is quite literally — under its own terms — a *disease;* all actions begin in *dis*-ease, proceed for maximum benefit to oneself, and occur within a climate of violence and the fear of violence. It did not occur to Mises (although it is something that occurs everyday) that actions could result from an abundance of contentment — love, the contemplation of beauty, and sacrifice — and proceed in an environment of cooperation and love. Rather, Mises constructs a theory that excludes every noble virtue and every unselfish act.

A Civilization of Love

John Paul II declared that a capitalism which represents the priority of capital over labor always represents an inversion of right values. Further, he condemned the notion that it is futile to address questions of justice within economics because the system is controlled by inflexible "laws" which dictate the outcomes in advance. But I am confident that the system is susceptible to change, and that now is the acceptable time. The first requirement of such change is that we recover our sense of freedom within the system. That is, we view economics as an arena of human freedom that allows us to construct systems which mirror our sense of justice. In order to do this we must recognize that economics serves human needs first and foremost. That is, we must end the tyranny of "things" over persons. We must rediscover the fact that the economy is about people, and people are what bring growth and stability.

In order to do this, we have to lose the assumptions of utilitarianism. Economics, indeed, civilization itself, is based not on utility but on love; this is not a pipe dream, but a reality because utility itself is based on love. Only because we love somebody is anything useful to us; the limiting case is self-love, where all things are done for self-interest, that is, utilitarianism. But such egocentrism, while always present to some degree in a sinful world, is the norm only in periods of decadence and decline. To reverse the decline, we will have to discover love of neighbor and the common good.

We must confront the confusion of means and ends and regain the confidence that we can build robust and affordable systems of transportation, education, health care, retirement, and work which are available to all.

We must recognize that the economy exists only to serve the needs of the family, or the whole system is just a pointless and unstable accumulation of things that have no meaning, and indeed no real utility. In other words, someone must shoot the Economic Stork.

Also required is some sense of the common good that is greater than the mere collection of individual choices. Here we must establish solidarity, which is the only basis for a vision of the common good.

Finally we must end the dependence on giganticism in government and industry through the principle of subsidiarity.

The Church's strategy for dealing with these issues revolves around the just wage and associating the means of production, insofar as possible, with the workers. The just wage is therefore the key. But here is precisely the point at which the Church finds itself most at odds with standard economic theories, and the question stands or falls on whether or not wages can be associated with justice, or are just the product of a mechanical system, and therefore beyond the reach of human freedom. This question we will take up in the next chapter.

Chapter 11

Marginal Productivity
and the Just Wage

As soon as the land of any country has all become private property, the landlords, like all other men, love to reap where they
never sowed, and demand a rent even for the natural produce.

—ADAM SMITH

THE CAPITALIST NARRATIVE

When we look at the tensions between Catholic teaching and capitalist
practice, we cannot escape the conclusion that the two seem to have irrec-
oncilable differences. On the one hand, we have the claims of a "positive"
science, deemed as certain as astronomy or physics, to distribute incomes
according to a "natural" and inflexible law that excludes all human intentionality. On the other hand, we have an ecclesial authority which places a
purely moral requirement on the distribution of incomes, namely the just
wage. At this point the question becomes categorical: either incomes are
distributed by an "automatically" operating "natural law," or they involve
human intentionality based on a concept of justice; there would seem to
be no middle ground. It is impossible that a natural phenomenon could be
modified by a moral diktat; the decree of the pope cannot place the sun at
the center of the universe.

We noted in chapter 2 that such differences, which do not seem to admit
of a rational resolution, could usually be traced to a difference in the narratives that are the hidden basis for each position. Capitalism is not different
in this regard, having its own myth which completely predetermines the vision of its adherents. The capitalist narrative starts with the autonomous
individual who freely decides all things based solely on utility to himself.
Utility, measured as pleasure or pain to the autonomous individual, answers
all questions of value; the individual, by his own choices, raises or lowers

171

himself by his own efforts, and his success or failure is his own. Any purely "social" values, if they can be considered to exist at all, are merely summations of the freely derived choices of individuals. Society as such is merely an epiphenomenon of individual choice. Using free choice and individual utility as the mainspring, a complete economics can be assembled using relatively simple mathematics, and this economics will result in a strict order — called "equilibrium" — which follows mechanically from the system: supply and demand will be in perfect balance with full employment of all resources including labor. The driving metaphor for this vision comes from Newton's laws of motion, in which a few simple laws provide an explanation for all the apparent complexity of the universe.[1]

In the same way the mathematics of marginal utility can resolve all supply and demand curves and reduce all the apparent richness of complexity of human exchanges to a few simple equations. Further, based on marginal utility, capitalism can make two purely *ethical* claims, namely, that price encodes all the relevant information, so that equal exchange (that is to say, corrective justice) is satisfied, and that the factors of production, capital and labor, get their fair shares, each gets what it produces, which satisfies distributive justice. Both of these claims are related to the miracle of marginal utility.

Price and Externalities

Concerning price, capitalism holds that, barring fraud, prices determined competitively under the rule of marginal utility encode all of the relevant information and hence give the purchaser all the information she needs to make a comparison between products. However, there is a great deal of information left out of the price, specifically the *externalities*, which by definition are excluded. For example, if I develop a way to make widgets at less than the current market price, the buyer can compare the prices offered by the various widget-makers and come to an informed decision. But if my "improved" method of making widgets dumps a hundred tons of lead oxide into the air and a hundred gallons of mercury into the stream, this information will not be encoded in the price; it will be "external," and the purchaser has no way of knowing, from price alone, the effects of the product. Nevertheless these effects constitute a real and palpable cost. The cost will be paid in the form of increased birth defects and miscarriages, lower IQs, and a host of other health concerns. But it will never show up in the cost accounting for the product, and hence the price will never reflect the costs, thereby rendering corrective justice impossible.

The question of externalities leads us to a general principle, namely that most of the problems of relating justice to economics are really problems of proper cost accounting. *All* products contain externalities. This is because every product is both the product of a particular firm and a social product. For example, every car bears the trademark of its maker, Ford or Honda or GM, but also the trademark of the society that creates it; the car depends on the existence of a road and highway system, insurance systems, gasoline distribution systems, a functioning police force, and a certain expectation of what transportation means on the part of the public. Some of these costs may show up (accidentally) in the tax rates corporations pay, and hence in the price, but many do not; they are external to the price. Moreover, there are costs to having a transportation system so dependent on one mode (e.g., higher levels of fossil fuel use) that are also external to the price. And all this is before efforts to "externalize" costs, such as getting the government to build roads to the plant, grant concessions or subsidies, or take over costs such as health care. Therefore the ethical claims of the price system cannot be justified as a simple matter of cost accounting. Some "social" mechanism is required to assure full cost accounting. But in the current environment, these social constraints, even when imposed in one country, can easily be circumvented by relocating production to another venue, one less sensitive to social costs.

Labor itself may be the biggest and most important externality. When an employer hires a worker, what she really wants is the work, not the worker. Compare work with any other commodity. If the price of steel, for example, does not cover the costs, then sooner or later, the producer will withdraw it from the market. The price must, over any appreciable length of time, cover all costs of production including depreciation of the equipment, labor and material, etc. Labor also has "production" costs, in the costs of a family, and depreciation costs in the form of health care and retirement. But unlike a bar of steel, a worker cannot withhold herself from the market for very long. The worker needs to eat each and every day and may be forced to work just for her daily bread, while the other costs are "externalized," either in the form of welfare, charity, or simply increased illness, poverty, and shorter life span. The question then arises, "How can the externalities be incorporated into the price system?"

The second ethical claim of marginal utility is that it ensures that the factors get their proper share; that labor gets that which labor produces and capital gets that which capital produces. Here "marginal utility" becomes "marginal productivity." Since each factor gets its marginal product, the resulting social product is correctly distributed. Hence distributive justice is satisfied and no further demands need to be made on the capitalist system. This is a powerful claim, and needs to be examined in great detail. At base is the question of whether marginal utility is a fact of "science," true for all times and places, or simply part of the overall cultural narrative. It is a categorical claim. If it is correct, then either the "just wage" is nonsense, or the market-determined wage is already "just."

MARGINAL PRODUCTIVITY

Historically, marginal productivity is a development of the Law of Rents. As the Law of Rents holds that the worker can earn no more than the produce of the least productive parcel of land, so the law of marginal productivity holds that a worker can earn no more than the least productive worker, the "last worker" hired. Marginal productivity is based on the intuitively obvious Law of Diminishing Returns. It is well understood that only so many workers can be set to work on a given process before their output starts to decline. For example, let's say one worker in a strawberry field can pick ten boxes in an hour and that this rate can be constant for the first ten workers hired. But at some point, the additional output (that is, the "marginal product") from the last person hired will decline; the additional workers will just start getting in each others' way. Let us say that the output declines to six boxes per hour for the eleventh picker, three boxes per hour for the twelfth, one for the thirteenth and none for the fourteenth; the fifteenth picker will actually decrease the overall output by some amount. If the pickers are paid the equivalent of three boxes per hour, then it makes no sense to hire the thirteenth worker; his wage would exceed the value of what he could add to production. The law of marginal productivity states that *all* of the pickers will be paid only what the last man that can be hired is paid, or in this case the equivalent of three boxes of strawberries per hour.[2]

J. B. Clark and the Distribution of Incomes

This was explicit in all of the theorists of the marginalist revolution, but John Bates Clark attempted to show that it was not only a scientific "fact," but revealed the very workings of the moral order; workers were paid the marginal product because that is all they deserved. While wages might *appear* to be based on free bargaining of the free market, they are in fact based on "a deep acting natural law" which dictates the outcomes for these "free bargains":[3]

Where natural laws have their way, the share of income that attaches to any productive function is gauged by the actual product of [that function]. In other words, free competition tends to give labor what labor creates, to capitalists what capitalists create, and to *entrepreneurs* what the coordinating function creates.[4]

Clark did not seem to realize that he had posed a "paradox of freedom"; in a free market, there would be no freedom in wages, interest, or prices. These would be set by an inexorable and unalterable law. When it came to price, whether the price of labor, capital, or products, freedom was enslaved to an immutable law.

In explicating this iron law, the task for Clark was to show that the marginal wage, the wage of the least productive person (or as Clark termed him, the "marginal man"[5]) represented the "specific product of labor," and of labor alone. His strategy was to start with the Law of Rents. As Ricardo noted that the least productive land commands no rent, Clark reasoned that the least productive tools and machinery also commanded no rents, and that workers could keep all the income they could get from them. This amount corresponds to the marginal rate for labor and is its natural wage.[6] How was this wage correlated to the "specific product of labor"? Clark argued that it was possible to fix the specific amounts of production that were separately attributable to capital and labor.[7] If the product of the one could be fixed, then the product of the other would be the remainder, since Clark only allowed for two factors of production, labor and capital, with land being just another kind of capital.[8] To fix the portion of the product attributable to labor alone, Clark reasoned that the "marginal man" could be hired "with no change in the amount or character of capital goods."[9] Therefore, the amount he added to production — and this amount alone — was the only part of production attributable to labor alone and constituted the "specific product of labor." Labor was therefore entitled by "natural law" only to this part of the produce. Clark made no attempt to fix the "specific product of capital"; he merely assumed it was the whole product minus the wages.[10]

Clark believed that the forces of free competition would force prices to equal the cost of production,[11] driving the rate of profit to zero, so that the entrepreneur would earn little more than the worker.[12] This introduces somewhat of a conundrum for the theory, since the whole system depends on the entrepreneur who seeks a profit, yet, to the degree that the theory works at all, no profit is possible.[13]

Since Clark had relied so heavily on the Law of Rents to determine the "natural" distribution of incomes, it was necessary to show that all income — whether from land, labor, or capital — was a form of rent. In so doing, he was attempting to complete the project begun by Nassau Senior.[14] Clark argued that since wages are a "differential gain," they are the same as ground rent. From this stunning non-sequitur, Clark concludes that:

> It is one of the most striking of economic facts that the income of all labor, on the one hand, and that of all capital, on the other, should be thus entirely akin to ground rent.[15]

Why the effort to equate all incomes with ground rent? Ground rent, as opposed to rent of human-made things like homes, buildings or machinery, is rent paid for the ground that stands beneath any productive asset. The problem with ground rent is that it has no economic function and hence represents a pure *economic rent*. Economic rent is an amount paid to a factor of production over and above that which is necessary to keep it in production; it is the very measure of economic inefficiency. But land has neither production cost nor depreciation cost. Thus the entire amount paid for such rent is economically and morally suspicious. No one claims that the landowner, merely by virtue of owning the land, adds any value to it; indeed, it is not contentious to point out that his title adds nothing productive to the land. The landowner's claim to all but the marginal product is a purely legal one, and neither a moral one nor an economic one. It is based solely on the monopoly status that land and the landlord enjoy.

The reduction of all incomes to rent also served a practical purpose: since all incomes are from the same source, they can be treated by the same mathematics. It has already been noted that Clark disembodied capital goods to treat them as a more abstract "capital" with no fixed content.[16] Clark performed the same courtesy for labor. He argued that labor was a "permanent" force[17] apart from any individual laborer and that it constantly changed its form.[18] This disembodying of labor and capital was the last bit of the theory necessary to unite all factors of production under the mathematics of the Law of Rents. In classical economics, it was necessary to have different explanations for the different forms of income; the Law of Rents for land, the Labor Theory of Value for Labor, and some sort of surplus value theory for profits. But now all three of these factors, in their disembodied states, could just be interchangeable "x's" in a production function solvable by differential equations.

Aristotle Overthrown

Clark believed that in the workings of marginal productivity he had discovered the workings of God himself; he published in purely religious journals claiming to have worked out the laws of the moral order, "natural laws" which were merely the working of God's plan and which would eventually lead to the New Jerusalem, the Kingdom of God on Earth.[19] But this would happen in a deterministic fashion, under the auspices of a mechanistic God. There was little room for any human or divine intentionality as the whole system would operate completely on "auto-pilot." It is therefore the supreme irony that Clark's implicit view of history was no different from that of Hegel or Marx.

Nevertheless, if Clark's claims are correct, then it is a remarkable achievement. All of economics, and all of justice, are reduced to the "science" of exchanges, that is, to corrective justice. Aristotle's claim that distributive justice has an irreducible cultural element would be false, and economics would be a completely self-contained science that is entirely free of moral, historical, or cultural elements. If Clark is correct, then Aristotle must be wrong. Any attempt to introduce normative considerations into economics would be, at best, counterproductive and, at worst, anti-scientific.

Clark was following in the tradition of Malthus, Say, and Senior in identifying the rules of economics with the moral order. Therefore we can conclude, with James Galbraith, that marginal productivity states a "theological position": *"From all according to their average product, to each according to his marginal product."*[20] Any attempt at redistribution would violate the theology and only result in making the problem worse; transfer payments raise the effective wage as effectively as wage increases and therefore raise unemployment. The ethical claim is that distributive justice is satisfied, and any further redistributions are excluded as counterproductive. To make it even worse, even charity is counterproductive. Thus, marginal productivity supposedly imprisons the wage system (and profits) in an iron grip that neither the government nor good intentions nor charity nor any other thing can mitigate.

THE CRITIQUE OF MARGINAL PRODUCTIVITY

The Reality Check

When examining any theory that purports to explain empirical reality, we need to examine it in two ways. First, we need to apply an *internal critique*, one aimed at noting whether the theory is logically coherent on its own terms. Second, we need to test the predictions of the theory against the real world to see if indeed the theory has any predictive or explanatory power. This we may call the *external critique* or, more simply, a *reality check*. Here we ask simply, "What would we expect to see in the world if the theory was correct?" In the case of marginal productivity, in economies where the wages tended to be at subsistence levels we would expect to see full employment, a high rate of labor force participation, little difference between the very rich and the very poor, and a full utilization of all economic resources. Conversely, in high-wage states we would expect to see low labor force participation, high unemployment, under-utilized economic assets, and high differentials between wealth and poverty. Yet, when we look at the real world, we find precisely the opposite, and we find this in nearly every single case. Now, in any single case there may be any number of *ad hoc* explanations for the divergence of actual results from the theoretical ones. However, when every single case seems to require an *ad hoc* explanation, we may begin to suspect that there is something wrong with the theory itself, no matter how logically consistent it may be.[21] Logic, after all, is only a test of validity and not directly a test of truth.

The Necessary Conditions

One critique of marginal productivity is conceded by all sides in the debate: the theory requires a long list of conditions to be fulfilled which cannot in fact be fulfilled. Some of these include perfect competition, constant returns to scale, full employment of resources, etc. Perfect competition, for example, is impossible even at a theoretical level because there are always barriers to market entry, aside even from the barriers created by market power and government action. Further, this assumption presupposes a large number of small firms such that none of them has much power to influence the market price to any great extent. But many industries are in fact composed of a small number of large firms with tremendous market power. As Paul Ormerod points out:

> By definition, any model necessarily abstracts from and simplifies reality. But the model of competitive equilibrium is a travesty of reality. The world does not consist, for example, of an enormous number of small firms, none of which has any degree of control over the market in which it is operating. Small firms may be fashionable at present, but it is large multi-national companies ... which dominate the world economy. It is entirely illegitimate to make the link between the model and the observed success of the Western market economies.[22]

Indeed, it is just this kind of market power which characterizes the American economy. What is needed then is an analysis of marginal productivity under conditions of monopoly, duopoly, oligopoly, and government power. In the absence of such an analysis, it is impossible to gauge just how far the departures from "ideal" conditions affect the operation of the theory; hence the arguments remain at the level of ideology and take on the shrillness that is typical of that form of argumentation.

Empirical Verification

An even more serious critique is the fact that marginal productivity is an empirical theory that simply does not permit of empirical verification. For all of its theoretical power, marginal productivity is not actually used by businesses, which is suspicious. The example of the berry-pickers previously given seems to be so obvious — to economists — that it needs no verification. But a *businessman* will immediately spot the fallacy. If an entrepreneur has ten workers in the field, it is highly unlikely that he has ten pickers. That is, he does not have a *homogenous* workforce as the theory presumes. Rather, he might have eight pickers and two supervisors, or one supervisor, seven pickers, and two performing a collection function, or some other configuration of labor. For a process that is losing money, the question becomes, "Who is the 'marginal man'?" Are there two many supervisors, or too few? Too many collectors, or too few? Too many pickers, or too few? Marginal productivity cannot answer these questions, cannot be computed, and therefore can give the businessman or -woman no useful information.

We could of course force a homogenization of labor on the formula by divorcing the work from the worker and reducing everything to some unit, let us say the wage of the lowest paid worker. So if our ten workers are divided into seven pickers (the lowest wage), one supervisor (who makes half as much again as the pickers, or 1.5 picker-units), and two collectors who make 25 percent more than the pickers (or 2.5 picker-units), we would have a total of 11 picker-units. Now we have a number to plug into the formula, but the formula can yield no useful results, just as before. For example, if we find that our picking operation is losing money, then we can run our productivity formula and discover, let us say, that we are 2 picker-units past our point of marginal productivity. But which two units? Do we have too much or too little supervision, collection, or picking? We have abstracted out the very information that would make the formula useful. And this is even before we add in the other factors of production, land and capital. Is the land just too expensive to grow strawberries? It turns out, as we shall see, that the problem of aggregating capital is even more difficult than the problem of aggregating different kinds of labor.

It comes therefore as no surprise that attempts to verify marginal productivity empirically have proven a failure.[23] As Garrick Small notes of marginal analysis in general:

> Some economists therefore have suggested that prices can sometimes be shown to behave *as though* firms were performing marginal analysis, even though it is known that they do not.... Apart from looking a lot like Ptolemaic astronomy, actual prices cannot be shown to be capable of being reliably predicted by marginalist methods because of the practical impossibility of generating the mathematical relationships with anything like the precision necessary to yield a specific price.[24]

The Social Nature of Production

The reason the individual factors of production cannot be computed has to do with the assumptions of the marginal productivity theory, assumptions which are hidden in most accounts but which Clark, at least, attempted to make explicit. Clark was searching for the amount that labor "separately" produced. He assumed that the "marginal man" could be added without any addition of capital and therefore represented "empty-handed labor."[25] This is simply empirically false. The "marginal man" is not added without an addition to capital; at the very least there is the capital represented by his wage, and he can produce nothing without consuming some capital in the form of tools and materials.

Clark did not actually attempt to compute the "separate product of capital" as he did for labor. Had he attempted to do so he would have discovered that the separate product of capital — or of labor — is the only precisely known number in all of economics: it is precisely zero. Take some item of capital, say a truck, and watch it all day with a careful eye to see what values it produces. There will be exactly none, unless and until a driver mounts the cab to make some deliveries. Take a pot of capital, let's say some cash, and fertilize it and water it with all the care you can. It will still refuse to grow. Unless and until someone takes the money out of the pot to purchase tools, materials, and the labor to work them, it will not produce any values. All production is *social;* it occurs at the intersection of land, labor, and capital, and nothing happens independently; hence there can be no "specific" or "independent" theories of production. The same rule applies to labor. "Empty-handed labor" is simply another name for "unemployment"; without capital, labor can produce nothing. The factors of production — capital, land, and labor —

do not in themselves even have a marginal product, only the process as a whole does. One particular arrangement of supervisors, collectors, and pickers will have a different marginal productivity than another arrangement, and it is only these various arrangements that can be compared. Marginal productivity for a given factor cannot be computed because it does not exist.

Therefore, management must use its best judgment in allocating the rewards in a way that best utilizes the company's resources and best encourages the contribution of the workers. There is no "natural" division of the product; it is a matter of distributive justice and, as Aristotle pointed out twenty-five hundred years ago, distributive justice follows no "natural" rule, but will always involve a cultural decision. Contribution to the production process is computed by merit, but merit will involve a judgment on the part of management, a judgment that can be reduced to no set formula.

Two Factors or Three? Or One?

The marginalist revolution reduced the three factors of production found in classical economics to two, labor and capital; land simply disappeared from economic theory and became another form of "capital." Clark carried the process further by "eliminating" labor and treating it as just another "bit" of the capital fund. This made the mathematics much simpler. But alas, it allowed for a clean break with reality. Land and capital are not identical and obey different economic laws. And labor is different from land and capital in ways too obvious to mention.

Marginal productivity might work very well for man-made things, at least in some circumstances. If the price of widgets is high enough to collect an economic rent, then widgets will attract capital and entrepreneurs, the supply will be increased and the price lowered. If the price is too low to pay for production costs and depreciation, producers will exit the market, lowering the supply and raising the price. Thus, the promise of marginal productivity is an economy free of economic rents with great equity and full employment. After all, equity equals equilibrium; they are practically the same word and very nearly the same thing. And economic rent is the enemy of both words. But the theory breaks down for land and labor. Since you can't manufacture land, no one can undercut the market, and hence marginal productivity will not apply; land, having no production or depreciation costs, will always earn a pure rent. Labor cannot be withdrawn from the market when the price does not cover production costs (the family) and depreciation (sickness and old age). Hence marginal productivity does not fulfill the basic requirements of any economy: to provide the necessities of life to all participants. Therefore marginal productivity cannot be a description of any reality. It describes a world where land is manufactured at will and workers, when not needed, can shut themselves off until the market improves. Hence, marginal productivity does not even rise to the level of good science fiction.

Marginal Productivity as Metaphor

When theories part from reality, they tend to become metaphors based on their own myths. And this is what has happened with marginal productivity. The theory states what turns out to be a metaphorical description, namely that the factors of production ("both" of them) produce what they get and get what they produce. This description implies that each factor "produces" something independently and its rewards can be computed as a factor share. But as we have noted, this is simply incorrect. Capital does not produce anything by itself. Production requires a responsible agent, that is, a worker, including the form of work known as management. Therefore, to describe capital as producing anything *ex nihilo* and by itself is a metaphor and not an empirical description of reality. In logic, this is called the *pathetic fallacy,* the attribution of human qualities to non-human things. Capital is not an agent of production; only humans can fill that role.

This first metaphor depends on a second one, the "distributive shares" metaphor, which states that each factor "gets" what it "produces." This is metaphoric because neither factor "gets" a share of the whole product; rather, the whole product is owned by the *residual claimant,* who has the legal liability to pay the suppliers of each factor, that is, the wages of the worker and the bills for the capital.[26] What the owner of the output, the residual claimant, is required to pay the factors of labor and capital is not a share of the output, but rather whatever the market demands on the basis of the power relationships involved, relationships that will normally be dominated by supply and demand but may also include such things as government regulation, custom, or hidden knowledge. The correct empirical description is, "the residual claimant owns the whole output of the production process and the responsibility of paying the liabilities for the use of labor and capital."[27]

Who is this "residual claimant" to the whole output? By custom it is the capitalist who owns the firm. By custom, the capitalist hires labor and claims the output. But this is a matter of custom, not economics. There is no *economic* reason why it can't be the worker who hires capital and claims the full output. In fact, that is a fairly common and largely successful form of organization, and we will examine successful firms built on just this model. For the present, it is necessary to separate the claims of science, metaphor, and culture and correctly identify which is which.

The Definition of Capital

As badly as marginal productivity works for labor, it does even worse at describing the productivity of capital. The marginalists have to aggregate capital into some common number in order to use it in the marginal productivity formula. But quite obviously, buildings and trucks and machinery are all different things and have different rates of return. So what number should we use to plug into the formula? All too easily we answer "price!"; but this doesn't work at all, because the price depends on the return. That is, someone would be willing to pay more for an asset that returned $100 per year than he would for one that returned only $50. How much an asset returns is supposed to be based on its marginal productivity, just as the wage is. But this turns out to be circular: the price depends on the productivity, but the productivity depends on the price.

Clark aggregated capital goods (trucks and buildings and so forth) into a mysterious fund called "capital," a fund that was distinct from any physical thing that was in the fund. The necessity of doing this is obvious: it is difficult to use a machine in the formula and would be much better if one had a number. But this aggregation makes even less sense than it did in the case of labor. We need to compute the formula to know what return to use in the formula, which means we need to compute it before we compute it. The whole logical structure is now shown to be totally incoherent. As Joan Robinson noted:

> We must agree (though mumpsimus will continue in the textbooks) that marginal productivity of capital in industry as a whole has been shown to be a meaningless expression. We must look somewhere else to determine the laws which regulate the distribution of the produce of the earth among the classes of the community.[28]

Summary: Equity and Equilibrium

We started with something that was — and is — intuitively obvious, the Law of Diminishing Returns, and tried to make it into a formula which solves all allocation, pricing, and distributive functions. At that point, the theory becomes incoherent. How could we have moved from the intuitively obvious to the patently incoherent so quickly? It is certainly true that the returns from any asset — be it land, labor, or capital — diminish as further units are added, so that at some point we cannot profitably employ an additional unit of that asset. But where does that point of marginal productivity come? It would greatly simplify the task of management if this could be known by a formula. If the marginal productivity of all factors could be known, then the proper allocation of resources would be equally obvious to the CEO and the janitor. The preparation of the most complex budgets would be a trivial matter: each function would state its marginal productivity, and the entire budget would be a matter of a few moments' work with a calculator. Executives would have even more excuse to spend their afternoons on the golf course than they already do, presuming there could be found a reason to hire executives in the first place.

Thankfully for the profession of management, the problem is not nearly that simple. Judgment — managerial judgment — is required for the proper allocation of resources and the compensation of employees. These judgments cannot be reduced to a formula. The problem is that the marginalist mathematics tried to reduce all production to exchanges and derive distributive justice formulaically from corrective justice. This cannot be done. Insofar as production is a *social process,* the distribution of rewards must be a social decision. In other words, the theory has reversed the natural order between distributive and corrective justice. Distributive justice must be prior because it deals with production, and production is prior to exchange; you must *make* something before you can *exchange* it.

In the same way, the theory assumes that equity will result from the attainment of equilibrium, when in fact the reverse is true: equity is prior to equilibrium. If we examine the assumptions of the marginal productivity theory, assumptions such as a large number of small firms and perfect competition, we find that they are assumptions more naturally connected with *equity.* But the theory is supposed to produce equity. Therefore, the whole theory assumes what is supposed to be its result as its starting point. The theory will have to be reconstructed, and reconstructed in the right order. That is, from distributive justice to corrective justice, from equity to equilibrium.

We can summarize our conclusions in this way: *Since all production is a social process, we can compute a marginal productivity only for a process as a whole, never for a factor within that process.* There is no "empty-handed labor" whose "productivity" can be calculated, nor any capital independent of labor that can produce any values. It is *only* the intersection of land, labor, and capital that produces economic values. This being the case, how then can we judge the relative compensations to be given to the factors of production? If marginal productivity formulas produce no useful results which can be examined by all sides, how then shall we construct a theory of compensation — that is, a distributive theory — that can be acknowledged by all parties to the production process?

THE JUST WAGE

Natural Law and Property

The neoclassical economists attempt to build a system based on natural law, but their concept of natural law hides a number of purely cultural assumptions, such as absolute property. The Christian idea of natural law views the law in light of the meaning and purpose of things, their *teleology*. Thus an economy cannot be merely the operation of "automatic" laws that have no necessary relation to the objective needs of human beings and their social situations, but is something subordinated to the ends and purposes of persons and societies. The perception of these ends and purposes will vary from culture to culture, but we can nevertheless detect some common threads: the necessity of providing for all citizens, the necessity of providing some rules of exchange, and so forth. But the most primary economic question that a culture must deal with is the question of property. The claims to some portion of the output of production are claims of property rights. Yet very little attention is given to examining the basis of property rights, so that in effect the whole theory rests on unexamined and wholly non-economic assumptions. Property is taken as a given or self-evident assumption, but is it? We have already seen that the system of property which we regard as "natural" is in fact a social convention of relatively recent origin and that many other property systems have existed and do exist.

We noted in chapter 5 that property rights are made up of two considerations: ownership and use, with the former subordinated to the latter, at least to some degree. The common use of property is part of the natural law, while the private ownership is a social convention, valid to the degree that it helps us to bring forth all the goods of the earth and make them widely available. Thus while property is conventional in itself, it can be used to serve the purposes of the natural law. However, this discussion refers to property in *things*, land or goods. But there is at least one form of property that is prior to both of these, and this form of property is completely natural. Thus while we have already discussed property under the headings of ownership and use, we can now discuss it under the headings of *natural property* and *conventional property*.

Natural Property

When we look at property, we can note that each person has a property in herself. This constitutes a "natural" property as it is self-evident and reducible to nothing else. Furthermore each person has a natural title in her labor and to what her labor produces. A person who makes something is considered the owner of that thing, to the extent that the labor and the materials are hers. Of course, people make most things in cooperation with others, so that the product is a social product, and hence no one person can claim the whole output, but only what is proportional to her contribution. This right to a proportional share is based on the fact that to produce something a person must contribute a portion of her life, and she therefore has a just claim to support for that portion of her life, her own property, which she has contributed to the product.[29] This leaves unanswered the question of the *level* of support, whether we will make of the worker a prince or a pauper, but unquestionably establishes a right to some level of support.

In producing anything, however, each person or each firm also makes use of two other factors: previously human-made things (capital) and land, which includes the raw materials that land supplies. How are these other factors to be compensated? Note that we are dealing with *three* factors of production, land, labor, and capital, rather than just *two,* labor and capital. Land is a gift of nature and labor the gift of the worker. But what about capital? Capital itself regresses to land and labor (and to previous capital, which regresses to land and labor), so that if we sort out the compensation between land and labor, we can also determine capital's compensation.

Conventional Property

We discussed labor's compensation as based on the portion of her life that a laborer contributes to the final product. But what contribution does the landowner make? In the first place, we note that the landlord makes neither the land nor the raw materials which can be extracted from it. His claim is a legal one, based on whatever operations of title prevail in his society, that is to say, on purely social conventions. So how does the landowner come into possession of the land, and what is the nature of his title? Almost all theorists, from John Locke to John Paul, agree that land was originally meant for common use and given to all; it is taken out of common usage by some variant of the Labor Theory of Value. For John Locke, this strips land of all communal values, but for Aristotle, Aquinas, and John Paul II, land can *never* lose its social values. The privatization of land is justified on pragmatic grounds alone, namely that this best serves the common use of land. Since the justification is only pragmatic and not "natural," it fails when land ownership no longer advances the common good. But whatever view of land one takes, what is obvious is that it arises not from natural law, but from social convention and positive law. Thus the compensation given to land is fixed socially, not "naturally."

If all values from land are "privatized," then the landlord will be able in principle to extract all marginal values and the Law of Rents will hold. But the entire structure of private ownership rests on convention and not on economic law; different conventions will yield different results, as we have already seen. These conventions, whichever ones a society chooses, will rest on moral considerations entirely. It may be the morality of the jungle where the strong prey on the weak in the name of pure self-interest, or it may be based on some vision of the common good and the natural right of people to the true products of their labor. The task of the social scientist here is not to arbitrate among these visions and pronounce an "economic" decision, but to compare the likely results of various social conventions using both theory and history as a guide. And in this case, we have fairly clear historical precedents. If, for example, the economic police had been on the job to enforce the Law of Rents in ninth-century England, Europe would still be mired in servility. The vast expansion of the ninth through the eleventh centuries simply would not have taken place; if the peasant was entitled to no more than subsistence, then that subsistence could have been as easily supplied by a scratch plow as by a moldboard plow, and he would hardly have bothered to innovate. Had the landlord received all the marginal values, there would be few values over the margin. Moreover, we can note the failure of the Statute of Laborers (1351) to control wages because the wage earner had alternatives in the form of the commons, customary rents, and secure tenures. The problem perceived by the authorities in the fourteenth century was how to dampen demand through control of wages. Two centuries later, when land had been privatized and the commons enclosed, the Law of Rents came into play, and the problem was how to prop up demand through the Poor Laws, the foundation of our modern welfare system; this system has continued to this very day, not because, as some suppose, of a "do-gooder" liberalism, but because hard-headed economics demands some prop to demand under conditions of marginal productivity and the Law of Rents. We have adopted Keynesian economics because it seems to work, but its true father is not Keynes, but Henry VIII.

Subsistence

Several points flow from the discussion so far:

1. The worker has a *natural* right to the values produced proportional to the share of her life that she surrenders to the production process.

2. The capitalist has the same rights proportional to his labor and to the capital he supplies, which regresses to prior labor.

3. The share of the landowner is set by social convention with a view toward the legitimate needs of the landowner and the common good. His right is not natural because he surrenders no portion of his life to supply land and raw materials, but is based solely on social conventions.

The question now becomes, "How we can place a monetary value on the natural property the worker has in the final product?" The answer is rooted in the share of his life that the worker surrenders to make the product. It would seem to have three parts: subsistence; a premium for training, skills, and responsibility levels; and something left over for savings to acquire his own property and provide for his own security in time of need.

Subsistence would seem to be the most "objective" of the three, but it turns out to be a slippery concept indeed. This is because humans have an amazing capacity for enduring hardships. Since survival is necessary, people are not free to withdraw their labor as conditions worsen. Therefore, they will continue to bid jobs down to the level of their daily bread if they have no other options. The free market is therefore not a very good guide to subsistence levels, since it tends to arbitrate power relationships rather than economic values and not only drive wages toward subsistence, but also drive subsistence itself to ever-lower levels. Further, subsistence has to be measured not just from the standpoint of the worker, but from the standpoint of his or her family. This is because the economy of exchange in any sane society will include support for the economy of use; it will include support for what Ivan Illich calls the right to "useful unemployment," that is, for people who produce use values outside of the exchange economy.[30]

Useful unemployment includes, pre-eminently, the domestic arts of the household. This is not just a moral and social issue, but an economic one as well. In many areas, such as child rearing, production for use is more economically efficient than production for exchange. Exchange systems impose an entry cost of their own. For example, mothers who enter the workforce often find that increased expenses for wardrobe, child-care, transportation, meal preparation, and house cleaning and maintenance often consume so much of their incomes that the benefits from their marginally calculated wages are marginal indeed. Another example of useful unemployment is education, something which adds to the productive stock of society. The best example of useful unemployment might be childhood itself, which should be free of undue burdens of work.

Regarding labor premiums for skills and responsibilities, the market seems to do well when these are correlated to scarcity, but otherwise not so well. Of course, many jobs will get much better than subsistence because of the political power of the groups involved or because of scarcity premiums; political power can come from unions or from laws which set wages, such as a minimum wage. Or the power may come from a particular position one has, as in the case of CEOs and senior executives working with overly compliant boards of directors.[31] Scarcity premiums are normally related to the cost of training or to some special talent that a worker has. It is important to note here that it is *not*, as generally supposed, the training itself or increased productivity which confers the higher wage, but solely the scarcity premium. This principle is evident when we look at two specific cases, software engineers and seamstresses. In the case of the programmers, the training required kept the numbers scarce for a long time so that engineers could easily command $40–$50 per hour. However, as the skills have become more general, and as their own work at building the Internet has made off-shoring more possible, the work is being outsourced to Indian programmers working for $10 per hour. A seamstress is also a highly skilled job; however, it is a skill that is routinely taught to nearly half the world's population from the time they are young girls. Hence, the supply is nearly infinite relative to the demand, and their skill commands no more than starvation wages. Clearly, it is the scarcity, and not the skill, that commands a premium. Nor can the wage differentials be laid at the door of "productivity" of the workers, because in the case of the Indian programmers, the productivity is assumed to be at least the same. Productivity may perhaps form the ceiling for the wage, but the actual wage is based on supply and demand, and only the scarcity, and not the productivity per se, commands a premium in the market.

Finally, there is the difficulty of determining a "savings premium." However, this might be tied to the rate needed to insure a decent retirement.

The problem then is to determine wage levels in accordance with the dignity of the worker and his or her family. In theory, one can support one's family in a lean-to in the park, trapping rabbits and wearing a loin-cloth; hence in theory very little cash is required. However, the city building inspector will not permit lean-to's and those who go for job interviews wearing loin-cloths tend not to get the best offers. In other words, there is a certain minimal standard that society establishes and which constitutes for that society a "dignified" existence. This varies widely from culture to culture, but is nevertheless knowable for any given culture. This means that there is a cultural aspect which is irreducible. The problem here is that a culture can set the bar too high or too low. How much do we really need in the way of clothing? What constitutes a decent home? Do we need a television? Or two? Cable? A computer? A certain number of trips to the movies? An argument can be made that a minimal participation in our culture requires at least some of these things. But whatever the answer, there is some standard below which we regard people as not being full participants in the society.

Measuring the Just Wage

But there is in fact a measure of the distance between the just wage and the prevailing wage, at least approximately and in the aggregate. This distance can be measured by the amount of transfer payments necessary to sustain demand. These transfer payments are of two types: welfare payments and consumer credit. Both of these constitute transfers of purchasing power between one group of citizens and another made in order to support demand; without these payments, there would be both a disastrous reduction in demand and a sudden implosion in the standards of society. To the extent that these things are necessary, they may serve as a proxy for the distance between social standards and actual pay. By the same token, to the extent that consumer credit exists merely to continue a cycle of pointless consumerism, it is destructive and needs to be excluded from any calculation of what a dignified life needs. Of course, some amount of consumer credit is acceptable, since it is proper to finance a long-lived item, such as a house or a car, over some portion of the life of that item. But when we end up paying next year for groceries we consumed yesterday, the situation has gotten out of hand, and all too frequently, that is what is happening; we are, too many of us, still paying for things we have consumed, discarded, or no longer care about. In any case, transfers, by subsidy or by credit, are required to insure purchasing power in the mass of people sufficient to keep the economy going; the distance measured by these transfers is an indication of the deficiency in the just wage.

The problem is complicated by consumerism, which makes the determination of the social component of the just wage much more difficult. Each of us receives ten thousand to twenty thousand messages a day urging us to purchase things that may not really contribute in any way to our well-being, but are in fact the mere trash and detritus of a marketing industry gone insane. Consumerism has another effect that is pertinent here, namely, that it can easily create the illusion of poverty where none exists. The more we identify our well-being and dignity with things rather than persons, the more dissatisfied we become with ourselves and our situations, and the more difficult it is to perceive a just wage. But suffice it to say that we need to concentrate on what is really helpful to our well-being as citizens and family members:

a proper measure of nutritious food, decent housing, transportation, education, health care, etc. This requires not only economic good sense, but a certain change of heart, a conversion, a certain realization that the good life is not really about goods at all, but about our role as persons and our relations to other persons and to God. This in turn requires a conscious effort to reject the messages which come at us on a moment-by-moment basis.

The just wage, then, is not so much a number as a criterion of judgment. We can say that the just wage is fulfilled under the following four conditions: one, that working families, as a rule, appear to live in the dignity appropriate for that society; two, that they can do so without putting wives and children to work;[32] three, that they have some security against periods of enforced unemployment, such as sickness, layoffs, and old age; and, four, that these conditions are accomplished without undue reliance on welfare payments and usury. While it may be difficult to give precision to any of these factors, it is certainly possible to make reasonable judgments and set reasonable standards.

Implementing the Just Wage

In the following chapters we will be looking at theoretical and practical approaches to the just wage and examining some actual implementations. For now, we can just touch on some of the possible solutions. The first "solution" is to do nothing, or rather, do more of the same. The proponents of this solution, largely neoconservative or libertarian theorists, believe that the current system can be made to work, although they can not always agree on how to do that. The general "get the government off my back" attitude misses the historical point that the government has been on everybody's back since the sixteenth century when the ownership system shifted from feudal to allodial, from a system of customary rights to the system of the Law of Rents. Almost immediately, a welfare system was necessary to support aggregate demand and insure against social breakdown. The system, and the debate about it, has continued for more than four centuries, with nearly every regime promising to reform it out of existence, while continuing it in practice. If the system hasn't worked in four centuries, there is little reason to believe that it will suddenly start working now. Madness can be defined as continuing to do the same thing over and over again and expecting different results.

Minimum wage levels pegged to a real consideration of poverty are a possible solution, but a messy and inefficient one. These levels will always depend on government mechanisms that are burdensome to those who must obey them, but easy to avoid for others. Further, the setting of a "poverty line" is a political process, and the public can be expected to be stingy when they are expected to provide support for all below this line.[33] Finally, a minimum wage treats all workers alike, when clearly this is not so; a high-school student working a part-time job and the father of a family have different requirements; setting the wage to benefit the one may harm the other. Still, in some situations, a minimum wage may be a necessary stopgap. Better, however, to find a solution that works "systematically," with the least possible amount of government interference.

Since the closure of the frontier and the enclosure of the commons, it has been difficult to find some refuge for the worker which would allow him or her to refuse a disadvantageous work contract. But the key seems to be in restoring the things that frontier and commons provided. We will have to discover the common-use values of land and find some way of distributing them. Indeed, the second part of the Church's strategy involves the wider distribution of property, and we should note here that the Church means productive property. For Leo XIII, writing in 1891, this meant land, as most people were still dependent on the farm or came from families that were. By our own time, "capital" had replaced land as the primary means of wealth. Thus John Paul II could broaden the definition to include plans to associate the workers with ownership of the company for which they worked.

The key point is that we must start with equity, since equity is prior to equilibrium. Where there are vast differences in wealth and poverty, where there is monopoly or oligopoly, where there is government-granted privilege, equilibrium will be unlikely, or will be maintained only by virtue of massive government intervention in the economy. For example, we can easily see the effect of a too-steep gradient (the difference between highest- and lowest-paid workers multiplied by the number of workers in each category) in pay scales.

Let O-A be the total amount paid in wages, O-B be the maximum number employed, and the arc A-B be the possible distributions of the wage fund O-A. The lines O-a, O-b, and O-c represent different gradients of wages and O-a', O-b', and O-c' different levels of employment corresponding to the different wage gradients. Obviously, the greater the equity, the larger the number of workers that can be employed. There needs to be a sufficient gradient to ensure that workers with greater skills and responsibilities have proper compensation; this is a requirement of equity. However, too steep a gradient will mean that some will go unemployed and equity will therefore be violated. There is no formula that can give the correct gradient; rather, it arises from how the culture views proper rewards. If it views everything in terms of money, then a steep gradient will be required to motivate people to

The Effect of Wage Distribution on Employment

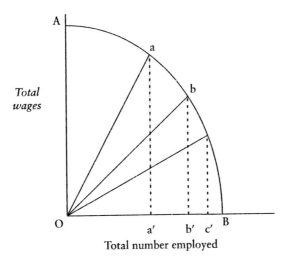

accept more responsibilities. However, this is rarely the case. Greater respect and recognition and job satisfaction, for example, are also great motivators.[34] Few people see their jobs solely in terms of cash, but also in terms of fulfilling higher-order needs such as fulfillment and self-actualization. This has profound impacts when considering job design as well as compensation packages.

In any case, we can begin to perceive, in a concrete fashion, the real relationship between equity and equilibrium. The remainder of our study will largely consist in examining practices and policies which contribute to equity, and thereby to equilibrium. But we can never lose sight of the fact that equity is not a by-product of equilibrium, but that equilibrium is dependent on some rough equity. There is a cliché in social justice: "If you wish for peace, work for justice." The economic equivalent is, "If you wish for equilibrium, work for equity." For equilibrium is economic peace and equity is economic justice, and you will never see the former without the latter. The two are practically the same words and very nearly the same thing.

Chapter 12

The Neoconservative Response

To try to run an economy by the highest Christian principles is certain to destroy both the economy and the reputation of Christianity.

—MICHAEL NOVAK

RESPONSES TO
CATHOLIC SOCIAL TEACHING

Since the social teaching of the Church is not in itself an "economic system," it calls for a faithful response from the laity in order to bring it to life in the world. The content of this response is not dictated in advance but depends on the skill and perceptions of the laity. There is not necessarily one "right" way to realize the teaching in the real world, but human ingenuity and the freedom given by a proper understanding of economics will allow a variety of implementations, as we shall see. This does not mean that all responses are equally effective or equally embody the spirit and content of the teachings; any implementation will start with a certain *theoretic* approach which will give the boundaries to that implementation.

D. Stephen Long has classified the responses to Catholic Social Teaching according to three major traditions. He calls these "the dominant tradition," "the emergent tradition," and the "residual tradition."[1] Long bases these classifications on the relation each tradition has to the dominant marginalist rationality of neoclassical economics. The dominant tradition, whether in its liberal, neoconservative, or libertarian strains, completely supports the utilitarianism of the marginalist revolution. In the emergent tradition, identified with "liberation theology," certain aspects of marginalism are retained, while the residual tradition completely rejects marginalism. Before looking at some practical applications of Catholic Social Teaching, we will look at some of the more important features of both the dominant and residual traditions; our bypassing of the emergent "liberation theology" is not meant to slight that view, which has important features of its own. But it is less

194

relevant to a study of the relationship between business and the Church's teaching, which is our main subject.

In this chapter, we will examine the dominant tradition through the lens of neoconservatism. This is not to imply that neoconservatism is the only strain within the dominant tradition, or even the best or most complete. There are indeed significant differences among the adherents of this tradition, mainly on public policy and economic matters, some being right-wing and some left, some neoclassical and some more Keynesian. Nevertheless, neoconservatism has come to enjoy overwhelming power and hence it is the strain of the dominant tradition that one is most likely to encounter; it has become the dominant strain within the dominant tradition. Indeed, the success of neoconservatism is remarkable. Its major intellectual lights (Michael Novak, George Weigel, Alejandro Chafuen, for examples) work for think tanks well funded by corporate America, and they have produced a large volume of influential works. There are also a number of influential neoconservative magazines, such as *Commentary, National Review, First Things, The Public Interest,* and *The Weekly Standard.* The last is funded by Rupert Murdoch, who also supports neoconservatism on the airwaves with the Fox News Channel. Neoconservatives occupy powerful positions within the Bush administration and were crucial in the decision to go to war in Iraq, as well as being leaders in the battles over the president's tax and Social Security policies. Neoconservative columnists such as David Brooks, George Will, Ann Coulter, and William Kristol are influential in public policy debates. Indeed, the close alliance between neoconservatism and corporate America is no accident, since neoconservatism is ideologically committed to supporting corporate capitalism.

The influence of the neoconservatives, however, cannot be explained totally by mere marketing or political muscle. Rather, the neoconservatives have tapped a strain in Christianity that has been present in one form or another since the Enlightenment, namely the attempt to reconcile the Church to Enlightenment thought, a movement that is sometimes called "modernism." Neoconservatism is, in a profound way, a right-wing version of the modernist crisis which was the subject of the first Vatican Council (1869–70). The modernists believe that the Church must accommodate itself to the modern world; they assert that a too strong insistence on dogmas is out of place in a pluralistic, multi-cultural, and democratic society. As Michael Novak puts it, the "writers of the biblical era did not envisage questions of political economy such as those we face today."[2] Furthermore, the Enlightenment beliefs of individualism, utilitarianism, and the divorce of faith and reason, ideas once considered controversial, have now become so commonplace that they are hardly subjects for debate anymore, but are the presumptions most people use in thinking and regard as self-evident. This shift in thinking has allowed the neoconservatives to make political alliances among a range of former liberals and social conservatives and become a powerful force. Many of the major figures in neoconservatism are former liberals who were disappointed with the results of the "nanny state," a circumstance that leads to the joke that a neoconservative is "a liberal who has been mugged by reality." But they have retained a basically liberal orientation, and that is especially true in regard to the Enlightenment dichotomy between facts and values. Recall Hume's "no ought from is" logic. Hume's disconnect of logic and morals relegated morals to the realm of private choice, while claiming an ability to look at "facts" or "natural law" unaided by authority or faith. This dependence on the so-called fact-value distinction is evident in the work that is often considered to be the founding document of neoconservatism, Michael Novak's *The Spirit of Democratic Capitalism*, a work that is highly indebted to Max Weber's *The Protestant Ethic and the Spirit of Capitalism*. And since Novak starts with Weber, so shall we.

WEBER'S QUESTION

Max Weber (1864–1920) was a sociologist of religion whose works occupy a pivotal position in the history of sociology; *The Protestant Ethic* is considered a classic in the field. The question that Weber poses is, "Why do Protestants in general and Calvinists in particular seem to do so much better in a capitalist economy than Catholics?"[3] Weber notes that "Protestants . . . have shown a special tendency to develop economic rationalism which cannot be observed to the same extent among Catholics."[4] Weber takes as his proto-typical capitalist Benjamin Franklin, whose "confession of faith" is that time is money, money begets money, idleness costs money, etc.[5] In considering Franklin, Weber notes:

> Let us pause a moment to consider this passage, the philosophy of which Kürnberger sums up with the words, "They make tallow out of cattle and money out of men." The peculiarity of this philosophy of avarice appears to be the ideal of the honest man of recognized credit, and above all the idea of a duty of the individual toward the increase of his capital, which is assumed to be an end in itself.[6]

The *summum bonum* of this ethic, "the earning of more and more money, combined with the strict avoidance of all spontaneous enjoyment of life," is "thought of so purely as an end in itself, that from the point of view of the happiness of, or utility to, the single individual, it appears entirely transcendental and absolutely irrational."[7]

Weber contrasts this attitude with the Catholic one that is more content with a sufficiency of income and a greater leisure and joy in living.[8] The Catholic businessman was more likely to be guided by traditional ideals than the Protestants, even though both were "capitalist." In speaking of the Catholic businessman, Weber says,

> The form of organization was in every respect capitalistic.... But it was traditionalistic business, if one considers the spirit which animated the entrepreneur: the traditional manner of life, the traditional rate of profit, the traditional amount of work, the traditional manner of regulating the relationships with labour, and the essentially traditional circle of customers and the manner of attracting new ones.[9]

Weber rejects the idea that the rationalism of the Enlightenment is sufficient to explain the acquisitiveness of Protestant capitalism.[10] Rather, he traces the differences in Catholic and Protestant capitalism to what he calls the "ethical peculiarities of Calvinism."[11] The most salient peculiarity was the Calvinist version of the doctrine of predestination.[12] In Weber's view, this doctrine replaced the "Father" God of the New Testament with a transcendental being, "beyond the reach of human understanding, who with His quite incomprehensible decrees has decided the fate of every individual."[13] The individual believer thus experiences an unprecedented inner loneliness: "No priest.... No Sacraments.... No Church..." can help him because none of these things are efficacious for salvation.[14] This doctrine leads, on the one hand, to a negative attitude toward all things sensual and emotional, and on the other "it forms one of the roots of that disillusioned and pessimistically inclined individualism" which is part of Puritanism.[15] The believer is required, however, to attain a certainty of his own election to salvation.[16] How is this to be done? The answer is through "intense worldly activity"[17] and success in the world. It is necessary to "prove" one's faith in worldly activity and to create a spiritual aristocracy of predestined saints within the world.[18] The gaining of wealth is a sign of God's election,[19] and it is to be combined with an asceticism which precludes idleness or the enjoyment of the wealth.[20]

Although the capitalist spirit begins with a religious spirit, that religious spirit dies out and gives way to "utilitarian worldliness":

> What the great religious epoch of the seventeenth century bequeathed to its utilitarian successor was, however, above all an amazingly good,

we may even say a pharisaically good, conscience in the acquisition of money.[21]

This brings us back to Benjamin Franklin, who was imbued with this spirit of capitalism from which the religious element was missing.[22] Victorious capitalism no longer needed religious support, and the freedom bequeathed by the religious spirit became a necessity that fixes man in an "iron cage" of mere acquisitiveness. In the last stage we become "Specialists without spirit, sensualists without heart; this nullity imagines that it has attained a level of civilization never before achieved."[23]

THE SPIRIT OF
DEMOCRATIC CAPITALISM

This then is the thesis that Novak uses for his starting point. Weber, he states, discovered a new spirit within capitalism. But whereas Weber constructed a critique of capitalism, Novak produces a paean; he specifically rejects Weber's conclusion that a capitalism based on the Protestant ethic leads man into an "iron cage."[24] Rather, he praises capitalism and urges the Church to embrace it; he finds an intellectual lacuna in the Church's rejection of capitalism and wants the Church to "learn from America."[25] The overriding theme of his book is that capitalism and democracy are inseparable, and that the Church ought to embrace both. Capitalism and democracy, Novak believes, spring from the same historical impulses that aimed at limiting the power of the state and liberated the energies of individuals.[26] Weber, for Novak, identifies capitalism as a new spirit in the world, one that depends primarily on sustained growth.[27]

The Fact-Value Distinction

Novak derives from the Weber the fact-value distinction. As Weber puts it, "The question of the relative value of the cultures which are compared here will not receive a single word."[28] For Weber, this distinction is methodological; he merely means that in examining the effects of Calvinism, he is not addressing its truth or falsity. But for the neoconservatives, the fact-value distinction is *ontological,* a part of what "is"; facts are one thing, and values are another, and the two are not connected. For example, in Alejandro Chafuen, we read that there are two kinds of natural law, the analytic and the normative. The analytic natural law is the law of nature and the normative law, the rules of conduct.[29] The analytic natural law describes a strict, unvarying regularity that holds in nature. Economic law, for Chafuen and the neoconservatives, falls under the analytic natural law, and hence "no ethical judgment can invalidate an economic law."[30] Therefore economics is sovereign and "value-free."[31] Chafuen admits that he cannot find this distinction in the Scholastics, but asserts that it is implicit.[32]

Since economics is sovereign and value-free, any attempt to impose an ethical or religious base is counterproductive. At the center of capitalism there is an "empty shrine" without religious symbols, which each person fills for himself;[33] social and economic life is no longer covered by a sacred canopy. "The system of democratic capitalism cannot in principle be a Christian system. . . . It cannot even be presumed to be, in an *obligatory* way, suffused with Christian values and purposes."[34] Indeed, an attempt "to try to run an economy by the highest Christian principles is certain to destroy both the economy and the reputation of Christianity."[35]

We can easily recognize in Novak's account of the fact-value distinction the dichotomies of the Enlightenment, the separation of faith and reason, the consignment of morality to the realm of private opinion, and the reduction of moral discussion to the attempt to impose one's will on others. Recall that this fragmenting of faith and reason left no place for morality to stand, save in the individual will, and especially the will to power. Since he believes that is so, Novak can say that "claims on the part of groups to represent 'conscience,' 'morality,' and 'principle' must be exposed for what they are: disguises for naked power and raw interest."[36]

The Ideals of Democratic Capitalism

Novak identifies six ideals from Weber that constitute capitalism. The first and foremost is the commodification of labor as a condition for its freedom. He believes that the only possibilities for labor are commodification or peonage.[37] The others ideals are reason, continuous enterprise, impersonality through the separation of the workplace from the household, stable networks of law, and an urban base.[38] Novak believes that Weber did not go far enough in his analysis of capitalism because he did not identify it as the system of economic and political liberty, describing it instead as the system of economic rationalism. Entrepreneurship, Novak believes, depends on practical intelligence and liberty, and these are sufficient to overcome the effects of what Weber calls the "iron cage."

Novak believes that a concept of sin is fundamental to economics and underlies all of its ideals; he believes that capitalism is the best system to confront the effects of original sin, not by repressing it, but by allowing it to flourish while placing a check on its power:

Every form of political economy necessarily begins (even if unconsciously) with a theory of sin. . . . The system of democratic capitalism,
believing itself to be the natural system of liberty and the system which,
so far in history, is best designed to meet the premises of original sin, is
designed against tyranny. Its chief aim is to fragment and check power,
but not to repress sin. Within it every human vice flourishes.[39]

Novak's exact meaning is not completely clear. He does not explain why
allowing "every human vice" to flourish will result in freedom or why the
flourishing of vice should be considered praiseworthy. But Novak's meaning
may be related to his view of the "doctrine" of unintended consequences,
which he derives from his reading of Weber. Weber noted that the attempt to
establish an acquisitive religion ended up destroying the religious base and
leaving only the acquisitiveness. Novak seems to be extending this to say
that any attempt to accomplish good things is likely to have unintended and
disastrous consequences. Therefore, in place of a system that emphasizes the
intentionality of acts or their goodness, the "best hopes for a good, free and
just society are best reposed in a system that gives high priority to commerce
and industry."[40]

In addition, Novak identifies pluralism, community, virtuous self-interest,
the communitarian individual, the family, and continuous revolution as the
ideals of capitalism. In all of this, he detects the hand of providence — that
is, God — working through a "system of natural liberty." In this, Novak is
echoing the religious rationalism of the eighteenth- and nineteenth-century
economists who identified economics with "nature and nature's god" and
who saw in such things as the Iron Law of Wages merely the workings of
God's will for the poor.

The Economic, Moral, and Political Orders

A society is built up from the economic, political, and moral orders, and
these orders are, for Novak, separate and distinct.[41] Novak laments the
encroachment of the political order on the economic and the growth of
the federal government; he notes the government's power to destroy whole
industries, such as the nuclear power industry.[42] In discussing the economic
system, Novak notes that it is not a democratic system; businesses should
not be run as democracies because democratic methods are not universally
desirable; organizing industry democratically would be a "grave and costly
error."[43] Further, the encroachments by government impose unacceptable
costs on business. Novak uses the example of requiring pollution controls
at Bethlehem Steel. In noting the "red dust" put in the air by the smelters,

he says, "Only in my adulthood was this same dust suddenly perceived as 'pollution.' "[44]

In discussing the moral-cultural order, Novak notes that it is "the chief dynamic force behind the rise of both a democratic political system and of a liberal economic system."[45] He laments that business is not sufficiently supported by the moral system and that businessmen are likely to be portrayed as villains. He finds that the cultural system does not have sufficient respect for businessmen, who, being men of action, do not make a moral presentation of themselves to the world. Novak laments the "burden of guilt" piled up on business for the problems of the Third World countries whose problems "[Third World leaders] do not consider attributing to themselves."[46] He therefore concludes that the moral-cultural system is insufficiently supportive of capitalism, and that "Democratic capitalism is more likely to perish through its loss of its indispensable ideas and morals than through weaknesses in its political system or its economic system. In its moral-cultural system lies its weakest link."[47]

A Theology of Economics

Novak places the "empty altar" at the heart of capitalism, which requires "not only a new theology but a new type of religion."[48] After all, the economy of the biblical nations was "an economy of caravans and traders," and biblical writers "did not envision questions of political economy we face today." This "new religion" cannot be associated with any particular denomination, since it is a religion of pluralism:

> Yet if Jewish and Christian conceptions of human life are sound, and if they fit the new social order of pluralism, the widespread nostalgia for a traditional form of social order may be resisted.... For the full exercise of their humanity, being both finite and sinful, free persons require pluralist institutions.[49]

It is Christianity that must fit into the new religion of pluralism while "nostalgia" for traditional forms must be resisted; the social order of pluralism becomes the standard by which we judge the faith. According to Novak, the emphasis on Scripture has resulted in a "gap between the Word of God and systems of economic, political, social, and cultural thought."[50] Since capitalism is necessary for political liberty and liberty necessary for capitalism, the role of the Church must be, *a priori*, to support capitalism.[51] Of critical importance to Novak's theology is the idea of man as co-creator with God. Capitalism, he believes, aids this relationship by allowing us to "create" as many goods as possible in an unending stream.

Novak's "new theology" depends on six doctrines, which he addresses "in their Christian form"[52] even though they represent for Novak something more universal. We must keep in mind, however, that for Novak capitalism does not depend on any specific religion and the "empty shrine" remains at its center.

The first doctrine is that of *original sin.*[53] An economic and political system must tolerate sin and allow vice to flourish; because of original sin, no system can be designed to suppress sin. The attempt to do so leads to the law of unintended consequences, the idea that the attempts to do good will only have bad results. Capitalism succeeds because it intends only the good of commerce, namely, goods, and hence ends up doing good, namely liberty.

The Trinity: Novak labels the Trinity a "symbol," since "no one has ever seen God."[54] The point of this symbolic Trinity is to teach us about pluralism and unity and to show us how to act in community without compromising individuality. "Experience and Scripture alike suggest that what is most real in human life, of highest value, is a community of persons."[55] Novak asserts that under capitalism, communities are transformed into "modalities unfamiliar in previous history" because they are not based on kith and kin, but on voluntary association.[56]

The Incarnation: Novak takes a rather pessimistic view of the Incarnation; it is no longer the salvific act of a loving God but the ultimate demonstration of the futility of good intentions:

> The point of the Incarnation is to respect the world as it is, to acknowledge its limits...and to disbelieve any promises that the world is now or ever will be transformed into the City of God. If Jesus could not effect that, how shall we?...The world is not going to become — *ever* — a kingdom of justice and love.[57]

Competition: "A political economy needs bold political leaders who thrive in contests of power....The will to power must be made creative, not destroyed."[58] Novak finds support for this belief in the parables of the talents, of the foolish and wise virgins, of the prodigal son, of the workers in the vineyard who all received the same pay, and in St. Paul's use of sports metaphors. The Christian is

> inspired to noble competition by the example of the saints who have gone before....The competition is relentless. Judgment is constant. Critics sometimes suggest that competitiveness is foreign to a religion of love, meekness, and peace. They have no idea how hard it is to be meeker than one's neighbor.[59]

For all these reasons, it seems wrong to imagine that the spirit of competition is foreign to the gospels, and that, in particular, competition for money is humankind's most mortal spiritual danger.[60]

The Separation of Church and State: Based on the "Render unto Caesar" text (Mt. 22:21), Novak believes that Christian values — or any other values — cannot be imposed on a society. The political system cannot be a Christian system. "On the question of abortion, for example, no one is likely ever to be satisfied with the law, but all might be well advised not to demand in law all that their own conscience commands."[61] The economic system needs special protection *from* religion because "No intelligent human order — not even within a church bureaucracy — can be run according to the counsels of Christianity."[62]

Caritas: The purpose of *caritas* is to teach us realism.[63] *Caritas* is at the basis of contractual communities, which Novak regards as higher than natural ones. "Yet when they form communities, they *choose* them, *elect* them, *contract* for them. The natural state of political community for persons is arrived at not by primordial belonging but by constitutional compact."[64] Our obligations in *caritas* are to raise the material base of society: "A system of political economy imitates the demand of *caritas* by reaching out, creating, inventing, producing, and distributing, raising the material base of the common good. It is based on realism."[65]

EVALUATING NEOCONSERVATISM

Capitalism and Natural Law

The major critiques of neoconservatism are two-fold: it is not new, and it is not conservative. Or rather, what it seeks to "conserve" is the Enlightenment, and what is new is the presentation of nineteenth-century liberalism as "conservative." As such, neoconservatism seeks to continue the project of the Enlightenment to subordinate society to a rationalistic economics, viewed as purely the operation of "natural law," and to continue the project of the modernists to subordinate the Church to the dictates of the Enlightenment. In fact, Novak himself states that "neoliberal" would be a better epithet than "neoconservative,"[66] and one is forced to agree that the tenets of liberalism describe more accurately the actual content of the movement.

Of that content, a dualistic view of natural law is crucial. The Enlightenment sought to cut natural law and morality free from the base of religion and Scripture, to find a principle analogous to Newton's laws of motion to govern the affairs of men. This dualism of physical facts and religious values is explicit throughout Novak's work. The "naturalness" of the capitalistic economic system is exempt from any critique and is indeed not really examined at all in the text, but merely assumed. Although other systems are critiqued, capitalism is assumed *a priori* to be the "natural system of liberty," and this "naturalism" isolates it from any theological critique because a "natural law" system is beyond such critique; one would not "critique" the theory of marginal productivity anymore than one would "critique" the orbit of Venus. But this immediately leads to a contradiction: If the theologian cannot comment on the economics, how can she give a theological defense or critique of *any* economic system? Wouldn't that be purely a matter for the specialists in that field, the economists? As long as the economists differ as much as they do, can a theologian committed to a "scientific" view of economics take sides on purely theological grounds? The very dualism which immunizes capitalism from critique also immunizes it from a defense, or even a comment, from theologians. It would be purely a matter for other specialists. The tenets of capitalism, such as marginal productivity, *cannot be assumed* to be a part of the "natural law," but *must be demonstrated* to be so, something which Novak never attempts, either on theological or economic grounds.

"Facts" Without Values?

Novak's dualistic view of natural law depends on a fact-value distinction which cannot be defended because there are no "naked" facts which stand apart from values. Take, for example, the statement, "The unemployment rate stands at 5.3 percent." This may *seem* like a statement of "objective" fact, but in fact it conceals a host of value judgments. We must ask, for example, "5.3 percent of what?" Of all citizens? Of all adults? Of all residents, legal or illegal? Of all people who may want a job? But how do we judge who wants and does not want a job? Is a person counted in the workforce if they have not sought a job in one week? In two? In ten? And so forth.[67] Every perception of a "fact" involves value judgments; facts do not stand apart from values but are dependent upon them. The idea of a "natural law" that can be perceived without values always ends up merely hiding the value judgments that a person is making behind a smokescreen of facts which are not facts, but judgments.

The Orders of Society

Novak separates society into economic, moral-cultural, and political orders. However, it is clear that he subordinates the moral and political orders to the economic. He laments the "encroachment" of the political order on the economic[68] and finds that the moral-cultural order is insufficiently supportive of capitalism, and, indeed, is the biggest threat to its survival.[69]

Novak discusses the moral and political systems entirely from the standpoint of the support they give, or ought to give, to the economic system. But certainly this is a reversal of the right order of values. There are indeed three such systems, and they are hierarchically arranged. But Novak stands the hierarchy on its head; he subordinates the political and spiritual to the economic. Surely the purpose of an economic system is to provide the necessary material base for the political system (humans living in community) and the moral system (humans' quest for ultimate truth and meaning).

The reason for this inversion of right order lies in Novak's dualism. In the fact-value distinction, only facts can have a real ontological status while values fall into the realm of wishful thinking. Novak makes facts stand over and against values, and hence values must in some way always support facts. But as already noted, these "facts" turn out to be value-judgments that are hidden behind a "scientistic" smoke-screen.

The Empty Altar and the New Religion

Since for Novak the economic system is a matter of pure natural law, it is not an arena of human freedom. Rather, it is "scientific" and hence religion must conform itself to the findings of this science, just as in the past the Church had to conform itself to the findings of astronomy. Conforming itself will require the Church to adopt not just a new theology but even a new religion, since writings from the pre-scientific days of the caravans cannot help us today. With that in mind, Novak reinterprets the traditional Christian doctrines so that they will be supportive of capitalism and analogous to doctrines from other religions.[70] But to accomplish this, he must drain the specifically Christian doctrines of any specifically Christian content. For example, he discusses the Trinity and the Incarnation as symbols only, the former a symbol of pluralism and the later a symbol of the futility of good intentions. According to Novak, because of the Trinity, "the mind becomes accustomed to seeing pluralism-in-unity."[71] It is not quite clear how the three divine, co-equal, and co-eternal persons constitute a form of pluralism. But Novak is certain that they represent the superiority of voluntary associations over natural ones. This appears to be Enlightenment "social contract" theory projected back on the Godhead. But the social contract is pure fiction, and the Trinity is not an analog for such associations: the Father does not offer to beget the Son or negotiate his being with him. For our part, when the umbilical cord was cut, we were not greeted by a lawyer, explaining to us our rights and responsibilities under the social contract. Rather, we were received into communities of kith and kin and received from them gifts of life and language and culture. It is under the aspect of gift (that is, grace) that we must relate Trinitarian love and community to economy. The question that the Trinity, the community of grace and love, poses for us is how we will be stewards of the gifts we have received and make them fruitful in a way that spreads God's gifts in the way he intends.

We can note Novak's pessimism on this very point; after all, he tells us, "If Christ can't bring about the Kingdom, how can we?"[72] This bleak assessment of the Incarnation is really the utilitarianism of Mises rooted in violence and a false idea of scarcity. If the Incarnation was to teach us about "limits" — if there is no hope for a kingdom of justice and love — then marginal utility is the real lesson of the Cross. It is quite true, as Novak says, that we do not strive for utopia, but we *do* strive for the kingdom. The kingdom really is advanced (or retarded) by our actions here in the world. Each one of us has the material responsibility to bring about the kingdom, not indeed everywhere, but in our own little corner of the world. The kingdom is a realistic hope because it is based on the true nature of humanity. Its achievement is the perfection inherent in human nature. Indeed, the full realization of the kingdom is obscured and delayed by sin, but its partial realization is ever present. We work with the full confidence that if we allow Christ to work through us, then we will really advance toward the kingdom.

As the doctrines of the Trinity and the Incarnation are drained of their meaning and allowed to stand as symbols for humanistic and capitalistic values (values which are deemed to be more fundamental) so too are the doctrines of charity, original sin, and the separation of realms. Novak also adds *competition* to the list of doctrines, which is certainly an innovation in Christian theology, or perhaps in any theology. One can chuckle at his idea of "competitive humility," but far more sinister is his use of this novel "doctrine" to sanctify the Nietzschean and Machiavellian "will to power."[73]

Novak passes off Catholic Social Teaching's resistance to liberalism with the statement that the popes have resisted liberalism because they confuse it with anti-clericalism and because they misunderstand "Anglo-Saxon cultures."[74] However, neoconservatism itself is largely irrelevant to the study of justice, and this by its own choice. Neoconservatives rarely speak on subjects like the "just wage," and then usually to question the whole idea or reduce it to irrelevance. From their perspective, this is perfectly logical. If liberalism is the true expression of Enlightenment rationality about the economy, then the concepts taught by the Church must be irrelevant at best and wrong at worst. Either marginal productivity rules our lives, or the freedom to construct just systems does. As a defender of the former view, neoconservatism, ironically enough, really has nothing to say to the businessman as businessman. All that a businessman needs to know comes from utilitarianism, and no one can add to this, certainly not priests and prelates. The purpose of neoconservatism is to serve this utilitarianism in the cultural and political spheres. Hence, its advocates absent themselves from the conversation about justice except to criticize those who view the economic sphere as an arena of human freedom where we can really use our creative talents to discover and implement just systems.

Novak's "altar" is not really "empty"; rather, Novak places the autistic, autonomous self on the altar so that each man can worship himself. And indeed, this is how it must be; man, being a spiritual being, cannot live without an altar. The altar cannot be "emptied"; it will have either an image of God as the mirror of man, or it will have merely a mirror, so that man can worship himself. It is almost too bad that the empty altar is not possible, because the nihilism of such empty worship would be preferable to the worship of the self.

Man as Co-creator

Novak identifies man as a co-creators of the world, and he is correct because humans do indeed have dominion over the earth with the task of bringing it to natural perfection. But this co-creation is not a matter of producing the biggest possible pile of goods; rather, it must be directed toward the good, the true, and the beautiful. Co-creation is the work of discerning the possibilities inherent in the true nature of things and then using our creative talents and efforts to bring these possibilities to fruition. Thus this co-creation is a theological matter and cannot be referred to economics alone; it is never a matter of merely producing whatever can be produced, but of producing things that truly advance human happiness and complete the order of creation.

To give a concrete example, Novak objects to the pollution controls at Bethlehem Steel. The question is, in the first instance, an empirical one: the "red dust" either is or is not pollution. But Novak does not face the empirical question; he merely complains that the perception of red dust as pollution is of recent origin, as if this were somehow germane to the debate. If it is indeed pollution (recently discovered to be so or not), then the discussion can proceed along both economic and theological lines. As an economic point, one would discuss the dust under the question of externalities; it would be a question of whether to place the costs of pollution on the polluters, in the form of removal technologies, or on the citizens surrounding the plant, in the form of higher cancer rates. As a theological question, one would ask both whether the red dust constitutes a true co-creation (perfecting the natural order) and where, morally, the costs should be placed. But Novak does neither; his point turns out to be ideological rather than theological, partisan rather than economic.

Allowing humans to fulfill their role as co-creators is indeed one of the jobs of economics. But there is a real question as to whether the concentrations of wealth and power lead to more co-creative energy or less. Moreover, it is not clear that capitalism alone provides the only route for such creative energy. For example, many of the major technical advances in our society in the last sixty years were the result not of the free market but of government-sponsored research. Nuclear energy, jet aviation, transistors, miniaturization, much drug research, the Internet, and thousands of other advances were the work of such non-market institutions as the government and the universities undertaking research that would simply have been too expensive and risky for a profit-oriented business.

Freedom, Formal and Material

For Novak, liberty is the highest good, but it is a freedom at odds with the Christian formulation. When the Enlightenment separated faith and reason, liberty lost its connection with virtue and became merely the formal ability to choose, not a freedom for any particular good.[75] Thus this "freedom" has no material content; it is a mere formality. But in Christianity, freedom has a material content; it is directed toward the virtues. Christian freedom is the liberty to explore truth and beauty in love. We have the ability to choose to do good or to do evil, but only one of these choices is true freedom. For example, we may choose to use cocaine or not, but one of these choices leads to slavery of mind and body; while the choice may involve a formal ability to choose, once the choice is made, we have enslaved ourselves and lost our freedom, at least to some degree. Christian freedom therefore can never be equated with the flourishing of vices. To illustrate the meaning of Christian freedom, take the freedom of a mathematician as an example. She is free to explore the infinite realms of her art; her research may range over number theory or lattices or topography or fields unimaginable to most of us. A lifetime would not be sufficient to scratch the surface of the truths to be revealed, and an eternity would be filled over and again with new wonders. But what the mathematician is *not* at liberty to do is to proclaim error; she is not free to say, "$1 + 1 = 3$." The very moment she does so, her very "being" as a mathematician is compromised and diminished. Her error will corrupt all of her subsequent calculations, and soon she risks her whole standing as a mathematician and becomes a slave of error. She of course has the *ability* to proclaim such error, but this ability is not liberty. Liberty consists of free acceptance of the truth.

The point here is that freedom can be adequately described not by the mere ability to choose, but by the object of the choices. In other words, there is both a *formal* aspect of freedom (i.e., the ability to choose) and a *material* aspect (the things actually chosen). Some human choices, namely the choice of vices, tend to slavery; others, the choice of virtues, tend toward true freedom. Thus to fully describe freedom, we need both the formal element (the ability to choose) and the material content of the choices (virtue or vice). The choice either to inhale cocaine as a powder or to smoke it as crack indeed involves "free choice," but not real freedom. In fact it is slavery. And here is the poignant and tragic situation of being human: our "freedom" paradoxically contains the possibility of the unfreedom of slavery. But until one realizes that the free choice is between freedom and slavery, one cannot frame the question correctly. True freedom is not compatible with the "flourishing of all vices."

In considering any individual in relation to society, one may indeed make an argument concerning the indifference of the system to particular choices. Further, it is quite true that the state, whatever forms it might take, does not endeavor to stamp out all vice; such a task is beyond both the capability and purpose of a state. However, social questions are also involved in every choice. Is it true freedom to be able to display pornographic images on billboards or the airwaves? Certainly there are commercial reasons for doing so, and one could argue, as Novak does, that commercial freedom must allow the flourishing of all vices. But such "freedom" leads to the cheapening of women and the commodification of sex. Such "freedom" advances the cause not of liberty but of slavery. Hence, it cannot be considered a purely "private" choice; *no* choice is purely private, but *every* choice has some public effect. We have already seen the problems of an undifferentiated "liberty" in regard to land tenure. The "freedom" of monopoly rights in land held without any claim of common values leads to the exclusion of others from owning anything at all and the imposition of the oppressive Law of Rents. Therefore, even at a purely practical level, the question of freedom is far more nuanced than neoconservatism will allow.

Novak is convinced that an attempt to concentrate solely on social justice will lead only to injustice, and he may be right. But then why would an attempt to base an economic system solely on one part of justice — namely liberty — be exempt from the law of unintended consequences? Indeed, if one flattens all questions to the merely formal without attending to the material, one will not even be able to see the law of unintended consequences in action. All consequences, intended or not, reveal themselves only in the material realm; absent the material there will be a blind spot in one's vision. For example, Novak reduces social justice to formal liberty: "Social justice means the freedom to choose one's own destiny, the right to the pursuit of happiness: The right to choose the meaning of life."[76] But even this limited definition ignores the material realm; to realize one's destiny, one needs material goods: an education, health care, meaningful work, and decent housing, among other things. If education is priced out of reach, health care unavailable, and one's job outsourced to India, then the formal ability to "choose one's destiny" will be an empty abstraction with no real meaning.

A *Pharisaically Good Conscience*

Weber noted that a practical result of Calvinism was to provide a "pharisaically good conscience" to a purely acquisitive spirit, the "Spirit of Capitalism." The thrust of Novak's argument is that the Catholic Church must also conform itself to this spirit and must provide the religious arguments for its defense. Businessmen and -women are themselves incapable of providing these arguments, Novak tells us, because they are men and women of "practical matters" unused to theoretical discussions. Aside from the condescension of this statement, it is questionable that theory and practice ought to be divided so that the Church has the role of defending businessmen, while the businessmen are relegated to mere practice. Indeed, businessmen and -women who do not understand the world about them and are concerned only with a pure acquisitiveness, are likely to be ineffective in business as well as incapable of meeting the demands of this increasingly inequitable, unstable, and dangerous world. The function of the Church is not to provide him or her with a defense that eases his or her conscience, but to form the conscience in the way of justice, a justice which, as it turns out, it also sound from a business and economic standpoint.

Chapter 13

Distributivism

It is a negation of property that the Duke of Sutherland should have all the farms in one estate; just as it would be a negation of marriage if he had all our wives in one harem.

—G. K. CHESTERTON

THE TRIUMPH OF LIBERALISM

The nineteenth century saw the triumph of liberal economic ideology, especially as expounded by the neoclassical school. Their teachings became the reigning orthodoxy, and in this case the religious term "orthodoxy" is appropriate because the economists, as we have previously noted, were merely interpreting the will of God expressed through the economic system. However, as much as liberalism triumphed in the realm of theory, it was problematic in the realm of practice. England became both richer and less stable, with widening gaps between rich and poor. The liberal victories, along with the destabilization of society, produced a reaction which in the nineteenth century primarily took the form of socialism of one sort or another. "Socialism" referred to a whole range of beliefs, from guild socialism to communes, from the "single tax" theories of Henry George to the "scientific" socialism of Marx and, most importantly for England, the "Fabian" socialist movement, which sought to impose socialism through slow and steady changes. The Fabian movement was able to attract some of the best talent in England to its banner and became a potent force in English political and intellectual life. By the turn of the century, communitarian and associative forms of socialism had been abandoned in favor of the state socialism advocated by the Fabians.[1]

All of these positions, capitalist, socialist, or Georgist, centered on the status of property, a question that has very nearly disappeared from contemporary debates. Into this highly polarized situation came Leo XIII's great encyclical, *Rerum Novarum*, which muddied the waters by opposing *both*

211

liberalism and socialism and by recalling the Scholastic distinction between the just ownership and the just use of property. As we have seen, Leo's solution was not a rejection of private property, as with the socialists, but its wider distribution through the mechanism of a just wage.

THE CHESTERBELLOC

If we could follow neither a socialist nor a liberal path, what was left? Was there a way to save property from the socialists and freedom from the liberals? This question motivated two great thinkers, G. K. Chesterton (1874–1936) and Hilaire Belloc (1870–1953). Both were former socialists who discovered the power of Catholic teaching as the way out of the seemingly intractable conundrum of property. Their solution has been labeled "distributivism." Belloc had been a brilliant student at Oxford and a protégé of Cardinal Manning. Denied a teaching position at Oxford because of his unfashionable views, he turned to politics, standing in 1906 for Parliament as a Liberal in a district that had never elected one. The district was also "non-conformist" in religion (we might say "evangelical" or "fundamentalist"), and Belloc's campaign agent advised him against mentioning religion. But that was not in Belloc's character. In his very first speech, he said:

> I am a Catholic. As far as possible I go to Mass every day. This (taking a rosary out of his pocket) is a rosary. As far as possible, I kneel down and tell these beads every day. If you reject me on account of my religion, I shall thank God that He has spared me the indignity of being your representative!

The incident is pure Belloc; he was, as we would say today, an "in your face" kind of guy, never one to shy away from a dispute or take the easy but popular answer. To everyone's surprise he was elected. Becoming disillusioned with the party system, he ran for re-election as an independent and won. But by 1910, he was fed up with politics completely and resigned from Parliament, which he felt was merely "secret government by the rich."[2] Belloc was a prolific and popular writer and poet, and his book *The Servile State* (1912) had a tremendous impact on Catholic thinking about freedom and justice.

Gilbert Keith Chesterton was a poet, novelist, and essayist whose unmistakable style combined a gentle wit with an ability to find the paradoxical in every situation. He became the great protagonist for the distributist position in such books as *The Outline of Sanity* (1926) and *What's Wrong with the World* (1910). During a series of famous debates between the socialist George Bernard Shaw and G. K. Chesterton, Shaw labeled the two distributist champions the "Chesterbelloc," a name which stuck. Distributivism became the leading interpretation of Catholic social thought until the time of Vatican II, when it began to be supplanted by more modernist interpretations of both the right and the left—typified by neoconservativism—or by liberation theology. Nevertheless, it is the distributist[3] interpretation that is the most widely *implemented* one and the one with the most practical impact in the world today, as we shall see.

The thesis of distributism is deceptively simple: States are characterized not just by the degree of political freedom granted to their citizens, but by the status of property. Property may be controlled by the state, owned by a few, or widely distributed, conditions that correspond to socialist, capitalist, and distributist states. Belloc worked out the implications of this thesis in his books *The Servile State* and *The Restoration of Property*.

THE SERVILE STATE

Belloc begins by recounting the history of Europe (which we have already covered): how Europe became a slave state at the close of the Roman Empire, how the serfs gradually won their political and property rights so that by the Middle Ages property was widely distributed, how this led to vast increases in productivity, trade, and the growth of cities. And how, finally, the system of widely distributed property came to an end with the seizure of the monasteries and the enclosure of the commons, events which led to the impoverishment of the mass of people. By 1700, power (and property) had passed to a new class, a class of capitalists;[4] the date is significant, because it is a date prior to the Industrial Revolution. This means that capitalism was not caused by industrialism, as some have argued, but the other way round.[5] Parliament, industry, commerce, the universities, the English Church, and the military all came to be dominated by members of this new class.

Belloc then goes on to note that from its very beginnings, capitalism destabilized England. We have already noted how the change in property led to the Poor Laws and the debasement of the currency. This change also destroyed the old system's organic way of dealing with poverty. But so many people were impoverished by the seizure that England was on the verge of social collapse. A "welfare" system was necessary and this was to remain so for four hundred years. Indeed, every attempt to establish a purely capitalistic system destabilizes society. At the same time, capitalism always becomes less "capitalistic"; it begins with an act of government violence and always demands more and more privileges and subsidies. By 1776, the extent of these privileges had been documented by Adam Smith in the *Wealth of Nations*. Capitalism, according to Belloc, is unstable for two reasons: divergence from its own moral theory and insecurity of two kinds.[6]

The moral theory of capitalism is based on freedom, but as ownership is more and more limited, more and more power passes to a small capitalist class and "freedom" at the practical level becomes problematic. The state increasingly becomes a tool to protect "contracts" which are increasingly *leonine,* that is, based on inequality.[7] One side may refuse the contract (the employer), but the other side (the worker) generally has no choice but to accept it because the alternative is starvation. The state can no longer be a neutral arbiter between classes but becomes a defender of one class, upon whom jobs and growth are increasingly dependent. This can be seen in the history of capitalism where, despite its moral claims, state power and capitalist power grow hand in hand. Adam Smith himself noted this problem when he said:

> Civil government, so far as it is instituted for the security of property, is in reality instituted for the defense of the rich against the poor, or of those who have some property against those who have none.[8]

In addition to this moral problem, capitalism also has two kinds of insecurity: insecurity for the workers and even insecurity for the capitalists. There is insecurity for the workers because the wage fetches less in old age, nothing in sickness, and jobs themselves are at the discretion of capitalists[9] (e.g., "outsourcing "). Where few possess the means of production, political freedom and economic security are impossible. A "perfect" capitalism is not possible because the mortality rates among the workers are simply too high.

But capitalism also produces insecurity for the capitalist. Competitive anarchy makes the system as unstable to owners as it is to workers and results in gluts and underselling. In addition, there is tremendous waste in advertising and commissions. Capitalism responds by becoming less capitalistic; it uses the law to raise barriers to competition and to limit liability; the corporation itself is an adjustment to the inherent instability of capitalism that allows investors to limit liability.[10] The ardent socialist does not fear a pure capitalism nearly as much as does the ardent capitalist. The gap between capitalist rhetoric and capitalist practice is evident in the astounding scale of government subsidy and privilege and in the sheer scope and size of government; corporate America does not hire battalions of well-paid lobbyists to ask for less government, but for more privilege, even as it hires armies of publicists to claim that it is doing just the opposite.

Stable Solutions

There is a deep conundrum, then, at the heart of capitalism, one that leaves it always unstable in its "pure" form. Chesterton summed up this conundrum as follows:

> Capitalism is contradictory as soon as it is complete; because it is dealing with the mass of men in two opposite ways at once. When most men are wage-earners, it is more and more difficult for most men to be customers. For the capitalist is always trying to cut down what his servant demands, and in doing so is cutting down what his customer can spend.... He is wanting the same man to be rich and poor at the same time.[11]

Given its instabilities, capitalism must, perforce, find some way of stabilizing itself. Belloc argues that there are only three stable solutions: slavery, socialism, or property (or some mixture of the three). "To solve capitalism you must either get rid of restricted ownership, or of freedom, or of both."[12] Of the three solutions, slave societies have shown themselves to be highly stable over long periods of time, but this solution is precluded by our Christian heritage. But the third solution, what Belloc calls the "proprietary state," is regarded as untenable by the intellectual and political elites, which leaves only the second, some sort of socialism. Thus in *practice* capitalism breeds a collectivist theory which leads to a *servile state*.[13] We may complain as much as we like about the growth of government, but all capitalist regimes, from Roosevelt to Reagan, from America to Sweden, encourage its growth.

And indeed the distributivist solution, that is, distributing property, appears to be difficult to implement. How are we to select the new owners? In absence of a just wage, workers cannot save enough to acquire significant property of their own. Further, the distributivist solution is highly disturbing to current power relationships. And will all people want to own? Many people have become accustomed to being wage-earners and no longer think, as they once did, in terms of making their own livings. These difficulties leave socialism as the easiest solution.

Socialism

Socialism is less "practical" than distributivism in the sense that socialism has never been tried, while distributivism has a real history and serves as a real model. We can examine the past and even the present to see how a proprietary state actually works and what its effects are. But socialism is easier to do; it works within existing arrangements; nothing really changes when the state buys up the waterworks or the trains; the same unpleasant boss that the clerk reports to remains in place; the same bureaucratic arrangements continue to hold. Therefore, the transition to socialism follows the line of least resistance.[14] But socialist practice does not really mean socialism, anymore than capitalist practice has anything to do with capitalism. In practice, socialism, like capitalism, merely means increased regulation, a solution that appeals to both corporate interests and socialist "reformers." Although the rhetoric is different, the results are the same. The "socialist" reformer continues to pile regulations on top of big business, a situation big business is more than content to see, because in return these regulations guarantee greater security from competition and hence greater security of profits. The capitalist becomes increasingly responsible for the welfare of the workers in return for a greater security of property and profits. In the end, you have neither socialism nor capitalism, but servility, the servile state.[15] The owners are free and economically control the unfree. The practical result of all of this is an increasing dependence of workers on the government and corporatist solutions. For example, health care, unemployment insurance, retirement benefits pass from control by the individual to control by the corporation or the state.

The most immediate losers in such a system are small businessmen. The cost of regulation is usually enough to discourage most would-be entrepreneurs from even thinking about starting their own businesses, no matter how much knowledge and skill they have in their own craft. Even the expense of filling out the paperwork, much less the cost of actually implementing the requirements, is large relative to a small business but small relative to a giant one. As a result, many people lose even the memory of ownership and think of themselves as mere wage earners. The instinct for property, and even its meaning, has been lost and with it the sentiment for freedom that only property can bring. The result is a system in which control passes to the owners of capital acting in concert with the state. The workers' needs are attended to, but at a cost of freedom. The system is stable but unfree.

UP FROM SERVILITY

At this point, some may be throwing up their hands and exclaiming, "Property? Look how many people in our country own their homes! Look how many own shares of stocks and bonds! And clearly everybody is free to start their own businesses and become as rich as Bill Gates!" As to our homes, it must be noted that "property" here means not a house per se, but the means of production. And whereas once the home was a place of work, zoning laws and business regulations make it useless or even illegal for use as a production center. The very topography of cities argues against the business use of a home; the house can no longer be a shop by the very decentralization of cities. Even the number of yard sales one may hold in a year is limited by local ordinances. It is true that the state bureaucratic apparatus has not yet adjusted to the Internet, so there are many home businesses that have escaped the ability of the state to control them or even locate them, but that is not yet a big enough factor to fundamentally change the situation. As for the supposed widespread ownership of stocks and other equities, the idea of any real widespread ownership is a myth. In 1998 the top 1 percent of people owned 42 percent of all shares, while the top 5 percent owned 67 percent, the top 10 percent owned 78 percent. Very few people beyond the top 10 percent own shares in sufficient amount to provide any meaningful income.[16] And the situation has deteriorated since 1998. Further, for many people their stocks are held by pension plans which are very likely to go into bankruptcy.

The libertarian may remark that while all this might be true, what is needed is a "return" to true free market principles. Now, I must say that I have a deep respect for libertarians, at least when they really are libertarian; certainly distributism and libertarianism share, at the very least, a suspicion of big government. Indeed, if one is going to proclaim free market principles, one ought to do so forthrightly and not, as is the practice of corporate America, preach one thing and practice another; there is always something to be said for intellectual honesty. Nevertheless, we cannot "return" to libertarian principles because we were never there; it is, quite literally, *utopia*, "nowhere." Capitalism begins with an act of government violence and grows along with government power. We may dream with either Karl Marx or Murray Rothbard that the state will wither away, or at least go on a diet, but that will never happen as long as corporate capitalists run the state.

The servile system has already begun. Indeed, it is already here. The differences between a "socialist" Europe and a "capitalist" America are merely differences of degree rather than of kind. Both depend on the same bureaucratic organization and social welfare systems. Belloc seems to have been absolutely correct in his predictions. The system needed help to stabilize itself exactly as Belloc said it would. But it is interesting to see exactly how it did stabilize itself. The real change came with the introduction of Keynesian economics, which made the government responsible not just for this or that social welfare program, but for making up shortages in aggregate demand by redistributive taxes. In other words, Keynesianism is itself "distributist," or rather "re-distributist," but it redistributes income rather than property. Therefore the debate, in practical terms, is not between distributivism and its opposite, but between kinds of distributivism, between redistribution of income and distribution of property. But one way or another, economic liberalism cannot provide stability on its own; it needs the help of distributists of one sort or another. Income redistribution, being a constant and ongoing process, will always require a vast state apparatus to assess the funds on the one hand and determine eligibility on the other.

Keynesianism has been adopted by nearly every regime, whether of the Right or Left, in Europe and America and large parts of Asia. Countries adopted this system because it seemed to work. The inherent instabilities of capitalism have been rendered less extreme, with depressions rendered much milder than the convulsion which shook this country and Europe at the end of the 1920s. Keynes had no problem with neoclassical economics as such; he was concerned with the problems of unemployment and poverty in the midst of plenty that such economics seemed to be causing, and felt that perhaps a little tweaking of aggregate demand by taxation and redistribution could cure this problem. But Keynesianism did enlarge state power, taxes, and the size of government to previously unimagined levels. We have become accustomed to having the government solve all problems and do so at the highest possible level. Even right-wing administrations have dropped all pretense of "federalism" and seek to intrude more and more on daily life; the teacher in his classroom, the cop on the beat, the shopkeeper in her store become increasingly the objects of federal concern and less of local regulation.

But today the future of the Keynesian arrangement seems in doubt. In both Europe and America, the costs of government seem ready to outstrip the ability of society to support them. Further, the willingness of corporate interests to continue the arrangement is ending; they have invested great sums and great energies in seeking an end to the system and their efforts are paying off. In America the taxes once broadly levied on incomes from both capital and labor are being narrowed to labor taxes alone, with capital increasingly exempted. This is consistent with the theory that growth comes from capital alone and capital cannot be taxed without limiting growth. And corporations are seeking to externalize social costs that have heretofore been part of the wage system, such as medical insurance, pensions, and unemployment costs. However, it is doubtful that shifting these responsibilities can be accomplished without introducing the very insecurities that occasioned the arrangements in the first place. Thus the Keynesian system seems to be caught in a conundrum, the very conundrum pointed out by Chesterton. It cannot continue its Keynesian bargain (and this is especially so in the face of global competition), and it cannot drop it without risking chaos. Is there no way forward from the servility of the modern state? Must we choose between corporate control and chaos?

THE ECONOMIC THEORY OF DISTRIBUTISM

While the distributist critique of capitalism might be trenchant, it would be useless if it did not have an economic theory of its own. Indeed, the charge against distributism was precisely that it is *not* an economic system, but merely a nostalgia for times long gone, or at best a form of agrarianism. This charge was especially pointed since both the socialists and the capitalists insisted on first-class economic research and the distributists did not seem to provide any.[17] While the Fabian socialists and neoclassical capitalists were producing first-rate economists, the distributists did not seem to be producing any at all, and hence it could be assumed that it was a "creed without a dogma."[18]

The charge is only partially correct. The distributists did not do the kind of economic research that the capitalists and socialists did. They did not do this kind of research because they regarded it as largely beside the point. The research program of the neoclassical economists concerned mainly issues of corrective justice, that is, of the rules of exchange, and the distributists had no quarrel with these rules; they regarded them as more or less fixed and self-evident. It required very little research to prove (against the socialists) that free exchange was better than government coercion, or to prove (against the capitalists) that markets were social institutions. It seemed to the distributists that the socialists and neoclassicists had deployed mighty weapons of research to "prove" the patently obvious.

Belloc did indeed produce an economics textbook, *Economics for Helen*.[19] The title was indicative of Belloc's feelings on the matter. "Helen" was taken to be an inquisitive high-school student to whom the rules of economics could be easily explained without a great deal of fuss. Belloc handled the whole of what would now be called "microeconomics" in a mere eighty-three pages, and he did not make any great departures from classical or neoclassical economic theory. But Belloc regarded these things as merely the "arithmetic" of economics, meaningless in itself until it was applied in practical situations in the political economy, that is, in the economy that actually exists in some polity or society.[20] For Belloc, economics are *architectonic*, a mere set of rules a society may use to construct a variety of economic systems in much the same way that an architect will use the laws of physics to construct an endless variety of buildings. In the same way, economics does not dictate one "right" system, anymore than there is just one "right" building. Any actual building, or any actual economic system, must conform to certain laws if it is to remain standing, but the actual shape of the building or the economy will be guided by human intentionality.

We must at this point recall Aristotle's distinction between corrective and distributive justice. Corrective justice deals with equality in exchanges, and hence can be handled (in principle) by simple mathematics with rules that are intuitively obvious to all participants in the market. Corrective justice, therefore, very easily lends itself to a "scientific" or mathematical treatment. But the situation is otherwise when it comes to distributive justice. Since distributive justice deals with distributions from a common fund, say the revenue of a state or the produce of a business firm, it requires some rule of distribution that cannot be based on number. For Aristotle, this rule of distribution should be, in justice, based on *merit*. However, merit cannot be reduced to arithmetic; different societies have different "yardsticks" by which to measure merit. In our society, "merit" equates to market power; people will obtain a price for their goods or their labor based solely on the market power associated with those goods or that labor. A seamstress has much skill but only a little market power, and hence her skills command only a little wage; her market "merit" and her family income are small. But lawyers or real estate agents, on the other hand, though they are as common as fleas, largely control access to the courts or the housing market, and hence their wages are high.

Within any actual political economy, the most important factor, the factor that would control all others, was *property*:

> The very first governing condition of economic production and distri-
> bution in the real world is the condition of *control*. Who *controls* the
> process of production in any particular Society? Who in it owns...the
> means of production, the stores of food and clothing, and houses and
> machinery? On the answer to that question depends the economic
> structure of a society. This control is called *Property*, and [is] the first
> thing we have to study in practical Economics.[21]

As a practical matter, the distribution of property will control all other distributions in society. It is only through wide distribution of property that the problems of the leonine contract can be avoided. Only if people have an alternative to the wage contract can they say "no," and only if they can say "no" can there be a real negotiation. For example, if a seamstress has enough capital to buy her own sewing machine, she is free to accept the wage offered or to enter the business herself as an entrepreneur. In other words, the legitimacy of the wage contract depends on the presence of a certain level of distributive justice *prior* to the negotiation of the contract.

We should now recall that the great neoclassical theorists — Marshall, Jevons, and especially Clark — tried to make corrective justice displace distributive justice. In Clark this took the form of using marginal analysis to compute the distribution of incomes. We have already noted the practical problems with this theory; now we can add another difficulty to it, namely the peculiar status of its starting conditions. For the neoclassical theorists, the market would, by itself, reach a condition of equity once a free market equilibrium was established. Therefore, equity depended on equilibrium. But equilibrium itself depended on a particular initial condition, namely that production be spread over a vast number of small firms. In other words, for the theory to work at all, the means of production (property) must be widely distributed throughout society.

We have now reached the point of supreme irony: as much as the neoclassical theorists may object to distributism, the neoclassical theory *presumes* the distributist theory. The neoclassical theory places equity *after* equilibrium, but assumes equity as its starting point, thereby placing equity *before* equilibrium! Equity, therefore, comes both *before* and *after* equilibrium, and the theory collapses into incoherence: equity in the theory depends on equilibrium, but equilibrium cannot be reached without equity as its starting point.

The distributist theory is much more straightforward: equilibrium depends on equity. All of the mechanisms of corrective justice, all of the "arithmetic" of economics depends on distributive justice. If there is at least a rough equity in society, then all the rules of classical and neoclassical economics will function, roughly, as the theories predict. But if this equity is absent, then neoclassical theories cannot establish it. Neoclassical economics are *Pareto optimal*. That is, exchanges cannot in general change the distribution of goods in a society. Pareto, and neoclassical theory along with him, merely restates Aristotle's observation that exchange takes place between equal values except in the case of fraud.

We may now locate the essence of distributivist economics and its major difference from neoclassical theories. The distributists place equity (distributive justice) prior to equilibrium (corrective justice). The neoclassical theorists do the reverse. Or more accurately, neoclassicism ignores distributive justice entirely, positing that it will result from corrective justice alone.

However, when the neoclassical theories are examined in detail, it is apparent that they unconsciously assume a just distribution, without which the free market could not really be "free," but only highly dependent on leonine contracts. The distributist, on the other hand, has no objection to neoclassical theory insofar as it confines itself to corrective justice (exchanges), but objects when it attempts to make corrective justice displace distributive justice.

THE OWNERSHIP SOCIETY

Those interested in just arrangements in society can only welcome the current rhetoric of "the ownership society." Thus far, the rhetoric occurs entirely within the debate over the future of Social Security. However, it is obvious that reserving a few dollars from the social taxes to buy a few shares of stock will not create an ownership society. That can only come from distributing real ownership of the means of production. While this may sound revolutionary, and is, it actually restores the balance that once existed. Hilaire Belloc was born in 1870 and could recall speaking with men who had been jailed for resisting the last of the enclosure movements. In other words, in his day there was still a real memory of an existing "ownership society," when ownership was considered a natural part of life and not something reserved to a special and limited class. That memory is gone, and too few men and women today imagine themselves making their own way with their own capital. Prior to restoring capital, the *sentiment* for ownership must be restored.

What would be the results of an ownership society? For one thing, insofar as real ownership is distributed, incomes would be more equalized, which would lessen the need of the government to be involved in the lives of its citizens. So long as there are great imbalances, there must be great redistributions or social chaos will reign. The government does not shrink because the government cannot shrink, not in the face of vast disparities between wealth and poverty. It is simply a practical question: the failure of aggregate demand would overwhelm the system, never mind questions of justice and equity.

A second result would be to bring equity to the labor contract, which today tends to be leonine. If the worker has the option of using his own capital to start his own business, the labor contract is more likely to be just; any contractual arrangement is a result of the bargaining power of the parties involved, and cannot be just if one party has no power.

Spreading ownership would also spread political power. States are always responsive to those who hold economic power, regardless of the political form of the state, monarchical, aristocratic, or democratic. The stranglehold which corporate interests have on government could be broken; indeed, it is not really possible to have a real democracy without some sort of economic "democracy" in the form of widely distributed ownership.

There would be particular advantages for businesses as well. They would be less and less responsible for the social welfare of their employees (who would often also be the owners, in whole or part); the income from capital, instead of being passed through the central government to be redistributed, would simply be a normal part of the compensation. Less reliance on taxation would lower the entry costs for businesses. These changes might not be an advantage to big business, but would be a great boon for small- and medium-sized ones, which are often drowned in paperwork and added costs. Further, a greater equality widens the base of the market, making investments more secure. Certainly, to the extent that there is equity in incomes, there is a wider market for any given product, except for high end luxury goods.

Further, in a system where workers own a significant or controlling interest in a firm, wage problems tend to disappear, and with them problems of social security and unemployment insurance. Recall David Ellerman's "residual claimant." When the claimants are the workers themselves, with a share of both wages and profits, the problem solves itself.

Leo XIII in *Rerum Novarum* viewed the just wage as the means of spreading ownership; Belloc reversed that by finding that wider ownership was the means of achieving the just wage. In this, Belloc appears to be correct, as John Paul II acknowledged when he called for associating the worker with the ownership of the workbench at which he labored. It should be clear that the only way to reduce the size of government and increase the range of freedom and justice is to eliminate the need for big government. But as long as there are great imbalances, there will be great bureaucracies.

But is any of this *practical?* Is it merely a pipe dream? Sure, it existed at one time, but times have changed. Can it exist again? As it turns out, not only is it practical in terms of history but also in terms of the current moment; there are indeed distributivist cultures and enterprises which can stand with the biggest and best that the capitalist system has to offer. We will examine these real case histories in some detail.

Part IV

The Practice of Justice
in the Modern Business World

Chapter 14

Taiwan and the "Land to the Tiller" Program

If property is good for Man, it is good for Everyman.

—G. K. CHESTERTON

LAND MONOPOLY AND LABOR MARKETS

We have seen that Catholic Social Teaching has made wider ownership of the means of production a keystone of its idea of justice. The Church has, of course, based this on its authority as a moral teacher, but that moral teaching would be suspect if it could not be shown to have a sound economic base. It is not that the Church makes its moral decisions based on some economic system, but rather that a true morality will eventually be shown to be consistent with economic theory. If the Church is correct in this view, then redistribution of land will be shown to be the basis of a just and stable economic order. Further, this view should be shown to be true both theoretically and in actual historical circumstances.

To some degree, we have already done this. We have seen how, theoretically, the Law of Rents is mitigated or abolished in the presence of a frontier or a commons. In such circumstances, wages stabilize at rates far above subsistence; when the frontier is closed and the commons enclosed, the Law of Rents takes over and wages tend toward subsistence. We have verified these purely theoretical conclusions by noting the experience of England in the fifteenth and sixteenth centuries. We noted that by the end of the fifteenth century, wages had reached nearly four times subsistence and attempts to enforce the Statute of Laborers were futile. But after all the land was "privatized" and the commons lost, wages dropped to bare subsistence levels and the Statute of Laborers became redundant. However, we do not need to look to sixteenth-century England for all of our data; we have enough examples in the twentieth and twenty-first centuries; we have enough data from our own time, both positive and negative. Examples of monopolistic land ownership are, alas, all too common and present themselves for our analysis.

The case for land redistribution can be made in purely neoclassical terms. Where there are few owners, and especially where the few combine to control the market, a monopoly in land is created which in turn creates a *monopsony* ("one buyer") for the labor market; land owners become "price makers" rather than "price takers."[1] Further, the economic control of the labor market is often reinforced by a series of institutional controls, such as the difficulty tenants or laborers have of obtaining credit, use of police power to prevent protests or unions, lack of education in rural areas, and discrimination. All of these obstacles leave sharecroppers or farm laborers at a disadvantage in wage or rent negotiations, making these contracts leonine. The effect is that the landowners can arbitrarily lower the cost of labor to below the marginal rate, reversing the situation in a theoretical "normal" labor market. Since actual wages are lower than marginal wages, wages would have to rise to the marginal rate to increase the amount of labor.[2] This has four consequences from a purely neoclassical perspective.[3] One, the cost of labor is lower than it would be in a competitive environment, resulting in exploitation of the farm worker. Indeed, the low wages make marginal costs higher than average costs. Two, total employment on the farms is lower than it would be because the higher marginal costs make it inefficient (in terms of profit) to fully utilize the land, resulting in surplus labor. The combination of surplus labor and lowered labor costs in turn lowers the *reservation wage* in urban areas, accentuating urban poverty. The reservation wage is the lowest amount a worker will accept, and it will depend on what his alternatives are. If the rate for farm work is lowered, the reservation rate for urban work will also be lower.

The third point follows from the second: since marginal costs are higher than average costs, total output is lower than it could be, resulting in production inefficiencies. Whenever labor costs are artificially controlled through monopoly or monopsony power, average labor cost is likely to be lower than marginal cost, meaning that optimal returns to capital are reached before full utilization of the resource. Which leads to four: although the farm is less efficient, the total profits are higher, which results in an inequality of income distribution and widespread poverty. In other words, the farm is made efficient not in terms of total output, but in terms of total profit.

The implications are that wider ownership of land would raise total output and average income by breaking the monopsony over the labor market. There would be a more equal distribution of income and a reduction in

The Effect of Monopsony on Output, Employment, and Profit

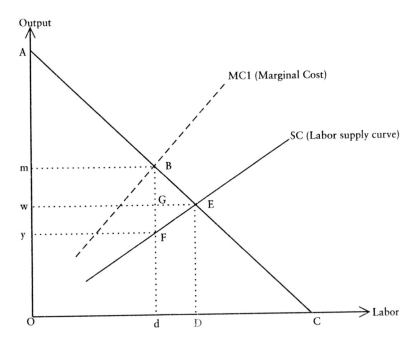

Taken from Keith Griffin, Azizur Rahman Khan, and Amy Ickowitz, "Poverty and the Distribution of Land," University of California, Riverside, October 2001

Normal (Free) Market (marginal costs coincide at equilibrium)	Monopsony (marginal costs higher than equilibrium)
Equilibrium at E, wage at Ow and employment at OD; therefore:	Equilibrium at B, wage at Oy, employment at Od; therefore:
1. Total output = OAED 2. Total wages = OwED 3. Total profit = wAE	1. Total output = OABd 2. Total wages = OyFd 3. Total profit = yABF

Hence, under monopsony

Decline in wage rates by wy (*exploitation*).
Total employment declines by dD (*underemployment*).
Output falls by dBED (*lower production*).
Profit increases by ywGF-GBE (*Economic rent*).

both urban and rural poverty. This in turn would broaden the market in the non-agricultural sectors, allowing for more secure investment opportunities, and advance the broadening of the economy away from the purely agricultural. However, there is a question of *how* to break up land monopolies. Three solutions have been put forward: a market-based solution, favored by the World Bank; a re-distributive solution, in which land is simply expropriated; or some combination of the two. All three have been tried extensively since the 1950s, when land reform achieved a high priority on the development agenda; the first two have been shown to have extensive problems. The World Bank solution hasn't worked for reasons which Belloc laid out in *The Servile State*.[4] In a market solution, by which landowners are simply given the market price for their land, nothing really changes. This is because the market price for anything is simply the same thing in a different form. The ownership of land or money is a claim on the output of society; the market price merely converts that claim from one form to another, from land to capital. The practical effects are that the oppressive rents are merely converted into oppressive interest payments. Nor is this effect mitigated by having the national governments pick up the debt, since governments can only pass on the cost to their citizens in the form of taxes. The market solution simply does not change the power relationships involved — which need to be changed — simply because that is not the function of the market; indeed, a free market depends on leaving power relationships exactly in place before and after a market trade. The World Bank solution has therefore merely saddled the so-called Third World with unmanageable debts, crippling interest payments, and even less of a prospect of being properly developed than they would have without the misguided "help" of the Bank.

But outright expropriation has it problems as well. This is because there is an immediate moral difficulty. It is certainly true that monopoly power is both morally repugnant and economically inefficient, and given that land ownership is a *social* convention society certainly does have the power to limit it. However, it is a stretch to then claim that the current owners have *no* rights whatsoever that society is bound to respect. Certainly, their monopoly rights ought to be terminated, having neither a moral nor an economic root. But neither can the current owners be reduced to penury without creating as great an evil, both moral and economic, as the one expropriation intends to correct. Outright expropriation turns to outright criminality, as it did in the communist nations or in places like Zimbabwe, because it begins in criminality, that is, with a denial of justice.

THE "LAND TO THE TILLER" PROGRAMS

That would seem to leave the third solution, a combination of market buy-out and expropriation. Like expropriation, this solution actually changes power relationships within a given society; like market-based solutions, it recognizes, partially, the rights of existing land owners. In such solutions, there is no magic formula as to the allocation of rights and power; it is arrived at on an arbitrary basis and is purely a matter of judgment. The primary examples of this form of land redistribution are Taiwan, Japan, and South Korea. The historical circumstances in which the redistributions took place are somewhat remarkable, involving the convergence of three events. The first was the explication of Chinese nationalism given by Sun Yat-sen (1866–1925), head of the Chinese Nationalist Party (the *Kuomintang*) which overthrew the Manchu dynasty in China and was in turn overthrown by the Chinese communists. The second was American ascendancy over the East after World War II. And the third was the imperative to effective action given by the fear of a communist victory in all three places, and the need to break the power of an oppressive land-owning class whose very existence had been the biggest practical argument in favor of communism.

Sun Yat-sen had made "land to the tiller" a foundation of the Chinese state, but the Kuomintang, at war with the communists, then the Japanese, and then the communists again, never had sufficient control of China to implement any actual reforms. Further, they depended to a large degree on warlords and large landowners, so that real reforms were politically impossible in any case. In 1949, the Nationalists were defeated by the communists and fled to the island of Formosa, now called Taiwan. The Taiwan that greeted the refugees was an agricultural and feudal society. The war had devastated production, which was at half its pre-war levels. Mostly it was a nation of small sharecroppers with most holding about 2.5–3 acres. Rents were 50–70 percent of the crop, and there was no security of tenure; the farmers could be evicted at will. Most of the land was owned by members of 20 families. Further, since the returns on land were so high, there was little interest in investing in anything but land. In addition, Taiwan had to absorb 2 million refugees from the mainland and bear the costs of defense. It was expected that Taiwan would soon fall to the mainland communists, as the Kuomintang had never proved very effective in controlling China. It was necessary to act quickly to reform Taiwan; it was the very failure to enact reforms which had made the Kuomintang unpopular in China and led to the victory of the communists. They could not make the same mistake twice.

Land reform was based on a program initiated in Japan by General Douglas MacArthur, who after the war was the virtual ruler. MacArthur's plan had both a political and economic purpose: politically, it weakened the landowning class that had supported Japanese militarism; economically, it distributed both income and incentives to innovate among the people. The success of the program in Japan encouraged its application to both Taiwan and Korea. Most of what we say here could apply to all three countries, but mostly we will look at the case of Taiwan.

Taiwan's land reform took place in three phases. In the first phase, starting in 1949, rents were reduced to 37.5 percent, and landlords were required to give six year leases. In addition, the tenants were no longer required to pay rents in advance. The farmers now had an improved income and at least some security of tenure. This also had the immediate effect of lowering land prices since the returns were now lower, which later facilitated the process of land redistribution. Further, during times of crop failure, tenants could apply for a reduction in the rents. The tenant also acquired the right of first refusal if the landowner attempted to sell the land.[5]

In the second phase (1951), public lands were sold to the farmers at a fixed rate of 2.5 times the average yield. These were lands that had been abandoned by the Japanese and taken over by the government; they represented 20 percent of all the arable land in Taiwan. Each farmer could buy 0.5–2.5 hectares of paddy land and 1–4 of dry land. The farmer was lent the money and could repay in kind over ten years. Approximately 266,000 families received land in this phase. The third phase (1953) was the "land to the tiller" proper. The landowners were forced to sell all their land over a small amount at the same terms the government had sold its own land, a price of 2.5 times the yield. About 166,000 families received land under this phase. So in total, about 432,000 families came into possession of their own land. The tenancy rate dropped from 64 percent to 17 percent and the farmers were now paying 25 percent for ten years rather than 50 percent forever.

Note that 2.5 times the annual revenue is a very low price to pay for any asset. Further, no account was taken of the externalities of any piece of land, which in a free market is usually a critical portion of the price. Land prices are normally set not by the productivity of the land, but by the externalities; things such as how close a piece of land is to a population center, the off-site improvements (such as roads or utilities), and so forth, are normally the major determinants of price; all of these were ignored. Thus the program can be considered a partial compensation and partial expropriation of the land.

As such, it actually changed the power relationships within the economy and the government.

The results were dramatic. Farm production increased as farmers used more fertilizer, went to multiple cropping with as many as four crops per year, and diversified production to higher value but more labor-intensive crops. Production increased at an annual rate of 5.6 percent from 1953 thru 1970. The farmers suddenly had something they never had before: relatively large amounts of disposable income. Now they needed some place to spend it. Providing products to buy would require an expansion of industry on the island, if the country was not to be dependent on imports. This necessary expansion was financed in a remarkably clever way. First, the former landowners were paid with 10 percent cash, 30 percent in stocks from four government-owned companies, and 60 percent in industrial revenue bonds. In other words, the government simply printed the money to buy the farms. Normally when governments merely print up some money to accomplish some project, the result is merely an inflationary spiral. But this did not happen. *Why no inflation?* This is where the Taiwanese strategy really becomes clever. The bonds that the landowners received were negotiable industrial bonds which they could then invest in any light industry they chose.[6] Indeed, there was nothing else they could do with the bonds; it was a case of "invest or die." The strategy was twofold: get capital, in the form of land, into the hands of farmers; get capital, in the form of industrial investment, in the hands of entrepreneurs. Note that the strategy provided both goods to buy and purchasers to buy them; it was a *binary* strategy, giving equal weight to production and consumption. A tremendous number of capitalists were created overnight; the former landowners, who previously had no interest in manufacturing, were converted into instant urban capitalists and had to find places to invest the proceeds from the land sales; the landless peasants became proprietors. By this method, the government provided support to Taiwan's fledgling industrial base. But the fact that the actual companies to invest in were picked by the former landowners meant better investment decisions than if the government had tried to pick the winners itself. Industrial production expanded, giving the newly empowered peasants some place to spend the money buying *locally* produced goods.

We can see the Taiwanese experiment for the conjuring trick it was: the government sold land it didn't own, bought with money it didn't have, and financed industries that didn't exist; the government managed both to expand the consumer market and to provide the industrial production necessary to serve that market and serve it from local resources. There was no inflation because the money supply expanded at the same rate as production by a sort of automatic method. Redistribution allowed for expansion of the consumer base which allowed for expansion of the industrial base. It is not often in business and economics that one gets to see solutions which are elegant and beautiful, but certainly the "land to the tiller" program qualifies. We can also note that all of this was accomplished with relatively little foreign aid or development assistance; the United States provided the 10 percent cash that the landowners received, but the rest was pure monetary "magic."

The story in Korea was much the same. In 1945, the American military government reduced the rents from 50–60 percent down to 33 percent. Later the provisional government forced the larger landlords to sell their land at a price of three times the annual output to be paid in fifteen years. However, the actual price was in reality only 1.8 times the produce, since the price was set using the depressed post-war averages.[7] In 1949 and 1950, there were further forced sales, the owners being compensated in bonds that could be used to buy the industries left behind by the departing Japanese, which represented 80 percent of Korea's industrial base.[8]

INDUSTRIAL POLICY

The benefits of land distribution would not have been half so great had it not been coupled with an intelligent industrial policy. The monetary conjuring trick which provided land to the peasants and capital to the entrepreneurs worked in concert with the industrial policy that began where Taiwan actually was: in a very primitive state. The "light industries" in which the bonds were invested were very light indeed. Few had more than 25 employees, and the average number was just eight. But a business — any business — always depends on a network of other businesses. To set up shop, one first needs land, then a building, office supplies, telephones, delivery services, furniture, machinery no matter how primitive, and so on. Business breeds business. But the Kuomintang was especially interested in a particular kind of business: import substitution. Since Taiwan's own industrial capacity was limited, most manufactured goods had to be imported. The government encouraged import substitution industries, first in such things that were easy to make, such as shoes, clothing and textiles.[9] Import substitution was a key part of development strategy; local resources were used to produce what had previously been imported, and a judicious but limited use of tariffs was designed to give local businesses the edge.

Taiwan was still a low-labor-cost state and hence there were transplant factories, what we now call "outsourcing." Manufacturers in Hong Kong and Japan contracted out some work to Taiwan. This gave the Taiwanese valuable experience in setting up factories and managing production. In learning how to make things cheaply for others, they learned how to make the same things for themselves. But the skills learned were then used to set up their own factories.

To encourage efficient use of the land, a *Georgist* tax policy was followed. *Georgism* was a nineteenth-century theory developed by Henry George (1839–97). George was probably the best-known and most popular economist of his day; some measure of his popularity can be gleaned from the fact that at his death, over one hundred thousand people filed past his coffin, while thousands more were unable to get into the hall. His major work, *Progress and Poverty*, was a best seller for many years, and his ideas had a tremendous influence up until recently. Basically, George noted that while the Law of Rents allocated all values above subsistence to the landlord, the landlord did not actually *do* anything to earn those values. George also noted that the landlord's claim to the land was based not on any natural right, but on government power alone. Further, the rent of land was due totally to the external factors: population and off-site improvements. In other words, the landlord added no values to the land per se. Yet, land tends to be taxed lightly while the improvements on land tend to be taxed heavily. For George, this reversed the logical order. Land should be taxed to its full rental value, while improvements should not be taxed at all; land after all is pure gift, while what a person makes off the land is his or hers alone, or should be. Thus Georgism is often called the *single-tax* theory, since there would be only land taxes. George believed that the single tax would force down the price of land by making it unprofitable to hold parcels for speculation, while encouraging development by leaving both labor and improvements to the land untaxed. One can say that George *socialized* the land while *privatizing* its development; it is an interesting view of the questions of the social and the private values of land that we have previously examined. Sun Yat-sen was an admirer of Henry George and made his ideas part and parcel of Chinese nationalism; hence George's theories were spread through the East. In fact, both Singapore and Hong Kong are based on Georgist principles. In pre-communist Hong Kong, all the land was owned by the government and leased to developers (which is equivalent to a 100 percent tax rate), while in Singapore, the government owns 65 percent of the land. Needless to say, both are very prosperous states. Georgism deserves a fuller treatment than this,[10] but for our purposes we can note that Taiwan followed a Georgist policy to encourage development while keeping other taxes relatively low.

EQUALITY AND DEVELOPMENT

Taiwan followed an import replacement scheme right up the industrial scale from cheap cloth shoes to shipbuilding, steel making, and electronics, and became a great trading nation. At the same time, Taiwan was able to create an economy with greater equity, in complete contradiction to the *Kuznets curve*. The Kuznets curve states that development and *in*equality first rise together before falling in later stages of development to form an inverted "U." Despite the lack of empirical evidence for this thesis, it is standard development dogma.[11] It is often used as an excuse for development programs which seem only to widen the gap between rich and poor without any discernable benefits to the people. But in Taiwan, along with Korea and Japan, rapid development and increased equality went hand in hand.

One of the standard measures of inequality is called the *Gini Coefficient,* which measures a society's distance from a "perfect" equality in income distribution; a Gini score of zero would indicate "perfect" income equality, and 100 would indicate a situation where one person had all the income. Taiwan measures .33 on this scale; the United States, by comparison, measures .464. The ratio in Taiwan between the earnings of the top 20 percent to the bottom 20 percent declined from 15 to 1 in 1950 to 5 to 1 by the 1970s. The current ratio for America is 14.6 to 1.[12] Taiwan has managed fifty years of high growth rates, increased equality, and low tax rates (comparatively). Unemployment was low to non-existent through most of Taiwan's post-war history. Before 2000, it rarely exceeded 3 percent and usually was less than 2 percent. Since 2000, the rate has risen as high as the low 5s before dropping back to the 4 percent range as Taiwan struggles to adjust to outsourcing to mainland China. By human measures, Taiwan's growth was also a great success. For example, the literacy rate increased from 45 percent in 1946 to 93 percent in 1989; life expectancy went from fifty-nine years in 1952 to seventy-four years in 1989 while the per capita caloric intake went from 2,078 calories to 3,070 in the same period. Living space per person went from 4.6 square meters to 23.8.[13] Further, Taiwan and the other "Asian Tigers" were able to achieve these successes despite having population densities among the highest in the world, a fact which contradicts the prevailing dogma that population density is an impediment to growth.

Taiwan is, of course, far from utopia. For one thing, its very success has brought with it a corrosive consumerism which threatens the very roots of the social order and cohesion upon which these decisions were made. For another thing, the ownership that was granted to farmers was not often extended to industrial workers. It is likely that coping with the challenge from China will require the same kind of redistributive programs for urban workers that were extended to farm workers. Nevertheless, Taiwan, Korea, and Japan have demonstrated the great effectiveness of redistributive policies in providing development with equity; these examples are sufficient to show that the Church's faith in redistribution and equity are not just sound moral imperatives, but sound economics as well. In only a single generation, Korea and Taiwan were able to transform themselves from feudal and highly unequal societies into industrial powerhouses while overcoming poverty and inequality. As such, redistribution of productive assets should provide a model for development. This is an especially important question, given the destabilizing inequality and lack of development that exist in the world today; moreover, the question is made more important today by both the phenomenon of "globalization" and the precarious security situation in the world. But despite the evident success of these models, they are not the models that have been followed by the World Bank and other development institutions; the latter have followed different dogmas, with tragically different results.

Chapter 15

Development and Globalization

They call it the free market, but I call it turbo-capitalism because it is so profoundly different from the strictly controlled capitalism that flourished from 1945 until the 1980s, and that brought the sensational novelty of mass affluence to the peoples of the United States, Western Europe, Japan, and all the other countries that followed their path.
— EDWARD LUTTWAK

THE GROWING GAP

Hardly a day goes by when we do not receive some reminder or appeal concerning "Third World" poverty. We are inundated with pleas for aid for disasters both natural and of human origin: tsunamis, AIDS, poverty, genocidal wars, you name it. One would think that these near-constant appeals would sensitize us to the situation of our poorer brothers and sisters throughout the world. Yet the results seem to be just the opposite. For one thing, the constant international appeals have made poverty something "remote" to us, something that occurs in "backward" societies far away, and not in our own country; in an era of globalization, however, poverty is not confined by national borders. In the same way, these appeals also "distance" our own involvement in this poverty; we assume that they relate to conditions for which we bear no responsibility. Indeed, we feel that we have done all that anybody could reasonably be expected to do. We have given to all the appeals — generously — and we have set up well-funded institutions such as the World Bank and the International Monetary Fund (IMF) to promote development. Further, we have "globalized" the economy and allowed the poorest of the poor to compete with us for our own jobs. If average Americans feel a certain "donor fatigue," they certainly have some excuse; if they feel that their own generosity has eroded their own well-being and stolen their own jobs, they are not far wrong.

238

The problem is real enough. According to the IMF, the gaps between rich and poor countries, as well as the income gaps between rich and poor people within countries, have all grown even in the face of enormous economic growth.[1] The Third World is saddled with un-repayable debts for loans which were supposed to increase the welfare of the people, but which instead have made real reform impossible due to the fiscal burdens of debt repayment. Given this situation (and few deny it), a growing chorus, which includes the Church, urges the West to merely cancel the debt and start all over again. Pope John Paul II put this project at the center of his millennium celebrations. But would merely canceling the debt achieve any real progress? As William Easterly points out, if the $2.3 trillion given so far hasn't improved the situation, will another $2.3 trillion work any better?[2] To update the dictum of Senator Everett Dirkson, "A trillion here and a trillion there, and pretty soon you're talking about real money." And yet the intractability of the problem is itself surprising, given the relative ease, cheapness, and success of development efforts in Korea, Taiwan, and Japan. Why was a little money so successful but a great deal of money so counterproductive? Why does it seem that the results are inversely proportional to the amount of money spent? Further, the problems have increased in the face of globalization which was itself considered to be part of the solution. Something has gone terribly wrong.

No longer can this problem be considered something "remote" because the realities of international trade put us in direct competition with people who are paid starvation wages; if their economies do not develop with justice, justice in our own country must suffer, as indeed it has. Where development has been just, as in Taiwan or Japan, their workers pose very little threat to us and even add to our well being; but where development has been unjust, as in Bangladesh, their poor and our poor and even middle-class workers must compete for the same jobs on unequal terms in a battle that forces us to adopt Third World standards of living. The problem then is not mere "development," but development with justice. Justice will benefit everyone; without it, the world will be destabilized with the result of constant war, depression, and the globalization of poverty. To understand the relation of justice and development, we must first look at the history of the problem and then at the way in which trade and development are actually related.

THE WORLD BANK

The relationship between development and justice is not lost on the major world agencies charged with development, particularly the World Bank. Yet the actual policies they have adopted have worked to undermine justice.

The World Bank was formed at the Bretton Woods Conference (1944) in a far-sighted effort to provide for post-war stability and a just world order, as well as to combat the growing influence of Soviet Communism. At first this policy worked very well. After World War II, the United States printed billions of dollars to send to the devastated nations of Europe, dollars which allowed them to buy machinery and materials from this country and each other. There was a mildly inflationary effect in the United States, but it was wisely considered a small price to pay for a peaceful and prosperous Europe, especially in the face of the Soviet threat.[3] Of course, the problem for Europe, even a Europe reduced to rubble by the war, was a relatively simple one: it was to rebuild the industrial structure that had previously been in place.

Since the successes in rebuilding Europe, the course of world development has not run so smoothly. In fact, it has been a nearly unbroken record of expensive failures, failures increasingly dominated by Western notions of industrial development. Before 1968, the Bank focused on large infrastructure projects, such as dams, highways, factories, airports, harbors, etc. But these "instant industrialization" projects simply did not work, except perhaps to disrupt economic arrangements which had existed for centuries. World Bank dam projects, for example, displaced 10 million people worldwide but enriched only small minorities. After 1968, the Bank concentrated on human development schemes involving education, health care, and birth control. These schemes turned out to cost more than even hydro-electric dams, but did little to aid development.

In the 1980s, the World Bank had another change of heart. At the urging of the Reagan administration, the Bank saw its role as establishing "free market" economies. As a condition of "rescheduling" or forgiving the unpayable debts from the Bank and the IMF, governments were required to balance their budgets, reduce social spending, and act against "wage rigidity," that is, high wages resulting from unions or government protections. Of course the great irony of the American insistence on these so-called "Structural Adjustment Programs" (SAPs) was that they were pushed by Washington at the precise moment when Washington was tripling its own debt with huge budget shortfalls and transforming the United States from a net creditor to a net debtor nation.[4] It is unlikely that the United States itself could have met the requirements of the SAPs it was enforcing on the Third World. But the SAPs were ironic in another sense. They were built on doctrinaire models of the "free market" economy, models that have never existed in practice. Contrary to the market myths, there have never been any successful economies of the type envisioned by the SAP models. Great Britain grew great not by *laissez-faire* capitalism, but by an aggressive protectionist mercantilism with imperialism. The United States grew rich on the vast wealth of "free" land and minerals conquered from the Indians combined with a protectionist policy. All the Western governments tamed the rough edges of a "pure" capitalism with varying degrees of Keynesian redistributive policies, the precise policies they were insisting that the Third World abandon. A relatively free market is a *necessary* but not a *sufficient* condition for prosperity; something further is required if chaos is to be avoided.

The effects which result from a doctrinaire concentration on pure free market solutions can easily be seen in a comparison between the countries which made the transition from communism to capitalism in the 1990s. In Russia, the government followed the "shock therapy" recommended by the IMF and the World Bank; the effects of this shock campaign on the Russian economy were only slightly less damaging than the effects of the "shock and awe" campaign on the economy of Baghdad. Harvard-trained *wunderkind* wrote plans for an economy they knew nothing about based on models which had never worked in practice. In the name of a free market, they ignored the long established series of *de facto* property rights which had grown up under the noses of the communist government.[5] Instead of a plan which recognized these rights, such as employee and management buyouts, cooperatives, employee stock option plans or other well-known and well-tested methods, a novel and untested voucher plan was concocted, one which dispossessed the current stakeholders and their *de facto* property rights in favor of a scheme that was easily manipulated by those with inside knowledge. The result was that the wealth of Russia was looted and passed into the hands of a small group of oligarchs, instant billionaires who gamed the system and outsmarted the IMF, the new Russian Federation, and the doctrinaire advisors who had dreamed up the scheme. The ordinary Russian was stripped of his ordinary and customary rights, and Russia has reverted to autocratic rule under a former KGB agent who appears intent on returning the country to the "good old days" when the government pulled all the strings and shut down dissenting voices.

By contrast, China neither sought nor accepted "aid" from the development agencies, but adopted a home-grown strategy of "incrementalism," an experimental approach involving continuous change in an attempt to discover what works and what doesn't on a small scale before transposing it to a larger scale.[6] The results were dramatically different from those in Russia, the beneficiary of the West's best advisors. In a little more than a decade, China became an industrial powerhouse, the prime financier of the

American debt, one of our biggest suppliers, and now a purchaser of important American assets, even strategic assets. This is by no means to endorse the Chinese brand of capitalism, but it is to point out how much better development goes without the aid of the development agencies.

Aside from the rise of the communist states, the World Bank represents the largest experiment ever attempted in social engineering. Underlying all of its various twists and turns of policy is the idea that there is a group of people, primarily Americans, who know what is best for the world, and that with the proper combination of money and incentives, "backward" nations can quickly be brought up to our level. When this fails to happen, as is usually the case, blame is laid on the failure of leadership in the recipient country and on their corruption and ineptitude. Certainly, when we read of the failures, the corruption, and the genocidal tribal wars, it is very easy for us to accept this version. However, in truth it is the very size and scale of the aid which funds and encourages the corruption and makes real reform almost impossible. The money is used as a tool of foreign policy to prop up dictators and strongmen considered "allies."

Take the case of the Volta River Dam in Ghana. After Ghana achieved its independence from Britain, its leader, Kwame Nkrumah (1909–72), wanted to leap immediately into the industrial age, a goal encouraged by the World Bank and other development agencies. Nkrumah was a Western-educated socialist, imbued with the then-fashionable ideas of industrialization and development. He had little feel for the native economy of Ghana built on the fecundity of the Volta river valley. Nevertheless, his plan was a reasonable one, at least according to the doctrines of the day. Ghana had large deposits of bauxite (aluminum ore), but processing the ore was an energy-intensive process. Nkrumah hoped that damming the Volta would produce enough electricity to process locally mined bauxite.

A plan was put together with the help of the World Bank and USAID (United States Agency for International Development). Ghana would put up 50 percent of the money and the aid agencies the rest. Kaiser Aluminum would build the plant. But Kaiser insisted that the electricity be priced below its cost, which made the dam a losing proposition. Nkrumah agreed to this demand because his real goal was to develop the bauxite mines and enter the modern age with high-value trade. However, after the dam and the smelter were built, Kaiser refused to accept local bauxite and shipped in ore from their own mines in other areas. This meant that the people of Ghana and the World Bank were merely subsidizing Kaiser and that little locally produced wealth would result from the project. Nkrumah, feeling increasingly beleaguered, became more erratic and threatened to go to the

Russians for help. However, that came to naught because he was removed in a military coup in 1966 which was rumored to be the work of the CIA. As luck would have it, the newly installed leaders did not want to develop the mines, and Kaiser was free to use Ghana as a cheap source of electricity and labor.

The lake behind the dam consumed 4 percent of Ghana's arable land and dispossessed eighty thousand farmers, who were given inferior land which could not support them. Half of them ended up as landless paupers, a situation which contributed later to tribal warfare in Ghana over land rights. Further, the dam was an ecological disaster for the fertile lands, which further exacerbated the problems of the existing economy. Ninety-nine percent of the dam's electricity output was consumed by the smelter, and the project contributed little, if anything, to the electrification of the country. Kaiser got a cheap source of labor, electric power at one-tenth of the world price,[7] and a pliant regime, while the Ghanaians ended up with few benefits, large debts, a military dictatorship, and a crippled native economy. But the Ghanaians got something else as well, something a little worse: they got the blame. It was easy to portray them as a hopelessly backward people given to corruption, incompetence, and warfare and unable to handle the demands of a modern society; it is easy to believe this because it perpetuates racial and ethnic stereotypes. Never mind that these things were largely imposed on them by forces outside their country and beyond their control.

If the World Bank approach hasn't worked, what would work? And what are we to do with the World Bank? Should it be abolished? The advice of David Ellerman, an economist with ten years' service at the World Bank, is that the Bank should be "decentralized with extreme prejudice."[8] It is not that the eight thousand employees of the Bank don't *want* to do the right things, it's just that the Bank is structured to do what it has been doing: move billions of dollars to pointless projects. As for the debts created by the Bank, it will do no good to abolish them, as Easterly points out, if this is merely a prelude to a new round of borrowing; there is simply no reason to believe that another trillion won't go the same way and have the same results as the last trillion. In order to understand what would work, we need to understand two things: how trade contributes to growth and how justice contributes to trade.

THE VALUES OF TRADE

Trade is indispensable to growth. No region is or should be self-sufficient. Regions which try to be self-sufficient, perhaps for political reasons, such as North Korea, or because they have been bypassed by development and roads, such as Appalachia, suffer a degeneration not only in economic terms, but in social and cultural terms as well. When one is required to be a jack of all trades, one is unlikely to be a master at any one of them. Trade exhibits a whole range of positive values, only some of which are purely economic, but all of which are vital to a healthy society. However, these same values can be perverted into their opposites by a lack of justice.

The Essential Goodness of Trade

In any given trade, both parties to the trade profit in some way. This is the lowest but most indispensable value, for without this mutual benefit, the trade simply does not take place. From the standpoint of the parties, this is the most important value, but from the standpoint of the society, it is the least important value, of interest mainly to the parties involved. But flowing from this "private" advantage, there is a range of higher values. The first are purely economic values: trade allows cities to specialize in what they do best from local resources; it extends the market for any particular good, so that it may be provided at a higher volume and lower price; it helps to smooth out production highs and lows because while the market for a commodity may be down in one region, it may be up in another. These and other purely economic benefits accrue to trade.

Aside from the economic values, there are social and cultural values. For example, trade establishes a constituency for peace; no one wants to go to war with a profitable trading partner. No matter what the tensions may be between particular nations, the persons on both sides who are trading partners are motivated to work for a peaceful resolution of any and all problems. For the same reasons, trade leads to an exchange of ideas and a broadening of culture, even (or especially) if one is trading with a cultural or religious "enemy." For example, after the collapse of the Western Roman Empire and the descent into the Dark Ages, the works of Aristotle were lost to the West. They were re-introduced into the West following the trade routes with the Muslims; the bridge that theology alone could not build was built by trade, and the Scholastic revolution in philosophy had its foundation in the trading fleets of Venice and the merchants of Toledo. Further, since development depends on constant innovations, there is a continuous improvement of the arts and sciences. This in turn gives an impetus to education as skilled workers and managers are required.

Perversions of Trade

Trade, then, promises to increase both the material and spiritual wealth of a nation. It exhibits a whole range of values from the purely economic to the purely intellectual. However, each and every one of these positive values can be perverted into its opposite by a lack of justice in trade. In a normal trade, equal values are exchanged; there is no way for one side to profit at the expense of the other side. When this balance is absent, when there is oppression or fraud involved, then the whole of trade becomes an exercise in oppression. Starting at the lowest level, oppression arises in trade when the values are not equal. This happens, for example, when some nations are forced to sell their raw materials or other products at below-market or controlled prices. Imperialism was built precisely on this principle. The other factor that perverts just trade is unjust labor markets. When workers cannot obtain a decent wage, it destabilizes trade in both countries. The immediate parties to the trade still benefit; in fact, their financial benefits are increased. The owners of the firm in the exporting country get a higher rate of profit due to their control of the labor market, while the importers get their goods at a lower cost. However, market equilibrium is lost. The workers in the exporting country do not make enough above subsistence to support local businesses, which will always depend on the earnings of the mass of workers and not just the elite of owners. At the same time, workers in the importing country will be forced to compete with subsistence laborers, leading both countries into a death spiral, with workers racing to the bottom in a competitive frenzy. This ultimately diminishes trade, as the income levels begin to sink among the mass of workers. While the rich may profit handsomely, they can never make up in their purchases the failure of aggregate demand provided by the mass of men and women. Adam Smith noted this fact when he said, "the rate of profit is highest in those nations going fastest to ruin."[9]

We can also note that the insecurity this induces among the workers eventually spreads to the owners, since their businesses are always at risk from competition from other unjust labor markets. The instability noted by Hilaire Belloc for both workers and owners is being played out before our very eyes as the American manufacturing base erodes, not because of inefficiencies, but because of a lack of justice in trade. Employers can stave off the disaster for a time by joining the downward spiral, for example by depressing their own workers' wages or by outsourcing the work, but these actions can clearly be seen as a mere stopgap, a way-station on the road to ruin. Let us be clear here: It is not that workers in all countries should be paid the same. Workers should be free to leverage their lower standards of living into a competitive advantage. But this only works if the object is to raise their material well-being above the level of subsistence as defined by their particular society. Obviously, this level will not include everything it includes in our society; it is unlikely to include a car, a big house, or even indoor plumbing. But if workers get subsistence and something to spare, the "something to spare" will support many local businesses, which will then raise the demand for labor and with it the average wage. Further, the excess over subsistence will contribute itself to trade, as workers, or at least the lowest level of businessmen, have incomes sufficient to buy foreign goods.

But if, on the other hand, workers can command no more than subsistence, then subsistence itself will be defined downward; the human capacity to endure hardships will allow for increasingly oppressive conditions. As this process continues, workers will lose what little bargaining power they have, because there will be no excess to support them in times of unemployment, and they cannot withhold their labor, even for a day. In such cases, the only thing worse than *being* exploited is *not being* exploited; one must work at the terms offered or starve. At this point, all the positive values of trade disappear into a black hole. Education will not be advanced because only the meanest labor is desired, labor which can be done by mere children, the easiest of all groups to exploit. Women will not be able to attend to the home, since they are the next easiest group to mistreat.

Previously, we saw how Taiwan and similar nations were able to leverage their low-wage situations into high-wage, high-value products. They did so by establishing, as well as anyone can be expected to, a just system and by having an object in mind, a public purpose for their economy. But when this common purpose is missing and everything turned over to mere private interest, the trading system works not to increase the well-being of all, but the well-being of a few and the misery of the many. Society then becomes the slave of an abstract economics and ripe for revolution and disorder. The course of business in states like Taiwan, which had some common purpose at the root of their business practice, soon moved from a low-wage to a high-wage status and improved the lot not only of their citizens, but of ours as well. We get goods at a lower price than we could make them, but they buy goods from us that they do not make. The connection between justice and trade is not something abstract; the businessman or -woman has a, interest in justice not as a matter of morality alone, but as a matter of shrewd business practice.

There are other perversions of just trade that we can note. For example, when one nation seeks exclusive control of lucrative trade routes or critical supplies, trade becomes not an inducement to peace, but a cause for war. The wars in the Middle East, for example, may or may not be about oil, but it is certain that without oil, any other issues would not have seemed as pressing as they were. History is littered with trade wars of varying types and intensities.

Fair Trade and Protectionism

If trade is not the problem, protectionism cannot be the solution. A nation that isolates itself from healthy and just competition for trade does so to its own ruin, as we can see in the case of North Korea. Protectionist tools can be useful for limited goals or short periods, but cannot be a general policy. However, the theory of free trade is often misunderstood; the theory is based on the work of Adam Smith and David Ricardo. Ricardo demonstrated that nations could benefit from free trade, but only under three conditions: capital must not be allowed to cross from high-wage to low-wage countries; each country must have full employment; and the trade must be balanced between the participating countries.[10] All three of these conditions are violated in current practice. Adam Smith allowed for protectionist tools in three cases. One case was for industries connected with the national defense: even if France could have made warships more cheaply than the English, it was not a good idea to outsource defense to the enemies. Since a merchant marine is necessary in time of war, it was legitimate, in Smith's opinion, to grant protections to the home merchant fleet. The second exception was to respond to barriers from other countries, for as long as they kept those barriers in place. The third exception was to impose the same burdens on foreign manufactures that were imposed on domestic ones. For example, if a certain product made locally was required to pay a certain tax or meet a certain standard, the same tax or standard could be levied on the imported product.[11]

Smith's exceptions and Ricardo's conditions, if interpreted too broadly, would cover the entire United States economy; indeed, it would be merely protectionism by another name. Virtually every product made in this country is covered by a wide range of regulations covering the environment, labor, health, safety, etc., standards that other nations do not and frequently cannot impose or enforce. We impose these regulations to ensure the safety of our workplace and the quality of our lives, but in other situations these regulations might constitute an intolerable burden on commerce. However, if these exceptions are treated with prudence, they become the foundation of a philosophy of *fair trade*, one that can advance both justice and trade at the same time.

For example, say that in a certain country, needle workers are paid ten cents for making a shirt that is exported to this country and sold at a final retail price of $20–$30 (a common case). Let us say further that this is a starvation wage for that society, but that a wage of thirty cents would afford some comfort and security as it is understood in that society. The difference of twenty cents would not make any appreciable difference in the competitiveness of the product. However, those twenty cents represent the difference between oppression and some small degree of freedom for the seamstress; they represent a better diet, improved housing, and perhaps some savings against sickness, unemployment, or even against the day when the worker will have enough to start her own small business. Under such circumstances, it is legitimate to impose a punitive tariff, let us say ten times the difference or $2 per shirt. That would raise the total labor-related cost (since the tariff is related to the labor rate) to $2.10 per shirt. The exporter would be faced with a choice of coming up with an extra twenty cents for his worker or with an extra two dollars for the American taxman. Quite obviously, he might be inclined to improve the lot of his workers rather than improve the finances of the United States government. The effect on the exporting country would be tremendous. With more to spend, there is more to support the local businesses, and hence increase the local market for labor — as well as everything else — and thus help to "naturally" raise the labor rate in that country. This in turn will break the exporter's death grip on labor and start the virtuous cycle that leads to the expansion of industry and the importation of foreign goods, perhaps even our goods. This is the same process we witnessed in the case of Taiwan: instituting justice at the lowest level provides a foundation for expansion of commerce at every level. By a tariff related to justice, rather than to mere commercial advantage, both sides will benefit commercially. And while there are certainly difficulties and opportunities for abuse, given that these are prudential and political determinations, it would certainly be a cheaper and more effective means of restoring equity in trade than the World Bank programs designed for that purpose which funnel billions into projects that accomplish little or nothing.

Americans, when they hear of the low wages paid for the goods they buy from other countries, frequently comfort themselves with the fiction, "But it's a good wage for that country." Usually, this is not the case. Indeed, the very economic logic used to justify the wages argues against its being above subsistence, and a downwardly defined subsistence at that. Without some power, either purchasing power or political power, the workers simply cannot bargain, and the wage contract is in fact leonine; workers must accept what they are given or accept starvation. Such a situation destabilizes both the exporting and the importing country; in fact, it destabilizes the whole world. People will endure much, but at some point they will give way to resentment and despair — and desperate people are more inclined to take desperate measures, are more inclined to hear the siren call of revolutionaries and warlords, and are far more likely to blame the West for imposing such harsh conditions on them. We face alternatives between reform and chaos.

Free trade purists might object to any restrictions or tariffs, but there is in fact a great deal of hypocrisy about free trade. In truth, there are no "free trade" agreements, despite the name. They are actually lengthy and complex agreements setting the terms of trade between nations, terms that usually favor the large nations and disadvantage poor ones. The Western countries have pressured the poor nations into "liberalizing" their trade barriers, while the Western nations are keeping up their own barriers. For example, the Western nations heavily subsidize their own agriculture, but since the chief exports of many of the poor countries are agricultural goods, they cannot compete against the subsidized prices and cannot obtain a fair market price. As Joseph Stiglitz notes:

> Looking at the "terms of trade" — the prices which developed and less developed countries get for the products they produce — after the last trade agreement in 1995 (the eighth), the *net* effect was to lower the prices some of the poorest countries in the world received relative to what they paid for their imports. The result was that some of the poorest countries in the world were actually made worse off.[12]

These subsidies for agriculture may or may not be justified, depending on one's point of view. But they cannot be considered "free trade." The American public pays twice: once in higher food prices and once again in the form of subsidies taken from their taxes. The justification is that farm subsidies "protect" the family farm, but the major benefits actually go to big "agribusinesses," such as Archer-Daniels-Midland and the like. If "free" trade allows such subsidies in the name of political expediency, certainly it should allow some in the name of just wages.

CITIES AND THE WEALTH OF NATIONS

Import Substitution

Key to the development question is an understanding of how and why trade creates wealth, or fails to create it. Unless this is clearly understood, the trade and development process will remain a mystery. Wealth first comes from the earth, in the form of fish, food, fibers, and minerals, but must be transformed into something useful by human ingenuity and work. While a portion of this work is done on the farm, in the mine, and by the fishing fleet, it can only be completed in cities. Only cities provide the density of innovative businesses and the concentration of markets that make real development and wealth creation possible. Cities are therefore a basic economic unit. Hence, it is the city, and not the nation, which is the basic economic structure (outside the family, of course). A "national" economy is a statistical illusion arrived at by summing up the various city economies.[13] In fact, the idea of a national economy creates real conundrums for its various parts, since the policies that work for one region of a nation frequently work against the interests of another region.

All cities, with minor exceptions, start out by importing goods, usually from the surrounding countryside, and processing them for trade. "Processing" here may mean only packaging or transshipping, but some "trade" activity takes place. In turn, cities exchange these goods for other goods which they import for their own use either in consumption or further production. This already implies that growth will depend, in the first instance, both on the productivity of those who work with the "natural" produce (farmers, fisherman, and miners) and on the ingenuity of the traders and the craftsmen. Recall that in the case of Taiwan the first step was to increase the rewards (and therefore the productivity) of the farmers. The second step was to encourage local manufacturing, no matter how primitive and crude it was at first.

This initial wealth provides the original capital for the city. But if trade is limited merely to what grows in the region, then it will, at best, wax and wane with the natural crops but never experience any real growth. Real growth comes from *import substitution,* the process of using local tools, materials, and methods to reproduce products that have previously been imported. Imports themselves provide some wealth and a comparatively few jobs; import replacement produces greater wealth and a large number of jobs. Import replacement requires a high degree of improvisation and a network of businesses. "Economic life develops by grace of innovating; it expands by grace of import-replacing."[14] It should be noted that import replacement does not diminish imports; on the contrary, the money earned from import substitution provides the cash to purchase different imports, each of which becomes another candidate for import replacement and another round of wealth creation.

If we analyze how the great trading cities became great, we will immediately understand how development proceeds and what retards it. If we take for example Venice, the cities of the Hanseatic League, or New York, they all follow the same pattern. They begin as "supply regions," processing the local produce for a distant market. With their earnings, they are able to import products from the distant market, either for their own use or for re-sale to other markets less advanced than themselves. But the next step is crucial: these trading cities begin to manufacture substitutes for the imported products and trade them to their more backward regions. This increases the industry of the city, lowers the amount it is importing for that good, and improves the earnings, so that local industries can both employ more people (ensuring that the city will grow) and earn more imports which will be candidates for further import replacement. This immediately gives a clue to what backward cities need more than anything else: they need each other.[15] It is unlikely that less-developed cities can profitably match the high-quality goods from industrialized countries. However, such goods are not what pre-industrialized regions really need. For example, everybody needs transportation. But not everybody needs the trucks, SUVs, and cars that pour out of Western and Asian factories. A pre-industrial city may need, for example, a low-tech multi-use tractor which can pull a plow, pull a cart with goods for market or with the family for Sunday Mass, or serve as a power source for a thresher or a well. The parts for such a vehicle could be partially imported (the power train, for example) and partially locally made. As time goes on and local wealth and skills improve, more and more local content can be added. The fact that the tractor would lack power steering, air conditioning, and high-fidelity audio would not be a drawback; the people do not need vehicles for sixty miles per hour, but for six, and for a variety of uses, not just one.

Of course, there are other kinds of cities besides import-replacing ones. There are supply regions, which process local goods for transshipment. These cities can be very wealthy but they will always have thin and fragile economies, dependent on the fortunes of the local produce. Further, when the product is critical and highly valued, it can be a curse. For example, there is hardly an oil-exporting country that is not both backward and re-pressive. In most cases, the very value of the oil suppresses the development of a diverse economy. In most oil-exporting countries, the mass of people are either poor or dependent or both. Then there are cities that get bypassed by new technologies, outdating what they used to produce. If the city does not find a new source of income, it will wither.

Transplants and Outsourcing

Even though import replacement has always been the basis of wealth, it is not the basis of most current development efforts. Local products are gener-ally judged to be too crude for the world market, which is likely to be true enough. Therefore, most "development" programs transplant factories to the region to make Western goods for Western customers, the ones deemed to have the money. The only local good supplied is labor, and that at the cheapest rate possible. Hence these factories contribute very little toward making the city an import-replacing city and therefore do very little toward developing the region. Transplants are not all bad, in moderation. They can serve as a technology-transfer tool when they introduce new methods and give the local entrepreneurs experience in setting up and running factories. But when an economy becomes dependent on transfers, the city merely serves as a colony for the home country, supplying nothing but cheap labor and experiencing little or no real development.[16]

From the standpoint of the outsourcing country, a small amount of outsourcing does little harm, if the profits are used to further develop the home country. But if they are used merely to finance a new round of outsourcing, then the home country ends up hollowing out its own manufacturing capabilities and lessening its own ability to serve as an import-replacing society.[17] The impacts of outsourcing as a development tool can be seen by looking at the "free-trade zones" in Central America. These zones were set up with money from the United States Government, acting through USAID, to be tax-free zones where foreign investors could set up factories, mainly to make goods for the American market. Major American labels, such as the Gap and Disney, subcontract their work to these *maquilladoros*. The net effect is that the United States government finances competition for our own manufacturers and workers. In 1990, USAID ran an advertisement for these free-trade zones in *Bobbin,* the trade magazine of the American Textile Industry. The full-page glossy ad showed a picture of a Salvadoran woman at a sewing machine, and the headline read, "Rosa Martinez produces apparel for U.S. markets on her sewing machine in El Salvador. You can hire her for fifty-seven cents an hour." A year later, they re-ran the same ad, only they had decided that Rosa was paid too much; the new ad said, "You can hire her for thirty-three cents an hour." The National Labor Committee computed that at one factory, the output was valued at $30,000 per day, while the total labor tab came to $180 per day, or a mere 0.6 percent.[18] Factor shares indeed!

Thirty-three cents an hour might be justified if it provides Rosa a decent living according to the standards of El Salvador. But it does not. Rosa lives in absolute poverty; her meager earnings provide little excess over subsistence to support the local economy, and the plant contributes nothing either to taxes or to import-replacing abilities. The primary labor force consists of girls thirteen to eighteen years old. They are given birth control pills each morning at some factories before being allowed in to work (they are told that they are "vitamin" pills), and if they still manage to become pregnant, they are given an injection with an abortifacient (they are told it is a "flu shot").[19] Nothing must be allowed to interfere with the logic of production. Of course, these young girls cannot attend school or have the life that any normal girl has a certain right to expect; both their childhoods and their futures have been stolen from them.

When justice is denied, the values of trade and development get replaced by the values of greed and oppression. Justice in exchanges depends on a ratio between both sides in which each gets its due. The buyer is willing to support the seller at some appropriate level in return for something which makes her life better. But when this ratio is broken, development becomes its very opposite. Both countries involved in the trade impoverish themselves; the individuals in the trade may profit but the societies are impoverished. Unjust trade becomes an instance of class warfare against the poor, and one side appears to have all the weapons. But it is inherently unstable and diminishes all who participate in it.

GLOBALIZATION AND "TURBO-CAPITALISM"

If trade is good, then globalization, being merely trade on a global scale, must also be good. In fact, without globalization, it is unlikely that the plight of the poor in the world would be such a pressing and immediate concern to us. However, if trade can be perverted, then globalization runs the same risks, and runs them on a global scale; when a system of exploitation becomes the norm of conduct, then a proper view of trade and development becomes impossible, and globalization itself becomes part of the problem. It appears that twenty-first-century globalization has taken the latter course: it has become a tool of exploitation and needs to be reformed. The solution is not to do away with globalization, an impossible task in the age of the electronic "global village," but to reform it by recalling the true values of trade. And as a practical matter, we really have no choice; the world is daily becoming more unstable, and the cry of the poor daily more desperate. If we do not act for reform, violence and chaos will overtake us.

Finding the way out will take an understanding of how we got in. This is not a difficult process because we can easily see how the course of trade developed since the Bretton Woods conference in 1944. That conference, acting with great wisdom, set up two international bodies, the World Bank (formally known as the International Bank for Reconstruction and Development) and the International Monetary Fund. The former had responsibility for development, and the latter for ensuring economic stability on a global basis. The guiding light of these organizations was a Keynesian view of economics, which recognized that markets by themselves were imperfect and that adjustments would be needed from time to time. Hanging over this conference was the memory of the cataclysm of the 1930s, the Great Depression, which was seen as part of the causes of the cataclysm of the 1940s, the Second World War. The world's leaders were determined never to let such a thing happen again.[20] These experiences had taught the world's leaders that for all the virtues of the market, there could be failures of international demand, a problem to be addressed by the IMF, and that the market was not always the best development tool, a problem to be addressed by the World Bank. The focus of these institutions was European, and in that context, the system worked very well: Europe, or at least Western Europe, recovered quickly as international trade expanded rapidly, and the wisdom of the leaders was evident to all. America in particular had demonstrated not only economic leadership, but moral leadership as well; its concern for justice turned out to be also a concern for practical economics and growth. The American people tolerated the extra expense and the corresponding inflation as the cost of a just world order, and the world was made better for it.

Although these institutions were designated as "world" and "international," they really excluded most of the world. As successful as they were in Europe, the same policies were counterproductive when operating in non-Western cultures. And of course the communist bloc was absent from the Bank and the IMF. Further, these institutions became subordinated to American foreign policy in the context of the great struggle with communism. In practical terms this meant that much of the money went to prop up dictators and tyrants in regimes deemed to be "on our side." More recently, the Bank has been used to prop repressive regimes such as those in Uzbekistan and Pakistan as an inducement to join, at least nominally, the "anti-terrorist" coalition. The Bank has been a camp-follower in America's foreign policy, diluting its role as a development agency.[21]

But the real change in the Bank's and IMF's operations came in the 1980s. This was the time of the so-called "Washington Consensus," implemented under the leadership of Ronald Reagan and Margaret Thatcher. The institutions founded to correct the imperfections of the market now became the missionaries of market perfection; no deviation from a rigid free market theory would be tolerated if a nation wished to receive aid. A purge was conducted at the World Bank with the old leadership replaced by missionaries of the new order.[22] The "Washington Consensus" was not really a consensus at all, since the Japanese and the Far-Eastern countries objected, pointing out that the policies which had made the "Asian Tigers" so successful were precisely the ones the Bank was rejecting.[23] As we have already noted, the first large-scale tests of these contending ideas came with the transition of the communist states to capitalism. The Asian model proved itself far superior. However, the Asians had little influence at the World Bank, which was and is mainly influenced by the United States. It has already been mentioned that Washington was preaching a doctrine for others it had no intention of following for itself. What was this doctrine?

Its adherents would simply call it the "free market," but Edward Luttwak calls it *Turbo-Capitalism:*

> What they celebrate, preach, and demand is private enterprise liberated from government regulations, unchecked by effective trade unions, unfettered by sentimental concerns over the fate of employees or communities, unrestrained by customs barriers or investment restrictions, and molested as little as possible by taxation. What they insistently demand is the privatization of state-owned businesses of all kinds and the conversion of public institutions from universities and botanic gardens to prisons, from libraries and schools to old-age homes into private enterprises run for profit. What they promise is a more dynamic economy that will generate new wealth — while saying nothing about the distribution of any wealth, old or new. They call it the free market, but I call it turbo-capitalism because it is so profoundly different from the strictly controlled capitalism that flourished from 1945 until the 1980s, and that brought the sensational novelty of mass affluence to the peoples of the United States, Western Europe, Japan, and all the other countries that followed their path.[24]

Following the prescriptions of turbo-capitalism, the IMF and the World Bank have become the chief enforcers of a dogmatic and abstract economic philosophy that is divorced from any actual conditions. The result is a system in which society exists to serve the needs of the economy, rather than the other way round.[25] The net effect is terrible deterioration of society. Crime rates sky-rocket as labor force participation plummets; jobs become less secure while employers can only survive by joining the outsourcing death-spiral. The wages of 70 percent of all Americans have remained stagnant or declined from the rates of the 1970s.[26] Since 1980, the share of income received by the top 5 percent of households has increased by 37.3 percent (from 15.8 to 21.7 percent) while the share of the bottom 20 percent has dropped by 23 percent (from 4.3 to 3.5 percent). In the same period, our Gini coefficient went from .406 to .462.[27] These growing inequalities, if they are not reversed, will have the effect of destabilizing society and remaking

America in the image of what we previously thought were "Third World" conditions; the inequality that the current notion of globalization is enforcing around the world is also being enforced on us. Clearly an abstract notion of "efficiency" is not sufficient to build a healthy economy, especially if "efficiency" is thought of only in terms of production and not distribution; to do this is simply to forget one-half of economics. Moreover, it is to set the wrong standard to judge an economy. If we do not have a purpose in mind, then we can never make a proper judgment on whether our efforts have been successful. If equity in distribution of incomes disappears as an economic goal, we will never be permitted to judge whether the economy is successful on this score or not. And if this element — which is precisely the moral element — disappears, then the rest of economics will be destabilized as well.

Therefore, we face a choice. We can continue down a road of turbo-capitalism, down a road on which there will be many losers and a few winners, or we can acknowledge that justice and equity are economic goals. And in a time of intense globalization, this is not just a choice for ourselves, but a choice made in solidarity with all the peoples of the earth. The international institutions, the World Bank, the IMF, and the WTO, can be dedicated to ensuring justice, or they can advance the cause of chaos. Some would have us believe that equity comes with a cost of unemployment, but this is simply not the case: equity and employment rise and fall together, and this is even more true in the case of equity in property than it is in equity in wages alone.[28] As matters now stand, America is busily hollowing itself out; its industries have been hollowed out by outsourcing, and it is losing its manufacturing capability; its finances are being hollowed out by a runaway consumerism financed by debt; its accounts are being hollowed out by deficits in trade balances and in the federal budget; its ability to provide a decent education to all (a foundation of a healthy economy) is diminishing; even on security matters, its army is overstretched abroad and the police at home are losing the battle. These are not the "inevitable" results of a process over which we have no control, but the results of conscious decisions we and our leaders have made about what the purpose of an economy should be. Those decisions can be reversed.

In 1914, Henry Ford scandalized the economic world by paying his workers the spectacular wage of $5 per day; the *Wall Street Journal* labeled it an "economic crime."[29] But Ford understood economics better than the economists and certainly better than the *Journal*; if the workers could not afford to buy his car, his business could not be successful; economics depends on efficiency in *both* supply and demand, and not on one factor alone. Ford's

Model T sold for $360, and a worker could buy it for seventy-two days' worth of work. We may be able to depress the wage for the mass of workers to subsistence levels, but we cannot then expect to sell them many Fords. But Ford's solution works only if the world is dedicated to moral values in the economy, to justice for all peoples. We have seen how this commitment to justice worked in the Asian economies of Taiwan, Korea, and Japan. Now we need to look at other ways of achieving the same goals in other situations, including our own.

Chapter 16

Micro-Banking

The best way to get a loan from a bank is to prove to them that you don't need the money.

THE $27 SOLUTION

We have been dealing so far with programs that move billions of dollars to development projects with results that are dubious at best. Now we will look at a program that deals not with billions but with hundreds and even with tens and twenties. It began with an academic economist and a $27 loan. The economist is Muhammad Yunus, who in 1972 became the chairman of the economics department at Chittagong University in Bangladesh. The country at that time was in the midst of a famine, and Dr. Yunus thought that it was his job to find some practical way to apply his training to the problem and come up with a solution. After working on the problem for several years without much success, he decided to do something rather amazing for an academic: he went into the village surrounding the university and talked to the poor. It was then that he met Sufiya Begum.

Sufiya made bamboo stools. She obtained the bamboo each day with a loan of twenty cents from a middleman, and at the end of the day, she sold the intricately woven stool back to the middleman for twenty-two cents; two cents was her entire earnings for a day's work. The professor asked if there was no other way for Sufiya to buy the bamboo. Could she not borrow the money? No, the moneylenders charged even more than the middlemen, 10 percent per week or even 10 percent per day. But Sufiya had no more time to talk to the professor, she had to finish the chair, or she wouldn't even get her two cents. The conversation was a revelation to Dr. Yunus:

> It was this knowledge that shocked me. In my university courses, I theorized about sums in the millions of dollars, but here before my eyes the problems of life and death were posed in terms of pennies. Something was wrong. Why did my university courses not reflect the

reality of Sufiya's life? I was angry, angry at myself, angry at my economics department and the thousands of intelligent professors who had not tried to address this problem and solve it. It seemed to me the existing economic system made it absolutely certain that Sufiya's income would be kept perpetually at such a low level that she would never save a penny and would never invest in expanding her economic base. Her children were condemned to live a life of penury, of hand-to-mouth survival, just as she had lived it before them, and as her parents did before her. I had never heard of anyone suffering for the lack of *twenty-two cents.*[1]

Dr. Yunus conducted a survey of the village and found that forty-two people borrowed a total of 856 *taka* — less than \$27 — everyday from the middlemen. All of the people who worked under the system lived the same kind of life as Sufiya Begum, a life of perpetual poverty. There was no way out of the system because the system itself insured that there was never any excess for the people to save and thus buy their own raw materials. This is what "subsistence" means; the dry economic term reflects a cruel and bitter reality. There is, at best, enough for the day and nothing to spare. Further, the "enough for a day" gets defined downward so that "enough" always means a little less than it did before; the human capacity to endure ensures that there will always be someone who can take a little less rather than starve. Dr. Yunus took \$27 from his pocket and lent it to the 42 villagers. But obviously he needed a permanent and wide-ranging solution, the kind of solution that a regular bank ought to provide.

Dr. Yunus went to the bank to find a solution, but the conversation took on a surreal quality. The bankers could not understand lending such small sums to illiterate people with no collateral. They thought the professor was making a joke.[2] Even filling out the banking forms would be an insurmountable barrier for most of the poor. And if the poor could get some one to fill out the forms, the cost of processing the forms would exceed the amount of the loans. But that was the minor problem. The real problem is that banks lend money on collateral, property they can take in the event of a default. In effect, this means that credit is limited to the rich; you get a loan from a bank by proving you don't really need the money. This proof is recorded in complex documents and reviewed by a careful process of lending committees, bank officers, and auditors. Of course, these are not unreasonable requirements; all of us would feel uneasy about putting our money in a bank without proper lending policies, collateral requirements, or review procedures. That would be as foolish as offering credit cards to unemployed university students. Nevertheless, the system excludes the poor, the very people who need credit the most.

The bankers, doing their best to be helpful, suggested that there be a guarantor for each loan. Dr. Yunus agreed to be the guarantor for each loan, but then presented the bank with a quandary: "I will not pay if there is any default." Of course, the bank could sue the professor, but the idea of suing to recover a small sum defaulted by a beggar was a practical impossibility and a public relations nightmare. Not unreasonably, the bank had great difficulties with the scheme. Nevertheless, after six months of back and forth negotiations, the bank finally approved the loan in December 1976.

THE GRAMEEN BANK

With money from the "regular" bank, Dr. Yunus founded the Grameen ("Rural") Bank, but he had no idea of how to run a bank, and nobody knew how to run a bank for paupers. The very idea seemed as preposterous as the established bankers thought it was. Yunus had to discover by trial and error the methods that would work and invent a whole system of banking that both met the needs of the poorest of the poor and the requirements of sound banking. All banking is based on *credit*, from the Latin *credo*, "I believe," as in, "I believe you can pay me back." Normally, this belief is established by collateral which automatically excludes the poor, the very group this bank was trying to reach. The Grameen Bank developed a method of forming groups of five borrowers who are to be responsible for each other; they are, in effect, collateral for each other. They help each other in business because they are all responsible for all the loans. Each group elects a leader and meets once a week to discuss business and make the weekly payments on their loans. All the loans in a particular group must be up to date before any member of that group can get further loans.

The loan procedures are very simple. All loans are for one year at 20 percent interest (since reduced to 16 percent)[3] with payment of 2 percent of the loan for fifty weeks plus interest of 2 *taka* for each 1,000 *taka* of the outstanding balance. This procedure makes the terms very easy to understand, something important when dealing with relatively unsophisticated borrowers. It also allows for easy supervision of the loans and a concentration on *credit discipline,* whereby borrowers learn to handle credit and to be responsible for their own business and that of their fellow members. Learning to use credit wisely, as every businessperson knows, whether here or in Bangladesh, is critical to the success of any business. And savings are critical as well. Five percent of the loan goes into a group fund which the members may borrow from to get over rough spots or to pursue additional business opportunities; this fund is under the control of the group itself.

When a group is first formed, only two of the members may get loans. If these two successfully make their payments for the first six weeks, then the other members may get loans. The groups not only allow the members to serve as collateral for each other, they serve a purpose of strengthening each member by making connections with other members. This encourages *solidarity* among the members of the bank. The solidarity is further encouraged by joining the five-member groups into larger groups of eight such borrowing circles, which elect their own leader and meet once a month with a bank officer to discuss bank business.

The bank does not give "job" training; rather, it assumes that all human beings have innate skills and just need capital to utilize those skills and acquire new ones. "Training programs" tend to perpetuate the interests of the trainers and raise bars to lending and development. But in the view of the bank, the poor are not poor because of poor skills, but because of poor and oppressive systems; they have no control over capital, and without such control, they lose control of their labor as well. And without such control, wages tend to a downwardly defined subsistence.

The Grameen Bank does not make "consumer" loans, which would make the bank an exercise in usury and obligate its members for useless things. They only lend for income-generating projects which can include education and decent housing, since many members work in the home. Buying a goat, buying raw materials for manufacture such as bamboo, cloth, farm implements, etc., things which can generate income and independence for the members are the focus of the loans. Such loans have the power to make real and positive changes in the life of the poor.

Take the case of Murshida. She was born into a poor family of eight children. At fifteen, she was married to an unskilled factory worker, who turned out to be a compulsive gambler and lost at the games what little money he made. He took to beating Murshida, and then sold the roof of their home during the monsoon season to pay his gambling debts. When Murshida confronted him, he beat her and divorced her on the spot, throwing her and the three children out of the now roofless house. For a while, she worked at spinning cotton into yarn on contract work, but did not earn enough to support her family. Hearing of Grameen Bank, she joined it, even though the village elders opposed the bank. With her first loan of 1,000 *taka*, she bought a goat and paid off the loan in six months with the profits from selling the milk. She now had a goat, a kid, and no debt. She then took another loan of 2,000 *taka* and bought raw cotton and a spinning wheel to make women's scarves. Her business grew so much that by 1999 she was employing as many as twenty-five women in making scarves. She also bought an acre of farmland with her profits and built a house with a Grameen Bank housing loan. She even set her brothers up in businesses that include sari trading and raw cotton trading.[4]

Murshida's story indicates not only the successes of the Bank but also the kinds of challenges that it faces. Concerning Mursida's success, we can note that it was not a matter of some vast program in which the G-8 leaders get together and decide to do expensive things for "less-developed" countries, something that always seems to involve moving billions of dollars from entrenched bureaucracies in the First World through corrupt governments in the Third World and finally back to Swiss banks in the First World without ever really improving anything, and many times serving merely to finance the very corruption the loans are trying to alleviate. This is likely an unfair description of *all* of the World Bank's and other agencies' projects, but it is general enough to illustrate the differences from Grameen. Grameen moves less than $100 to women like Murshida to allow them to unlock their own human potential and liberate themselves and their families from a system that oppresses them. True development is always *self-development,* a do-it-yourself project; it cannot be imposed from on high and from a foreign source. It has to come from both within the country and within the person. Certainly, aid agencies can help, but they can never impose development on a person or a country.

Nevertheless, although Grameen relies on the individual's initiative and creativity to break through the wall of poverty, the process still relies on a social structure capable of delivering the credit and dedicated individuals willing to work with and support the poorest of the poor. Dr. Yunus says that Grameen does not believe in charity, but it seems to me that they have discovered charity of a deeper sort. Certainly, they reject the charity of handouts, which merely finances dependency. But they do practice that charity based on *solidarity* with the poor. That is to say, in order for the Grameen program to work, it requires a cadre of dedicated people willing to see things from the viewpoint of the poor. In order to free the poor, they must in some sense become poor; this is the deeper level of charity, not the charity of writing checks but the charity of true involvement. In Murshida's case, it was necessary for the Bank's workers to break through the opposition of the village elders and the general low status that women have in Bangladesh. This requires more than the mere opening of a branch bank. It requires people of a certain sort. It requires the Bicycle Bankers.

THE BICYCLE BANKERS

Grameen bankers faced all sorts of obstacles. There was of course opposition from the traditional bankers, on whom Grameen was dependent in the early years. Grameen did not obtain its independence from the banks until 1983, and even then it was a quasi-governmental project, subject to bureaucrats in the capital. But there were even more serious problems. This was banking in a rural, village environment. Village elders and religious leaders were often suspicious of Grameen, seeing it as something perhaps connected with the West, or with Christianity, or with some other alien doctrine. Furthermore, Grameen sometimes had to operate under conditions of communist insurrection, where murder and violence were common, or after the floods or tsunamis that periodically ravage a low-lying country like Bangladesh. These conditions require an uncommon sort of banker; they require bankers who can go door to door in a village on their bicycles to work with clients who are, at least initially, destitute. They must work with these people on a daily basis, attend their weekly meetings, the monthly center meetings, and keep a handle on the businesses of the up to 400 borrowers for whom each banker is responsible.

One of the greatest challenges to the bank is that of reaching women borrowers. Like many traditional cultures, there are in Bangladesh tremendous barriers not only to women handling money, but even to their being seen in public unless escorted by a male relative. But the Bank thought it was important to reach women for two reasons. The first was that women are the poorest of the poor, and the poor are the mission of the Bank. But the second reason was business-related. Women are more closely tied to their families and more likely to work hard, repay the loans, build businesses, and re-invest in new loans. The money they make is more likely to go to food, housing, education, and business expansion. It was not an easy task to reach women, either as borrowers or as employees of the Bank, but getting women to work as branch managers was key to getting women to become borrowers. In that culture, women are discouraged from working outside the home, and in many villages the idea of a woman tooling around the village on a bicycle and doing business with men and other women was positively scandalous. Many women faced intense pressure to refuse such jobs or to quit them. Nevertheless, the Bank persevered. Although they were originally a very small percentage of the borrowers, women are now 95 percent of the bank's 4.6 million members.

Capital: Social and Financial

Grameen gives high priority to building not just financial capital, but social capital as well. The Bank actually begins building social capital with the formation of the five-borrower groups even before any loans are given. It thereby recognizes a principle that social capital precedes financial capital. This social capital is further advanced by the centers, the combination of eight groups which elect their own officers and set their own social agenda, a process which develops leadership; the goal is to develop a social agenda owned by the borrowers rather than imposed by the bankers. The leaders of the centers gather annually for a conference, and, over the course of the years, they have codified their social agenda into "The Sixteen Decisions":[5]

We shall follow and advance the four principles of the Grameen Bank — discipline, unity, courage, and hard work — in all walks of our lives.

Prosperity we shall bring to our families.

We shall not live in a dilapidated house. We shall repair our houses and work toward constructing new houses at the earliest opportunity.

We shall grow vegetables all the year round. We shall eat plenty of them and sell the surplus.

During the plantation season, we shall plant as many seedlings as possible.

We shall plan to keep our families small. We shall minimize our expenditures. We shall look after our health.

We shall educate our children and ensure that they can earn enough to pay for their education.

We shall always keep our children and the environment clean.

We shall build and use pit latrines.

We shall drink water from tube wells. If they are not available, we shall boil water or use alum to purify it.

We shall not take any dowry at our sons' weddings; neither shall we give any dowry at our daughters' weddings. We shall keep the center free from the curse of the dowry. We shall not practice child marriage.

We shall not commit an injustice, and we will oppose anyone who tries to do so.

We shall collectively undertake larger investments for higher incomes.

We shall always be ready to help each other. If anyone is in difficulty, we shall all help him or her.

If we come to know of any breach of discipline in any center, we shall all go there and help restore discipline.

We shall introduce physical exercises in all our centers. We shall take part in all social activities collectively.

These "decisions" are not, of course, loan requirements, but something the elected leaders urge on the bank membership. In doing so, they recognize a reality that economics has discarded: the relationship between the moral and the economic aspects of life. It is not sufficient merely to have sufficient capital. Even financial capital is a social commodity because it is a part of our relations with society. As such, it cannot be abstracted from a given set of social circumstances and culture. The Grameen Bank has a goal of making every branch poverty-free. This lack of poverty is not defined by a certain level of income, but by specific and concrete criteria, which the Bank defines as:[6]

Having a house with a tin roof.

Having beds or cots for all members of the family.

Having access to safe drinking water.

Having access to a sanitary latrine.

Having all school-age children attending school.

Having sufficient warm clothing for the winter.

Having mosquito nets.

Having a home vegetable garden.

Having no food shortages, even during the most difficult time of a difficult year.

Having sufficient income-earning opportunities for all adult members of the family.

How successful has Grameen been? We can get some idea by looking at the numbers. Since its inception, Grameen has made $4.8 billion in loans, of which $4.3 billion has been repaid.[7] In May 2005 the Bank disbursed $53.3 million in loans and received $41.3 million in payments. It has a total of $358 million in loans outstanding and a total of $372 million in deposits, of which $245 million is from members. Half of the 1,500 banking centers are self-supporting, with more in deposits than in loans. Grameen housing loans have built 621,000 homes. There are 756,000 groups, 88,000 centers, and 1,500 branches operating in 53,000 villages. Obviously, Grameen has had a tremendous influence on Bangladesh. Why does such a "cheap" program have such positive impacts when programs involving billions — or even trillions — do little good and much harm? One obvious conclusion is that money is only part of the solution, and not even the greatest part. Money is an indispensable part of development; its availability is a necessary condition, but not a sufficient one.

Chapter 17

The Mondragón Cooperative Corporation

We can speak of socializing [the means of production] only when
... on the basis of his work each person is fully entitled to consider himself a part owner of the great workbench at which he
is working with everybody else. —POPE JOHN PAUL II

AGENCY AND ORGANIZATION

Two problems dominate all workplace relations: the agency dilemma and
the organizational structure. Often these are treated as separate issues, but
in fact they are tightly connected. *Agency* refers to situations in which one
person (the "agent") is acting on behalf of another person (the "principal").
It is the duty of the agent to carry out the wishes of the principal and to look
after the latter's interests. Within the firm, managers are agents of the stock-
holders, and the employees are agents of the managers. These relationships
take place within the context of an organizational structure. Both agency
and organization lead to certain tensions: In the case of agency, it is the
conflict between the interests of the agent and those of the principal, and in
the case of the organization, it is the tension between control and freedom.
Each of these tensions imposes its own costs and inefficiencies on a firm, but
taken together they may determine not only the character and the success
of the firm, but also the character of the economic life of a whole nation,
since the national economy is composed largely of a series of firms.

The Agency Dilemma

There are two kinds of agents: profit takers and employees. The former
seeks to provide a product or service for a price, and the latter agrees to
follow instructions for a wage. Both cases lead to a dilemma: people are
inclined to opportunism, seeking their own interests and disregarding, as

267

far as possible, the interests of their principals. The problem is to induce the agent to act so as to maximize the principal's interests.[1] Agency theory tries to find ways to negotiate and monitor contracts so as to reduce the injury to either party through incentives and sanctions. Conventional theories of agency are based on the underlying utilitarianism of economics. Work is regarded as a disutility, and people have to be induced by a wage to overcome their aversion to work.[2] Further, the agents must be closely monitored, and a package of incentives and sanctions devised. Such mechanisms are costly; incentives often raise costs to the point where the principal is better off performing the function himself or abandoning the project. Sanctions are often resisted by agents to the point that makes them self-defeating.[3] The more there is a divergence of interests between the agent and the principal, the higher the costs will be to overcome that divergence.

We see in the agency dilemma how bad theory leads to bad practice. The model of the human being as *homo economicus,* motivated solely by profit and averse to work, leads to practices which make the theory a self-fulfilling prophecy; workers are not to be trusted and must be carefully monitored, with suitable rewards and punishments applied. But this is simply a bad model. People may indeed be averse to hard toil, but they generally want to work, want to have some way of affecting the world and expressing themselves. The real question here is whether human motives are internal or external. Since people, by and large, *do* wish to work, the problem is somewhat different than the one addressed by utilitarian economics. The real problem is harmonizing the interests of the agent and the principal, the worker and the owner. If a worker or manager does not have internal "ownership" of the goals and purposes of a firm and its owners, motivation must be supplied externally by complex systems of monitoring, rewards, and sanctions, systems which have their own disutility and inefficiencies.[4] Most of the fads in management theory involve ever-greater and more complex refinements of the monitoring system (e.g., "management by objectives"). But if the worker seeks more from work than a wage, if she seeks not only the means of support but also the means of expression, development, and fulfillment, then a different set of systems and structures will apply.

Organization

Connected to the problem of agency is the problem of organization; it is the organization that establishes and enforces the agency relationships. Any organization must contend with two opposed issues: order and freedom.[5] Without order, things will simply collapse and nothing can be accomplished. But order by itself tends to be rigid. A firm that concentrates on order alone will be static and lifeless and well on its way to disappearing. Growth requires innovation, which is to say it requires some "order-breaking" mechanism:

> There must be plenty of elbow-room and scope for breaking through the established order, to do the thing never done before, never anticipated by the guardians of orderliness, the new, unpredicted and unpredictable outcome of a man's creative idea.[6]

The problem for a firm is to strive continuously for *both* the necessary order and creative freedom. We may associate "order" with the administrator and the accountant, while "freedom" is associated with the entrepreneur. Every firm needs both administrators and entrepreneurs. In a small firm, it is easier to manage the tension between freedom and creativity, but the problem is exacerbated in large-scale organizations. The sheer size of large organizations implies a rigid bureaucracy and the need for ever more complex monitoring systems, systems capable, by their sheer weight, of stifling freedom and creativity. In the modern world, it is unlikely that large-scale organization can or should disappear. Part of the solution, then, would seem to be to find "smallness" within large bureaucratic organizations, to find freedom within order. E. F. Schumacher suggests that the large firm be organized as a series of semi-autonomous "quasi-firms."[7] However, this decentralization, while necessary, is not in itself sufficient; large firms commonly go through a wave of centralization, which is then followed by a wave of decentralization, like the swing of a pendulum. The movement in each direction is accompanied by excellent arguments, all of which are true since the goals of order on the one hand and freedom on the other are both true. The problem is that firms force themselves to choose between these perfectly reasonable goals. It is "either/or" thinking, when what is needed is "both/and" thinking.[8]

Schumacher suggests that to achieve both freedom and order, large-scale organizations need to combine decentralization with the Principle of Subsidiarity, which Schumacher defines as:

> The higher level must not absorb the functions of a lower one, on the assumption that, being higher, it will automatically be wiser and fulfill them more efficiently. Loyalty can grow only from the smaller units to the larger (and higher) ones, not the other way round—and loyalty is an essential element in the health of any organization.... The burden of proof lies always on those who want to deprive a lower level of its functions and thereby its freedom and responsibility in that respect;

they have to prove that the lower level is incapable of fulfilling this function satisfactorily.[9]

This is not to say that the higher level cannot take any functions from the lower — else it would be without authority or function at all — but the presumption is always in favor of the lower unit, and the burden of proof must be on the higher unit. The "center" needs to be able to issue orders down the chain of command; at the same time, it is remote from the actual operations. Commands issued at the top, while they may be justified in the general case, may not work out well in any particular case. The lower level units need methods of making exceptions to general commands. The primary grounds for exceptions are profit; a lower level might be justified in taking a different course when the command will negatively affect their profitability. This in turn implies that each unit has its own set of books, both balance sheets and profit-and-loss statements. Units showing good profits should have greater freedom of action while those losing money would be more closely monitored. Profit here serves as a Principle of Vindication.[10] A lower unit that can improve its profitability by making an exception should have a strong case for the exception, and central management should always be willing to negotiate its commands with any particular unit, while concentrating on those things absolutely necessary for proper order.

The agency relationship exists within the context of the firm's organizational structure, and the two issues cannot easily be divorced in practice, however much they are divorced in the various theories of management. A bureaucratic organization will tend to impose its will in a top-down method and follow a theory of agency which is suspicious of the worker and stifling of freedom. But an organization with insufficient controls from the top will lead to disorder and may even miss criminal activity in lower levels. This delicate balancing act puts management in a very difficult situation. Indeed, there seems at first glance to be no natural solution and certainly no easy answer to the problems of agency and organization. Within the purely corporate structure, as we have traditionally understood it, the problems seem intractable.

Yet there are other kinds of corporations which seem to have the potential to solve these problems. Pre-eminent among them is the cooperative, that is, a firm in which the workers own the company. The cooperative corporation mitigates the agency problem because the agents and the principals are the same persons. This mitigation of the agency problem allows cooperatives greater freedom and flexibility in solving the organizational problem. Indeed, cooperatives seem to enjoy a competitive advantage over traditional forms of corporate organization. Cooperatives are common enough in small-scale production and in consumers' cooperatives, both formal and informal. But is it a flexible enough organizational model for large-scale production?

We can give a definitive answer to that question. The Mondragón Cooperative Corporation (MCC) of Spain, which has a fifty-year history, has proven a durable and successful firm, or rather collection of firms. One measure of its success is its sheer size: at the end of 2004, it had €18.6 billion (US$22.3 billion) in assets, €10.5 billion (US$12.6 billion) in sales, and 71,000 employees.[11] The corporation manufactures appliances, electronics, car parts, and even full factories to order; it provides engineering, banking, and insurance services; it runs a university, a technical college and several training institutes; it has a retail division with markets, supermarkets, and hyper-markets. It is a major competitor in European and international markets; half of its sales are from exports. If it were an American company, its sales would place it at 154 on the Fortune 500. Thus we can safely say that the MCC, with its fifty-year history, diverse product line, and large employee base, serves as a test of worker ownership. Its history helps us to understand, in practical terms, how the basic agency dilemma can be overcome within a cooperative organization.

THE HISTORY OF THE MCC

The Origins

The story of this remarkable company begins with a rather remarkable man, Fr. José Maria Arizmendiarrieta, who was assigned in 1941 to the village of Mondragón in the Basque region of Spain. The Basques constitute a separate group in Spain with a language unrelated to Romance languages (or anything else) and a long history of independence and resistance. They resisted the Romans, the Goths, the Muslims, the Spanish, the French, the Falangists (the Spanish Fascists under Franco), the communists, and anybody else who has ever tried to rule them. The Basque region had been devastated by the Spanish Civil War (1936–38); they had supported the losing side and had been singled out by Franco for reprisals. Large numbers of Basques were executed or imprisoned, and poverty and unemployment remained endemic until the 1950s. In Fr. José's words, "We lost the Civil War, and we became an occupied region."[12] However, the independent spirit of the Basques proved to be fertile ground for the ideas of Fr. José. He took on the project of alleviating the poverty of the region. For him, the solution lay in the pages of *Rerum Novarum, Quadragesimo Anno,* and the thinkers who had pondered the principles these encyclicals contained. Property, and its proper use, was central to his thought, as it was to Pope Leo and to Belloc and Chesterton. "Property," Fr. José wrote, "is valued in so far as it serves as an efficient resource for building responsibility and efficiency in any vision of community life in a decentralized form."[13]

Fr. José's first step was the education of the people into the distributist ideal. He became the counselor for the Church's lay social and cultural arm, known as "Catholic Action," and formed the *Hezibide Elkartea,* The League for Education and Culture, which established a training school for apprentices. He helped a group of these students become engineers, and later encouraged them to form a company of their own on cooperative lines. The engineers agreed to do so, but had no specific plan or product in mind. In order to establish a factory, it was necessary to obtain a license from the government, which was not always cooperative toward the Basques. But when a nearby stove factory went bankrupt, they raised $360,000 from the community to buy it (1955).[14] This first of the co-operatives was named *Ulgor,* which was an acronym from the names of the five students of Fr. José who were the founders. It was first organized as a conventional business because there was no legal form for cooperatives, nor would there be until 1959. As the cooperative movement grew in the Basque country, it formed a number of innovative institutions providing support structures for the cooperatives and the workers. These support cooperatives demonstrate the innovation and flexibility of the cooperative movement, as well as its dedication to the welfare of the workers.

The Support Cooperatives

The *Caja Laboral Credit Union: Ulgor* did well, but by itself it was not enough to really change things. What was needed was a source of financing for cooperatives. The founders needed their own bank. When Fr. José suggested this to them, they resisted; they did not wish to become bankers. "Our initial reaction," said one of the founders, "was one of annoyance and we literally sent Don José packing."[15] So Fr. José solved the problem in a very "un-priestly" way: He simply forged their names on the application for a credit union charter, which was granted. His students had the option of either repudiating the charter (thereby sending their mentor to jail) or getting down to the business of banking. They chose the latter, and it turned out to be a master stroke. The bank, called the *Caja Laboral,* became a "factory factory," spinning off new cooperatives across the Basque region. It became the backbone of the cooperative movement, institutionalizing the entrepreneurial and import-replacement functions.[16] A group of workers wanting to start their own cooperative would pick a product to produce and a manager and go to the bank with their plan. If the proposal was sound, the bank would assign an advisor — called a "godfather" — to the group and the due-diligence phase would begin with marketing studies and all the usual startup activities. At the completion of the studies, the whole plan would be presented to the bank which would rule on the loan.

The bank also served as the integrating force for the growing number of cooperatives. The bank held the retirement funds and each member's share capital, as well as the reserves for each cooperative. The bank also provided oversight for all the cooperatives, especially those in financial trouble. In such cases, the bank would take over day-to-day operations until the health of the cooperative returned. As one of the institutions common to all the cooperatives, it supplied a level of business expertise to the fledgling movement that might otherwise have been lacking. Its success can be measured by the fact that of the hundreds of cooperatives started, only a handful have gone out of business. Today, the bank has over €10 billion in assets.[17]

The *Lagun-Aro Social Insurance Cooperative:* In 1959, the Spanish government refused to allow the members of the cooperatives to join the Spanish Social Security system. Making a virtue of necessity, the cooperatives formed their own social insurance cooperative. Originally established as the Social Insurance Division of the *Caja Laboral*, it was spun off to its own cooperative, the *Lagun-Aro*. The functions of this cooperative have varied over time. Originally it provided retirement funds and health clinics, functions which the Basque government took over in 1987. It now provides life insurance, leasing, and consumer finance functions. Currently, *Lagun-Aro* has nearly €3 billion in assets.[18]

The *Hezibide Elkartea Education and Training Cooperative:* From the very beginning of his service in the Mondragón parish, Fr. José stressed the importance of education. It is no surprise then that the educational efforts preceded the cooperatives. It was the school for apprentices that formed the founders of the cooperative movement, and the emphasis on education continues. The original school for apprentices has become Mondragón University, with over four thousand students. In addition, the cooperative operates a wide range of educational institutions from pre-school to adult education, a network of primary and secondary schools, professional and vocational training institutes, and a language center. The students at Mondragón University have their own cooperative, *Alecoop*, which Fr. José founded in 1966 so that students could support themselves. One measure of the success of the educational programs came in 1993 when the Basque government demanded that any school receiving government funds must join the government system. Eighty percent of the schools voted to turn down the government money and retain their independence.

The *Ikerlan and Ideko Research and Development Centers:* Important to the success of the cooperatives was keeping up with technology. At Fr. José's urging, cooperatives were established to provide research and development efforts to the industrial cooperatives. Currently, a network of ten research centers provides support for electronics, computer-aided design and manufacturing, energy systems, renewable energy sources, machine tool technology, and thermo-plastics.

The support cooperatives demonstrate the advanced thinking and organizational flexibility of the movement. The cooperatives have a comprehensive approach to economic questions which include everything from pre-school education to retirement pensions, all handled within a cooperative environment. Their services exceed by far the services provided by traditional corporations and do so on an "economic" basis, fulfilling the twin requirements of social responsibility and economic rationality.

The Recession of the 1980s

Organizations are best judged on the way they handle adversity. Many forms of organization will appear to work well when times are good, but the real test comes in hard times. For Mondragón, this test came in the early 1980s, when Spain was hit by a severe economic recession. Unemployment rates soared to over 20 percent. The cooperatives did not escape these problems. For the first time, they faced problems of negative profits and surplus labor. But the cooperative model proved resilient. The *Caja Laboral* and the *Lagun-Aro* provided a firm base to fight the effects of the recession. Unemployment cover, something not previously necessary, was provided by the *Lagun.* Since wages were a share of the profits and many cooperatives had negative profits, the *Caja* capitalized the wage packets. The bank also made loans to workers on generous terms, sometimes even at a zero interest rate. Because of profit-pooling, the better-off cooperatives could transfer funds to those having difficulties. Surplus employees were given preference for openings at other cooperatives, and the accumulated capital of the workers was used to weather the storm. It is important to note that all of these policies, some of them harsh, were adopted by the General Assembly, the body which represented all of the worker-owners. The democratic and cooperative model proved itself flexible and responsive to the crisis, and in the second half of the 1980s, Mondragón resumed its positive growth.[19]

ORGANIZATION

Up until 1991, the cooperatives had been joined mainly through the Bank, a series of inter-cooperative agreements, and regional organizations based on geographic proximity. But the success of the cooperatives and their sheer size made that organization somewhat cumbersome. At congresses held between 1987 and 1991, the cooperatives agreed to reorganize themselves into the Mondragón Cooperative Corporation that we know today. The first task was to codify the principles handed down from Fr. José and honed by the experience of the members.

The Basic Principles

The Basic Principles were adopted by the 1987 General Assembly:[20]

1. Open admission: The cooperative is open to all men and women without regard to race or creed.

2. Democratic organization: All members are equal and the principle of "one person, one vote" rules, regardless of seniority, position, accumulated capital, etc.

3. Sovereignty of labor: "Work is placed top of our scale of priorities, since we believe that it is the key to transforming nature, society and even people themselves. As work is held to be the principle generator of wealth within the co-operative company structure, the corresponding distribution model should coincide with the degree of labour provided. Given the importance attached to the concept of work, the co-operatives are committed to widening the scope of job opportunities for all members."

4. Subordinate and instrumental character of capital: While capital is necessary for business, it is always considered subordinate to labor; it is worthy of remuneration, but contributions to share capital do not give members the right to participate in the management of the cooperative; only work does that.

5. Participatory management: All members have the right to participate in the management of the cooperatives, which implies the proper organizational structures, professional and social training for members, transparent information policies, and internal promotions.

6. Payment solidarity: Wages should be sufficient, comparable with those of other salaried workers in the region and in keeping with the means

of the cooperative. Payment should correspond to an internal frame-work based on solidarity, reflected in a smaller difference between the top and bottom of the pay scale than is commonly seen in the business market.

7. Cooperation between cooperatives: This is not only a requirement of worker solidarity, but also a basic requirement for efficient business practice. Some practical aspects of this principle are profit-pooling within subgroups, ease of transfer of worker members between coop-eratives, and the development of synergies derived from overall size. Cooperation with other cooperative entities in Spain, Europe, and the rest of the world is promoted through agreements to promote joint development.

8. Social transformation: Mondragón is more than a mere business enter-prise; it seeks social transformation with the aim of building a freer and more just society.

9. Universality: Mondragón has strong local roots in the Basque country, but has a universal vocation to work in solidarity with all those who desire economic democracy and who share the common objectives of peace, justice, and development.

10. Education: Without attention to education and the development of each person, the goals of the cooperative are unattainable. Special at-tention is paid to the education of young people, upon whom the future of the cooperative experience rests.

Organizational Structure

All of the principles would be abstract and meaningless if they were not embodied in appropriate structures and institutions. It is here that the co-operative demonstrates its superiority to traditional business methodology, which is normally a top-down organization with, frequently, little or no in-put from the workers and, perhaps, an antagonistic relationship with the unions, assuming there are unions. Needless to say, Mondragón, with its worker-owners, is organized on different principles.

The basic building blocks are the industrial cooperatives which are owned and operated by the workers. The worker-owners share in the profits and losses and have an equal say in the governance. There are no outside share-holders. The workers join in the *Cooperative Congress*, which is the highest authority in the MCC. Annually it meets to review the performance of the cooperative and elect a *Governing Council*, which conducts the affairs of the cooperative between meetings. Voting for the council is by one member/one vote rules, and terms are for four years. The Council appoints the manager. The manager may attend council meetings but has no vote. The Congress also appoints an audit committee, the watchdog committee which monitors the financial performance of the cooperative.

Another body, the *Social Council*, is elected from the shop floor with a representative from every 20 or 30 workers. While the General Congress represents the workers as *owners*, the Social Council represents the owners as *workers*. The two bodies reflect a reality that while the workers and the owners are the same persons, they have different functions at different times and these different functions need to be represented in different ways. The Council, therefore, functions in a manner analogous to a union, without the in-built antagonism, and advises management on such issues as job design, working hours, pay rates, health and safety issues, etc. The Council provides management with direct experience from the workers on working problems.

Each of the cooperatives is a member of one of three groups, the financial, industrial, and distribution groups. The industrial cooperatives are further organized into seven sub-groups by type of product (automotive, machine tools, household, etc.). The purpose of the groups and subgroups is to facilitate planning and share expertise.

In lieu of wages the worker-owners receive *anticipos*, a monthly advance on the profits. The level of the advances, following a principle of "external solidarity," is set at the prevailing rate for work for similar jobs. The advances are set by a committee composed of the human resources director and seven members of the Social Council. Overall, incomes are kept as equal as possible. In addition, 45 percent of the cooperative's earnings are credited to the members as capital held in individual accounts. The accounts earn interest at an agreed-upon rate. Members may draw upon the interest or use the accounts as collateral for personal loans, but the principle cannot be touched until retirement. Ten percent of the earnings go into a social fund, and the rest is reinvested in the cooperative.

WORKERS AS OWNERS

We began this discussion looking at the problems occasioned by the agency dilemma and traditional organizational structures. The cooperative is one form that gains significant competitive advantages from its ability to overcome the inefficiencies associated with these two problems. When the workers are the owners, the dichotomy between agents and principals is mitigated or may disappear entirely. However, that does not happen automatically as a result of the workers being owners, but must be embodied in the organization and culture of the firm. Worker ownership is not a magic wand. Still, it provides a powerful tool which, when intelligently embodied in the organizational reality of the firm, grants not only significant business benefits, but social benefits as well. The program of social insurance, education, training, and research and development would simply be too expensive for most companies organized on traditional lines. Many of these costs are simply placed on the government or ignored altogether. But the founders of Mondragón refused to see a dichotomy between "business" and "social" issues. Rather, they treated them as part of a whole. Indeed, it is a mystery as to why they should be treated any other way. After all, the same wage which provides us our daily bread must also educate our children, provide for our old age, and support us in times of need. We all need to earn that wage in some sort of productive environment which is itself always dependent on social institutions, be they government or "private." Current models "privatize" the "business" part but make public the social concerns, as if there were a different source of funds for each or as if people could be divided into their "public" and "private" selves. Indeed, even business is neither wholly public nor wholly private, but is *social;* it always takes place within a context that presumes certain institutions.

Catholic Social Teaching stresses the just distribution of property, a requirement that some find problematic. But in the cooperatives, we see this teaching implemented within a healthy, vibrant, and innovative business environment. Mondragón's success proves there is no inherent contradiction between justice and good business; indeed, the cooperatives seem to enjoy a competitive advantage based on eliminating the agency dilemma and the organizational inefficiencies which result from it. The cooperative organization is a thoroughly democratized one, something many observers find impractical or undesirable. For example, Michael Novak speaks for many when he says, "To organize industry democratically would be a grave and costly error, since democratic procedures are not designed for productivity and efficiency."[21] Mondragón's success would seem to contradict Novak's pessimism.

Recall that in speaking of marginal productivity, we noted that while the traditional model has capital hiring labor and keeping the whole product, one could also draw the model with labor hiring capital and keeping the whole product. This is the model for Mondragón. It works.

Not every company can transform itself into a cooperative. Nevertheless, there are lessons from the Mondragón experience that can be applied in each and every company to a greater or lesser degree. If, as we have argued throughout this book, economics and justice are not opposed, but complementary, then a proper view of one should reinforce a proper view of the other. The proper view should always be able to accommodate both sound business practice and social justice.

Chapter 18

The Just Wage and Business

You can't have high productivity with faceless people.

—JACK STACK

THE JUST WAGE AND BUSINESS

Most students of business will not have the opportunity to apply their skills in situations such as that of the Mondragón Cooperative, land redistribution programs, or micro-banking. Indeed, the only relevant data so far might be that which concerns globalization, since many businesses, if not most, find that cutthroat competition with Third-World labor is the overriding reality of their situation. Our workers are pitted against theirs, to the disadvantage of both, and the entrepreneur who wishes to survive has little choice but to recognize this reality and act accordingly. However, an economy that takes this route has taken the short route to social chaos and economic ruin. The current implementation of globalization is not a "reality" in the sense of something given by nature and therefore intrinsic to the "real," but rather something created by human beings in a particular historical and cultural moment. Cutthroat globalization is "real" only because it is perceived to be real; that is, enough people accept it and treat it as "reality" so that it does indeed become a reality. People despair of a solution because they confuse a social "reality" with a natural one. Cutthroat globalization is not "real" in this latter sense.

Nor is it permanent. Indeed, the process is so destabilizing that it will either find a way to heal itself or it will collapse into chaos and war, a process that seems to be happening before our very eyes. Healing the wounds of globalization will require the application of the principles we have dealt with so far, and will require their application at the level of the individual business or corporation. Moreover, when we examine the sources of the present "reality," we find that it does not really add to corporate or human values, but is a detriment to them. Recognizing real values does not detract from business values, but enhances them. Our present "reality" turns out to be based on mistakes about the nature of work and the nature of social organization, mistakes that are easy enough to overcome and, in the process, to enhance the value of the firm.

VALUES AND CORPORATE VALUE

A globalization that depends on exploitation has the power it does because of the misunderstanding of what actually builds corporate value. That is to say, the relationship between values and value is misunderstood. Milton Friedman famously remarked that corporations have "one and only one social responsibility," which is to "increase [the corporation's] profits."[1] It is not that Friedman denies the other values that business brings to society, but he proposes one and only one measure, a measure equivalent to the price of the stock. As we shall see, this single measure hasn't even worked well for the shareholder, especially not the small shareholder. Further, this single measure involves the logical error known as the *fallacy of composition*, the belief that the whole is never more or less than the sum of its parts. But mostly, the statement is wrong because it is simply bad economics and bad business practice. The statement is predicated on the belief that growth is a function of the increase in capital. However, this theory has been shown to be false at a merely empirical level. As discussed in chapter 10, capital is responsible for no more than one-third of economic growth.[2] There are at least two other factors of even greater importance. The first involves the general climate of social cohesion, law, and prosperity of the society. Without stable laws and general prosperity, business is difficult or impossible. A corporation may be able to increase shareholder value by sending its work to foreign or domestic sweatshops, but in doing so it destabilizes society and thus destroys the very conditions which make business possible. Recognizing this dependency of business on overall stability involves recognizing the practical importance of the principle of solidarity.

Further, the real source of economic growth — and, therefore, the real source of increase in shareholder value — is not physical capital, but human capital, the rearing, socialization, and education of children and the creativity and dedication which workers bring to their jobs. But modern firms often have a difficult time taking full advantage of this source of growth. What George Goyder says about shop-floor workers is true of workers generally:

> There is a large reserve of productivity latent in human attitudes on the shop-floor. It is the single biggest resource we have. If we could tap that resource, the growth of productivity would be explosive. Nothing

holds us back from increased production but ourselves.... No expert known to the writer who has quantified the reservoir of productivity latent in shop-floor attitudes has put the potential increase below thirty per cent. Some have given a much higher figure.[3]

The question, then, is how we call forth all the values which the worker has to give. Or asked another way, how do we increase the value of a company, its shareholder value included, by increasing social stability and worker development? I believe that there are three key issues: proper job design, proper organization, and proper ownership. These are the factors which are largely within the control of the corporation. There are, of course, other factors which the corporation cannot control; the corporation is the direct employer of the workers, but some part of the problem depends on the *indirect employer* (see chapter 7), the collection of rules and social norms that also contribute to the wage contract. Nevertheless, the direct employer not only has direct responsibility, but direct control of the key organization, design, and ownership issues. In this chapter, we will deal with the first two issues and leave ownership for the next chapter.

PRINCIPLES OF THE JUST WAGE

We have, thus far, presented the just wage as a moral requirement of a just and stable economic order. However, it is never sufficient to state an abstract moral principle without reflecting on the principles necessary for its implementation. Morality is the field of human action, and hence an "abstract moral principle" is almost a contradiction in terms. To have any real meaning, a moral principle must attain a concrete existence in our actions and our institutions. This requires, in turn, that we reflect on the principles needed for implementation. Helen Alford and Michael Naughton have identified three principles necessary for the implementation of the just wage: the principle of *need*, the principle of *equity* or *contribution*, and the principle of *economic order*.[4]

The Principle of Need

For most people, the wage is the only way they have of fulfilling their material needs. From the standpoint of the economy as a whole, wages are the major means of distributing the output of production to the mass of people. Thus, from both the standpoint of the individual worker and the society at large, there is a need for a just or living wage. From the individual standpoint, the worker surrenders a portion of her life to the production process and hence has a right to be compensated at a rate that will allow her to sustain herself, grow, and develop during that portion of her life.[5] From the standpoint of society, it is required that new workers be brought up and educated. Thus, combining both aspects, we may say that the just wage is the amount necessary to sustain the individual worker and her family.

In a country like the United States, the problem of the "living wage" would seem to be no problem at all. Not only is there sufficient wealth, but the increases in productivity would seem to be able, by themselves, to lift all workers out of poverty. Unfortunately, the majority of productivity gains have gone to a relatively small group of workers at the top, while wage inequality is actually increasing. Indeed, the real hourly pay of workers at the bottom has fallen at the same time their "fringe" benefits (like health care) are being drastically reduced or cut entirely.[6]

The Principle of Equity

The principle of need defines what is due to a person simply because he is a person. The principle of equity, on the other hand, defines what is due to *this particular person*, based on her individual contributions. Each person has a different level of skills, gives a different level of effort, and has different talents. A wage, to be just, must honor these different contributions that each person makes.[7] If we were to look at need alone, all wages would be equal. But such equality would violate equity, since persons must be honored in their individuality, with their individual contributions both recognized and compensated.

Inequitable pay is likely one of the largest problems in the corporate world today, especially in the widening gap between worker and executive pay. Executives like to talk a good game; "they sermonize on the importance of employees' contributions, but pay as if the executive is the Lone Ranger of corporate success."[8] Without a principle of equity, the right relationships are impossible to establish as employees become convinced that pay is not based on performance and contribution, but on status and power alone. And when employees feel that their contributions are not being rewarded, they tend to make fewer contributions.

The Principle of Economic Order

The principles of need and equity are also necessary conditions for economic order; the firm must generate sufficient values to be able to pay just and equitable wages. No economy that excludes a large portion of its workers from a living wage can hope to achieve equilibrium, and if contributions are not seen to be compensated, they will soon cease to be given. However, while they are *necessary* conditions, they are not *sufficient* conditions. Just and equitable wages cannot be determined apart from a firm's resources and level of profit. In other words, the just wage must also be a *sustainable* wage; it must be determined in light of the economic health of the firm. To be sure, a just and equitable wage will contribute to the health of a firm, and even confer a competitive advantage. However, justice in pay has to be combined with creativity in product design, manufacture, marketing, and service. Now, it is likely that equitable pay will help to call forth these innovations, but it will also require knowledge of the production process in modern business to see what the bars are to justice and equity at the practical level.

JOB DESIGN

The Division of Labor

The most common understanding of the role of labor in the production process is given by the "division of labor," especially as that theory is expounded by Adam Smith in *The Wealth of Nations*. Smith devotes the first three chapters of his book to this topic and treats it as the foundation both of all wealth and of the "natural" distribution of rewards "among the different Ranks of the People."[9] Smith illustrates this principle with the famous example of the pin factory. There are 18 steps in the manufacture of pins, and each step is assigned to a different worker. Thus, one person pulls the wire, another straightens it, yet others cut the wire, sharpen it, prepare it for attachment of the heads, and so forth.

Smith believed that there were three advantages to this system:

> First, to the increase of dexterity in every particular workman; secondly, to the saving of the time which is commonly lost in passing from one species of work to another; and lastly, to the invention of a great number of machines which facilitate and abridge labour, and enable one man to do the work of many.[10]

Whether or not these advantages are real, or are really attributable to the division of labor, there are also some disadvantages, some of which Smith recognized and some of which he did not. The first disadvantage is that labor is "de-skilled." There are no longer "pin-makers," workers thoroughly knowledgeable and skilled in the art of making pins, but only a collection of people with single, narrow tasks: wire-pullers, sharpeners, etc., each with a simple and repetitive task to perform. Such de-skilled labor quickly loses it bargaining power as each low-skilled person is easily replaced. This leads to another consequence. We may recall that work is both transitive and intransitive; that is, while we work to form the world, our work is at the same time forming us. Part of our work goes out of us into some object in the material world, but another part stays within us, and is part of our development and growth. But when our work is confined to one or two simple operations, there is little opportunity for growth and development. Smith himself came to recognize this problem; in the second edition of his great work, he added the following qualification to his theory:

> In the progress of the division of labour, the employment of the far greater part of those who live by labour…comes to be confined to a few very simple operations, frequently to one or two.…The man whose whole life is spent in performing a few simple operations…has no occasion to exert his understanding or to exercise his invention in finding out expedients for removing difficulties which never occur. He naturally loses, therefore, the habit of such exertion, and generally becomes as stupid and ignorant as it is possible for a human creature to become.[11]

This loss of innovative spirit leads to a third difficulty. As workers cease to be "pin-makers" and become instead "wire-pullers" or "sharpeners" or one of the other eighteen jobs involved in the process, then knowledge of the process is lost among the workers. This means, in turn, that a new function is required, that of the professional manager. When workers had knowledge of the whole process, then "management" was a minor consideration, and any one of the workers could, in theory, manage the process; management was a negligible expense. But with the loss of knowledge, management becomes the decisive factor and a huge overhead cost. Part of the gains in efficiency from the division of labor is lost to the need for increased management overhead.

The resulting increase in the need for, and power of, professional management leads to yet another difficulty: agency problems are increased. When managers become both numerous and important, they form a new group, a group with its own narrow interests. They are supposed to be fulfilling only the interests of the owners, but in fact they have their own set of interests. Therefore the overheads associated with agency are increased. Further, this division of the roles of worker and manager creates tensions and resentments on both sides.

Management seems to be an overhead expense with no natural limits, short of bankrupting the company. Indeed, the rise of managerial power has spawned a new class of *über*-managers whose pay and privileges dwarf those of line workers to an unprecedented degree. As John Bogle assesses their newfound power:

> Over the past century, a gradual move from *owners' capitalism* — providing the lion's share of the rewards of investment to those who put up the money and risk their own capital — has culminated in an extreme version of *manager's capitalism* — providing vastly disproportionate rewards to those whom we have trusted to manage our enterprises in the interest of the owners.[12]

How "disproportionate" are these rewards? Consider that in 1980, the average CEO pay was 42 times that of the average worker. By 2000, CEO pay had ballooned to 531 times that of the worker average.[13] During the same period, the pay of the average worker increased at the minuscule rate of 0.3 percent per annum; CEO pay increased 8.5 percent per annum, or 28 times faster.[14] But that is only part of the compensation, since the executives often live a lavish lifestyle at company expense, a lifestyle not counted in the computation of their pay, but a real cost nevertheless. The monies paid to the *über*-managers can only come from the rewards due either to the investors or the workers, or both; all parties are short-changed. Although there are many reasons for the rise of this new class, the de-skilling of labor, and therefore its loss of power, is one important reason.

Finally, when work no longer fulfills the worker, when he ceases to be, or to have a chance to be, a real craftsman and becomes a mere servo-mechanism of the assembly line, then his only compensation for the job is expressed by the wage. This leads to constant wage pressures. Combined with the division of management from labor, the resulting tensions form a constant pressure for unionization which is, from a management standpoint, an undesirable outcome and an unending source of friction.

Nevertheless, the division of labor has become a bedrock assumption of industrial production. It has the status of a dogma, not to be questioned. Therefore, we need to question it.

The Sequencing of Tasks

No one can deny that modern industrial technique has efficiently produced a vast collection of goods and increased the overall wealth of society. And if we were to look at most of these highly productive factories, we would be likely to observe that they are run according to the precepts of the dogma of the division of labor. But you would not find it in all highly productive factories. In at least some, you would find increasingly popular methods such as "human-centered design" or "cellular manufacturing," methods which violate the central tenets of the division of labor. In the light of alternative methods, is the division of labor really as necessary as it seems?

Smith placed a dichotomy between minute specialization and the crafting of each separate pin. But this is a false dichotomy; it was never a case of one person making one pin at a time versus a group of specialists making thousands. Rather, it is a question of the sequencing of the tasks, whether by a few craftsmen or by a group of specialists. The real efficiencies come from properly sequencing the tasks. Thus, a single craftsman who draws out all the wire for a batch at one time, then straightens the whole batch, then cuts the wire, etc., will achieve the same efficiencies as does the division of labor.[15] The division of labor succeeds not because of the specialization of jobs, but because it also sequences the tasks. This sequencing eliminates the set-up times between tasks, one of the three reasons that Smith claimed for the superiority of the division of labor. The other two were the dexterity that a worker acquires when doing a single task and the amount of innovation that specialized labor brings to the assembly line. The argument for the former is unconvincing; a craftsman becomes accomplished at the various tasks of his trade without being forced to specialize.

As for the latter argument, innovation brought about by specialization, the opposite seems to be the case: specialization decreases innovation, as Smith himself came to recognize when he noted that the specialized worker loses the habit of innovation and becomes "as stupid . . . as it is possible for a human being to become." A craftsman might, for example, notice that the pulling, straightening, and cutting of the wire might be combined, with a few mechanical changes, into one operation. The specialist either doesn't notice this, or if she does, she fears it because it means the elimination of two jobs. This is borne out by the history of industry in the nineteenth and twentieth centuries, when workers opposed or even sabotaged machinery precisely because they perceived, often quite correctly, that such innovations were not in their best interests. Of course, there has been a great deal of innovation in industry, but it does not ordinarily arise from the shop floor. Rather, it depends on the fact that inventors are granted a monopoly for a period of time in the form of a patent.[16]

Recognizing the true source of industrial efficiency gives us tremendous freedom in job design. The division of labor concentrates on separation and isolation, reducing the worker to a "cog" in the assembly line. It therefore loses most of the values that the worker can contribute, save for the value of his muscle-power. Thus it throws away one of the most important assets of a firm. The separation of tasks, on the other hand, allows us to design jobs

that call for a greater development of the worker and hence for more productivity. Management overhead can be greatly reduced, and a workforce
more knowledgeable about the process can contribute more in the way of
innovations. The shop floor workers can be the authors of their own jobs.
And with such "authorship" comes a kind of authority. We can begin, at this
point, to see the outlines of possible solutions to the problem of low wages.

Job Design and the Just Wage

Modern corporate culture has been largely formed by the tenets of the division of labor. But this is not in any way a "natural" principle; rather, it is
the product of a particular culture and a particular cultural attitude toward
work and the workers. For example, in the guild system, the master was also
a "worker" working alongside his apprentices, and the hierarchy was both
vertical and temporary. Each apprentice worked in expectation of becoming
his own master, and the master had the job of communicating the necessary
skills. Management overhead was practically nil and there were, of course,
no "unions" because the workers and masters had the same set of interests
and were joined in the same organization.

   In recent years, serious challenges to the division of labor philosophy have
arisen with several different strategies, such as "human-centered design" and
"cellular management." These strategies aim at fostering worker skills and
development "so that the worker controls the technology and not the other
way around."[17] Workers are organized into "cells" and each cell is given
a certain amount of autonomy and accountability. Without going into the
technicalities of these methods, we can note the way they differ from the
division of labor theories. Instead of decreasing the skills of the workers,
the purpose is to increase them; instead of concentrating all accountability
in the hands of the managers, it is placed at the lowest practical level. As
an example of how these job design strategies may be used, we can take the
case of Reell Precision Manufacturing (RPM).

   RPM established a "target wage" for its lowest-paid employees based on
a rough idea of a reasonable standard of living. In 1996, this target wage
was $10.91 per hour, or $22,500 per year. However, RPM could not simply
raise minimum wages to this amount; to do so would simply put the entire
company at risk, making everybody worse off. Instead:

> Reell redesigned its manufacturing work to include more skill and de-
> cision making from employees, thus creating organizational conditions
> which require less supervision, allow faster set-up times, and reduce

the need for quality inspection. Together, these improvements reduce overall costs, allowing Reell to pay its target wage.[18]

By simply redesigning jobs, RPM was able to meet both its moral and its business obligations. That is, they were able to meet both the principle of need and the principle of equity. But in doing so, they also built a better business; that is, they met the principle of economic order. Here, I think, we have a general principle: while a "moral" requirement may seem "extrinsic" to business, that is, something outside its proper realm and concern, it is actually an *intrinsic* requirement of a sound economy, if the requirement is properly understood. This should not come as a surprise. All proper relations between humans are properly regulated by justice. Business is certainly a set of human relations and is therefore properly regulated by justice.

This failure to understand the proper relationship between business and justice means that we often end up asking the wrong questions. For example, the "realistic" businessman asks how a just wage can be made compatible with good business in an age of global competition. This is the wrong question. The proper question is how global competition can be made compatible with the just wage and good business. It is beyond doubt that when a company lays off ten thousand workers, it also lays off ten thousand customers; they are the same persons. When the jobs are "outsourced" to countries with subsistence labor rates, we do not get back the ten thousand customers; at best we get back a handful of top managers and owners in the outsourced company. The bulk of the workers just make too little to consider buying our products. At the heart of the problem lies Chesterton's conundrum: you cannot pay a man like a pauper and expect him to spend like a prince. Now, a few companies may be able to outsource some of their work without too much of an effect on the overall economy. But when it becomes widespread, when a nation swaps its capacity to make things (the only sure way to wealth) for some short-term and private gains, then that nation is on the short road to ruin. It may be able, for a time, to sustain itself by borrowing, but sooner or later, the creditors will call in their notes, with catastrophic results. Moreover, inequality will multiply, with its inevitable burden of social unrest and resentment.

ORGANIZATION AND CULTURE

The Fallacy of the Flow Chart

Any firm of any appreciable size is likely to have a flow chart which describes the hierarchical relations within the firm in neat little boxes and clear lines of authority and communication. The flow of authority is thus clearly defined in a quasi-militaristic fashion, with all of the "troops" organized in their platoons, companies, and battalions, and authority flowing from the "general" at the top down to each "private" soldier. The generals give the orders and the troops execute them. The only problem is that anyone who has actually worked in a company knows instinctively that this is not true. Moreover, such a person knows that knowledge of the competitive battle does not reside exclusively at the top, nor does the necessary information flow either up or down the "chain of command" in a clear and unambiguous fashion. The official flow chart, in other words, expresses not the reality of the firm, but only the delusions of the managers. In order to get a correct view of what actually happens in a firm, we will have to examine the sources of authority.

Recall the discussion of authority under the heading of *The Entrepreneurial Firm* in chapter 11. We noted two sources of authority, one from the entrepreneur who is the "author" of the firm (and therefore its originating authority), and one from the process of production itself, that is, from the shop floor:

> This is the authority of the process itself. The shop-floor worker knows what has to be done and has often discovered, or will discover by trial and error, how best to do it. This knowledge represents the accumulated wisdom of shop-floor experience and it is part of the task of the foreman to see that it is communicated upwards to management.[19]

Given these two forms of authority, the "top-down" interpretation of the flow chart is counterproductive and never quite true. The dual authority exists whether or not management recognizes it. Many a top manager has discovered that resistance to his orders and ideas has killed or crippled a project or plan. His response is often to insist on greater discipline within the organization and tighter control. And just as often, he discovers that this only makes things worse, only hardens the attitudes and stiffens the resistance. When authority is viewed in a top-down manner only, then the natural response from the other authorities is resistance. What is required is an acceptance of authority, one that doesn't depend solely on fear of losing one's job, but rather on social cohesion. Nothing creates a sense of social cohesion as does a sense of shared purpose. This shared purpose is, in turn, created by shared risks and rewards; this is what creates the requisite loyalty in a firm. Indeed, if workers feel that all of the rewards of increased productivity will go only to the top, then they will have little incentive for increasing productivity, and much incentive to resist it.

Order and Creativity

The problems of recognizing multiple sources of authority and the creation of a shared purpose are the primary organizational challenges. In the family firm, this sense of shared purpose is obvious and intuitive, and little attention need be paid to the problem. But as organizations grow large and complex, the common purpose becomes more and more difficult, especially in firms that have a quasi-military, top-down organizational model. We have already seen in the last chapter how an organization based on the principle of subsidiarity mitigates the agency problem and creates a sense of shared purpose. We can now see how that same organizational model helps to recognize the multiple sources of authority. The organizational issue is critical because workers can only make a full contribution if they have responsibility for improving their jobs. However, authority is the corollary of responsibility; no one can hold somebody responsible for something over which he had no authority. We can now see why the principle of subsidiarity is the primary principle for organizations. The fine balance between the requirements of order and creativity cannot be achieved by the quasi-militaristic organization, nor can it be achieved by an "anarchical" one, which gives free rein to creativity without requiring accountability. The principles involved in the Mondragón organization can indeed be applied to a more conventional firm, at least in part, and can be applied so as to grant a competitive advantage.

Creativity and Culture

All human activity takes place within a culture, and businesses in this regard are no different from any other human activity. Building a business is largely about building a business culture. Cultures are based on shared values and expressed or known through the human relationships based on those values. For example, if we take Milton Friedman's single measure of value (shareholder value), we announce to all the employees that the most important persons in the firm are the persons not actually in the firm. The difficulty is that the human relationships built on such a model will be inhuman; people will not be valued in themselves, but will tend to be faceless cogs in a profit-making machine. One can certainly make a principled defense of this view; one can certainly argue that all values should be the values of the owners. However, this involves some ambiguous questions of "ownership," questions we shall deal with in the next chapter. But it also presents serious problems in bringing forth the best from employees, which is precisely the factor upon which shareholder value most depends. As Jack Stack put it, "You can't have high productivity with faceless people."[20] If, as we have argued, value is based on human work and creativity, then we have an immediate problem with Freidman's diktat. The shareholders represent only the capital in a firm, and usually they represent even less than that; they represent only the *original* capital of the firm, capital which in most firms has long since been consumed. The rest of the capital comes from re-tained earnings and borrowing. Thus, at highest rating, Friedman reduces all values to the partial values of remote owners. But since the employees of the firm produce, at the lowest rating, two-thirds of the value of a firm, the interests of two-thirds of the firm is ignored. Thus, even from a narrow standpoint of shareholder value, this subordination of values cannot be the best description of building values in a firm.

What kind of culture, then, does build the maximum values? Jack Stack, the founder and president of the Springfield Remanufacturing Company (SRC), identifies the primary management task as follows:

> People can accomplish almost anything if they have a common pur-pose, a higher goal, and they all know what it is, and they're going after it together. *Everybody needs to be going somewhere.* People need a des-tination, or they get lost. It they have one, however, and if it's really their own, there's no telling what they can do. They can survive the darkest hours, beat the longest odds, scale the greatest heights.[21]

Building a *common purpose,* a goal that is owned and shared by all members of the firm, is the primary task in building a company culture, and hence of building the firm. What Mr. Stack especially wished to avoid was what he called "employee thinking," that is, thinking only about one's job or at best, one's department, without considering the common purpose, the good of the whole firm.[22] Yet, this is precisely the kind of thinking that most of us have been taught, both formally and informally. It is the kind of thinking implicit in Milton Friedman's shareholder model of the firm. After all, if only the interests of the shareholders count, then there can be no common purpose that involves all members of the firm. But this kind of thinking, Mr. Stack says, is capable of destroying the company from within.[23]

What Stack set out to create was a community of entrepreneurs, rather than just a collection of people with jobs; indeed, SRC wanted to do away with "jobs" and the employee mentality altogether.[24] But the primary prob-lem is that people have been trained to see themselves in terms of jobs rather than as entrepreneurs; they see themselves as merely performing a function for somebody else, usually somebody very remote. Creating this community meant realizing that the business was not an end in itself, but a means to an end, "a tool that allows us to accomplish the things that matter most to us, and those things must transcend business to have real meaning and value."[25] To accomplish this goal, to create this community, SRC used two means: education and equity sharing.

To educate the members of the firm (it would be wrong to say "employees"), Stack invented a system of informal but continuous education he called *The Great Game of Business*. If the workers are going to take responsibility for the firm, they must know the rules of business, and the *Great Game* was the means of teaching them these rules, from the simplest to the most complex. As Stack evaluates the results of this "game," he notes that "we've had dozens of employees rise from the shop floor . . . to top management positions, and they're far better qualified than a lot of MBAs I see."[26] The game requires that the firm practice *open-book management*. If all members of the firm are to be responsible for the firm, then they all must have equal access to the books. Further, you cannot truly educate employees unless they can see how their actions affect the firm, and this is impossible without looking at the books. But the greatest benefit, as Jack Stack notes, is that "when you open your books — really open them — you also open your mind, and neither your mind nor your books will be closed again."[27]

Continuous education and open-book management frees the firm from the constraints of the division of labor, which confines each worker to just one task, and from the quasi-militaristic "top-down" management, which confines responsibility to just one group. The results of this culture at SRC have been nothing short of phenomenal. In twenty years, they went from sales of $16 million to $185 million, with similar results for profit and shareholder equity. But it is in the area of shareholder equity that the firm really stands out, because all of the shares are owned by the workers. The company has 727 worker-owners, of whom only five were original members of the firm. The other 722 shareholders own 64 percent of the firm.[28] This point is crucial, because "owning their work" must involve real ownership, and not just some psychic substitute. Equity sharing defines the community,[29] a community built on the premise that all the members of the community must share in the wealth that the community creates.[30] This notion of sharing, or "distributive justice," has been an intrinsic part of our understanding of justice from the time of Aristotle until relatively modern times. However, in the modern world, the concept of ownership changed radically. It is hard for us to see this change, because we regard current notions as natural and intuitive, and thus have difficulty in recognizing just how artificial our notions are. Since ownership is the most basic of all economic relationships, we need to examine it in greater detail in the next chapter.

Chapter 19

Building an Ownership Society

> Property in the hands of labor is freedom;
> Labor in the hands of property is slavery.
> — DMYTRI KLEINER

During the debates on privatizing Social Security, there was much rhetoric about "building an ownership society." Now, anyone interested in either social justice or the proper operation of an economy must welcome this discussion. However, it is obvious that buying a few shares of stock with a portion of retirement funds is not sufficient to create the ownership society. What then is an ownership society? I take it to be a society in which ownership of productive assets, such as land or tools, is widespread among the population. Too often the political and economic debates revolve around the theoretical differences between socialism and capitalism. However, the *practical* differences between these two may be more apparent than real. This is because in capitalist *practice* (as opposed to theory), ownership of the means of production has come to be vested in collectives of immense size and power. These institutions resemble a communist state more than most communist states do, because ownership is vested, not in individuals, but in an immense collective entity. Indeed, the corporation has done more to "collectivize" production than any communist collective ever did. Thus the real debate is, or should be, between *concentrated* ownership (whether in the hands of state or corporate bureaucrats) and distributed ownership. In order to understand this issue, we need to examine four issues: the connection between private property and the common good; the rise of corporate power; the distinction between ownership and use; and finally the practical ways of building an ownership culture at the level of both the individual firm and the society in general.

PRIVATE PROPERTY AND THE COMMON GOOD

It is well understood that the simplest method for calling forth creativity is simply to give people ownership of that which they create. People simply care more for their own property than they do for the property of another. Recall the experience of ninth- and tenth-century England. When the serfs achieved economic control of their own plots, that is, the right to receive all surplus values above the customary rents, there was an explosion of technological advances which have come to be called "the second agricultural revolution"; the entire wealth of the High Middle Ages was built on this revolution. Property relations are the most basic of all economic relations, and all economic outcomes will depend, to a large extent, on the division of property, including both physical and intellectual property. But as we saw in chapter 5, there have been a variety of legal and social forms for property ownership, and each form has different economic consequences and results in a different form of social organization.

In traditional Christian thinking, private property is a sacred right, but exists under what might be called a "social mortgage." As John Paul II expressed the relationship:

> Christian tradition has never upheld this right [to ownership of property] as absolute and untouchable. On the contrary, it has always understood this right within the broader context of the right common to all to use the goods of the whole of creation: *the right to private property is subordinated to the right to common use,* to the fact that goods are meant for everyone.[1]

When we deal with "small" property, the property people have in their own homes, tools, and personal effects, there are few real issues which arise. However, as productive property gets concentrated in the hands of a relative few, then the issues become more significant and have a greater, indeed decisive, economic impact. If the pope is correct, then there must be some means of distinguishing between legitimate and illegitimate ownership of the means of production. John Paul II gives us this general criterion:

> Ownership of the means of production, whether in industry or agriculture, is just and legitimate if it serves useful work. It becomes illegitimate, however, when it is not utilized or when it serves to impede the work of others, in an effort to gain a profit which is not the result of the overall expansion of work and the wealth of society, but rather is the result of curbing them or of illicit exploitation, speculation or the breaking of solidarity among working people. Ownership of this kind has no justification, and represents an abuse in the sight of God and humanity.[2]

While the idea of limits to ownership may strike the modern ear as strange or even threatening, the idea of unlimited ownership has definite economic consequences. Indeed, such ownership presents a great challenge to economic stability and social order. The reason for this is easy to see if we recall that the major presupposition of "free market" economics is that production is spread over a vast number of firms. But as the means of production become more and more concentrated, this becomes less and less likely, and the neo-classical system simply fails to achieve the equilibrium state at which it aims. Therefore, this is a question not only of justice, but of practical economics.

The major means for concentrating ownership in the modern world is the corporation. Of the hundred largest economies in the world, fifty-one are corporations; they have revenues (and powers) greater than most nations.[3] In addition to their economic power, their political power is formidable. For example, in 2000, business interests donated $1.2 billion to candidates in national elections, which was 75 percent of all political donations.[4] There are thirty-five thousand registered lobbyists in Washington, largely employed by corporations. This represents an enormous investment, and corporations expect a return on this investment, a return they get in the form of favorable laws, lowered taxes, compliant regulators, and outright subsidies. The corporation is, arguably, the dominant social institution of the modern world, dwarfing both state and church in social influence. Further, modern corporations embody a concept of ownership that is unprecedented in world history.

When we own something, we have a collection of rights and duties. We have the rights of use and control and the right to receive a share of the wealth that the property creates. We also have some responsibilities. If the property causes harm to another, we have personal liabilities. For example, if one owns a lot in the city, and he neglects it so that it becomes overgrown and a haven for vermin, the owner can be held personally liable if someone is bitten by the vermin. And, in most cultures, property has some sort of public obligations that vary in their form from culture to culture. Within corporations, however, ownership has a new and unique meaning which changes or abolishes each one of these traditional aspects of ownership. In order to understand how this came about, we need to examine the history of this institution.

A SHORT HISTORY OF CORPORATIONS

English Roots

Although corporations are so ubiquitous that we have come to think of them as "natural," their existence and powers have always been both problematic and controversial. The term "corporation" originally referred to monopolies granted by royal charter, most notably to the medieval guilds. These charters created monopolies as quasi-governmental entities in specific geographic areas for a specific trade. The rights and duties of the guild were specified, and the charters could be revoked if the guild exceeded its authority or no longer served the public good.

Beginning in 1555 with the establishment of the Moscovy Company, corporate charters were granted for trade monopolies to specific areas. The logic of these monopolies was that long-distance trade was a highly risky undertaking, unlikely to attract the necessary capital without being a monopoly. One of the more famous corporations was the East India Company, established in 1601 to trade with India. This corporation maintained its own army and navy, minted its own money, conquered India for the English crown, and generally served as the government in the areas in which it operated. Since it operated mainly outside of England, its extensive abuses were largely ignored. These abuses have recently provided the now-deceased company with a role in popular culture, namely to serve as the villains for the *Pirates of the Caribbean* movies, even though the company operated in India and not in the Americas; nonetheless, to make the pirates look good, the producers had to find somebody who was worse.

Counterattack

In 1776, two blows were struck against corporate power. The first was the publication of Adam Smith's *The Wealth of Nations*. Smith hated both the corporate monopolies and the general idea of the limited-liability joint-stock company. He did allow that there were four cases in which they might be justified. The first was for developing new trade routes, but this would be a temporary monopoly only. The others were for national banks, insurance companies, and canals. Aside from these exceptions, he wrote, "I have not been able to recollect any other in which all the three circumstances requisite for rendering reasonable the establishment of a joint stock company concur."[5] Smith believed that these monopolies were part of a process by which governments made things difficult for the poor.

> Civil government, so far as it is instituted for the security of property, is in reality instituted for the defense of the rich against the poor, or of those who have some property against those who have none.[6]

The second blow in 1776 against corporate power was the American Revolution. It was a rebellion against the abusive power of the English crown, a power that usually operated through the chartered corporations. The Navigation Acts required that all goods exported from Europe or Asia to America had first to pass through England, usually on corporate-owned ships. The colonists had to ship all their goods on English ships and were forbidden from the manufacture of many items; these had to be bought from England. The colonies were viewed strictly as a cheap source of raw materials and a high-markup market for English manufactured goods.[7] The corporations were far more damaging to colonial interests than was the Stamp Tax, and it was East India Company tea that the "Indians" dumped into the harbor at the Boston Tea Party, thereby rendering it, as one wag put it, "undrinkable, even for Americans."

In early America, corporations were severely limited, a fact which expressed the American experience with the oppressive power of English corporations. No mention is made of corporations in the Constitution, even though James Madison suggested that the granting of charters should be a federal right. But to most of the founders, federal charters smacked of royal privileges, and the power was left to the states.[8] The states, for their part, wrote very restrictive charters indeed. The corporations could only exist for a limited amount of time, had to be dissolved if their charters were not renewed, could not make political contributions,[9] and could not own stock in other companies. The investors were personally liable for any criminal acts of the officers and for any debts incurred by the corporation. The charters could be revoked at any time, a power the states exercised from time to time. All investors, regardless of their contribution, had equal voting rights. Each corporation was limited to conducting only those businesses authorized in the charter, and there were limits on the amount of debt they could incur. By 1800, there were only 200 corporate charters granted.[10]

The Rise of Corporate Power

Things slowly began to change, however, as the corporations gained more and more power. As the nineteenth century progressed, the character of America and England was changing. These were nations of small producers and farmers in the first half of the century. But this era of self-sufficiency was coming to a close. As factories grew in size, people were becoming more and more dependent on businesses for jobs.

Meanwhile, the corporations were expanding their powers through both the courts and the legislatures. The Civil War proved a boon for corporate power, as the combination of military spending and outright corruption allowed them to amass great wealth and power. Abraham Lincoln viewed the rise of corporate power with great alarm, and toward the end of his life he made a prediction about the eventual results of this power:

> Corporations have been enthroned.... An era of corruption in high places will follow and the money power will endeavor to prolong its reign by working on the prejudices of the people... until wealth is aggregated in a few hands... and the Republic is destroyed.[11]

A decisive moment came in 1886, in the case of *Santa Clara County v. Southern Pacific Railroad*. As late as 1855, in *Dodge v. Woolsey*, the Supreme Court had ruled that the Constitution conferred no inalienable rights on corporations. But the *Santa Clara* case completely reversed that decision and ruled that corporations were "legal persons" and therefore entitled to the rights of real persons. These rights included free speech, which meant that the corporations could freely engage in all sorts of political activities. It also meant that liabilities were limited to the "legal person" and not to the actual persons who claimed the rights (but not the responsibilities) of ownership.[12] The investor's liability was now limited to the amount of money he had paid for the stock. This was an enormous change. Think about owning some productive asset. Let's say you are a blacksmith who owns an anvil and, through your negligence, the anvil falls from its pedestal and crushes somebody's foot. You would hardly be able to say to the victim, "I'm sorry, but I am liable for damages only up to the value of the anvil," as if the anvil had been harmed rather than the foot. But this is precisely what happens in corporations; the investors are liable only for the money they have invested and not a cent more. This meant that corporations could acquire tremendous wealth without owners bearing the liabilities that normally attach to owning any property.

But even paying the price of the anvil for damages was offensive to corporations. In a series of decisions, pro-corporate courts struck down any limits on corporate power. Sympathetic judges ruled that workers were responsible for their own injuries on the job and struck down wage and hour laws as unconstitutional. This was happening at a time when industrial accidents were commonplace; between 1888 and 1908, seven hundred thousand workers were killed in on-the-job accidents, an average of one hundred per day.[13]

At the same time, checks on corporate power were eroding at the state level. In 1889, New Jersey passed the "General Revision Act," which permitted corporations to grow to unlimited size, removed all time limits on their charters, reduced shareholder power, and allowed companies to buy or merge with other companies. A "race to the bottom" followed, with most states gutting their corporate laws. The winner of this dubious race was Delaware, where in 1899 the "General Incorporation Law" allowed corporations to write all their own rules of governance. It is no accident that nearly 60 percent of the Fortune 500 companies are incorporated in the State of Delaware. This was the age of the "robber barons" who used the corporations and the trusts to depress wages, control prices, and make huge fortunes.

Corporations could now grow as large as they pleased. And they did. Between 1895 and 1904, 1,800 companies were consolidated into 137 mega-corporations, and corporations were becoming the dominant institution of business and society.[14] But they had not completely captured the political realm. For the next ninety years, there would be a see-saw battle between pro- and anti-corporate forces. Anti-trust laws were passed, and Presidents Theodore Roosevelt and Woodrow Wilson sought to curb corporate power. But after Wilson, the counterattack died out, and by the 1920s a string of pro-corporate presidents grew more favorable to — and dependent on — corporate power. President Coolidge declared "The business of America is business," and business, by that time, meant the corporation. However, the Great Depression changed the power equation once more. The government became an economic force in its own right through massive public works programs and, later, through massive military spending. In the last analysis, however, the New Deal actually favored the large corporation. The increased regulation made competition from smaller companies more difficult, while the government preferred dealing with large and stable organizations rather than with the chaos of free competition.

After World War II, the corporations held enormous power, but that power was somewhat balanced by both union and government power. There was a sort of "controlled capitalism," which seemed to operate within a social contract that "brought the sensational novelty of mass affluence to the peoples of the United States, Western Europe, [and] Japan."[15] Adding to the forces of social stability was, paradoxically, the external threat of communism, which seemed to be on the march throughout the world; after the war, China, North Vietnam, Korea, Cuba, and Eastern Europe fell under communist domination, and socialism seemed to be gaining footholds in Africa, South America, and South Asia. In such perilous times, a "social contract" approach was deemed necessary. But beginning around the mid-1970s, there was another sea-change. Confidence in the social balance was shaken by the phenomenon of "stagflation," the disastrous combination of stagnant growth and rapid inflation. The idea of a controlled capitalism was falling into disrepute, while an ideology of unshackled capitalism was arising, spear-headed by Milton Friedman, a Nobel Prize winner.

The Triumph of the Corporations

When Margaret Thatcher became Prime Minister of England in 1979 and Ronald Reagan was elected president in 1980, the corporate-friendly ideology became, once again, the dominant force in government. For the next quarter-century there would be a steady erosion of regulations, a steady shifting of tax burdens from corporations to individuals and from wealthy individuals to the middle class, and a steady increase in the privileges and subsidies given to large corporations. In the same period, the power of organized labor declined as companies downsized and outsourced, and "free trade" (so-called) allowed corporations to operate as supra-national entities, with no particular ties or loyalties to any one country.

Accompanying this victory was a strange political alliance of corporations, libertarians, and social conservatives. I call this alliance "strange" because each of the groups would seem to have basic interests contrary to the others. Libertarians are, of course, the group most devoted to "free-market" economics. However, by free-market theory itself, corporate power works against the free market, not in favor of it. This is precisely why Adam Smith, the grandfather of all free-market theorists, opposed corporate power. To the extent that firms grow large enough to affect the market by their own actions, that is, when they become *price-makers* rather than *price-takers*, the free-market theory simply breaks down. The same problem exists with so-called free trade. The theory, as it appeared in Ricardo, assumed that capital could not move from high-wage to low-wage countries. Otherwise, it is not really "trade" at all, but merely the arbitrage of labor rates. The problem with the libertarians is not so much a failure of their ideology, but a failure to be true to their own first principles, without which their ideology simply does not function as intended.

The political alliance with the social conservatives, or the "religious right" as they are sometimes known, is even more strange than the alliance with libertarians. Corporations have never shown much restraint in the kinds of marketing they do or the kinds of products they sell, and the marketing they do and the products they sell are often destructive of the "family values" that are at the heart of social conservatism. In return for their support of corporatism, the social conservatives do get some support on such "hot-button" issues as gay marriage or abortion. However, this support often has the quality of "tokenism," since the concerns of the social conservatives are, at best, peripheral to the concerns of most corporations. The Fox empire provides a wonderful example of this; they support "family values" on their news channel and work to break them down on their entertainment channels.

Nevertheless, the alliance is a brilliant political achievement and has as-sured the triumph of corporate power in America and, indeed, throughout the world. Rare is the political candidate, of either party, who can hope to run without corporate support, and rarer still is one who wins without it. Almost every corner of political and economic life is dominated by a corpo-ration, and there seems to be no serious challenge to their authority on the horizon; even some churches emulate the organizational style and marketing technique of corporations in a bid to become "mega-churches."

That having been said, we may also note that often times a "complete" victory is the prelude to a complete catastrophe. The world that has been created by such corporatism does not seem to function very well and grows more unstable everyday. In this country, we have been saddled with debts we cannot pay and wars we cannot win. The bland assurances from Washington that we will "grow our way out of debt" are contradicted each budget cycle by new rivers of red ink, while at the same time our manufacturing resources, the only real way to grow out of debt, are being systematically looted, dis-mantled, or sold to foreign firms. We have as much of a chance of winning the "Battle of the Budget" as we have of winning the "Battle of Baghdad." Consumer spending is rising while the wage of the average worker is stag-nating; only rising consumer debt holds up consumption. Income inequality has risen to levels not seen since just before the Great Depression. Indeed, if we were living within our means, we would already be in a recession. For these reasons, and many more, a profound crisis seems inevitable. Then the libertarians may rediscover their roots and the social conservatives may discover that they are dupes, and the grand coalition will fall apart.

OWNERSHIP AND USE

The Decline of Real Ownership

The trajectory we have traced in this brief history is one of the movement of limited-purpose, tightly controlled local monopolies into supra-national organizations with revenues and powers that exceed those of most nation-states. In the process, the nature and meaning of "ownership" have fundamentally changed. In the past, property was held by those who used it, and property was considered necessary to ensure that those who tilled the soil or made the goods would receive the fruits of their labor. Ownership was active, meaning the personal use and management of resources. Further, the ownership of a "thing" lasted only as long as the thing was in existence; when the plow was worn-out beyond repair, it was discarded. While this seems too trivial to mention, consider how "capital" works. In supplying capital to a firm, one supplies the ability to buy the tools and materials that are consumed in the process of production. In return for buying these consumed items, the capitalist receives ownership in perpetuity, long after his capital has been consumed.

In short, work and ownership became separated, a situation we now view as "natural," although it is anything but. Ownership now designates the right to receive an annuity from the profits with no corresponding obligations of work, management, or responsibility. As R. H. Tawney notes, "Property was to be an aid to creative work, not an alternative to it."[16] Ownership of a business once designated active control of that business, but now, as John Bogle notes:

> The position of ownership has changed from that of an active to that of a passive agent. The owner now holds a piece of paper representing a set of rights... but has little control. The owner is practically powerless to affect the underlying property through his own efforts...the "owner" of industrial wealth is left with a mere symbol of ownership while the power, the responsibility and the substance which have been an integral part of ownership in the past are being transferred to a separate group in whose hands lies control.[17]

Mr. Bogle is well qualified to comment on these matters, being himself a successful investor and the founder and CEO of the Vanguard Funds, one of the leading groups of mutual funds. Mr. Bogle laments, at great length, the way shareholders, the nominal "owners" of a firm, have been short-changed both by the *über*-managers of the firm, who appropriate the lion's share of the rewards to themselves, and by the securities industry through high management and intermediation fees. Bogle proposes a complex set of "reforms" to ensure that the stockholder will get a greater share of the rewards, displacing both the managers and the financial intermediaries. However, while many of these proposed reforms are certainly worthwhile, they will not change the nature of the system and will not really affect the outcome very much. For Mr. Bogle has correctly identified the effects, but is mistaken about the causes.

Bogle would like investors to be more "active" in managing the companies they "own." But in fact, this is simply impossible. A person with a diverse portfolio of investments cannot possibly be an expert in all the various disciplines represented by that portfolio. Further, even if the investor had the expertise, there is very little he could do with it. In any large enterprise, the voice of an individual investor will count for little, even if he had the means to make himself heard, which he usually doesn't. This is not completely the result of a conspiracy on the part of managers or mutual funds; it is a perfectly natural and necessary process. Whenever ownership is concentrated in large institutions, the owners must grant control and use to another group. Think about a person using his own property for production. In this case, ownership, control, use, and responsibility will all reside in the same person. However, there is, of necessity, a limit to the amount of property he can use. At some point, he cannot put an additional increment of property into production without surrendering some degree of control and use. Therefore, if property accumulates in one entity, then control and use will slip away from the owners and to the managers. There is simply no other way things can work.

Indeed, this is the way it has always worked. Consider a feudal society in which the king owned all the land. The actual use of the land was given to others. The barons to whom the king gave estates were, in law, *tenants-in-chief,* and they, in turn, granted the land to other tenants. The lion's share of the rewards went neither to the king nor to the tenants-in-chief, but to the actual tenants who actually worked the land. The question becomes, then, who *should* receive the rewards? The king? The baron? The peasant? In this situation, we have little difficulty in conceding that the one who actually works the land should receive the rewards, subject only to what is necessary to support the state, represented by the lords and, ultimately, the king. However, we have some difficulty in applying this rather obvious principle to corporations. Nevertheless, it is worth examining in more detail.

Stocks and Stock Markets

Were the *über*-managers to give a defense of their privileges, they might say to Mr. Bogle and the stock-holders something like this: "You take no interest in the company, you endure no burden for its management, you bear no risk for its debts. Yet, in return for your piece of paper, you want a greater share of the rewards. But your piece of paper represents capital which we long ago consumed and for which we have paid, and continue to pay. Yet, you still have your capital intact, and probably a handsome increase in its market value. Therefore, the dividends we pay you, although but a pittance of the profits, are still a more-than-adequate reward for the work you do not do, the risks you do not bear, and the capital you no longer provide. Like the soldiers in the Gospel of Luke, you ought to be content with your pay and say no more!"

This is indeed a coherent argument. It goes to the question of who should rule the corporation and how the rewards and responsibilities ought to be apportioned. Ownership in corporations is vested, for the most part, in those who provided the original capital or, occasionally, subsequent infusions of capital. This seems "natural" to us, but in fact it is a social custom, one dictated by neither natural law nor economic theory. In economic theory, capital can hire labor through a wage payment and claim all the rewards, or labor can hire capital through an interest payment and claim all the rewards. Or they can both claim the rewards through some sort of sharing of ownership. But in any case, economics per se takes no stance on the issue. But from the standpoint of *political economy*, or what we might call macroeconomics or social theory, it makes a great deal of difference, and these differing methods of ownership greatly affect the kind of society that results, the allocation of rewards and responsibilities, and ultimately, the stability of the economic and political systems.

In the current system, ownership resides in the original investors, or in those to whom the original investors have sold their interest, usually on the stock market. Buying stocks in a company is called "investing," but that is a misnomer; it is properly called "speculating." An investor is one who provides firms with the capital they need to continue in operation, to grow and expand. A speculator provides the firm with no capital at all, but merely makes a bet on what the firm will be worth at some point in the future. The stock market, for the most part, is analogous to a used-car lot. When one buys a used Ford off the lot, Ford receives no money. Likewise, when one buys a "used" share of Ford on the stock market, the Ford Motor Company receives no funds. It is true that existing companies can raise funds in the stock market by issuing new shares, but they rarely do so, even when the stock market would be the most efficient way to raise funds; current owners generally do not like to issue new shares because it dilutes their ownership rights. Capital needs for most companies are met by retained earnings, banks, bonds, or venture capitalists. Therefore, the money "invested" in the stock market does not, for the most part, perform the functions of true investment, but rather competes for funds that could go to expanding the economy.

There is a curious problem with ownership residing solely in the original investors. Production occurs at the intersection of capital and labor, both of which are consumed in the process of production. The original capital represented by a share of stock has been consumed, no less than the original labor that consumed it. We would consider it strange if a worker were to go the Ford Motor Company and say, "Ten years ago, I contributed some work to your company, and you should continue to pay me." Yet we have no problem when a shareholder says, "Fifty years ago, a person from whom

I bought a share of your stock contributed some capital to your company, and you should continue to pay me for it." We have no problem with this because it is customary, in our culture, to award ownership to original investors. Yet, it would be difficult to distinguish between the two cases; the worker was paid for his work and the capitalist for his capital. Whether or not one is willing to defend the customary arrangement, it is necessary to acknowledge that it is merely customary, and not something dictated by natural law or economic necessity. Once we have acknowledged this, then we can discuss whether this custom is the best from both the social and economic standpoints.

Property, Private and Social

One point we can dispose of very quickly: this is not an argument about "private property" per se. Although much ink is spilled in such discussions, it is not an issue here. There is no suggestion here that property in itself represents a social evil. On the contrary, it represents a social good and a necessary one. And more, it represents a sacred right, one not to be tampered with by law or custom. It is as natural for a person to say "this is my home" or "this is my book" as it is for him to breathe. Property in the hands of labor is freedom. A person with his or her own tools or land is free to work for himself or for another. In such circumstances, any wage contract he accepts is likely to be fair, and he will require no union or government official to arbitrate on his behalf. Therefore, the question is not whether property should be private, but how to divide property among private owners and how to distribute the wealth created in production.

We take it as an absolute and self-evident principle that wealth should go to those who produce it. There simply is no other defensible principle of distribution. If an able-bodied man should receive something for which he did no work or to which he contributed no capital, then he has stolen it. On the other hand, if a man does not receive his rightful share of what he has worked to produce, he has been robbed. Both wealth without work and work without wealth are instances of theft; in the first case a man receives what he does not earn, and in the second he earns what he does not receive.

If a man or a woman produces something by himself or herself, that thing is his or hers, wholly and entirely. If she grows some vegetables on her own land, using her own tools and her own labor, then the entire product is hers and no one else may rightfully claim a share. There are few who would argue with this principle. However, most production is *social;* it requires that groups of workers come together with tools, raw materials, and plans. Further, production presumes a wider social context of laws, markets, roads, coinage, schools, families, and so forth. There is now no single "owner" to which the wealth can be attributed, but a collection of "owners." The output of a production process is not a private property, but a social product of many property owners within a social structure. Therefore, the division of the social product depends on who can claim a property in the social product, and to what degree. If we accept as the rule that "wealth belongs to those who create it" when dealing with individual producers, we can then restate the rule for social products as, "Wealth belongs to those who create it, in the same proportion that they contribute to its creation." If this is the rule, and it seems unassailable, then we must ask how wealth is created.

The Source of Wealth

Two things, and two things alone, are combined to produce wealth: the gifts of the earth and the labor of humans. That's it. There is nothing else. No one, anywhere, can possibly point to any human value which is not the result of human labor, whether physical or mental,[18] combined with the things given freely by nature. Since the gifts of the earth are free, all costs, as well as all values, are the result of work alone. Two objections might be raised at this point. One, that the gifts of the earth are not free, but have a cost, and two, that production requires capital as well as labor.

Concerning the first point, we can point to a confusion about the cost of natural resources. Some natural things necessary for production, such as sunlight and air, require no labor and hence have no cost. Other things, such as the food, fiber, and mineral wealth of the earth, require work to make them available. Nature herself makes no charge and has no cost. The cost of natural goods is merely the labor required to make them available. There is no "exchange" with nature; she makes no charge, but only offers a challenge to the ingenuity of humans to use her resources.

Concerning capital, we must note that capital itself is merely an intermediate product of labor held out from current consumption to be used in future production. In order to plant a crop next year, the farmer must reserve some seed-corn from his harvest this year. In the same manner, tools, machines, buildings, and all the other things consumed in production which go by the name of "capital" are, in fact, the results of labor in the current or a prior period.

At this point, the utilitarian economist is throwing up his hands in dismay because he sees the Labor Theory of Value in all this, a theory which the utilitarians abandoned 150 years ago. The economist would be right; this is precisely the Labor Theory. However, one can debate as much as one likes the merits of the Labor Theory of Value as a pricing or allocation mechanism. But one can never get around the simple, empirical fact that all values stem from labor and from no other source. No one has ever yet or ever will find an exception to this rule. There is simply no wealth without work, nor can there be. Some may appropriate the work of others to make themselves wealthy, but the wealth itself depends on work. Therefore, the only real question is whether or not the wealth will be awarded to those who worked to create it.

Since labor is the source of all wealth, it is likewise the source of all property. Therefore, labor cannot be denied a property right in the wealth it creates. Moreover, since labor is the resource which creates wealth, then the maintenance of labor, the just wage, is simply an economic necessity. New laborers must be raised and educated, and older ones must be provided for in their infirmity. Any "economic" theory which ignores this, which attempts to reduce labor, the source of all values, to a mere "factor of production," a mere thing, will simply result in an incomplete description of any actual economy.

The Rights of Capital

If all values are traced to labor, where does that leave the capitalist and his rights? Does the person who provides capital have no rights at all, no property in the social product? Currently, capital claims all the profit from production; under the rules herein advanced, should it in fact claim none of them, as the communists would have it? We can note that the question only arises when "capital" and "labor" are conceived of in entirely different terms. Only then can there arise the question of the rights of one party held over and above the rights of the other party. But, as we have seen, capital is nothing other than that which is saved out of prior labor. Therefore, the rights of capital are nothing more or less than the rights of labor itself! The rights of capital are neither *opposed* to the rights of labor nor superior to them, they are *identical* with them. Once it is recognized that the rights of both labor and capital spring from the same source, there can be no question of one side or the other appropriating all the rights for itself.

Therefore, we may note with John Paul II that capital cannot be separated from labor, nor labor opposed to capital; an economic system can be right only if it overcomes this opposition.[19] There can be no opposition because not only do their rights spring from the same source, but also because they are mutually dependent; there are no "independent productivities" that either side can advance in support of its claims. Capital without labor is inert; labor without capital is unemployed. Therefore, we can now ask, "What are the rights of capital (or labor)?"

I believe that there are three rights each side may claim. The first is a right to receive a payment for the services rendered, a wage in the case of labor and interest in the case of capital. The second is a right to a degree of control sufficient to insure the interests of both sides. And the third is a claim of the final product proportional to the contribution of each. Along with each of these rights goes a corresponding responsibility. Corresponding to the first, there is a duty to conscientiously perform the work (a duty that falls more heavily on labor than on capital); corresponding to the second right is the duty to act always for the common interest; and to the third, the duty to claim no more than one's proportion of the output.

There is also one other right that must be claimed by both parties, and that is the right of renewal. It is actually more of a necessity than a right. Capital must be renewed, otherwise production could not continue. Labor must be renewed, otherwise humanity would cease to be. There must be a new generation of workers. This is the basis of the claim that a just wage must be sufficient to support a family and the education of the children. Without this, an economy simply has no point. In the case of capital, the original capital must be restored to its original owner or retained by the company for further expansion. In the former case, this restoration of capital extinguishes any ownership claims of the capitalist; if the capital remains with the company as retained earnings, then the ownership claim continues as well.

Time Limits on Ownership

There is, however, one right which both sides claim and neither should. That is the right of perpetual ownership. Property rights in production are based on labor, and labor alone. But labor, whether in the form of work or of capital, is extinguished in the process of production. New labor and new capital must constantly be supplied to a firm. The labor and capital that was supplied yesterday is already gone, and with it any claim to a property right in the output. A worker has a property claim only for as long as he provides actual work, and an investor has a claim only for as long as the capital she supplied survives. The problem with current notions of ownership is that they are based on the ownership of land. But land is not consumed in production; it is, relative to production, an "eternal" asset. Ownership of a firm, therefore, should be confined to those who have current usufruct, that is, fruitful use of the property, by the provision of either labor or capital.

The basis of this claim of perpetual equity is, as we have seen, rather dubious. It is neither equitable nor efficient to require firms to continue to pay for assets they have consumed, depreciated, and discarded.[20] Further, it reserves control of a firm to absentee landlords, unconnected themselves with the actual business. As George Goyder puts it:

> It is iniquitous to give control over an organization dependent upon the daily cooperation of free men and women to absentee landlords from now until doomsday. We must choose between the perpetual [ownership] and freedom, for the two are in the long run incompatible. Either capitalism will accept the demands of natural justice, or it will cease to exist and be replaced by a collectivist system likely to be a good deal worse.[21]

There is a third possibility which Goyder, writing in the late 1980s, did not consider, but is the one which is, in fact, coming to pass. That is of a corporate collectivism which subordinates workers, investors, government, and even churches to its own purposes,[22] purposes that reflect neither the interests of the shareholders, nor the workers, nor the society at large, but only the narrow interests of the *über*-managers.

Stock ownership should be, therefore, time-limited. It should extend for a certain period of time, after which the company would have the right to purchase the share on behalf of the employees at a price based on either that share's proportion of the book value of the company or of the retained earnings, whichever is higher. Note that the price would not be based on the "market price," because the market price is set as an estimate of future earnings, and it is precisely the unjust claim to future earnings which is being extinguished.

Such a system would entirely change the nature of stock market investments. Currently, owners of stock receive very little in the way of dividends in most cases. Indeed, one can argue that just as companies refuse to pay a just wage for workers, they refuse a "just dividend" for investors. If the claims of both workers and investors are based on the same source, labor, then one would expect that dividends and wages would be somehow "normalized" to each other; the labor represented by capital would earn something that approximated the wage of the labor represented by actual work. In the current system, most of the "profits" of investment are not profits at all; they are the result of pure speculation and gambling. That is to say, the price of a stock is based on an estimate of its future worth. If the seller guesses better than the buyer, the seller gets a "profit," but the buyer takes a loss, and there is no real net gain. A shareholder may hold a stock or sell it short, but in either case, such gambling is not to be confused with the serious job of investing, that is, the job of supplying capital for the expansion of work and business.

If shares were time-limited and the shareholder's proportionate share of the book value of the company were returned to him, then his profit would be an actual profit, based on a real increase in value and not on somebody else's loss. Let us say that share warrants were customarily of ten years' duration.[23] That means that every ten years an investor's capital would be returned to him. He would then have to find new investment opportunities, which means finding another company (or even the same one) in which to invest. This means that companies would be receiving new infusions of capital when and if they went to the stock market.

The concept of a time-limited ownership may strike some as a radical departure from economic practice, but in fact it is not. Indeed, as Shann Turnbull points out, "All negotiable equities have limited economic life except land, collectables, and interests in corporations."[24] For example, patents and copyrights are time-limited property rights; when one writes a book or discovers a cure for cancer, one receives a property right only for a certain period of time, after which the book or the cure enters into the public domain and anyone may appropriate it. It would seem indefensible that one who provides a perpetual asset, like a cure for cancer, should receive a temporary right, while one who provides a temporary asset, like a bit of capital, should receive a perpetual right.

THE OWNERSHIP SOCIETY

The Need for Wide Ownership

The degree of the distribution of property is the basis for the economic organization for any society. Where ownership is narrow, slavery in one form or another is the result; where ownership is extensive, liberty is the result. Since property in land, capital, and education is necessary for production, and production is necessary for life, those who would live must go to those who have capital and offer them their labor in return for life. Should those with property accept the offer, the worker will live, and live at whatever level is acceptable to the owners of capital. If the worker can go to many employers, her wage contract is more likely to be just, that is, is more likely to give her an equitable share of what her labor creates. And if the worker can use her own land, tools, and skills to make her own products, then she may sell her produce directly to the public, rather than just her labor to a capitalist, and claim the entire proceeds of the sale, save what is claimed by the community to support public necessities, such as roads, defense, and education.

Thus we may conclude that property in the hands of labor is liberty, while labor in the hands of property is slavery. If the worker can make his own way in the world with his own tools, he will be free; if his tools are owned by another, he himself will be owned, for all practical purposes.

At this point, the objection will be raised that ownership is already widespread in our society. Indeed, this notion is central to our view of ourselves as a nation and an economy. And there is some basis for this view. After all, nearly 52 percent of all households own some stock, either directly or indirectly.[25] Homeownership is widespread and everyone is free to start their own business, which many do. However, effective ownership is actually concentrated in a small number of persons. Concerning stocks, 62 percent are owned by the top 5 percent of all households, and 77 percent by the top ten percent. That leaves very little for the bottom 90 percent of the population.[26] For the most part, stock ownership provides little income and less security for the mass of people. As for homes, they are no longer centers of production; they are consumer items rather than means of production. And while many people do indeed have a small business, the space for such businesses is shrinking, as mega-corporations move into areas that were traditionally left to small businesses.

The task of natural justice is to ensure the widest degree of ownership possible. But this is also a task of practical economics. The neoclassical theory only works to the degree that property is widespread; competitive equilibrium assumes dispersed ownership of the means of production. To the extent that this assumption is not correct, the theory breaks down. Just as the neoclassical theory is powerless to explain the conundrum of rising productivity and falling real wages, so it is powerless to explain the discontent which is settling on the planet like a plague. Without recovering their own roots, the standard economic theories become meaningless abstractions of real use only to ideologues seeking to attack or defend a particular political viewpoint. The ownership society is necessary to reestablish the relevance of neoclassical economics.

Employee Stock Ownership Plans (ESOPs)

Establishing the ownership society means reestablishing the connection between ownership and use, between wealth and work. This is accomplished by giving to labor a portion of the wealth it creates, in the form of full or partial ownership of their firms. Currently, the major legal framework for accomplishing this is the Employee Stock Ownership Plan, or ESOP. An ESOP is essentially a *leveraged buy-out* (LBO) of a firm on behalf of the employees. An LBO is simply a technique of using the firm's assets as collateral for a loan with which to buy the firm. Much the same thing happens when one buys a house or a car with borrowed money; the home or the auto is pledged as collateral for the loan. But unlike a mortgage or a car loan, an LBO uses the company's own income to repay the loan.

Typically, an ESOP works in four stages. First, the current owners agree to sell the company, in whole or in part, to the employees and establish a trust fund to accomplish this. Second, the fund borrows money from a bank or other financial institution. Third, the fund uses the money to buy stock at market prices, either from the existing owners, or as new shares of treasury stock. And fourth, the dividends earned by the fund's stock are used to retire the debt incurred in acquiring the stock. As the debt is retired, shares of stock are transferred to individual employee accounts. Eventually, the loan is repaid, and the employees come into ownership of the firm. As the employees retire, they sell their shares back to the company to be purchased by new employees in the same way. The current law for ESOPs provides for tax advantages for the loans necessary to purchase the company, which helps lower the cost of acquisition.

ESOPs are quite common, and are often extremely successful at both transferring ownership and improving productivity and profits. However, along with the successes there are often spectacular failures. One problem arises from the fact of tax-advantaged financing. Some companies use this as simply a lower-cost financing method without any real intention of transferring effective ownership. ENRON was an ESOP, at least in name if not in fact. The second problem arises from the market pricing of the shares. The idea of an LBO is to use future incomes to buy current stock. However, market prices for an equity are, in theory, simply the net present value of all the future cash flows. If the market is "efficient" in pricing the stock, nothing will actually change; dividend payments to the current owners will simply be replaced by interest payments to the bank, and the process of acquiring the company will be painfully slow. Supporters of ESOPs would like to be able to go directly to the Federal Reserve Bank and borrow money at zero interest plus a service charge; this would certainly change the dynamics of the ESOP and make it a much more effective tool.

In general, for any LBO, ESOP or otherwise, the buyer must find values in the firm not contemplated by the sellers when they set the price. This is why so many LBOs are accompanied by mass layoffs, breakups, and other techniques to find more values in the firm than were contemplated in the price. An LBO simply won't work in an "efficient" market. In an ESOP, this additional value could be the increased productivity and dedication that an employee-owned company can bring to the marketplace. Actual experience has shown that this is often the case; employee-owned companies simply produce more value than traditional capital ownership.

Another problem occurs from the fact that ESOPs are usually used as substitutes for retirement plans. This exposes the employees to the "all the eggs in one basket" problem, which means that if the company fails, so does the retirement plan. Further, when a large group of employees retire at the same time, the company could be forced to raise cash to buy out their interests, thereby burdening the company with additional debt.[27]

Despite the difficulties, an ESOP can be an effective tool when combined with the management approaches of the previous chapter, and when the share prices approximate the book value rather than the market value. After all, the whole point is to end claims on the future profits of the firm, but the market price attempts to include the discounted value of these claims.

Further refinements are needed, and a great number of things could be done, if the public had a mind to, and a mind to force their elected leaders to mind their wishes. The use of zero-interest loans for employee acquisitions would be a great advance. Better would be time-limited shares, with the firm buying up shares as a matter of course on behalf of their employees. But if existing owners did not wish to time-limit their shares, tax law could be used to encourage them. For example, "book-value" sales of shares to a company on behalf of employees could be done without capital gains taxes. Dividends on shares less than ten years old could be made tax-free, while those on shares older than ten years could be made punitive, making the share too expensive to hold. Employee-owned companies could be converted into cooperatives along the lines of Mondragón. What is lacking is not the means, but the will. The great problem is that most people regard perpetual ownership of firms by those who provided the original capital as the "normal" order of things, not knowing how abnormal it is. And they are likely to regard an attack on such ownership as an attack on property itself. It is not. It is, rather, a defense of property, property that is proper to work, rather than a way of avoiding work.

The Problem of Size

One of the major obstacles to the ownership society is the tendency of corporations to grow to enormous size. This tendency strikes at the very roots of economic order, that is, at the neoclassical ideal of competitive equilibrium. To the degree that production occurs within, or is controlled by, a limited number of corporate collectives, competition is diminished as the economic space for smaller firms disappears. The mega-corporation creates its own economic gravitational field which draws competitive firms to itself, like a black hole. This happens for a variety of reasons. Among other things, large corporations have easier access to credit; they can more easily take a loss by underselling smaller firms until the smaller ones go out of business; they can get better terms from suppliers, or even dictate the terms to suppliers, terms that are not available to smaller customers; and they are more likely to control the political process in their own favor.[28]

The problem of size was recognized early on by the founders of neoclassicism, but they could provide no solution from within economics. And indeed, from within economics, there is no solution; there is no mechanism within the theory that can limit the size of any enterprise, yet if an enterprise grows to such a size that it obtains effective control of the market, the theory breaks down. Indeed, when A. E. Marshall, one of the founders of scientific neoclassicism, looked at the problem, he abandoned the language of science entirely in favor of the language of metaphor. He compared the economy to a forest which, even though it is dominated by large trees which get most of the sunlight and nutrients, nevertheless allows new trees to grow. This use of metaphor, while it may be aesthetically pleasing, is scientifically vague and is, in any case, belied by actual events. The commanding heights of the American economy have come to be dominated by corporate collectives that more resemble the model of European socialism rather than a free market. The major difference is that while the Europeans attempt to exercise some political control of the corporate collectives, in America the corporation is more likely to control the political process.

It is in the political economy rather than in economics that we must look for safeguards. That is, we must trust in legal limits rather than in anything intrinsic to economics per se. The major mechanism for ensuring free competition is the anti-trust laws. These laws are often viewed as "anti-business," but nothing could be further from the truth. If being "pro-business" means "expanding the space for an ever-wider variety of businesses," then the anti-trust laws are pro-business, even if they are anti-mega-corporate. Indeed, one can be pro-business or pro-corporate collectives, but one cannot be both.

Unfortunately, the anti-trust laws have gone out of fashion, even among neoclassical economists. In ignoring monopolies and oligarchies, they betray the very roots of neoclassical theory and turn it into a meaningless abstraction, a mere ideology. Indeed, some so-called "free market" economists, such as Edward Younkins, will argue that monopolies are "efficient" so long as they are not government monopolies; they argue that perfect competition is an impossibility and therefore we ought to allow both monopolies and collusion.[29] But the free market cannot exist in the face of monopoly, monopsony, and oligarchy, whether they are "government" or "private."

You can have free markets or you can have monopolies, but you cannot have both; a choice must be made.

PROPERTY AND FREEDOM

If property is good, it is good for everybody. But to the extent that production is confined to corporate collectives, the opportunities for meaningful ownership, meaningful competition, and meaningful markets are diminished and replaced with a kind of privatized socialism. Indeed, ownership itself actually disappears, to be replaced by a financial abstraction known as an equity share, a share that claims perpetual rights that no natural system of ownership could ever claim, since no claim to ownership could outrun the life of the thing owned.

Within these corporate collectives, neither those who provide the capital nor those who provide the labor get their full rights; rather, a new class arises, the class of *über*-managers that appropriates to itself rewards all out of proportion to its contributions. This is a natural result of the decline of real ownership; as ownership becomes an abstraction, the power of the nominal owners declines in the face of the actual users, the managers.

Workers with their own property are more secure in their work, more secure in times of illness or economic trouble, and more secure in old age. They are less likely to be mere dependents of the state or of the corporate collectives. In a word, they are more *free* than people without property. And it is precisely free people that a free market requires. Collectivization of property, whether by the government or by the corporations, is the enemy of both free people and free markets.

Chapter 20

The Vocation of Business

The society or culture which has lost its spiritual roots is a dying culture, however prosperous it may appear externally. Consequently the problem of social survival is not only a political or economic one; it is above all things religious, since it is in religion that the ultimate spiritual roots of both society and the individual are to be found. —CHRISTOPHER DAWSON

THE FREE MARKET AND FREEDOM

The Street Car Conspiracy

In 1922, Alfred P. Sloan, the president of General Motors, had a problem. The company had lost $65 million, an enormous sum of money in those days, and Sloan concluded that the market was saturated. Although only one in ten Americans owned a car, all who wanted one seemed to have one already, and the automobile business would be a slow-growth, replacement business. At that time, 90 percent of all trips were taken by rail, mostly electric rail and trolleys. There were twelve hundred separate street-car companies, and virtually every city of over twenty-five hundred people had an electric trolley line. So long as there was a viable alternative to the automobile, the growth of the industry would be limited. Sloan, therefore, set out to eliminate the alternative.[1]

Sloan set up a special unit within GM with the goal of first destroying the electric trains and replacing them with buses, and then eliminating the transport companies entirely. GM's first move was to attack the sources of the trolley lines' financing; GM used its leverage with the railroad companies and banks who were often the primary investors in the trolley lines. For example, they went to the Southern Pacific Railroad, the owner of Los Angeles's Pacific Electric trolleys, and threatened to move their freight business to another company if PE did not scrap the trolleys and convert to buses. They went to banks that lent money to street car lines and promised

317

them millions in additional deposits if they would convince the rail lines to convert to buses. Finally, GM lobbied congress to pass a law forcing local electric companies to divest themselves of street car company stocks; since the trolleys were large consumers of electric power, electric companies were often heavy investors in them.

When these tactics were of no avail, they formed holding companies to buy up the rail lines. These companies were usually formed in partnership with Firestone Tire and Rubber, Standard Oil Company, and other similar firms. These holding companies always followed the same pattern. They would buy up the local street car company, tear up the tracks and scrap the trolleys, and purchase buses from GM to replace the whole system. Since the tracks and trolleys represented the bulk of the capital of the companies, the immediate effect was to wreck the finances of the company so that bankruptcy was the predetermined outcome.

The results were dramatic. In city after city, as the street car lines went bankrupt, automobile sales exploded; sales in the cities with ruined transportation companies doubled, then doubled again, and kept climbing. Automobile ownership, which was relatively static between the late 1920s and the late 1940s, exploded in the 1950s until nearly every family had at least one car, if not two or three.[2] The success of GM's strategy can be judged by the fact that car ownership is still much lower in cities that have viable public transportation systems. In New York City, for example, only 46 percent of households owned cars in 2000, while in Manhattan the number was only 23 percent.[3]

But the results went far beyond the transportation industries. The very shape of our cities, indeed the very shape of our lives, has been determined by Sloan's strategy. The needs of the automobile determined, to a great extent, all government policy. The car, unlike the railways, required expensive road beds that only the government seemed capable of building and maintaining. The roads, in turn, led to an expansion of populations into suburbs, which in turn required more roads. The automobile quickly exhausted domestic supplies of oil, which required us to intervene in distant lands to secure supplies. And there are few today who would deny the automobile's effect on climate change. This is an impressive set of consequences from one business decision.

There are many who argue that Sloan's strategy does not constitute a conspiracy in the criminal sense, but was merely good business practice. They point to the fact that while GM was convicted of an anti-trust violation, that conviction was overturned on appeal. The problem with this argument is that it may be true. Sloan may have been doing nothing more than exercising his freedom under the rules of the market. If Sloan were engaged in an illegal conspiracy, it would be bad, but if that's the way the system is supposed to work, then it is worse. If the "private" decisions of a few powerful individuals can determine the urban, political, geopolitical, and climatological realities of the nation and the world, then "freedom" becomes a very paradoxical quality, because the "freedom" of a few limits the freedom of all. So long as viable alternatives existed, the decision to purchase a Ford was a free decision. But as soon as the alternative is eliminated, freedom also disappears; as a car becomes a necessity, it ceases to be a free choice. One is still free to choose the model and color of the car, but not the fact of the car; one *must* have a car to participate in social and economic life. So we are presented with a paradox: the freedom of Alfred P. Sloan has the potential to limit the freedom of everyone else and to result in conflicts and climate change that no one is free to avoid. The question that immediately arises is, "Can this really be an adequate notion of freedom?"

A "Natural" System of Liberty?

Neoclassical economics has always rooted itself in the purely moral claim, first advanced by Adam Smith, that the market constitutes a "perfect system of natural liberty." Freedom consists in the free exchanges between individuals, from which liberty would arise spontaneously; the consumer would be king and the economy would serve the king in liberty. This definition of liberty rests on three assumptions: a negative definition of freedom, individualism, and a lack of an objective or common good. Freedom is defined negatively as simply the absence of coercion; as long as a choice is not coerced, then it is free. Freedom is nothing more than pursuing what you want without interference from others.[4]

The second assumption is that of the autonomous individual; individuals are autonomous and sovereign and have no connections other than those which they choose for themselves. And the third assumption flows from the second: there is no end or *telos* apart from individual desire. Hence there can be no "common good," no "sacred canopy," only an "empty shrine," as Michael Novak puts it, in which each individual places his or her own private idols. There are no objective goods, only individual wants; individual utility — hedonism — is all, and no other standard can be permitted.[5]

However, this is an inadequate definition of freedom, one that always leads to "unfreedom." If Mr. Sloan is "free" to eliminate the alternatives to his product, not to mention altering the geopolitical and climatological landscape, then his freedom comes at the expense of the freedom of all. We can note how well this notion of freedom accords with the decline of moral dialogue. If there are no objective notions of justice available to us, then "morality" will be nothing more than an attempt to impose one's will on everybody else. Alfred Sloan was able to do this in a spectacular fashion. When taken in this way, the "freedom of the market" means the freedom one has to impose one's will upon the market and eliminate the alternatives. "Freedom" thus means "unfreedom."

This paradox of freedom and its opposite has always been implicit in neoclassicism. The laws of marginal utility, for example, are presumed to act in a deterministic way so that outcomes are determined in advance. J. B. Clark, for example, noted that while wages might *appear* to be based on free bargaining, they are in fact based on "a deep acting natural law" which dictates the outcomes for these "free bargains."[6] But if everything is determined in advance of bargaining, where is there room for freedom? This paradox lies at the heart of the human condition. If we mean by "natural" the physical laws that determine the material world, then there is no "natural liberty." The order of nature is deterministic. Everything in nature follows a strict order of cause and effect, and no degrees of liberty are allowed; the planet Venus, which has for millions of years followed a precise orbit, is not allowed to decide that it wants to follow a different course today. Freedom, on the other hand, is intentional; it involves human intentionality in the creation of free systems. There is no "natural" freedom, only supernatural, because freedom itself is an attribute of God alone, and only by participation in the divine can human beings, and the systems they build, achieve some measure of freedom. Thus freedom cannot arise spontaneously, but can only come when people deliberately act to create freedom. But what does this freedom consist of?

Rediscovering Freedom

Free-market economists are certainly correct to root the discussion of markets in the notion of freedom. However, they are wrong to believe that the question of freedom can be resolved from within economics itself. As soon as one says "free market," one is in the midst of a theological discussion on the nature of freedom. Economists must defer to philosophers and theologians on this topic. As it is now, the economists are simply talking beyond their expertise and training. This is not to say that the economist has no role in this discussion, but the economist's role is limited to taking the different notions of freedom, building economic models of them, and comparing the results.

In order to discover real freedom, we must first break the bonds of autonomous individualism. Autonomy in the strict sense is simply impossible. We are social beings in a social context. Our desires are largely formed by our society and culture. We are, all of us, "beings-in-relationship" with others. There is a certain degree of autonomy possible within each person, but it is a relative autonomy, not an absolute one. Hence, autonomy alone cannot form the basis of a free economics. We are beings-in-relationship; economics forms one aspect of our relations with others and, like all other human relations, it is governed by the virtue of justice.

The negative definition of freedom denies any natural ends or purposes to freedom, but roots it merely in an undifferentiated and subjective notion of choice; it therefore excludes any notion of justice. It roots freedom in pure desire without considering the content of that desire. But without some notion of a proper purpose, how is it possible to judge when an economy is properly functioning? Without a notion of a purpose, arbitrary measures, such as profits or growth, are substituted for real measures. But both growth and profits are not the ends of an economy, but the means to the ends. The ends of an economy are, self-evidently, the material provisioning of society and the fair return of rewards to those who contribute to material abundance. These ends are directly related to freedom, since without a material sufficiency no one can be free, and without a just return each person is robbed.

In order to judge whether a choice leads to freedom, we must ask whether that choice fulfills the proper ends and purposes of human beings. So, for example, the choice of whether to inhale cocaine in crack or in powder form is a "free choice" from a market perspective. In comparing the cases of Rosa Martinez, working at a *maquilladoro* for starvation wages, and a worker-owner in the Mondragón Cooperative, the market economist would judge them both as "free" because neither was coerced into work by the government. But this is nonsense. Rosa was coerced into work by the threat of starvation, and she has no property in her work which grants her a fair return for her labor. The worker-owner, on the other hand, has a property in her work and a just wage. Only one of these workers can be judged to be "free" in any rational sense.

The choice of an addictive substance is a free choice, but one that destroys freedom since it is merely the choice of the particular form of slavery. Therefore free choice, though necessary for freedom, is not sufficient for freedom; we must also look at the content of the choice, at the ends to which it is directed. Thus we can fairly judge that the *maquilladoro* directs Sra. Martinez toward slavery, while Mondragón directs the worker toward freedom. We can distinguish Mondragón and the *maquilladoro* not on the basis of choice, but on the basis of whether each choice fulfills real human ends. On this basis only the former choice constitutes freedom. As Hilaire Belloc noted, "Economic freedom can only be a good if it fulfills some need in our nature."[7]

True freedom requires proper material means and proper spiritual ends. We need proper means because although freedom is a spiritual quality, it has a material basis; even our spiritual lives have a material basis. A man who has not enough to eat, who cannot feed or clothe his family, cannot be free. He must accept whatever is offered. Now, it is the function of an economy to produce and distribute the material goods which we all need. Thus any economy must be judged on how well it fulfills this function. If a particular economy depends on exploitation, if it depends, for example, on outsourcing its work to people earning starvation wages, then it may be a "free market," but it cannot be an economy of freedom. An economy may produce goods in abundance, but if it distributes those goods so that some live in luxury and others live little better than slaves, then it is a slave economy and in describing it we need to dispense with any fictions based on freedom.

THE VOCATION OF BUSINESS

Justice and Economics

Throughout this work, the idea has been advanced that justice and economics, equity and equilibrium, are intimately related. Without equity, an economy cannot achieve equilibrium and will be unstable. Without justice, one cannot achieve equity. An economy may achieve high rates of growth; it may return great profits to the investors. But without justice, it will not be a free economy, and without equity, it will not be stable. Some economists, no doubt, will find this dependence on justice to be problematic; they fear that such dependence will compromise the "scientific" nature of economics. But this is simply a misunderstanding of science. Every science looks to a higher science for its standard of truth. The standard model of economics, in refusing to acknowledge any higher standard, is simply insufficiently scientific. Without recognizing their dependence on justice, neoclassical models suffer not from too much science, but from too little.

But it need not be this way, for indeed, when we examine the neoclassical model of competitive equilibrium, we find the requirements for justice buried within its starting conditions. There cannot be a concentration of wealth and power or the model simply does not work. If economic scientists would be attentive to the requirements of their own models, there would be no question about the relationship between justice and economics. But alas, too often they are not. In this regard, economics is unique among the sciences in its inattention to its own starting points. It is the only science that is reluctant to measure the distance between the ideal and the actual conditions. In physics, for example, rocks and feathers fall at the same rate, under conditions of an absolute vacuum. However, this never actually happens because nature abhors a vacuum and we never actually see one. Anyone who would use this principle in practice must give a precise measure of the distance between the ideal and the actual conditions. Thus an airplane designer will use air pressure as the precise measure of this distance. In calculating how fast his 777 will fall and what forces he must overcome, he does not use the ideal alone, but the ideal modified by the actual.

In economics, the starting condition for competitive equilibrium in a free market economy is that production is spread over a vast number of firms, none of which have any real market power. But like the ideal vacuum in physics, this doesn't happen in the modern economy, or very rarely. Like the engineer of the 777, we must measure the distance from the ideal, such as the degree of monopoly, oligarchy, and collusion in the market, before we can reach any conclusions or design systems or policies that work on this market "air pressure." But too often, economists refuse to form a precise measure of this distance, and prefer to reason in an absolute vacuum.

A free market requires free men and women, and it is pointless to speak of a free market in an economy of exploitation. To be free in an economic sense, men and women require both a sufficiency of means and equity in the rewards. The means of production are physical capital and education, and equity means a just share of the output. Without these, we will have neither free human beings nor free markets. A just wage and well-distributed property are the prerequisites to a free economy.

The Commitment to Freedom

But while the economy requires justice, the plain fact of the matter is that an individual business does not. That is, if one adopts the goal of profits as the sole measure of business, then justice is, in some sense, optional. A man can be dishonest or indifferent to justice and still make a great fortune. An economy mired in injustice is on the road to ruin, but a man mired in injustice may be on the road to Nob Hill. Further, his advantage is likely to be greater the more honest his competitors are. If one factory owner fires all of his workers and moves production to a country where the workers are exploited, he will obtain a big advantage over his competitors. True, a certain number of potential customers are lost, but this will not be significant if other producers keep their production at home. However, if all the producers move to an exploitative labor market, then there will be a failure of demand that will have to be made up, in the short term, by government spending or consumer credit and will, in the long term, threaten the economy with collapse. The point here is that justice cannot be made "automatic." It is a virtue, a product of human intentionality. Economic systems can advance or retard the cause of justice, but the need for virtue cannot be eliminated. No amount of tinkering with economic rules or systems can eliminate the need for just men and women.

We are not called upon to change the world; the world is not given to us. There is little we can do, directly, for the Indian seamstress working for starvation wages; she is not in our domain. Of course, there is *something* we can do always, indirectly. We can be aware of her; when we dress in the morning we can look at the labels and be aware of the people whose poverty contributes to our wealth, and we can say a prayer for them. But directly, it is not our responsibility. Nevertheless, each of us has a responsibility for some little corner of the world, and for that we *will* be held accountable. That corner is in our domain and so we can always do something about that. There is a scary line in the Bible, perhaps the scariest of all the sacred sayings: "From those to whom much is given, much will be required" (Luke 12:48). We are given everything, and especially the secret knowledge that the "least of our brothers," the one most wretched and needy, is really Christ in clever disguise, and we will be judged *solely* by how we respond to the needs of this "Christ." Here the question of the vocation of business is connected with our own eternal ends.

To accomplish anything, however, we must discover our own freedom. We must first decide, and we must first decide to accept responsibility. We must reject the idea that we are powerless pawns in a socioeconomic game whose rules are fixed and whose only object is acquisition. We must discover our freedom of action. In many cases, this will be small. But in some cases, certainly, it will be significant.

Each one is given some task to perform, some job, some mission that only he or she can do. It will be something that in the whole history of the human race, only one person can do. Each person, alone of all humanity, will have the training and experience, will be in the right place at the right time to accomplish this mission, whatever it happens to be. This is our calling, our vocation. But in order to accomplish this, each of us will have to remove the impediments to freedom that exist in each one of us. What kind of impediments?

The world is full of people who want us to be something that is of no particular use to us. They want us to seek our happiness in things, because things can be sold but happiness is unprofitable. Indeed, advertising is built on building discontent; it teaches us to be always unhappy with our lives, our looks, our status and so forth, and to seek products which will, they say, ease this unhappiness. They are more than happy to sell us something to buy temporary happiness in this or that thing, and then buy it again in another thing. We must not become what somebody else wants us to become if we are to become great; as good as that may be for the economy, it is deadly for the soul. And it is in the soul that all great works, and all evil ones, originate. Therefore, in order to accomplish anything, there must be *metanoia*, a change of heart, a conversion. There must be a commitment to true freedom.

The importance of this task cannot be underestimated. The world we live in is a world mostly built by businessmen and -women. Every age has a dominant profession, a profession more responsible than the others for the sum of things. In some ages it is the priest, in others the warrior, and in still others it is the scholar. But our age is an age of commerce, and in this age the businessman and the bureaucrat will be the determinative professions. Therefore whatever we do, no matter how unimportant it may seem, is of global significance and lasting consequence. We build the world that is, and we can blame no others; we must take the responsibility on ourselves.

Notes

1. Justice and Economics

1. D. Stephen Long, *Divine Economy: Theology and the Market*, ed. Catherine Pickstock, John Milbank, and Graham Ward, *Radical Orthodoxy* (London and New York: Routledge, 2000), 175.

2. *Final cause* is one of the four "causes" of Aristotelian analysis. The other three are *formal cause*, the plan, blueprint, or idea of any particular product; *efficient cause*, the agent who actually makes the product (that is, labor, including the form of labor known as management); and *material cause*, the materials and instruments used in the production of the product (i.e., capital).

3. Robert W. Faulhaber, "The Rise and Fall of 'Self-Interest,'" *Review of Social Economy* 63, no. 3 (2005): 421.

4. Ibid.

5. E. K. Hunt, "The Normative Foundations of Social Theory: An Essay on the Criteria Defining Social Economics," *Review of Social Economy* 63, no. 3 (2005): 427.

6. Ibid.

7. Ibid.

8. Ibid., 428.

9. Ibid.

2. The Modern Moral Dialogue

1. Alasdair MacIntyre, *After Virtue: A Study in Moral Theory*, 2nd ed. (Notre Dame, IN: University of Notre Dame Press, 1984), 10.

2. Ibid., 8.

3. Ibid., 9.

4. Ibid.

5. Ibid., 10.

6. Frederick D. Wilhelmsen, *Man's Knowledge of Reality* (Englewood Cliffs, NJ: Prentice-Hall, 1956), 12.

7. Ibid.

8. MacIntyre, *After Virtue*, 44.

9. Ibid., 45.

10. Ibid., 46.

11. Ibid., 48.

12. Ibid., 49.

13. E. K. Hunt, *History of Economic Thought: A Critical Perspective* (Armonk, NY: M. E. Sharpe, 2002; reprint, updated 2nd ed.), 131.

14. Ibid., 143.

15. Ludwig von Mises, *Human Action: A Treatise on Economics,* 4th rev. ed. (San Francisco: Fox & Wilkes, 1963), 735.

16. MacIntyre, *After Virtue,* 15.

17. Ibid., 58.

18. John Milbank, *Theology and Social Theory: Beyond Secular Reason* (Oxford: Blackwell, 1990), 41.

19. Ibid., 84.

20. It must be noted, however, that the chain of reasoning which arrives at the Big Bang is itself based on a narrative of empirical reason, which cannot be logically demonstrated.

21. Milbank, *Theology and Social Theory,* 330.

22. This assumes, of course, that Adam Smith really *is* the founder of capitalism. Most of his book, *The Wealth of Nations,* is in fact a polemic against the prevailing commercial practices and the system he most admires is the agricultural; he considers the world of manufacturing and commerce peripheral to the productive world of the farm. Cf. Book IV, Chapter IX.

23. Helen J. Alford, O.P. and Michael J. Naughton, *Managing as If Faith Mattered: Christian Social Principles in the Modern Organization* (Notre Dame, IN: University of Notre Dame Press, 2001), 46–64.

24. Ibid., 47.

25. Ibid., 55.

26. Ibid., 56.

27. Ibid., 57.

28. See chaps. 13–18.

3. Justice in Economic History

1. Schumpeter passes over the economic history of the Roman Empire because it produced no economists. In doing so, he did not quite get his own joke. After all, if one of the longest periods of peace and prosperity in human history can be accomplished without the aid of economists, then perhaps it is the economists, and not the historians, who are superfluous. Joseph A. Schumpeter, *History of Economic Analysis* (New York: Oxford University Press, 1994).

2. D. McCloskey, *The Secret Sins of Economics* (Chicago: Prickly Paradigm Press, 2002), 29–30.

3. Robert Solow, "Economic History and Economics," *American Economic Review* 75, no. 2 (1985): 330.

4. This derives from a phrase originally used by George Stigler, "the Economist as Preacher." Stigler believed that the best economist wasn't the one who discovered the truth about economic reality, but the one who best persuaded others to his point of view. Truth becomes subordinate to persuasion or marketing. I am using "the preacher as economist" and "the economist as preacher" in quite a different sense from what Stigler intended, one much closer to John D. Mueller, *Redeeming Economics: Free Markets and the Human Person* (Washington, DC: ISI Books, forthcoming, 2007).

5. Aristotle, *Nicomachean Ethics*, ed. Richard McKeon, trans. W. D. Ross, *Introduction to Aristotle* (New York: Modern Library, 1947), 1139a, 10.

6. Ibid., 1129b, 25.

7. Aristotle, *Politics*, ed. Richard McKeon, trans. Benjamin Jowett, *An Introduction to Aristotle* (New York: Modern Library, 1947), 1252b, 11.

8. Ibid., 1253a, 26.

9. Aristotle, *Ethics*, 1130b, 31–33.

10. Ibid., 1131a, 25–29.

11. During the Middle Ages, the term "corrective" justice became "commutative" justice due to a mistranslation. The word Aristotle uses is διόρθωτικός (diórthotikós), "corrective" (LSJ). Although the term "commutative" has become more common, we will use the term "corrective" as closer to the original sense in Aristotle.

12. Aristotle, *Ethics*, 1132b, 19–21.

13. Ibid., 1133a, 25–31.

14. Ibid., 1133b, 18–20.

15. Aristotle, *Politics*, 1256b, 9.

16. Ibid., 1257b, 19–20.

17. Ibid., 1258a, 1.

18. Ibid., 1257b, 39ff.

19. R. H. Tawney, *Religion and the Rise of Capitalism* (New York: Mentor Books, 1954), 34.

20. St. Thomas Aquinas, *Summa Theologica*, trans. Fathers of the English Dominican Province, 5 vols. (Allen, TX: Christian Classics, 1981), II–II, 83, 6.

21. Mary L. Hirschfeld, *Standard of Living and Economic Virtue: Building a Bridge between St. Thomas Aquinas and the 21st Century* (2005 [cited December 17, 2005]); available at *www.nd.edu/~econplcy/workshops/documents/jsce_paper.pdf*.

22. Ibid.

23. Aquinas, *Summa Theologica*, II–II, 77, 4.

24. Albino Barrera O.P., *Modern Catholic Social Documents and Political Economy* (Washington, DC: Georgetown University Press, 2001), 57.

25. Jarrett Bede, *Social Theories of the Middle Ages: 1200–1500* (Westminster, MD: Newman Book Club, 1942), 122.

26. Quoted in Bernard W. Dempsey, S.J., "Ability to Pay," *Review of Social Economy* 63, no. 3 (2005): 341.

27. Aquinas, *Summa Theologica*, II–II, 77, 1.

28. Ibid., II–II, 77, 1, r. 1.

29. George O'Brien, *An Essay on Medieval Economic Teaching* (1920; reprint, Kitchner, ON: Batouche Books, 2001), 59.

30. Ibid., 64. There have been attempts to equate the "common estimation" with the market price so that the just price is "just the price" fixed by the free market. See, for example, Alejandro A. Chafuen, *Faith and Liberty: The Economic Thought of the Late Scholastics* (New York: Lexington Books, 2003). However, this thesis is hard to credit, not only in the light of the specific denial of utility pricing, but also for the fact that if common estimation and market price were the same, then the vast literature of the Scholastics on the subject would be merely tautological.

31. Amintore Fanfani, *Catholicism, Protestantism, and Capitalism* (Norfolk, VA: IHS Press, 2003), 59.

32. Hirschfeld, *Standard of Living and Economic Virtue.*

33. Hunt, *History of Economic Thought*, 33.

34. Max Weber, *The Protestant Ethic and the Spirit of Capitalism*, trans. Talcott Parsons, 2nd Roxbury ed. (Los Angeles: Roxbury Publishing Co., 1998), 53.

35. Milbank, *Theology and Social Theory*, 39.

36. Ibid., 37.

37. Mueller, *Redeeming Economics*, 49.

38. Hunt, *History of Economic Thought*, 45.

39. Mueller, *Redeeming Economics*, 62.

40. Hunt, *History of Economic Thought*, 51.

41. Ibid., 53.

42. Adam Smith, *An Inquiry into the Nature and Causes of the Wealth of Nations* (1776) (Amherst, NY: Prometheus Books, 1991).

43. Ibid., I.VIII, 70.

44. Ibid., I.VIII, 68.

45. Ibid., I.VI, 52.

46. Ibid., I.VIII, 69.

47. Ibid., I.VIII, 70.

48. Mueller, *Redeeming Economics*, 45.

49. Smith, *The Wealth of Nations*, I.X, 137.

50. Ibid., I.XI, 219.

51. Ibid., I.VIII, 83.

52. Ibid., I.VIII, 86–87.

53. Mueller, *Redeeming Economics*, 117.

54. Quoted in Richard T. Gill, *Evolution of Modern Economics* (Englewood Cliffs, NJ: Prentice-Hall, 1967), 51.

55. Ibid., 31.

56. Adam Smith, *The Theory of Moral Sentiments*, 6th ed., *The Conservative Leadership Series* (Washington, DC: Regnery, 1997), IV.I, 249.

57. Smith, *The Wealth of Nations*, IV.II, 351–52.

58. Ibid., V.I., 55.

59. Ibid., I.X, 151.

60. Ibid., I.II, 20.

61. Hunt, *History of Economic Thought*, 80.

62. Ibid., 100.

63. Ibid., 67.

64. Ibid., 69.

65. Garrick Small, *An Aristotelian Construction of the Social Economy of Land* (Sydney, Australia: University of Technology, Sydney, Australia, 2000), 252.

66. Ibid., 255.

67. Ibid., 256.

68. Hunt, *History of Economic Thought*, 96–97.

69. Mueller, *Redeeming Economics*, 72.

70. Hunt, *History of Economic Thought*, 102.

71. Small, *The Social Economy of Land*, 242.

72. Hunt, *History of Economic Thought*, 104.

73. Ibid., 245.

74. Christopher Lasch, *The True and Only Heaven: Progress and Its Critics* (New York: W. W. Norton, 1991), 150.

75. Milbank, *Theology and Social Theory*, 202.

76. Lasch, *The True and Only Heaven*, 318.

77. Hunt, "The Normative Foundations of Social Theory: An Essay on the Criteria Defining Social Economics," 432.

78. Quoted in Gertrude Himmelfarb, *The Idea of Poverty: England in the Early Industrial Age* (London and Boston: Faber and Faber, 1984), 105.

79. Ibid., 122.

80. Quoted in Hunt, *History of Economic Thought*, 78–79.

81. Ibid., 79.

82. Milbank, *Theology and Social Theory*, 42.

83. Himmelfarb, *The Idea of Poverty*, 107. The importance of original sin to economics will become a key tenet of the neoconservative theology of economics. See Michael Novak, *The Spirit of Democratic Capitalism* (New York: Simon & Schuster, 1982), 349–51.

84. Hunt, *History of Economic Thought*, 86–87.

85. Ibid., 155.

86. Larry J. Sechrest, "Jean-Baptiste Say: Neglected Champion of Laissez-Faire," Ludwig von Mises Institute, *www.mises.org/content/jean-baptiste.asp*, cited December 28, 2005.

87. Hunt, *History of Economic Thought*, 138.

88. Quoted in Ibid., 139.

89. Ibid., 147.

90. Ibid., 143.

91. Ibid., 145.

92. Of course, it will be pointed out that the principle is itself "value-laden," since it suggests that human beings "ought" to be fed and the race "ought" to continue. As it turns out, all principled statements about human beings and their institutions are value-laden.

93. Hunt, *History of Economic Thought*, 150.

94. Ibid.

95. Quoted in Ibid., 142.

96. Quoted in Ibid., 140.

4. The Disappearance of Justice

1. Hunt, *History of Economic Thought*, 251.

2. Ibid., 253.

3. Paul Ormerod, *The Death of Economics* (New York: John Wiley & Sons, 1994), 52.

4. Ibid., 87.

5. John Bates Clark, *The Distribution of Wealth: A Theory of Wages, Interest, and Profits* (New York: Augustus M. Kelly, 1899; reprint, 1965), v.

6. Hunt, *History of Economic Thought*, 309.

7. Ibid., 429.

8. Clark, *The Distribution of Wealth,* 111.

9. Joan Robinson, "Euler's Theorem and the Problem of Distribution," *Economic Journal* 44, no. 175 (1934): 399.

10. See chapter 11.

11. James E. Alvey, "A Short History of Economics as a Moral Science," *Journal of Markets and Morality* 2, no. 1 (Spring 1999): 62.

12. One wonders how nature assures that she is getting a fair price, and who negotiates the contracts on her behalf.

13. Lawrence A. Boland, *The Principles of Economics: Some Lies My Teachers Told Me* (London and New York: Routledge, 1992), 17.

14. Robert H. Nelson, *Economics as Religion: From Samuelson to Chicago and Beyond* (University Park: Pennsylvania State University Press, 2001), 102.

15. Hunt, *History of Economic Thought,* 402.

16. John Maynard Keynes, *The General Theory of Employment, Interest, and Money* (San Diego: Harcourt, 1964), 378. What Keynes refers to as "classical" theories, we now label "neoclassical."

17. Ibid., 17.

18. Ibid., 264.

19. Ibid., 247.

20. Ibid., 249–50.

21. Ibid., 339.

22. Ibid., 28.

23. Hunt, *History of Economic Thought,* 145.

24. Ibid., 132.

25. Keynes, *The General Theory,* 170.

26. Ibid., 247.

27. Ibid., 293.

28. Ibid., 315.

29. Ibid., 316.

30. Ibid., 321–22.

31. Ibid., 320.

32. Ibid., 352. The distinction between the MEC and the interest rate is crucial to Keynes's analysis of usury; see chapter 10.

33. Ibid., 319.

34. Ibid., 318.

35. Ibid., 258.

36. Ibid., 9.

37. Ibid., 262–65.

38. Ibid., 265.

39. Ibid., 267.

40. Ibid., 379.

41. Ibid., 129.

42. Ibid., 324.

43. Ibid., 31.

44. Ibid., 372.

45. Ibid., 325.

46. Ibid., 376.

47. Ibid., 374.

48. Ibid., 380.

49. Ibid., 374.

50. Clark, *The Distribution of Wealth*, 16.

51. Hunt, *History of Economic Thought*, 417.

52. Edward Luttwak, *Turbo-Capitalism: Winners and Losers in the Global Economy* (New York: HarperCollins, 1999), 27.

53. Hunt, *History of Economic Thought*, 467.

54. D. McCloskey, "The Rhetoric of Economics," *Journal of Economic Literature* 21 (1983): 488.

55. Novak, *The Spirit of Democratic Capitalism*, 185.

56. Nelson, *Economics as Religion*, 173.

57. Ibid.

58. Hunt, *History of Economic Thought*, 472.

59. Nelson, *Economics as Religion*, 178.

60. Ibid., 180.

61. Ibid., 183.

62. Jennifer Roback Morse, *Love and Economics* (Dallas: Spence Publishing Company, 2001), 229.

63. "If we take in our hand any volume; of divinity or school metaphysics, for instance; let us ask, Does it contain any abstract reasoning concerning quantity or number? No. Does it contain any experimental reasoning concerning matter of fact and existence? No. Commit it then to the flames: for it can contain nothing but sophistry and illusion." (David Hume, *Enquiry Concerning Human Understanding*)

5. *Property, Culture and Economics*

1. Walter Brueggemann, *The Land* (Minneapolis: Fortress Press, 1977), 4.

2. Norman C. Habel, *The Land Is Mine: Six Biblical Land Ideologies* (Minneapolis: Fortress Press, 1995).

3. All biblical quotations are from the New American Bible.

4. This applies to agricultural land only; the regulations for city land are different, and the right of redemption expires after a year, and such land is exempt from the jubilee.

5. Small, *The Social Economy of Land*, 116.

6. Ibid., 118.

7. Garrick Small, "Contemporary Problems in Property in the Light of the Economic Thought of St. Thomas Aquinas," in *Congresso Tomista Internazionale* (Rome: 2003), 8.

8. Small, *The Social Economy of Land*, 143–44.

9. Ibid., 144.

10. Milbank, *Theology and Social Theory*, 333.

11. Small, *The Social Economy of Land*, 145.

12. Milbank, *Theology and Social Theory*, 351.

13. Small, *The Social Economy of Land*, 124.

14. Fernand Braudel, *The Structures of Everyday Life,* vol. 1 (New York: Harper and Row, 1982), 120.

15. Francis Oakley, *The Medieval Experience* (Toronto: University of Toronto Press, 1988), 83.

16. Richard Steckel, "New Light on the 'Dark Ages': The Remarkably Tall Stature of Northern European Men During the Medieval Era," *Social Science History* 28, no. 2 (2004).

17. Hilaire Belloc, *The Servile State* (1913; reprint, Indianapolis: Liberty Classics, 1977), 47.

18. Ibid., 44–45.

19. The figures for the fees and services come from James E. Thorold Rogers, *Six Centuries of Work and Wages: The History of English Labour* (1884; reprint, Kitchner, ON: Batouche Books, 2001), 37–45.

20. Bede, *Social Theories of the Middle Ages: 1200–1500,* 139.

21. Rogers, *Six Centuries of Work,* 56.

22. Belloc, *The Servile State,* 49.

23. This system survives at the college level. We spend four years getting a bachelor's degree and a further three to get a master's because this was the length of time for an apprentice to become first a "journeyman" and then a "master." The "colleges" were originally guilds of scholars who earned their livings by teaching.

24. Rogers, *Six Centuries of Work,* 223.

25. G. M. Trevelyan, *Illustrated English Social History, Volume One* (Harmondsworth, UK: Penguin Books, 1964), 31.

26. Rogers, *Six Centuries of Work,* 227.

27. Ibid., 250.

28. Ibid., 389.

29. Trevelyan, *English Social History,* 33.

30. Ibid., 37.

31. Small, *The Social Economy of Land,* 129.

32. Trevelyan, *English Social History,* 208.

33. Belloc, *The Servile State,* 64.

34. Ibid., 66.

35. Tawney, *Religion and the Rise of Capitalism,* 120.

36. Belloc, *The Servile State,* 64.

37. Which leads to the lament:

> *We hang the man and flog the woman,*
> *Who steals the goose from off the common;*
> *But let the greater villain loose,*
> *Who steals the common from the goose.*

38. Rogers, *Six Centuries of Work,* 343.

39. Ibid., 344.

40. Ibid., 389.

41. Trevelyan, *English Social History,* 232.

42. Rogers, *Six Centuries of Work,* 445.

43. Tawney, *Religion and the Rise of Capitalism,* 120.

44. Small, *The Social Economy of Land,* 149.

45. Ibid.

46. Clark, *The Distribution of Wealth*, 120.

47. Hernando De Soto, *The Mystery of Capital: Why Capitalism Triumphs in the West and Fails Everywhere Else* (New York: Basic Books, 2000), 49.

48. Ibid., 50.

49. Ibid., 5.

50. Ibid., 33–34.

51. Ibid., 191.

52. Tawney, *Religion and the Rise of Capitalism*, 127–28.

6. Rerum Novarum: *A Scandalous Encyclical?*

1. Quoted in Race Matthews, *Jobs of Our Own: Building a Stakeholder Society* (Sydney, Australia and West Wickham, UK: Comerford and Miller, 1999), 22.

2. Ibid., 23–24.

3. Ibid., 31.

4. William Murphy, "In the Beginning: *Rerum Novarum* (1891)" in *Building the Free Society: Democracy, Capitalism and Catholic Social Teaching*, ed. George Weigel and Robert Royal (Grand Rapids: Eerdmans, 1993), 8.

5. Ibid., 9.

6. Ibid.

7. Ibid., 10.

8. Ibid., 11.

9. Donal Dorr, *Option for the Poor: One Hundred Years of Catholic Social Teaching* (Maryknoll, NY: Orbis Books, 1992), 21.

10. Murphy, "In the Beginning: *Rerum Novarum* (1891)," 22.

11. For example, see Thomas E. Woods, Jr., "Catholic Social Teaching and Economic Law," *www.lewrockwell.com/woods/woods8.html*.

12. Dorr, *Option for the Poor*, 16.

13. Ibid., 29.

7. Laborem Exercens: *Work as the Key to the Social Question*

1. The terms "liberalism" and "capitalism" are used interchangeably.

2. See Alford, *Managing as If Faith Mattered*, 99–124.

8. Centesimus Annus: *The Uncertain Victory*

1. For example, see George Weigel, "The Virtues of Freedom: *Centesimus Annus*," in *Building the Free Society: Democracy, Capitalism, and Catholic Social Teaching*, ed. George Weigel and Robert Royal (Grand Rapids: Eerdmans, 1993).

2. For example, see Michael Budde and Robert Brimlow, *Christianity Incorporated: How Big Business Is Buying the Church* (Grand Rapids: Brazos Press, 2002), 109–28.

9. *The Social Teachings and Economics: Ideas in Tension*

1. When referring to "economics" in this context, we mean primarily *neoclassical* economics. There are of course many other schools of thought — Keynesian, Institutional, Marxist, Neo-Ricardian, etc. Neoclassicism is, for the moment, the

dominant but by no means unanimous view; it was chosen because it forms a convenient counterpoint to Catholic Social Teaching.

2. Paul Heyne, Peter Boettke, and Dave Prychitko, *The Economic Way of Thinking*, 10th ed. (Delhi: Pearson Education (Singapore) Pte. Ltd., 2003).

3. Ibid., 275.

4. See, for example, Adam Smith: "The wages of labour are the encouragement of industry, which, like every other human quality, improves in proportion to the encouragement it receives.... Where wages are high, we always find the workmen more active, diligent, and expeditious, than were they are low" (*The Wealth of Nations*, I.VIII).

5. Mueller, *Redeeming Economics*, 194.

6. Heyne, *The Economic Way of Thinking*, 285.

7. There is extensive literature on this topic. See, for example, Daniele Checchi and Cecilia Carcia, "Labour Shares and the Personal Distribution of Income in the OECD," 2. "Contrary to the textbook approach in macroeconomics where factor shares are taken to be constant, variations in the labour share across countries and over time are large." Also, the measurements of inequality, such as GINI coefficients and top-to-bottom decile or quintile ratios vary widely. Naturally, economists of all persuasions fiercely debate the interpretation of these data, but however one decides the issue, it is certainly not as intuitively obvious as the authors of *The Economic Way of Thinking* believe it to be.

8. See chapter 2.

9. Charles M. A. Clark, "Catholic Social Thought and the Economic Problem," *Oikonomia*, no. 1 (2005), *www.pust.edu/oikonomia/pages/febb2000/Clark.htm.*

10. Ibid.

11. Ibid.

12. Robert L. Heilbroner and William Milberg, *The Making of Economic Society*, 11th ed. (Englewood Cliffs, NJ: Prentice Hall, 2002), 6.

13. Ibid., 7.

14. Ibid., 8.

15. Clark, "Catholic Social Thought and the Economic Problem."

16. Ibid.

17. Ibid.

10. Toward an Evolved Capitalism

1. Heyne, *The Economic Way of Thinking*, 4.

2. Ibid., 5.

3. Ibid. It is interesting that neoclassical economists claim the ability to explain all other social phenomenon, but bristle when other social professions attempt to comment on economics.

4. Ibid., 7.

5. Ibid., 5.

6. Mises, *Human Action*, 13.

7. Ibid., 41.

8. Ibid., 42.

9. Ibid., 120.

10. Ibid., 93.

11. Ibid., 13.

12. Ibid., 21.

13. Ibid., 57.

14. This, by the way, is the normal course of philosophic error. It is ordinarily not a question of being absolutely wrong, but of being relatively right. Every thinker starts with some truth; indeed, it is difficult for humans to start anyplace else, aside from cases where actual malice or deliberate deceit is involved. The error comes in taking the small truth and making it stand for the whole of truth.

15. Heyne, *The Economic Way of Thinking*, 5.

16. Mueller, *Redeeming Economics*, 75.

17. Ibid., 184.

18. G. K. Chesterton, *The Collected Works of G. K. Chesterton* (San Francisco: Ignatius Press, 1987), 59.

19. Edward N. Wolff, *Top Heavy: The Increasing Inequality of Wealth in America and What Can Be Done About It* (New York: New Press, 2002), 8–17.

20. A "ponzi-scheme" is an investment swindle in which high profits are promised from fictitious sources and early investors are paid off with funds raised from later ones. It is named after Charles Ponzi, famous for organizing such investment schemes.

21. For a good survey on the history of the notions of usury, see D. Stephen Long, "Avarice as a Capital Vice," unpublished (2005).

22. Keynes, *The General Theory*, 351–52.

23. Faulhaber, "The Rise and Fall of 'Self-Interest,' " 418.

24. Nelson, *Economics as Religion*, 280.

25. Faulhaber, "The Rise and Fall of 'Self-Interest,' " 421.

26. Ibid.

27. Mueller, *Redeeming Economics*, 75.

28. Quoted in Ibid., 190.

29. Ibid., 193.

30. See chapter 3.

31. George Goyder, *The Just Enterprise* (London: Andre Deutsch, 1987), 30.

32. Ibid.

33. Ibid., 31–32.

34. Ibid., 33.

35. See chapter 17.

36. David Herrera, "*Laborem Exercens*, 'Traditional' Organizations and the Democratic Mondragón Model" (paper presented at the Work as the Key to the Social Question Conference, Vatican City, September 12–15, 2001), 243.

37. Mueller, *Redeeming Economics*, 90.

38. Mises, *Human Action*, 168–69.

11. Marginal Productivity and the Just Wage

1. Charles M. A. Clark, "Economic Insights from the Catholic Social Thought Tradition: Towards a More Just Economy," (2005), 2–7.

2. Bradley R. Schiller, *Essentials of Economics*, 2nd ed. (New York: McGraw-Hill, 1996), 172.

3. Clark, *The Distribution of Wealth*, 2.

4. Ibid., 3. Italics in original.

5. Ibid., 94.

6. Ibid., 97.

7. Ibid., 47.

8. Ibid., 190.

9. Ibid., 101.

10. Ibid., 195.

11. Ibid., 16.

12. Ibid., 111–12.

13. Hunt, *History of Economic Thought*, 306.

14. See page 58.

15. Clark, *The Distribution of Wealth*, 191.

16. See page 66.

17. Clark, *The Distribution of Wealth*, 157.

18. Ibid., 158–59.

19. Nelson, *Economics as Religion*, 102.

20. James K. Galbraith, "The Importance of Being Sufficiently Equal," in *Should Differences in Income and Wealth Matter?* ed. Ellen Frankel et al. (Cambridge: Cambridge University Press, 2002), 202–3. Italics in original.

21. Boland, *The Principles of Economics*, 206.

22. Ormerod, *The Death of Economics*, 48.

23. Anwar Shaikh, "Laws of Production and Laws of Algebra: Humbug II," in *Growth, Profits and Property*, ed. Edward J. Nell (Cambridge: Cambridge University Press, 1980).

24. Small, *The Social Economy of Land*, 159.

25. Clark, *The Distribution of Wealth*, 171.

26. David Ellerman, *Intellectual Trespassing as a Way of Life*, ed. Philip Mirowski, The Worldly Philosophy: Studies at the Intersection of Philosophy and Economics (Lanham, MD: Rowman & Littlefield, 1995), 108.

27. David Ellerman, *Property and Contract in Economics: The Case for Economic Democracy* (Malden, MA: Blackwell Publishing, 1993), 132.

28. Joan Robinson, "The Measure of Capital: The End of the Controversy," *Economic Journal* 81 (1971): 602.

29. Small, *The Social Economy of Land*, 242.

30. Ivan Illich, *The Right to Useful Unemployment and Its Professional Enemies* (London: Marion Boyars, 1978).

31. John C. Bogle, *The Battle for the Soul of Capitalism* (New Haven: Yale University Press, 2005).

32. This is not to be taken as an argument against child labor per se, but only against child labor in an adult context that lends itself to exploitation. Children in fact need to work, certainly inside the home and to some extent outside of it; it is part of the socialization and education process. One of the advantages of having mothers employed in the home is that they can supervise and enforce children's work.

33. However, we can note the brilliant suggestion of John D. Mueller to set the standard income tax deduction equal to the poverty line. Suddenly there would be a great interest in the poor and their line, interest that is largely lacking right now, and the general public would have an incentive to be more generous.

34. In this respect, the experience of the Japanese economy is enlightening: "The Japanese have understood that what people are largely pursuing in the workplace is not so much money as the respect of the people around them, and therefore maintain a sophisticated — indeed, bizarrely over-elaborate to the Western eye — economy of *respect* in addition to the economy of money. They have understood that a large part of what money-seeking individuals really want is just to spend that money on purchasing social respect, through status display or whatever, so it is far more efficient to allocate respect directly. Did you really think people as obviously intelligent as the Japanese were doing all those odd-looking bows for nothing? Sure, these behaviors are derived from tradition, but there's a reason they kept these traditions and the West hasn't. Interestingly, this understanding on their part of the need for unapologetic status differentials contradicts the emphasis in Western socialism on a *culture* of equality." Robert Locke, "Japan, Refutation of Neoliberalism," *post-autistic economics review,* no. 23 (2004), *www.paecon.net/PAEReview/issue23/Locke23.htm.*

12. The Neoconservative Response

1. Long, *Divine Economy,* 5.

2. Michael Novak, *The Spirit of Democratic Capitalism* (New York: American Enterprise Institute/Simon and Schuster Publication, 1982), 335.

3. Weber, *The Protestant Ethic and the Spirit of Capitalism,* 35.

4. Ibid., 40.

5. Ibid., 50.

6. Ibid., 51.

7. Ibid., 53.

8. Ibid., 41.

9. Ibid., 67.

10. Ibid., 76.

11. Ibid., 87.

12. Ibid., 103.

13. Ibid., 103–4.

14. Ibid., 104.

15. Ibid., 105.

16. Ibid., 111.

17. Ibid., 112.

18. Ibid., 121.

19. Ibid., 162.

20. Ibid., 167.

21. Ibid., 176.

22. Ibid., 180.

23. Ibid., 182.

24. Novak, *The Spirit of Democratic Capitalism,* 47.

25. Ibid., 249.

26. Ibid., 14.

27. Ibid., 38.

28. Weber, *The Protestant Ethic and the Spirit of Capitalism*, 29. It is an irony that Weber is not actually able to remain "value-free" in practice. *The Protestant Ethic* reads very much like a judgment on capitalism and Puritanism, which even Weber admits: "But this brings us to the world of judgments and of faith, with which this purely historical text need not be burdened" (182). Indeed, the whole "fact-value distinction" is taken more seriously in critiques of Weber than it was by Weber himself.

29. Chafuen, *Faith and Liberty*, 20.

30. Ibid., 24. Italics in original.

31. Ibid., 25.

32. What Chafuen fails to recognize is that the possibility of two natural laws was indeed known to the Scholastics in the form of the doctrine of the double truth (e.g., Siger of Brabant, 1235–82), but was condemned as a heresy by the Church in 1277.

33. Novak, *The Spirit of Democratic Capitalism*, 70.

34. Ibid., 351.

35. Ibid., 352.

36. Long, *Divine Economy*, 11.

37. Novak, *The Spirit of Democratic Capitalism*, 43. It is clear that Weber regards this new-found "freedom" of labor as only a mere formality (Introduction, p. 21) rather than an actuality. He does not present the dichotomy between the commodification of labor and peonage that Novak credits to him.

38. Ibid., 43–45.

39. Ibid., 350.

40. Ibid., 89.

41. Ibid., 171.

42. Ibid., 173.

43. Ibid., 178.

44. Ibid., 179.

45. Ibid., 185. Italics in original.

46. Ibid.

47. Ibid., 186.

48. Ibid., 69.

49. Ibid., 69–70.

50. Ibid., 335.

51. Long, *Divine Economy*, 14.

52. Novak, *The Spirit of Democratic Capitalism*, 337.

53. Ibid., 349–51. Novak actually makes this fourth on his list; however it is presented first in the text, and so will be listed first here.

54. Ibid., 337.

55. Ibid., 338.

56. Ibid., 339.

57. Ibid., 341.

58. Ibid., 344.

59. Ibid., 347.
60. Ibid., 349.
61. Ibid., 351.
62. Ibid., 352.
63. Ibid., 354.
64. Ibid., 355.
65. Ibid., 357.
66. Ibid., 406, n. 2.
67. See chapter 8.
68. Novak, *The Spirit of Democratic Capitalism*, 171.
69. Ibid., 182.
70. Ibid., 334.
71. Ibid., 337.
72. Ibid.
73. Ibid., 344.
74. Ibid., 246.
75. Long, *Divine Economy*, 15.
76. Ibid., 47.

13. Distributivism

1. Matthews, *Jobs of Our Own*, 95.
2. Ibid., 82.
3. The terms "distributivism" and "distributism" are used interchangeably; the former is more grammatically correct but the later is more widely used. We will use both.
4. Belloc, *The Servile State*, 96.
5. Ibid., 83.
6. Ibid., 108.
7. Ibid., 111.
8. Smith, *The Wealth of Nations*, V. I, 5.
9. Belloc, *The Servile State*, 113.
10. Ibid., 115–19.
11. Chesterton, *The Collected Works of G. K. Chesterton*, 59.
12. Belloc, *The Servile State*, 122.
13. Ibid., 125.
14. Ibid., 129–30.
15. Ibid., 146.
16. Wolff, *Top Heavy*, 30.
17. Matthews, *Jobs of Our Own*, 59.
18. Ibid.
19. Hilaire Belloc, *Economics for Helen* (London: J. W. Arrowsmith, Ltd., 1924).
20. Ibid., 87.
21. Ibid., 93.

14. Taiwan and the "Land to the Tiller" Program

1. Keith Griffin, Azizur Rahman Khan, and Amy Ickowitz, "Poverty and the Distribution of Land," *Journal of Agrarian Change* 2, no. 3 (2002), 289.
2. Ibid., 289.
3. Ibid., 289–91.
4. Belloc, "Appendix on 'Buying Out,' " 163–70.
5. Griffin, "Poverty and the Distribution of Land," 304.
6. Jane Jacobs, *Cities and the Wealth of Nations: Principles of Economic Life* (New York: Vintage Books, 1985), 100.
7. Griffin, "Poverty and the Distribution of Land," 306.
8. Ibid., 306
9. Jacobs, *Cities and the Wealth of Nations*, 100.
10. See Henry George, *Progress and Poverty*, originally published in 1880 and available in many editions. As a sidelight, one element at least of Georgism remains in popular culture, the board game "Monopoly." It was originally developed by Georgists as a teaching tool.
11. Klaus Deininger and Lyn Squire, "Economic Growth and Income Inequality: Reexamining the Links," *Finance and Development* (International Monetary Fund, March 1997); see *www.imf.org/external/pubs/ft/fandd/1997/03/pdf/deininge.pdf*.
12. Carmen DeNavas-Walt, Bernadette D. Proctor, and Robert J. Mills, *Income, Poverty, and Health Insurance Coverage in the United States: 2003* (Washington, DC: U.S. Census Bureau, Current Population Reports P60-226: U.S. Government Printing Office, 2004), Table A-3, p. 37.
13. Shirley W. Y. Kuo, "Economic Development of the Republic of China on Taiwan," in *Agriculture on the Road to Industrialization*, ed. John W. Mellor (Baltimore: Johns Hopkins University Press, 1995), 334.

15. Development and Globalization

1. IMF Staff, "Globalization: Threat or Opportunity?" (International Monetary Fund, April 12, 2000, corrected January 2002), *www.imp.org/external/np.exr/ib/2000/041200.htm*, p. 3. The situation is actually worse than the IMF presents it, because the IMF cannot determine the starting place of the incomes of people in most countries. Many or most of these societies had large amounts of production for use rather than for exchange. When, for example, farmers are dispossessed of their land and have to take jobs to buy food, it shows up as in "increase" in wages and in the economy when in fact it is a loss.
2. William Easterly, "A Modest Proposal," *The Washington Post*, March 13, 2005, available at *www.washingtonpost.com*. See also, Easterly, "Think Again: Debt Relief," *Foreign Policy Magazine* (March 2005); see *plato.acadiau.ca/courses/pols/Grieve/Debt%20relief%20easterly.html*.
3. Luttwak, *Turbo-Capitalism*, 202.
4. See Congressional Budget Office, "Revenues, Outlays, Deficits, Surpluses, and Debt Held by the Public, 1962 to 2004," *www.cbo.gov/showdoc.cfm?index=1821&sequence=0#table1*. In 1980, the debt of the United States was $712 billion; when Reagan left office, it was over $2 trillion; when the elder Bush left office, it was

$3 trillion. By the end of 2004 it was nearly $4.3 trillion. President Bush's own estimates are that this will grow to $5.7 trillion by 2008 (OMB, "Analytical Perspectives: Budget of the United States, Fiscal Year 2006," *www.whitehouse.gov/omb/budget/fy2006/pdf/spec.pdf*, p. 245), estimates which are generally regarded as low and do not include the cost of the war in Iraq. Further, these debts are only the "on-budget" items and do not include the nearly $2 trillion in "off-budget" liabilities for the bonds held by the Social Security system or the as yet unknown liabilities for the health care systems.

5. David Ellerman, *Helping People Help Themselves: From the World Bank to an Alternative Philosophy of Development Assistance* (Ann Arbor: University of Michigan Press, 2005), 198–99.

6. Ibid., 196–98.

7. Jacobs, *Cities and the Wealth of Nations*, 105.

8. Ellerman, *Helping People*, 245.

9. Smith, *The Wealth of Nations*, Bk. I, Ch. XI.

10. David C. Korten, *When Corporations Rule the World* (San Francisco: Berrett-Koehler, 1995), 78.

11. Smith, *The Wealth of Nations*, Bk. IV, Ch. III, 360–63.

12. Joseph E. Stiglitz, *Globalization and Its Discontents* (New York: W. W. Norton, 2003), 7.

13. Jacobs, *Cities and the Wealth of Nations*, 32.

14. Ibid., 39.

15. Ibid., 149.

16. See ibid., 93–104.

17. In light of this, the policy of the American government to exempt from taxation all profits from outsourced factories so long as the profits are not repatriated is counterproductive and encourages further outsourcing. It is in fact one of the myriad ways in which the government encourages and subsidizes outsourcing.

18. National Labor Committee Video, *Zoned for Slavery: The Child behind the Label* (Crowing Rooster Arts, 1995).

19. Ibid. It is surprising that with power of the pro-life movement that there have not been protests about the practices of these American-supported zones.

20. Stiglitz, *Globalization and Its Discontents*, 11–12.

21. Ellerman, *Helping People*, 242.

22. Stiglitz, *Globalization and Its Discontents*, 13.

23. Edith Terry, "How Asia Got Rich: World Bank vs. Japanese Industrial Policy: Japan Policy Research Institute Working Paper N. 10," (JPRI: June 1995), available at *www.jpri.org/publications/workingpapers/wp10.html*.

24. Luttwak, *Turbo-Capitalism*, 27.

25. Ibid., 61.

26. Ibid., 63.

27. DeNavas-Walt, *Income, Poverty, and Health Insurance Coverage in the United States*, 25.

28. Galbraith, "The Importance of Being Sufficiently Equal," 209; Deininger and Squire, "Economic Growth and Income Inequality: Reexamining the Links," 38.

29. Luttwak, *Turbo-Capitalism*, 82.

16. Micro-Banking

1. Muhammad Yunus with Alan Jolis, *Banker to the Poor: Micro-Lending and the Battle against World Poverty* (New York: Public Affairs, 1999), 48, italics in original.
2. Ibid., 51–55.
3. The Grameen Bank Web Site, "Credit Delivery System," *www.grameen-info .org/bank.cds.html.*
4. Yunus, *Banker to the Poor,* 199–201.
5. Ibid., 135–37.
6. Ibid., 202.
7. All numbers are from The Grameen Bank Web Site, "Statement No. 1, Issue Number 305, June 12, 2005," *www.grameen-info/bank/May05US$.htm.*

17. The Mondragón Cooperative Corporation

1. Matthews, *Jobs of Our Own,* 10.
2. Ellerman, *Helping People,* 65.
3. Matthews, *Jobs of Our Own,* 12.
4. Ellerman, *Helping People,* 26.
5. E. F. Schumacher, *Small Is Beautiful: Economics as if People Mattered* (New York: Perennial Library, Harper and Row, 1973), 243.
6. Ibid., 243.
7. Ibid., 245.
8. Ibid., 243.
9. Ibid., 244.
10. Ibid., 246.
11. Mondragón Cooperative Corporation, "Most Relevant Data to 31-12-2004," *www.mondragon.mcc.es/ing/magnitudes/cifras_i.html.*
12. Matthews, *Jobs of Our Own,* 184.
13. Ibid., 185.
14. Ibid., 195.
15. Ibid., 205.
16. Mondragón Cooperative Corporation, "The History of an Experience," *www.mondragon.mcc.es-historiaMCC_ing.pdf,* 6.
17. Mondragón Cooperative Corporation Website, "Most Relevant Data to 31-12-2004," *www.mondragon.mcc.es/ing/magnitudes/cifras_i.html.*
18. Ibid.
19. Mondragón Cooperative Corporation, "The History," 11–13.
20. Ibid., 35–37.
21. Novak, *The Spirit of Democratic Capitalism,* 178.

18. The Just Wage and Business

1. Milton Friedman, "The Social Responsibility of Business Is to Increase Its Profits," *New York Times Magazine,* September 13, 1970.
2. Mueller, *Redeeming Economics,* 75.
3. Goyder, *The Just Enterprise,* 31.
4. Alford, *Managing as If Faith Mattered,* 130.

5. See chapter 11 on "Natural Property."
6. Alford, *Managing as If Faith Mattered*, 134.
7. Ibid., 139.
8. Ibid., 139–40.
9. Smith, *The Wealth of Nations*, 9.
10. Ibid., 13.
11. Ibid.
12. Bogle, *The Battle for the Soul of Capitalism*, xix.
13. Ibid., 17.
14. Ibid., 18.
15. Stephen A. Marglin, "What Do Bosses Do? The Origins and Functions of Hierarchy in Capitalist Production," *Review of Radical Political Economics* 6, no. 2 (1974): 70.
16. Ibid., 90. Monopolies are not necessarily the best way to ensure the flow of inventions. As Stephen Marglin notes, "An invention, like knowledge generally, is a 'public good': the use of an idea by one person does not reduce the stock of knowledge in the way that consumption of a loaf of bread reduces the stock of wheat. It is well understood that public goods cannot be efficiently distributed through the market mechanism; so patents cannot be defended on efficiency grounds." Two counterexamples to patents suffice to make the point. For the first, recall the revival of agriculture in the ninth and tenth centuries, a revival which depended on an explosion of innovation, none of which was patented and all of which was freely shared. But the wealth of the High Middle Ages and the expansion of trade and urban life depended on these innovations. A second example comes from our own time with the success of open systems software, such as Linux, where nobody has an exclusive right and any improvements to the system must be offered free of charge.
17. Alford, *Managing as If Faith Mattered*, 118.
18. Ibid., 136.
19. Goyder, *The Just Enterprise*, 31.
20. Jack Stack, "Springfield Remanufacturing Company — the Great Game of Business," in *Curing World Poverty: The New Role of Property*, ed. John H. Miller (St. Louis: Social Justice Review, 1994), 239.
21. Jack Stack and Bo Burlingham, *A Stake in the Outcome: Building a Culture of Ownership for the Long-Term Success of Your Business* (New York: Doubleday, 2003), 21.
22. Ibid., 57–60.
23. Ibid., 60.
24. Stack, "The Great Game of Business," 239–40.
25. Stack, *A Stake in the Outcome*, 5.
26. Ibid., 9.
27. Ibid.
28. Ibid., 3.
29. Ibid., 14.
30. Ibid., 185.

19. Building an Ownership Society

1. Pope John Paul II, *Laborem Exercens* (1981), 64. Italics in original.

2. Pope John Paul II, *Centesimus Annus* (Boston: St. Paul Books and Media, 1991), 43.3.

3. Marjorie Kelly, "The Divine Right of Capital," *www.citizenworks.org/corp/dg/s2r1.pdf.*

4. Lee Drutman, "The History of the Corporation," *www.citizenworks.org/corp/dg/s2r1.php.*

5. Smith, *The Wealth of Nations,* V. I, 3.

6. Ibid., V. I., 5.

7. Korten, *When Corporations Rule,* 55.

8. Bogle, *The Battle for the Soul of Capitalism,* 128.

9. Drutman, "The History of the Corporation."

10. Korten, *When Corporations Rule,* 56–57.

11. Quoted in ibid., 58.

12. Drutman, "The History of the Corporation."

13. Korten, *When Corporations Rule,* 59.

14. Drutman, "The History of the Corporation."

15. Luttwak, *Turbo-Capitalism,* 27.

16. R. H. Tawney, *The Acquisitive Society* (Mineola, NY: Dover Publications, 2004; reprint, 1920), 59.

17. Bogle, *The Battle for the Soul of Capitalism,* 31–32.

18. The distinction between physical and mental work is less clear than might be supposed. Even the meanest labor, which we typically call "mindless," does in fact require a mind; even the most mental work requires that the mental effort be expressed in some physical product. Writing a book is an example of "mental" work, but I can assure you that it is physical as well.

19. John Paul II, *Laborem Exercens,* 58.

20. Shann Turnbull, "Should Ownership Last Forever?" *Journal of Socio-Economics* 27, no. 3 (1998): 15.

21. Goyder, *The Just Enterprise,* 61.

22. Cf. Budde, *Christianity Incorporated.*

23. Although the capital goods purchased by investment have useful lives of varying lengths, there are good technical reasons for choosing ten years as the time horizon suitable to induce investment capital. This discussion is beyond the scope of this book, but cf. Turnbull, "Should Ownership Last Forever?"

24. Ibid., 4.

25. Edward N. Wolff, "Changes in Household Wealth in the 1980s and 1990s in the U.S." (2004), *www.levy.org/default.asp?view=publications_view&pubID=fca3a440ee.*

26. Ibid.

27. Stack, *A Stake in the Outcome,* 137–41.

28. Hilaire Belloc, *An Essay on the Restoration of Property* (Norfolk, VA: IHS Press, 2002), 43–44.

29. Edward W. Younkins, "Antitrust Laws Harm Consumers and Stifle Competition," *Le Québécois Libre,* no. 116 (2002).

20. The Vocation of Business

1. Bradford Snell, *The Streetcar Conspiracy: How General Motors Deliberately Destroyed Public Transit*: see *www.lovearth.net/gmdeliberatelydestroyed.htm* (cited August 2005).

2. Kenneth L. Hess, "The Growth of Automotive Transportation" (1996). See *www.klhess.com/car_essy.html*.

3. Census Bureau, *HO 41 Tenure by Vehicle Available, Data Set: 2000 Supplementary Survey Summary Tables (www.factfinder.census.gov)*.

4. William T. Cavanaugh, "The Unfreedom of the Free Market," in *Wealth, Poverty and Human Destiny*, ed. Doug Bandow and David L. Schindler (Wilmington: ISI Books, 2003), 106.

5. Ibid.

6. Clark, *The Distribution of Wealth*, 2.

7. Belloc, *The Restoration of Property*, 30.

Bibliography

Alford, Helen J., O.P., and Michael J. Naughton. *Managing as If Faith Mattered: Christian Social Principles in the Modern Organization.* Notre Dame, IN: University of Notre Dame Press, 2001.

Alvey, James E. "A Short History of Economics as a Moral Science." *Journal of Markets and Morality* 2, no. 1 (Spring, 1999).

Aquinas, St. Thomas. *Summa Theologica.* Translated by Fathers of the English Dominican Province. 5 vols. Allen, Texas: Christian Classics, 1981.

Aristotle. *Nicomachean Ethics.* Translated by W. D. Ross. Edited by Richard McKeon, *Introduction to Aristotle.* New York: Modern Library, 1947.

———. *Politics.* Translated by Benjamin Jowett. Edited by Richard McKeon, *An Introduction to Aristotle.* New York: Modern Library, 1947.

Barrera O.P., Albino. *Modern Catholic Social Documents and Political Economy.* Washington, DC: Georgetown University Press, 2001.

Bede, Jarrett. *Social Theories of the Middle Ages: 1200–1500.* Westminster, MD: Newman Book Club, 1942.

Belloc, Hilaire. *Economics for Helen.* London: J. W. Arrowsmith, Ltd., 1924.

———. *An Essay on the Restoration of Property.* London: The Distributist League, 1936. Reprint, Norfolk, VA: IHS Press, 2002.

———. *The Servile State.* London: T. N. Foulis, 1913. Reprint, Indianapolis: Liberty Classics, 1977.

Bogle, John C. *The Battle for the Soul of Capitalism.* New Haven: Yale University Press, 2005.

Boland, Lawrence A. *The Principles of Economics: Some Lies My Teachers Told Me.* London and New York: Routledge, 1992.

Braudel, Fernand. *The Structures of Everyday Life.* Vol. 1. New York: Harper and Row, 1982.

Brueggemann, Walter. *The Land.* Minneapolis: Fortress Press, 1977.

Budde, Michael, and Robert Brimlow. *Christianity Incorporated: How Big Business Is Buying the Church.* Grand Rapids: Brazos Press, 2002.

Cavanaugh, William T. "The Unfreedom of the Free Market." In *Wealth, Poverty and Human Destiny,* edited by Doug Bandow and David L. Schindler, 103–28. Wilmington: ISI Books, 2003.

Census Bureau, *HO 41 Tenure by Vehicle Available, Data Set: 2000 Supplementary Survey Summary Tables (www.factfinder.census.gov).*

Chafuen, Alejandro A. *Faith and Liberty: The Economic Thought of the Late Scholastics.* New York: Lexington Books, 2003.

Checchi, Daniele, and Cecilia Carcia. "Labour Shares and the Personal Distribution of Income in the OECD" (October 2005), *www.vcharite.univ-mrs.fr/PP/penalosa/ workingpapers/Checchi-GarciaPenalosa.pdf.*

Chesterton, G. K. *The Collected Works of G. K. Chesterton.* San Francisco: Ignatius Press, 1987.

Clark, Charles M. A. "Catholic Social Thought and the Economic Problem." *Oikonomia,* no. 1 (2005), *www.pust.edu/oikonomia/pages/febb2000/Clark.htm.*

————. "Economic Insights from the Catholic Social Thought Tradition: Towards a More Just Economy." 2005.

Clark, John Bates. *The Distribution of Wealth: A Theory of Wages, Interest, and Profits.* New York: Augustus M. Kelly, 1899. Reprint, 1965.

De Soto, Hernando. *The Mystery of Capital: Why Capitalism Triumphs in the West and Fails Everywhere Else.* New York: Basic Books, 2000.

Dempsey, Bernard W., S.J., "Ability to Pay." *Review of Social Economy* 63, no. 3 (2005): 335–46.

Drutman, Lee. "The History of the Corporation." See *www.citizenworks.org/corp/ dg/s2r1.php.*

Ellerman, David. *Intellectual Trespassing as a Way of Life.* Edited by Philip Mirowski. The Worldly Philosophy: Studies at the Intersection of Philosophy and Economics. Lanham, MD: Rowman & Littlefield, 1995.

————. *Property and Contract in Economics: The Case for Economic Democracy.* Malden, MA: Blackwell Publishing, 1993.

Fanfani, Amintore. *Catholicism, Protestantism, and Capitalism.* Norfolk, VA: IHS Press, 2003.

Faulhaber, Robert W. "The Rise and Fall of 'Self-Interest.'" *Review of Social Economy* 63, no. 3 (2005): 405–22.

Friedman, Milton. "The Social Responsibility of Business Is to Increase Its Profits." *New York Times Magazine,* September 13, 1970.

Galbraith, James K. "The Importance of Being Sufficiently Equal." In *Should Differences in Income and Wealth Matter?* edited by Ellen Frankel et al. Cambridge: Cambridge University Press, 2002.

Gill, Richard T. *Evolution of Modern Economics.* Englewood Cliffs, NJ: Prentice-Hall, 1967.

Goyder, George. *The Just Enterprise.* London: Andre Deutsch, 1987.

Habel, Norman C. *The Land Is Mine: Six Biblical Land Ideologies.* Minneapolis: Fortress Press, 1995.

Heilbroner, Robert L. and William Milberg. *The Making of Economic Society.* Eleventh ed. Englewood Cliffs, NJ: Prentice Hall, 2002.

Herrera, David. "*Laborem Exercens,* 'Traditional' Organizations and the Democratic Mondragón Model." Paper presented at the Work as the Key to the Social Question Conference, Vatican City, September 12–15, 2001.

Hess, Kenneth L. "The Growth of Automotive Transportation." 1996. *www.klhess .com/car_essy.html.*

Heyne, Paul, Peter Boettke, and Dave Prychitko. *The Economic Way of Thinking.* 10th ed. Delhi, India: Pearson Education (Singapore) Pte. Ltd, 2003.

Himmelfarb, Gertrude. *The Idea of Poverty: England in the Early Industrial Age.* London and Boston: Faber and Faber, 1984.

Hirschfeld, Mary L. "Standard of Living and Economic Virtue: Building a Bridge between St. Thomas Aquinas and the 21st Century" 2005. *www.nd.edu/~econplcy/workshops/documents/jsce_paper.pdf* (accessed December 17, 2005).

Hunt, E. K. *History of Economic Thought: A Critical Perspective.* Armonk, NY: M. E. Sharpe, 2002. Reprint, Updated 2nd edition.

———. "The Normative Foundations of Social Theory: An Essay on the Criteria Defining Social Economics." *Review of Social Economy* 63, no. 3 (2005): 423–46.

Illich, Ivan. *The Right to Useful Unemployment and Its Professional Enemies.* London: Marion Boyars, 1978.

John Paul II, Pope. *Centesimus Annus.* Boston: St. Paul Books and Media, 1991.

———. *Laborem Exercens,* 1981.

Kelly, Marjorie. "The Divine Right of Capital." *www.citizenworks.org/corp/dg/s2r1.pdf.*

Keynes, John Maynard. *The General Theory of Employment, Interest, and Money.* San Diego: Harcourt, 1964.

Korten, David C. *When Corporations Rule the World.* San Francisco: Berrett-Koehler, 1995.

Lasch, Christopher. *The True and Only Heaven: Progress and Its Critics.* New York: W. W. Norton, 1991.

Locke, Robert. "Japan, Refutation of Neoliberalism." *post-autistic economics review,* no. 23 (2004), *www.paecon.net/PAEReview/issue23/Locke23.htm.*

Long, D. Stephen. "Avarice as a Capital Vice." Unpublished. 2005.

———. *Divine Economy: Theology and the Market.* Edited by Catherine Pickstock, John Milbank, and Graham Ward, *Radical Orthodoxy.* London and New York: Routledge, 2000.

Luttwak, Edward. *Turbo-Capitalism: Winners and Losers in the Global Economy.* New York: HarperCollins, 1999.

MacIntyre, Alasdair. *After Virtue: A Study in Moral Theory.* 2nd ed. Notre Dame, IN: University of Notre Dame Press, 1984.

Marglin, Stephen A. "What Do Bosses Do? The Origins and Functions of Hierarchy in Capitalist Production." *Review of Radical Political Economics* 6, no. 2 (1974): 60–112.

Matthews, Race. *Jobs of Our Own: Building a Stakeholder Society.* Sydney, Australia and West Wickham, UK: Comerford and Miller, 1999.

McCloskey, D. "The Rhetoric of Economics." *Journal of Economic Literature* 21 (1983): 481–517.

———. *The Secret Sins of Economics.* Chicago: Prickly Paradigm Press, 2002.

Milbank, John. *Theology and Social Theory: Beyond Secular Reason.* Oxford: Blackwell, 1990.

Mises, Ludwig von. *Human Action: A Treatise on Economics.* 4th revised ed. San Francisco: Fox & Wilkes, 1963.

Morse, Jennifer Roback. *Love and Economics.* Dallas: Spence Publishing Company, 2001.

Mueller, John D. *Redeeming Economics: Free Markets and the Human Person.* Washington, DC: ISI Books, Forthcoming, 2007.

Nelson, Robert H. *Economics as Religion: From Samuelson to Chicago and Beyond.* University Park: Pennsylvania State University Press, 2001.

Novak, Michael. *The Spirit of Democratic Capitalism.* New York: Simon & Schuster, 1982.

O'Brien, George. *An Essay on Medieval Economic Teaching.* Kitchner, ON: Batouche Books, 2001.

Oakley, Francis. *The Medieval Experience.* Toronto: University of Toronto Press, 1988.

Ormerod, Paul. *The Death of Economics.* New York: John Wiley & Sons, 1994.

Robinson, Joan. "Euler's Theorem and the Problem of Distribution." *Economic Journal* 44, no. 175 (1934): 398–414.

———. "The Measure of Capital: The End of the Controversy." *Economic Journal* 81 (1971): 597–602.

Rogers, James E. Thorold. *Six Centuries of Work and Wages: The History of English Labour.* Kitchner, ON: Batouche Books, 2001.

Schiller, Bradley R. *Essentials of Economics.* 2nd ed. New York: McGraw-Hill, 1996.

Schumpeter, Joseph A. *History of Economic Analysis.* New York: Oxford University Press, 1994.

Sechrest, Larry J. "Jean-Baptiste Say: Neglected Champion of *Laissez-Faire.*" Ludwig von Mises Institute, *www.mises.org/content/jean-baptiste.asp* (accessed December 28, 2005).

Shaikh, Anwar. "Laws of Production and Laws of Algebra: Humbug II." In *Growth, Profits and Property,* edited by Edward J. Nell. Cambridge: Cambridge University Press, 1980.

Small, Garrick. *An Aristotelian Construction of the Social Economy of Land.* Sydney, Australia: University of Technology, Sydney, Australia, 2000.

———. "Contemporary Problems in Property in the Light of the Economic Thought of St. Thomas Aquinas." In *Congresso Tomista Internazionale.* Rome, 2003.

Smith, Adam. *An Inquiry into the Nature and Causes of the Wealth of Nations.* 1776. Amherst, NY: Prometheus Books, 1991.

———. *The Theory of Moral Sentiments.* 6th ed. *The Conservative Leadership Series.* Washington, DC: Regnery, 1997.

Snell, Bradford. *The Streetcar Conspiracy: How General Motors Deliberately Destroyed Public Transit. www.lovearth.net/gmdeliberatelydestroyed.htm* (accessed August, 2005).

Solow, Robert. "Economic History and Economics." *American Economic Review* 75, no. 2 (1985): 328–31.

Stack, Jack. "Springfield Remanufacturing Company — The Great Game of Business." In *Curing World Poverty: The New Role of Property,* edited by John H. Miller, 235–46. St. Louis: Social Justice Review, 1994.

Stack, Jack, and Bo Burlingham. *A Stake in the Outcome: Building a Culture of Ownership for the Long-Term Success of Your Business.* New York: Doubleday, 2003.

Steckel, Richard. "New Light on the 'Dark Ages': The Remarkably Tall Stature of Northern European Men during the Medieval Era." *Social Science History* 28, no. 2 (2004): 211–29.

Tawney, R. H. *The Acquisitive Society.* Mineola, NY: Dover Publications, 2004. Reprint, 1920.

——. *Religion and the Rise of Capitalism.* New York: Mentor Books, 1954.

Trevelyan, G. M. *Illustrated English Social History,* Volume One. Harmondsworth, UK: Penguin Books, 1964.

Turnbull, Shann. "Should Ownership Last Forever?" *Journal of Socio-Economics* 27, no. 3 (1998): 341–63.

Weber, Max. *The Protestant Ethic and the Spirit of Capitalism.* Translated by Talcott Parsons. 2nd Roxbury ed. Los Angeles: Roxbury Publishing Co., 1998.

Weigel, George. "The Virtues of Freedom: *Centesimus Annus.*" In *Building the Free Society: Democracy, Capitalism, and Catholic Social Teaching,* edited by George Weigel and Robert Royal, 207–23. Grand Rapids: Eerdmans, 1993.

Wilhelmsen, Frederick D. *Man's Knowledge of Reality.* Englewood Cliffs, NJ: Prentice-Hall, 1956.

Wolff, Edward N. "Changes in Household Wealth in the 1980s and 1990s in the U.S." (2004). *www.levy.org/default.asp?view=publications_view&pubID= fca3a440ee.*

——. *Top Heavy: The Increasing Inequality of Wealth in America and What Can Be Done about It.* New York: New Press, 2002.

Younkins, Edward W. "Antitrust Laws Harm Consumers and Stifle Competition." *Le Québécois Libre,* no. 116 (2002).

Index